# LIS Interrupted

# LIS Interrupted

Intersections of Mental Illness and Library Work

*Edited by*
*Miranda Dube*
*Carrie Wade*

Library Juice Press
Sacramento, CA

Published in 2021 by Litwin Books.

Litwin Books
PO Box 188784
Sacramento, CA 95818

http://litwinbooks.com/

This book is printed on acid-free paper.

Library of Congress Cataloging-in-Publication Data

Names: Dube, Miranda, editor. | Wade, Carrie, editor.
Title: LIS interrupted : intersections of mental illness and library work /
  edited by Miranda Dube, Carrie Wade.
Description: Sacramento, CA : Library Juice Press, 2021. | Includes
  bibliographical references and index. | Summary: "Provides a collection
  of both personal narratives and critical analyses of mental illness in
  the LIS field, exploring intersections with labor, culture, stigma,
  race, ability, identity, and gender"-- Provided by publisher.
Identifiers: LCCN 2021007453 | ISBN 9781634001083 (trade paperback ;
  acid-free paper)
Subjects: LCSH: Librarians--United States--Psychology. | Librarians--Mental
  health--United States. | Library science--United States--Psychological
  aspects. | Information science--United States--Psychological aspects.
Classification: LCC Z682.35.P82 L57 2021 | DDC 025.501/9--dc23
LC record available at https://lccn.loc.gov/2021007453

# Contents

# A Letter to the Reader

Dear Reader,

Thank you for picking up this book. Regardless of how or why you have arrived here in this moment—if it's to see yourself in the pages, learn more about mental illness, improve your library praxis, none or any combination of the above—we want to express our gratitude towards you.

Brave and vulnerable people opened up their minds to write this book. They have invited us to witness their challenges and triumphs as they navigate both mental illness and the Library and Information Science (LIS) field. Authors featured here have dedicated their time and energy to help the field, both as individuals and as a community. Being brave and vulnerable is not just limited to the authors of these chapters though. You, dear reader, are brave and vulnerable. Willing to talk about mental illness, and reflecting as both humans and professionals to examine how we can improve the world for ourselves and our colleagues, is a brave and vulnerable act.

This book has been organized into three sections: "The Process of Becoming," "Critical Perspectives and Narratives," and "The Situated Experience."

The first section, "The Process of Becoming," focuses on folks entering the world of library work—from their experiences as graduate students to establishing themselves as new professionals. Kaelyn Leonard tells of their experience working towards a master's degree in library and information science (MLIS) as a person with ADHD. Zoë Nissen opens up about their experience developing and recovering from an eating disorder (ED) as they attended graduate school and entered library workplaces. Karina Hagelin shares their radically vulnerable experience with assault and mental illness, and provides ways we can begin practicing the same within libraries. Marisol Moreno-Ortiz outlines the ways they navigated their mental health as a new career Diversity Scholar. From the Fortunoff Video Archive of Holocaust Testimonials comes Christy Bailey-Tomacek whose own experiences with difficult mental illness has helped create an emotionally safer workplace amongst coworkers handling and transcribing materials related to human trauma. Nina Clements helps us understand that there is never a clear ending when it comes to disclosures and mental illness. Chelsea Tarwater invites us to witness the darkest moments of their depression and sing story time songs as we go. The section closes with Allison Rand, present for the Boston Marathon bombings, who discusses how the resulting Post-Traumatic Stress Disorder (PTSD) has impacted their life.

For "Critical Perspectives and Narratives" the book takes an analytic turn. This section contains chapters that challenge norms and practices in libraries by examining our foundations. It opens with Alice Bennett who examines mental health disclosures in the context of western academic libraries in Higher Education. Carolyn Hansen reviews outdated and problematic catalog headings, specifically focusing on Library of Congress subject headings. Michelle Ashley Gohr and Andrew Barber use critical theories to address concerning trends in librarianship that focus on class and alienation of paraprofessionals and other library workers in the neoliberal landscape. Pamela Andrews and Melissa Freiley analyze librarians' use of humor on Twitter in relation to librarian stereotypes and mental illness. Sara Harrington explores how emotional labor, gender, and mental illness intersect in the LIS field. Brady Lund discusses communication disorders and provides suggestions for improvements the LIS field can make to reduce barriers. Stacey Astill considers the impact of health news on library staff who experience anxiety. Ian Ross Hughes questions aspects of the in-person interview and provides ways to reduce barriers in order to hire the most qualified candidates. Stephanie S. Rosen, through highlighting their personal experience, provides us with a path to understanding healthy care work in LIS. Marie Campbell, Clayton Hume, Max Powers, and Ann Sen conclude this section with an analysis of their shared experience and formation of a solidarity network as co-workers co-experiencing workplace anxiety under toxic leadership.

To close out the book is the third section and a return to personal narratives with "The Situated Experience," which focuses on established professionals who have coexisted with their conditions and careers. It begins with Chaundria Campos, a black woman and veteran with PTSD, who discusses workplace resources as the classic line that seldom helps. Jasmine Rizer explores how ongoing mental health issues has affected their decisions of how and why they have chosen to be open or not in the workplace. Evelyn E. Nalepinski outlines ways we can turn the misfit nature of librarianship into a more inclusive space for neurodivergent individuals. John Cohen illuminates how their experience with bipolar disorder has positively improved their ability to lead. Jodene R. Peck Pappas examines their experience as a cataloguer who also has Obsessive-Compulsive Personality Disorder (OCPD) and depression. Jess Alexander concludes this section with their recount of their battle with The Machine That Goes Beep—a villain to the author's neurodivergent brain.

There are many ways to read this book: you may choose to read one chapter, all chapters, or somewhere in between. You may choose to mark up the pages with your thoughts. You may choose to read this cuddled up under covers alone or in a group of trusted friends. There is no right or wrong way to engage with this book, just like there is no right or wrong way to experience, learn about, or reduce stigma around mental illness. We hope if anything resonates too deeply, or creates feelings of unease, that you will have a trusted confidant to process with, or a tried and true way to provide yourself care that you can utilize.

We encourage you to practice mindfulness, to breathe and ground yourself as you explore the lives and experiences of others. Understand that one life is not a universal experience either—each glimmers as its own unique set of circumstances and conditions to create the lives presented here. Similarly, the thoughts and ideas presented here will hopefully open you up to new possibilities as well.

We are honored that you have picked this book up, and hope you find something befitting your needs in its pages.

*With care and gratitude,*
*Miranda Dube and Carrie Wade*

# The Process of Becoming

# The Space Between Neurodiversity and a Degree: Misinterpretations of ADHD in Higher Education

**Kaelyn Leonard**

*Content Warning*  Discussions of academic despair, ADHD diagnosis parameters, and minimization of mental illness.

## Personal Reflection

Obtaining a Masters in Library and Information Science (MLIS) is a step towards being something— purveyor of knowledge, finder of things, or solver of mysteries. However, as an MLIS student, I often feel removed from that identity. Students are pre-professionals who carry the weight of expectation. We are expected to produce answers, solve problems, and generally navigate channels in order to find the information we need at any given moment. But what happens when you can't?

The picture of what neurodiversity means is abstract. For me, it is a vast pool of frustration that bleeds rivers of questions I can't answer, no matter which search strategy I use. Can a concept grid showcase the synonyms of hyperfocus? Will a Boolean search highlight if I can be productive today OR emotionally stable tomorrow? I watch neurotypical people admire the way the storm clouds roll over the surface of the water. They don't know that the storms brew in my chest, in my brain, in every cell of my body until I am nothing but the rain that they'll complain has spoiled their day.

Mental illness can rob you of everything. I once thought the worst thing it could take from me was normalcy, but as I entered higher education, I learned that normalcy was just the facade we are fed as children, not the goal. It robbed me of something I've always depended on: words. A vocabulary to define my illness and symptoms. What about spoons[1] to make it through the day? Without either of these, I wondered how I could muster the power to overcome the voice that told me that I just wasn't sick enough. I wanted the truth to be simpler— for my struggle to beg for last-minute extensions and my resistance to seek accommodation services to be unfounded.

I never expected that voice in my head to be proven right— the one that whispers what-ifs and who-knows from the irrational epicenter of thought. I thought all I wanted was for my doubts to be wrong. In so many moments that I had to hold myself together, my list of wants became longer. I wanted to be seen and heard and understood. I wanted to find a space that I could *exist* in, even if I didn't *fit* there, because I had worked for it just as much as anyone else. But people have a way of only hearing what's convenient. Things that cannot be seen, heard, or universally understood remain an inconvenience for those who don't experience it. A certain subset of illnesses did not earn the moniker of 'invisible' by being accepted and understood; they lingered in spaces that destroy us while our too-tight smiles remain on armored display.

## Experience and Criticisms

In the higher education system, there's a presupposition that everyone will fit the mold. The system isn't built for exceptions. There is an unspoken expectation that students will bend and bend, surpassing all forms of reason, but miraculously never break, to fold themselves into whatever available space exists. Combined with the nature of graduate studies, where failure and missteps are not an option, my experience was steeped in imposter syndrome from the start. As a first-generation student, I didn't know the rules of the game. I didn't

---

1 Miserandino, Christine. "The Spoon Theory." *But You Don't Look Sick?*, April 26, 2013. https://butyoudontlooksick.com/articles/written-by-christine/the-spoon-theory/.

have the checkmarks on a list: the vocabulary, the documentation, or perhaps most insulting of all, the money.

While a student could theoretically contact their instructors individually regarding accommodations, there is a power imbalance that leaves many (like myself) feeling insecure about disclosing a sensitive part of their identity to someone who has substantial influence over their education, letters of recommendation, and future job prospects. The ADA disclosure that every syllabus must include seemed like nothing more than an inconvenient footnote. Without an established relationship of trust, support, or mentorship, I hesitated with the weight of what one email or phone call could cost me. As an online student in a distance program, the space between the physical campus and my point of existence had never seemed as vast as when I looked across cyberspace into an empty address book. A formal request for accommodations, processed by a dedicated department which promised not to disclose specific diagnoses in order to protect the student's privacy, sounded ideal in comparison. It was when I sought accommodations that I realized not all is as it *appears* on the surface, and that even those who are supposed to support us can fail.

To an English major, vocabulary is something that seems illimitable. I was unprepared for two words to be my undoing: "Unspecified ADHD." These words would haunt me throughout my petition for accommodation services. They would be thrown in my face as something the counselor had "never heard of." I would be needled about "what that even meant." Again and again, I would be left searching for something that had never failed me before: words. My official diagnosis, in its most unembellished form, was nothing more than an unspecified version of an acronym. According to the DSM-V:

314.01 (F90.9) UNSPECIFIED ATTENTION-DEFICIT/
HYPERACTIVITY DISORDER

This category applied to presentations in which symptoms characteristic of ADHD that cause clinically significant distress or impairment in social, occupational or other important areas of functioning predominate but do not meet the full criteria for ADHD or any of the disorders in the neurodevelopmental disorders diagnostic class. The unspecified ADHD category is used in situations in which the clinician chooses not to specify the reason that the criteria are not met for the ADHD or for a specific neurodevelopmental disorder, and includes presentation in which there is insufficient information to make a more specific diagnosis.[2]

The use of "unspecified" in my ADHD diagnosis, rather than Inattentive or Hyperactive, was the stone that made all of my efforts come tumbling down.

To specify Inattentive, Hyperactive, or Combined Presentation ADHD, a person must present six symptoms within the given category defined by the DSM. I didn't know then what I do now— that my *specifics* align with the Predominantly Inattentive Presentation of ADHD. The way I kick myself about missed grammar errors that remain in a paper is echoed in "often fails to give close attention to details or makes careless mistakes in schoolwork, at work, or with other activities."[3] My chronic inability to keep track of time and deadlines harkens to "often has trouble organizing tasks and activities." The looming danger of opening my phone or a new tab is a reminder of "is easily distracted." My physician chose not to define my life by a single visit, while an accommodations counselor tried to undermine my academic experience with a single word.

Even when I screamed that I was drowning in a sea of deadlines, my achievements were weaponized against me. The counselor assigned to me insisted that someone sporting a 3.7 GPA at a full credit load during their first semester of graduate school, dinged by a single A-, wasn't someone with the marks of struggle. The four months I spent sleeping a mere three to five hours a night in order to pore over textbooks and PDFs for six to eight hours a day, reading and rereading the same lines of words that should have made sense but instead seemed to morph and swim before my eyes, was diminished to a mere difference in student study habits. My reality turned into an unfathomable tale of woe—an absolute impossibility that I was working harder than I ever had to gain that shred of success. When did it become a merit badge to make it through the sleepless nights? Why would the impact on my mental and physical health rank as utterly inconsequential, as long as I could produce the quintessential good work?

---

2  *Diagnostic and Statistical Manual of Mental Disorders: DSM-5.* (Arlington, VA: American Psychiatric Association, 2017). https://www.virtualeduc.com/v7/resources/data/ADD/DSM5_Presentations.htm.

3  "Symptoms and Diagnosis of ADHD | CDC." Centers for Disease Control and Prevention. https://www.cdc.gov/ncbddd/adhd/diagnosis.html.

The format and delivery of online coursework varies between pro-grams, instructors, and individual courses. One semester's format does not dictate the next. During that first arduous semester, I had lectures in the form of PDFs and PowerPoint slides, analytical formats that were familiar to me. This had allowed me to survive but did not prepare me for any other instruction style. The shift, and accompany-ing struggle, of my second semester came with lengthy audio record-ings. Words would fade into static, lulling me into nothing more than a sea of meaningless noise. I felt myself slipping from the first day and dismissed it as an overload of information. Only, how long is "new" information a continual sensory overload? How many times could I blame archival repository planning, or RUSA guidelines, for the way that I couldn't grasp the critical words of my professors after endless hours of listening to the same fifty minutes over and over again?

My difficulty with the audio aspects of my coursework were the incit-ing incident that pushed me to seek accommodations for my ADHD. At nearly the midpoint in the semester, I felt hopeless and afraid of failure. I thought I was asking for something simple: transcriptions of the recorded lectures. Note-taking services were advertised clearly as an available resource, and a common recommendation for students with ADHD is assistance with note-taking in the classroom.[4] Although I was an online student, I was assured by my advisor that accommo-dations were still made available. Then again, nothing is ever as sim-ple as it seems.

I never expected to be met with an outright dismissal of my inability to successfully listen to recorded lectures. In truth, hearing this from someone who is in a position to assist students with various disabilities made my blood boil. They disclosed that note-taking services existed only for campus students, effectively "othering" me for my position as an online distance student. No amount of advocating for myself, point-ing to institutional documentation, or referring to my own document-ed illness could sway this person. People with ADHD do not have that problem, they stated as though it were fact. Instead, they were quick to impress upon me that I must want more time on tests— something I never once asked for in my request—because "that's what people with ADHD need." What people with ADHD *need* varies from individual to

---

4   "Recommended Accommodations for College Students with ADHD." ADDA–Attention Deficit Disorder Association. September 20, 2017. https://add.org/recommended-accommoda-tions-college-students-adhd/.

individual. What I needed, so very desperately at that critical point in my graduate career, was institutional support.

Higher education institutions are failing their neurodivergent students by relying on textbook presentations of mental health disorders to be the sole presentation. Policies and procedures that are supposedly built to support and protect students of *all* backgrounds are not infallible. This is particularly true if they are drafted without the input of the communities they serve. A step in the right direction would be hiring consultants to review current procedures, policies, and proposed accommodations. Moreover, consultants would be invaluable in the revision and drafting of documents necessary for Disability and Accessibility Services (and similar offices). Having input from people who are affected by the specific disorders minimizes the risk of overlooking lesser-known symptoms and invalidating students' personal experiences.

The gross misunderstanding of how ADHD impacts student performance, especially at the graduate level, is something that I believe needs to be better represented. Executive dysfunction presents in a palette of greys, not black and white. The graduate school success recipe looks something like this: one part constant emotional drain of having no work/life balance, equal parts intellectual demand for every course, and a healthy pour of self-imposed desire for perfection. It would take years of practice to master without a mental disorder—ADHD adds in layers of complications to every step. Rejection sensitivity lurks in every feedback bubble, waiting to see if there's a disagreement with my assessment of a collection's current holdings that could paralyze me. Emotional dysregulation runs rampant when I'm struggling to meet my own impossibly high standards. Hyperfocus is my backhanded blessing that might allow me to dedicate twelve consecutive hours to the paper that I just couldn't get started until the morning it was due. Even if I am more than my ADHD—bright, successful, or perhaps seemingly unaffected on the surface—I also am who I am *because* of it.

The logistical and emotional roadblocks that ADHD presents, paired with a glaring lack of systemic support from the institution I was pouring thousands of dollars and countless hours of dedication into, could have been enough to break me. I won't lie—they nearly were. I asked myself how I could ever entertain the possibility of academic librarianship, of becoming a cog in the broken machinery of academia that is built to chew up neurodivergent people like me. I questioned how I was supposed to succeed without effectively risking the entirety of my future by outing myself to each and every instructor as someone with a mental illness.

Among swaths of uncertainty, I clung to something I knew: My ADHD had not stopped me from earning a bachelor's degree. Being told what I am or am not only drives me to prove myself that much more, and if my life-long love for the pursuit of knowledge had brought me to an MLIS, it would have to be enough to help me continue on the path of earning it. I turned to the thing I do best—the very skill a library science program teaches you to hone to the sharpest edge—research. I found something that exceeded my wildest dreams: Otter. An AI voice-to-text software that transcribes from audio files in real time, it was a solution that hadn't been offered to me, even by a trained disability counselor.[5] Yet, it was the only thing that allowed me to finish my semester, allowing me to read my lectures rather than lose hours that bled into days in tears of frustration.

Maintaining that 3.7 GPA throughout my first year of my MLIS, once thrown in my face as an impossibility for someone with ADHD, has become one of my proudest achievements. It is something I fought for—against a system that should have listened to me, against an illness that manipulates my neurological functions, and against the expectation that only those who thrive on organization and logic have a place in a field with "science" in the name. If libraries and archives can be for all, so can library and information science. There is space in the world of LIS for those with ADHD—intense dedication to tasks, unique approaches to problem solving, and resilience have all proved to be invaluable skills in my professional experience. My intuition when something was amiss has been the undercurrent that swept me toward solutions. My burning rage and disbelief at the misunderstanding of my illness urges me to speak that much louder. I refuse to shy away from a critical part of who I am.

## Suggestions for Future LIS Students

Neurodivergent students looking ahead to their graduate school applications, question the institutions you plan to apply to. You do not need to be a current student to ask questions that impact future decisions

---

5   For information on this program, see Otter Voice Notes. https://otter.ai/

regarding your education—a prospective student is just as deserving of information. Be direct when asking what accommodations the institution offers for specific mental disorders and learning disabilities. If you have a concern regarding possible accommodations for a symptom that is outside the scope of the textbook definition, advocate for yourself. If they are the right fit for you, they should have no problem disclosing processes, procedures, and resources. If you will attend as a distance student, it is prudent to ensure that the same accommodations will extend to you. Neurotypical is not synonymous for successful. Your voice, your perspective, your passion, and your insight belong in the field of Library and Information Science— with or without the support of your institution.

## Acknowledgements

The support of my partners, Zach and Lily, was instrumental when it came down to mustering the courage to submit my work to *LIS Interrupted*. They reminded me every step of the way that there is something larger at work than a single story. I also owe my editors, Miranda and Carrie, my depthless gratitude for encouraging me to push my boundaries as a writer.

*Bibliography*

*Diagnostic and Statistical Manual of Mental Disorders: DSM-5*. Arlington, VA: American Psychiatric Association, 2017. https://www.virtualeduc.com/v7/resources/data/ADD/DSM5_Presentations.htm.

"Recommended Accommodations for College Students with ADHD." ADDA–Attention Deficit Disorder Association. September 20, 2017. Accessed August 01, 2019. https://add.org/recommended-accommodations-college-students-adhd/.

"Symptoms and Diagnosis of ADHD | CDC." Centers for Disease Control and Prevention. Accessed July 31, 2019. https://www.cdc.gov/ncbddd/adhd/diagnosis.html.

# There's no Dublin Core Element for "Body Issues"

**Zoë Nissen**

*Content Warning*   Eating disorders, discussion of food/disordered behaviors, guilt, body size/type, body-shaming. Mentions of alcohol use, suicide, depression, and anxiety.

Let's face it: I've never had a great relationship with food. It's ingrained in my family that you finish what's on your plate. Yet I grew up in the late 90s and early 2000s when it felt like the entire United States was talking about the "obesity epidemic" and how we as a country needed to get more fit. We were all watching The Biggest Loser and it felt like a new fad diet cropped up every day. As a kid I liked to eat, and I wanted junk food more than anything in the world—probably because Cheetos and Oreos were verboten in our house. I inherited a penchant for large meals and full-bodied wine from my father's side of the family and a lust for chocolate from my mother's. I also inherited a compact frame designed for life in harsh European climates, clinging on to weight in order to keep me warm in freezing temperatures—I guess genetics didn't get the memo that I was born in the middle of the California desert at the peak of summer.

As I grew up, my woman-identified body began to look different from some of the other woman-identified bodies around me. My thighs commanded attention. A muffin top spilled over my jeans. I felt like every other teenage girl was perfect and had a flat stomach, perky chest, and a nice petite butt that meant that they never had to walk sideways between the rows of desks in our overcrowded classrooms in order to avoid knocking someone's notebook off. I tried to focus my attention outside of my body, and for a time I succeeded. While school wasn't always my favorite, playing music and writing stories brought me joy and confidence. Around my senior year of high school, though, a comparative voice started whispering in my head. It got progressively louder and louder as I went through college even though I still played my instruments, wrote stories, and even found a new source of happiness in dancing. It hit fever pitch during the second semester of my third year of undergrad when my then-boyfriend voiced my worst fears: that the size of my thighs made it difficult for him to love me.

I've always been straight-sized[1]. I've never had to deal with institutionalized discrimination due to my weight. Men on the street have made inappropriate comments about the size of my butt, but I've never had to browse the accessories section of a store while my friends shop the racks because nothing on them will fit me, or purchase a seatbelt extender or an extra seat on a plane. Doctors have told me that I could stand to lose a few pounds, but always treat me for the condition I've come in to complain about instead of prescribing weight loss as a cure-all. My body type is not the Western ideal, but it has never been held up as a picture of "what not to do."

But despite knowing all of that, that comment from my boyfriend shook me to my core. We had been together since high school and while I knew that most of those relationships don't stand the test of time, I wanted us to be different. I wanted us to be endgame. In my panic, I decided to focus the rest of my college career on one thing: losing weight. Yes, I had classes to attend and a senior thesis to write, but this was going to be my golden ticket. If I had the right body, then maybe he would finally pay attention to me in the way I wanted. If I had the right body, then he would treat me like his girlfriend instead of his therapist. He'd show me off. He'd be proud of me.

---

1 The retail industry separates women's clothing by size. In the United States, sizes 0 to 12 (sometimes 14) are considered "straight" sizes, whereas larger sizes are considered "plus" sizes. Plus size garments are often separated out into separate sections in retail stores, or into separate stores altogether, whereas straight sizes are not. For more discussion of size inclusion/exclusion consult Nittle, "Is Inclusive Sizing Just Another Trend?", 2018.

We broke up the week after I graduated. That decision had been per-colating for years, but my rapidly deteriorating mental state finally spurred me to take the plunge and tell him that, after seven years, I couldn't be with him. I was so burned out on having to be everything for him. And I was so, so, *so* undernourished. All I wanted was to fo-cus on my body. My brain didn't have enough energy to care about an-other person.

Yet I didn't snap out of it after breaking up with him. Now that we weren't together, I needed to get not just a "revenge body," but my revenge career, my revenge *life*. I needed to show him what he threw away. I'd be smart, successful, and most of all—I'd be hot.

For the next year, I threw myself headfirst into my plan. I had worked in my college's library since my junior year, and with my charm and knack for cataloging I had managed to snag a full-time position as a Project Assistant working with the Special Collections department on a weed-ing project. I worked hard to learn all that I could about resource de-scription and librarianship. I wrote and rewrote my application essays for graduate school programs, most located outside of California. I was no longer attached to someone who wanted to work in Hollywood, so I could go anywhere—and maybe finally afford to live without room-mates who kept me up until three in the morning playing acoustic gui-tar (badly).

While I was busting my ass to get my career going, I kept up the ap-pearance of being a semi-successful twenty-something postgrad. I still played in the community wind ensemble I joined in college and met up with friends for drinks and nights of dancing. But inside my head, every waking moment, my thoughts always spiraled back to two things: exercise and FOOD.

Most folks with eating disorders don't fit neatly into one category. Most of us run the gamut of diagnoses, and the diagnostic criterion are inherently flawed anyhow. The latest DSM *still* thinks BMI is a use-ful measure to assess body weight for height and an anorexia diagno-sis *still* requires an "abnormally low weight"[2]—let's not get me on my semantic soapbox of what "normal" and "abnormal" entail. Just like we all have different stories of how we got sick, our sicknesses all

---

2   "Feeding and Eating Disorders," in *Diagnostic and Statistical Manual of Mental Disorders :
    DSM-5.*, Fifth edition. (Arlington, VA: American Psychiatric Association, 2013).

manifest differently. Mine crept up on me slowly, my revenge-body fantasy going from "eating healthy" to full-blown restriction. By the time I began purging I knew I had an eating disorder, but getting help seemed impossible. My wellness was not a priority.

When I got into the University of Wisconsin-Madison's Library & Information Studies program, I was ecstatic. I finally had my ticket out of the Los Angeles cesspool. I could run away. I could reinvent myself. This could be my transformation; the ultimate thing I had worked so hard to achieve. That summer, my father and I packed my tiny hatchback to the brim and sped 2,000 miles across the country into my new life.

I got "lucky"—students in my grad program were fairly open about mental health issues. After a well-known student died by suicide just two months before my cohort started classes, it felt like a revolution was happening. Everyone I knew was in therapy, we talked about depressive episodes and anxiety attacks and how to access mental healthcare during our *orientation day*. This was something I'd never experienced before. I'd always been taught to keep my issues to myself.

I'd been binging and purging regularly for about three years at this point, though I was starting to acknowledge that I'd actually done this on and off since I was about fourteen. In part due to a fellow incoming student's openness about her experiences with anxiety and depression, I worked up the guts to the University Health Services office and tell them I needed help finding a therapist. It was hard for me to even articulate what I needed—I remember being very quiet for most of that appointment, feeling numb and scared and worried about what lay ahead—but I did it. I did it because I needed to finally take charge of my well-being. I was in a new city, 2,000 miles away from my family, I was single, and I hadn't become close friends with anyone yet. After years of masking my pain as anger and taking it out on other people there was finally no one to take it out on—I had to confront it myself. I had to deal with what was happening with me before it completely consumed me. Thinking about food and worrying about my body already took up so much mental space. I wanted to be able to give that space to my degree, to my work.

I'll also admit that a lot of my motivation was shame. What was I going to tell my professors when I said I needed extensions on assignments? When I finally did muster the courage to ask for what I needed, my professors—even ones I liked, professors who championed mental health resources on campus and supposedly believed there was no shame in asking for help—wanted an explanation. I was so embarrassed that I spent my weekends in a haze of alcohol-assisted binging and purging. I was so ashamed that this was me—wasn't I smarter than this? Movies and TV tell us eating disorders are for shallow girls, tragic girls who only care about their looks, anorexic perfectionists and bulimic cheerleaders like in *Heathers*. I'm an intelligent woman, a graduate student at an R1 university, I'm a feminist! My brain is more important than what my body looks like!

But yet there I was. "Smart," by all that is measurable, yet still sick.

In a hotel room in Sacramento over the winter holidays, I broke down and told my parents that I had an eating disorder. I had spent the previous night obsessively trying to "burn off" my food after eating a very full plate at dinner and several desserts. I was angry that they didn't see this as self-destructive, and angry with myself for overeating. Some offhand comment from one of my parents set me off—I honestly can't even remember what it was now, or who said it, just that it was rooted in diet culture—and suddenly I was crying and telling them what I had kept secret for the past several years.

When I went back to school for the spring semester, I started actively working with my therapist to quiet the voices in my head, the critical one that told me my body was never good enough, and the self-destructive one that said, *fuck it, we can always purge.* Together we started looking for the root causes of these behaviors and figuring out what voids I was trying to fill when I binged, purged, or restricted. As I was learning in school how to organize information and communicate it in a meaningful way to other people, I was learning how to communicate meaningfully with myself. I learned how to reward myself with things other than food. Through a lot of pain and frustration, I learned to listen to what my body had to tell me, and I learned to forgive myself when I misinterpreted the messages. During the day I'd read all of the articles I had to for class (okay, I would read one article and pick out my one talking point for class discussion), and in the evenings I'd read *Health at Every Size, Brain Over Binge,* and any other recovery manual I could get my hands on so I could understand what was happening in my body and in my brain. I wanted to know that one day, the calorie calculator in my head would be silent, that after a large meal I would relax and enjoy my dining companions' company, and a walk would be a relaxing, amiable activity. I picked up my dance practice again, but this time instead of pursuing ballet and hip-hop I joined a community of bellydancers focused on the pursuit of body liberation. I started reading books on fat positivity and their authors' unapologetic rebellion tapped into my punk-rock roots—I wanted to be radical and supporting bodies that weren't the thin ideal was the most radical thing I could do to my eating disorder. I intentionally gave myself plenty of opportunities and spaces to practice new skills and thought patterns, and I was incredibly fortunate to have a community of people willing to support me on this journey.

Grad school was a bubble. A difficult bubble full of stress and breakdowns, but at least I had space in the day to make time for things like going to therapy and eating mindfully. My public services job was mainly evenings and my other positions offered me a flexible schedule. I could roll into class, sit next to one of my friends, and tell them how I'd cried on the bus on the way over here and have them go "Girl, same." During conferences, a friend and I would check in with each other about our mental well-being because professional expectations were a trigger for both of us. We were radically honest with each other and vented our frustrations about the people around us who were constantly demanding our attention when our under-resourced brains were working overtime just to keep us afloat. We took to Twitter to complain about our mental states, our struggles on our public accounts as out-in-the-open as possible, and left comments saying "I see you" on each other's updates. We felt safe expressing ourselves, even if our selves were scary sometimes. We were rejecting the tired narrative that grad students must let their mental health fall to the wayside during school. We wanted it all. We *needed* it all, if we were to make it through the next two years.

Sometimes I wondered if I should put it all on pause to pursue inpatient treatment. I stretched myself across multiple jobs, professional organization activities, and convinced myself that it would be a huge loss to my career if I took a break. That I wasn't "really" sick enough—I was still making it to my jobs, I wasn't deathly underweight, I hadn't reached a "breaking point" where my sickness consumed my life. It was more of a constant, low-level hum of anxiety, like bass from your neighbor who listens to talk radio.[3]

---

3  If you put your schooling on pause or ended it completely to pursue recovery, please know that I am SO PROUD of you. You are doing the thing that I was not brave enough or honest with myself enough to do.

For better or for worse, I pulled myself through my degree. At gradu-ation every student got to make a brief thank-you speech, and in ad-dition to my parents and cat I thanked my therapist for the time she spent with me, because without weekly sessions with her I do not know if I would have made it through the program at all. I vowed that no matter where the job market would take me, I would never let my-self work anywhere that would rewind the time I spent working on myself. Up there on that stage, I could see how far I'd come from the scared, anxious, woman I'd been in Los Angeles.

Fate *would* have it this way, though. Fate *would* take me back to the city where I nurtured my sickness, would make me leave the Midwest—where in the winter I actually NEEDED to gain weight so I wouldn't feel my insides freeze, talk about exposure therapy—to go back to South-ern California, where I thought I had left my demons in the dust. I never thought I'd live here again—what *librarian* can afford to live in Los An-geles?!—so I never thought I'd have to confront this past. Even though my grad school identity as "eating disorder girl" was exhausting, at least I had done all the work of telling people about it already. In my job hunt and in securing a position, I went through it All. Over. Again.

The interview process was exhausting enough. The interview meal al-ways throws me for a loop—are they judging me for how much I'm eat-ing? Do they think I should have ordered a salad? Everyone else or-dered salad and I ordered pasta, was that wrong? Do they think I'm fat? I know the statistics, the heavier you are the harder it is to get a job[4]. I consciously know that I'm not even close to the part of the spec-trum where weight-based job discrimination becomes really A Thing, but I am five feet tall and have what Shakira would call very honest hips. The night before I had my first on-campus interview, I had din-ner at an Italian restaurant in Southern California with a *very* tall, *very* conventionally attractive, *very thin* woman who is the head of the li-braries. Even though I had made tremendous strides in my recovery, I could not fight off the thought that I was a schlub in comparison. During this meal in the back of my head I was trying to balance be-tween wanting to restrict my food intake so this woman didn't think I was a glutton, and wanting to eat everything on my plate out of ner-vousness because food is soothing and what else am I supposed to do

---

4   Lynn K. Bartels and Cynthia R. Nordstrom, "Too Big to Hire: Factors Impacting Weight Dis-crimination," *Management Research Review* 36, no. 9 (January 1, 2013): 868–81, https://doi.org/10.1108/MRR-06-2012-0134.

with my hands at the dinner table anyway? What does hunger feel like again? What is a fullness cue? I'm nervous and when I'm nervous my body shuts these things down, because that's what I taught it to do for so many years and I am still in the process of unlearning. When I get in high-stress situations, my brain works overtime. I try to tell myself that it's okay if I don't get this part of recovery right today, I try to console my mind that is doing backflips upon itself with kind words. I try to be gentle with myself, to not judge myself, to put my wellness first.

And while all of that is going on, I'm supposed to be job-flirting? Thank you, next.

Thankfully, I didn't get the position with the intensely triggering dinner, but that doesn't mean that the job I *did* get didn't come without its own host of issues. I view my eating disorder the same way I view my queerness—I'm going to talk about it, I'm not ashamed of it, it's just a part of me, but it sure does make a lot of YOU people uncomfortable. In starting my new job at possibly the most Los Angeles of Los Angeles universities, I had to remember that not everyone knows the phrase "diet culture" and not everyone knows that restricting foods only makes you want them more and starts the binge-restrict cycle, and not everyone has read *Health At Every Size* and knows that fat-shaming is bad[5], skinny teas are bad[6], keto is bad[7], all of your obsessions with weight and size and beauty, they're freaking *bad*. I guess I'm "lucky" that my inner circle of friends out here all have clawed through recovery from various levels of disordered habits and they "get it", but so many people at my workplace and in the professional world just *DO NOT*.

This is what's fucked—one of many things that are fucked, emotionally and systemically—about a profession primarily composed of women and femmes: whether consciously or not, we still do that thing where we're supposed to bond with each other over hating our bodies.

---

5   Michael Hobbes, "Everything You Know About Obesity Is Wrong," News, *The Huffington Post*, September 19, 2018, https://highline.huffingtonpost.com/articles/en/everything-you-know-about-obesity-is-wrong/.

6   Claudia McNeilly, "Why Instagram's Favorite Diet—'Teatoxing'—Won't Actually Help You Lose Weight," News, *Teen Vogue*, August 12, 2016, https://www.teenvogue.com/story/tea-detox-teatox-bad-for-health-dangers.

7   Joanna Clay, "Is the Keto Diet Safe? USC Experts Have Some Serious Concerns," News, *USC News*, February 19, 2019, https://news.usc.eduhttps://news.usc.edu/154342/is-the-keto-diet-safe-usc-experts-have-some-serious-concerns/.

Conversations about "losing those last ten pounds" are common in my work breakroom, and I am supposed to murmur sympathetically that I, too, possess an unworthy fleshsuit. A colleague complains that we shouldn't have food-related rewards, not because they play into a narrative that food is something you need to earn instead of an essential part of functioning, but because "they'll make us fat." This isn't a generational thing, or a not-woke-enough thing—it's even gotten the ardent feminists. My coworker discusses the Vagina Monologues with me, then mentions that she's jealous of my standing desk because "Americans are so fat because we sit all day." And when I try to interrupt those thought patterns—despite the fact that whoa, that was just a huge trigger out of left field!—by saying something like "hm, I don't think it's fair to demonize a food group" or "I mean, I don't think being fat is the worst thing we can be," people look at me like I've suddenly started speaking in an obscure foreign language they don't know. And to them, I guess I have. Instead of going "ugh, yeah, I totally need to quit eating sugar, too," or "yeah, it's great that I can stay fit even at work," or "yeah, I need to watch my figure, too," I've deviated from the standard narrative. They don't know what to do. No one's ever said that to them before.

Figuring out these boundaries is *hard*. When I encounter a trigger it's like a siren going off in my brain. I can't breathe. My vision gets cloudy. I know that what they're saying is harmful, can't they see that it's harmful? I did so much work to train my brain not to say these things to me, but now here they are, out there coming at me from my colleagues who I thought were safe and understanding but apparently not. I'm caught between the fight and freeze responses. As an eating disorder survivor, I'm feeling attacked and want to yell at them for hurting me. As an educator, I feel the need to tell them that their assumptions just straight-up aren't true. But as someone experiencing a moment of trauma, I'm having trouble tuning out the wailing alarm in my head. I'll stutter and stumble, trying to educate but forgetting the perfect wording as shock radiates through my entire being. And then my triggering colleague will look at me strangely, as if I'm the one spouting misinformation and hoax. When I try to set a boundary and tell my colleague, "maybe I'm not your best audience to talk to about running all the time," I feel like I'm labeled a bitch. A failure. A mess. Uneducated. Unprofessional.

I believe in being honest with people. But now, I also believe in protecting myself.

It's not my job to educate you about this.

It's not my job to educate you about this.

*It's not my job to educate you about this.*

It's not my job to educate you about this, but that doesn't mean it hurts any less when you don't educate yourself. I've already done more labor than necessary by telling you that I had an eating disorder. It's your turn to do some labor and find out what it means. We're librarians for shit's sake. Do your own damn research.

Every time I "come out" I get the same look—pure panic in a colleague's eyes. They don't know how to handle it. They don't know how to handle *me*. They don't believe it. They don't believe *me*. I field comments like, "But you don't look sick!" "But I've seen you eat!" "But you dance all the time, it doesn't matter what you eat!" and frankly, it is exhausting.

What exactly are you looking for when you say these things? Do you want it to go away? Do you want proof? How do you want me to prove it? Do you want me to scream the internal monologue that I rehearse every time I have to go to a meeting or event where food will be served so I don't eat too much or too little? How about the next time I get stressed out I'll have you sit in front of me while I recite the stream-of-consciousness thoughts that bubble up telling me that surely, the way to smooth things over with this co-worker/boss/friend/bus driver is if I change my body! Maybe I'd get respected if I wasn't so dang hippy! And then I'll yell the self-soothing platitudes as loud as they sound in my head to beat back those thoughts and that, colleague, is why my eyes go dark when you talk about how you're "so bad" that you skipped the gym once this week.

And it hurts, colleague. It hurts when I hear you talk this way about yourself, because friend, your body is the least interesting thing about you. You are funny and smart and kind, and I hate watching you self-harm like this (yes, it's self-harm). I know how much that path hurts because I've been down it, but you're not ready to admit that it hurts yet and that scares me. I don't want you to feel what I've felt. I wouldn't wish that on my worst enemy. And then I feel like I have to start thinking, "well, grad school wasn't The Real World™, you were sheltered and guess what, diet culture exists and you just have to DEAL WITH IT," but then there's also, "why can't The Real World™ just exist without diet culture?" Why is asking for a shift in thought processes suddenly too much? Why is it, that I, that we, the sick people, have to accommodate those that are not? Or at least, those that haven't recognized that they are sick yet. Why do I have to remain quiet, maintain the status quo?

When I tried staying quiet, it just made me sicker. I can't be a stereotypical mousy metadata librarian. I can't help but be loud about this.

Now that I'm nearly a year into this position, some of my hard work is starting to pay off. I've decorated my cubicle with cutesy mental health stickers and put up posters declaring it a body-positive zone. I've found my social sea legs here and can weave awareness into my wit—if you try to humblebrag about not having eaten all day because you've been so busy I have no problem telling you that's not cute and pulling a snack from my purse for you like a total Mom. I'm perfectly fine walking away from holiday party conversations that turn to techniques on how to "burn off" the snacks, because I'd rather be rude than hurt myself. I've even found some colleagues that I'll be able to vent about it with later, other stereotype-defying librarians and archivists who have their own experiences that have made them stronger. We all carry something with us that informs who we are, and those things never fit into pre-determined boxes anyway.

Thinking about the discourse on mental health in libraries also makes me think of the conversations happening about how the core of information organization in the West is biased. If we can have conversations about disentangling ourselves from outdated subject headings, we can have conversations about disentangling ourselves from the way we try to label each other. We can unlearn what a person with an eating disorder looks like or acts like, and even unlearn our preconceptions as to what eating disorders even *are*. Trust me, I do metadata. I like order. I like neat labels that help make things findable. I like norms and standardization. But with this, I just can't uphold the typical categorizations. I can't make myself conform to the stereotype of librarians of old as the buttoned-up rule-following spinster, or to the new stereotype of the people-pleasing perfectionist. My grad cohort spoiled me too much, it embraced the loud, rowdy, sometimes messy person that I am. I've fought too hard to let diet culture beat me. I'm not going to gloss over my experiences and just "stick it in the notes field." I refuse to be cataloged under a certain subject heading, a certain diagnosis, nothing so simple can quite contain me.

## My Recovery Resources

Note: These are a list of books that helped *me*, a white, cis, straight-size woman, in my recovery from my eating disorder. I cannot stress enough that every person's journey is unique, so the content in these books may not apply to your situation and this list is meant simply as a jumping-off point. I encourage you to find resources that work for you and share them widely!

Bacon, Lindo. *Health at Every Size : The Surprising Truth about Your Weight.* Dallas, TX: BenBella Books, 2010.

Baker, Jes. *Things No One Will Tell Fat Girls : A Handbook for Unapologetic Living*, 2015.

Hansen, Kathryn. *Brain over Binge : Why I Was Bulimic, Why Conventional Therapy Didn't Work, and How I Recovered for Good.* Columbus, GA: Camellia, 2011.

Stanley, Jessamyn. *Every Body Yoga : Let Go of Fear. Get on the Mat. Love Your Body.* Workman Pub Co, 2017.

Taylor, Sonya Renee. *The Body Is Not an Apology : The Power of Radical Self-Love / Sonya Renee Taylor.* First Edition. Oakland, CA: Berrett-Koehler Publishers, 2018.

Wolf, Naomi. *The Beauty Myth: How Images of Beauty Are Used against Women / Naomi Wolf.* First Perennial edition. New York: Perennial, 2002.

## Acknowledgements

Thank you to (in no particular order): my colleagues in Wisconsin, California, and the virtual world who have let me be loud about the frustrations recovery entails; the fat activists and scholars whose work I have learned and benefitted from; my mom and dad who continue to grow and educate themselves and instilled in me the importance of lifelong learning; my friends who loved me enough to stick around through my entire healing process (and a special thanks to those who didn't ditch me pre-recovery when I was honestly pretty triggering to be around—the coven knows who they are); Miss Martini for being the best cat and making sure I always have at least one good thing in my life per day; Dance Life in Madison, Wisconsin for giving me a safe place to get back in touch with my body and the Los Angeles bellydance community for encouraging me to grow; my therapist in graduate school, who while not an eating disorder specialist educated herself on what I needed; Miranda and Carrie for putting this collection together; and everyone in the library/archives world that is open about their mental health. Our collective voice is loud and together we can change this culture.

## *Bibliography*

Bartels, Lynn K., and Cynthia R. Nordstrom. "Too Big to Hire: Factors Impacting Weight Discrimination." *Management Research Review* 36, no. 9 (January 1, 2013): 868–81. https://doi.org/10.1108/MRR-06-2012-0134.

Clay, Joanna. "Is the Keto Diet Safe? USC Experts Have Some Serious Concerns." News. USC News, February 19, 2019. https://news.usc.eduhttps://news.usc.edu/154342/is-the-keto-diet-safe-usc-experts-have-some-serious-concerns/.

"Feeding and Eating Disorders." In *Diagnostic and Statistical Manual of Mental Disorders : DSM-5.*, Fifth edition. Arlington, VA: American Psychiatric Association, 2013. AUTHOR NEEDS TO BE CITED.

Hobbes, Michael. "Everything You Know About Obesity Is Wrong." News. The Huffington Post, September 19, 2018. https://highline.huffingtonpost.com/articles/en/everything-you-know-about-obesity-is-wrong/.

McNeilly, Claudia. "Why Instagram's Favorite Diet—'Teatoxing'—Won't Actually Help You Lose Weight." News. Teen Vogue, August 12, 2016. https://www.teenvogue.com/story/tea-detox-teatox-bad-for-health-dangers.

# Surviving to Thriving: Creating a Culture of Radical Vulnerability in Libraries

**Karina Hagelin**

*Content Warning*  Discussion of sexual violence, post-traumatic stress disorder, borderline personality disorder, anorexia, self-injury, suicide, and substance abuse disorder/addiction.

## Introduction

This chapter will walk through my own journey and build upon those experiences to offer tangible, concrete suggestions for creating a culture of radical vulnerability in libraries. To provide a shared vocabulary for readers, a glossary is included following the conclusion.

I offer my experiences, my truth, and my tenderness in the spirit of cultivating radical vulnerability. My softness and my openness have been weaponized against me but I still believe wholeheartedly in sharing these gifts with the hope of creating space for others to do the same. I call this radical vulnerability, which I see as a praxis and strategy of sharing openly about experiences, identities, and stories that have been stigmatized and weaponized against us, in order to keep us quiet, small, and powerless. Some of these topics include mental health and illness, disability, addiction, failure, trauma, and abuse. Speaking up is a tactic to actively destigmatize and normalize these experiences while creating a space for others to do the same, with compassion, care, and empathy. It's not only okay to share about these things, it's important in the way that it can change and even save lives. It allows us to see these moments as sites of growth and transformation, rather than sources of shame. There is power in sharing your story. This is why I offer you mine.

## Claiming Crazy

I am mad crazy.

Let me be clear about what I mean when I say "mad crazy." I mean waking up in the middle of the night, screaming my lungs raw, because I had another night terror about the rape. I am talking about struggling to hold onto reality because the memories of what happened to me feel so real it's like they're happening all over again. The urge to dissociate, to escape and disappear into myself, sings to me like a siren to a sailor. I mean shutting the door to my office so I can sob uncontrollably because something benign and harmless didn't feel benign and harmless, so I'm having a panic attack, inducing a feeling I can only describe as "I'm going to die." I mean struggling with actually wanting to die because that's historically felt like a better alternative to the life I'm not really living, just barely surviving.

I am mad crazy. I am reclaiming those slurs in the name of mad pride and liberation which offers a life free of shame. I am also a librarian who has worked in the library and information science (LIS) field for the past decade, both as a library worker and librarian.

## Surviving

Things have always been hard for me. Growing up, I struggled with borderline personality disorder as a result of childhood trauma. For me, this manifested as an intense fear of abandonment accompanied by horrific mood swings, feelings of emptiness, suicidal ideation and suicide attempts, impulsive and self-destructive behaviors, episodes of stress-related paranoia, and outbursts of anger. It was really tough to survive when I was in the midst of ongoing trauma and I felt everything so intensely, so profoundly, that if I my feelings were a dial, I was turned all the way up to an 11. And I was doing it all without any support, community, or professional help.

In 2011, my life changed. I was raped by a friend. That was my breaking point. The point of no return. The collapse of my life as I knew it. A sense of knowing that if I didn't get help, I would die. That night pushed me over the edge, becoming my catalyst to seek help and begin the journey into my healing process. These days, my comrades, especially those who also struggle with mental illness, remark how healthy my coping skills are—but things weren't always like that.

To try and cope, I began self-harming and using heroin with benzodiazepines, such as Xanax and Klonopin. It was the only way I knew how to survive. I stopped eating to try and maintain a sense of control over my life that was quickly spiraling out of control, developing anorexia that turned me into a walking skeleton. I was angry, afraid, and alone, pushing everyone around me away. And to be honest, I didn't have to try that hard. Folks in my community didn't want to deal with the "drama" of my rape, the resulting post-traumatic stress disorder, and the drug addiction that was ruining my life. I was the "crazy girl," the "unstable junkie," the "drama queen." The warm blanket of heroin, much like a child's security blanket, made my fears and anxieties melt away. Everything was okay, at least for a few hours, until it wasn't again. Reality was so incredibly painful that I couldn't handle it. Two years of my life went by like this, self-medicating so I wouldn't kill myself. The positive feelings never lasted and I did end up attempting suicide. Several times. I wasn't really living my life—I was just barely surviving it.

During all of this, I was still attempting to go to college, work, and be "normal." The day after I was raped, I took my midterms like nothing had happened, despite my thighs being marred with deep black and blue bruises. A professor I looked up to asked if I needed help after noticing my thighs. I said I was "fine," that everything was "fine," because that's what I wanted to believe. I desperately wanted to believe that I was okay, that everything was normal, that things were "fine," because I couldn't accept my reality: the one crumbling down around me. She told me about a campus organization that supports survivors of sexual and interpersonal violence.

I ended up going to the campus center that supported survivors, not knowing what to expect but desperate for help and healing. I was willing to try nearly anything. The staff were educated, compassionate, and empathetic care workers who were able to provide the help I needed without judgement, blame, or pressure. I was in control of my healing process here.

The organization set me up with a trauma therapist who helped me save my life. I connected with an amazing psychiatrist who helped me find the right medications, and a substance abuse counselor who helped me patch myself up and work on my recovery through a harm reduction lens. I learned skills like distress tolerance, grounding, and dialing down, in addition to dialectical behavioral therapy (DBT) techniques to help me cope. I became involved in survivor and recovery support groups, so I knew I wasn't alone, that my struggles were not unique, and that I had a community. I worked with this program and team for eight years, only leaving their care when I moved away for my first professional LIS position. While I recognize I did most of the work and heavy-lifting, I know that they helped save me from myself during the darkest and most painful years of my life.

## To Thriving

Today, I am sober and in recovery, I haven't self-harmed in years, and I'm eating again (although some days it's still a struggle). I didn't think I'd make it to 25 but I recently celebrated my 30th birthday, surrounded by friends. I live with my three rescue cats, Cashew, Chickpea, and Boo, in a gorgeous, colorful, apartment that feels like the first home I've ever known. I have a job I love in a field I am passionate about. I create artwork about healing as resistance, radical vulnerability, and queer femme joy that has resonated with and impacted hundreds of other survivors.

Things aren't perfect—and they will never be. Healing isn't a linear process. I have good days and bad days. I trust that my baseline for wellness will continue to expand and stabilize as I heal. I am proud of the progress I've made, as a little work each day has added up to monumental change. I, like so many others, have put in this profoundly difficult work and yet, I've noticed our community, profession, and field haven't.

## Creating a Culture of Radical Vulnerability in Libraries

Library work cultures normalize ableism by encouraging surface-acting which manifests in "fake it til you make it" thinking—it encourages a person to force a smile during a challenging experience at work when actually feeling frustrated[1]. Surface-acting has tremendous challeng-

---

1   Alicia A. Grandey, "When 'The Show Must Go On': Surface Acting and Deep Acting as Determinants of Emotional Exhaustion and Peer-Rated Service Delivery," *Academy of Management Journal* 46, no. 1 (February 1, 2003): 86–96, https://doi.org/10.5465/30040678.

es as the expectation to perform sanity and/or able-bodiedness, is stifling and isolating for those of us who are disabled, crazy, and/or sick. Simply being asked "How are you today?" is a huge stressor. The expectation is to say I'm "Good!" or "Great!" when in reality, I'm struggling with being present.

As librarians, we're expected to put on a shining face for our patrons and colleagues rather than "cause discomfort" if they were actually faced with our real-life human struggles (physically, emotionally, mentally, etc.). This prioritization of others' potential discomfort with our very real anguish is dangerous, and creates a culture of silencing, fear, and stigma. As a community, we need to foster a culture of radical empathy and vulnerability, without the fear of repercussions from colleagues, supervisors, and/or HR. Cultivating a culture of radical empathy and vulnerability isn't an easy task but it's something to work toward. A little progress each day can add up to big changes in the lives of our peers and colleagues.

As librarians and library workers, we need to commit ourselves to creating a culture that radically celebrates vulnerability, compassion, and empathy—a culture that allows folks to bring their whole, authentic selves to work. We need to show up for each other. I think sometimes people are afraid of doing it "wrong"—but showing up is what's important, letting your colleague know they're not alone, that you see them, and that you're someone they can go to and trust. Doing so from a genuine place of care and concern is essential.

We can also participate in trainings on Mental Health First Aid or speak to our local survivor support organization or counseling center about how to best support colleagues if we're nervous. These trainings should be offered periodically, and everyone should be encouraged to attend to improve the overall health of our workplaces. I'm incredibly grateful for the colleagues and comrades who have supported me in bringing my whole self to work. They've made it a possibility for me. I hope I can pay their kindness forward by cultivating a similar culture wherever I go.

Something that seems small, but that deeply affects me and many other mentally ill folks, is the usage of ableist slurs, such as crazy and insane, as descriptors—usually not in the positive sense, never in the reclaimed sense. People have used these slurs to discredit me and my experiences as a crazy, disabled, and sick/chronically ill queer femme. They are both harmful and hurtful. It's important to learn new language, to question why we feel it's necessary to use ableist slurs, and to interrupt ourselves and others when we slip up.

There are many resources available to help us communicate more compassionately, such as Lydia X. Z. Brown's article "Ableism/Language". This living document they've created—with the help and input of many different disabled people—is an ever-growing, expanding, and changing glossary that includes lists of ableist words and phrases—including slurs—as well as words which people can consider using instead. It's important to note that when talking about a disabled person, folks should reflect whatever language the disabled person prefers to use to describe themselves[2]. For example, many people consider "person with a disability" to be correct. The reality is people—and the language we use—are messy, incoherent, and constantly changing. The idea that there is a "correct" way to do things also relies on ableist ideas about what is "right". The focus needs to be on inclusivity, not correctness. Part of being inclusive is being willing to listen to disabled people, so if you're unsure of what language to use, just ask.

Another challenge is the built environment itself, the physical structures and spaces in our workplaces. In the past, I've had offices with doors, allowing me to close myself off to the world when necessary, whether to regroup or cry. Open layouts are becoming more common, with cubicles lacking real walls and doors, rendering this type of coping skill impossible. If an open layout is absolutely unavoidable, there needs to be multiple rooms available to workers. A good example of this is the University of Maryland's iSchool's "quiet room," complete with a desk, stuffed animals, tissues, and snacks. Students, staff, and faculty can sign up for chunks of time to use the room however they wish. I often used this space as a place to cry and calm down during panic attacks or to rest when my lupus became too much to bear. This was a crucial resource to me as a graduate student and a model for how to create a more inclusive, accessible workspace.

Open layouts and cubicles can be difficult for people with PTSD or other mental illnesses. As a survivor, I need to have my back to a wall to feel safe and reduce hypervigilance. In my current open workspace, it is impossible to have my back to a wall. Currently, there is a printer behind the barrier that separates me from the rest of the library,

---

2   Lydia XZ Brown, "Ableism/Language," accessed December 1, 2019, https://www.autistichoya.com/p/ableist-words-and-terms-to-avoid.html.

which generates high foot traffic behind me. This increased my hyper-vigilance and worsened my ability to cope with my PTSD. I decided to hang up prints of affirmations from one of my zines, "The Little Book of Work Affirmations," to block the glass barrier and create a sense of privacy. Changing my office space was helpful but it shouldn't be something we have to do to feel safe and productive at work. When new workers start, we should be mindful of any environmental needs before placing them and be willing to move folks around to accommodate any accessibility needs. For example, my PTSD is always worse during October, the anniversary of my rape. Since this has historically been an incredibly difficult time for me, my supervisor has offered to switch spaces with me during this time, trading her closed office for my cubicle for a few months. This is one of the ways we can intervene with built spaces to create safer ones.

There are many ways we can create change, whether through altering built spaces or changing our culture. It takes all kinds of strategies to create effective cultural shifts and changes. I want to emphasize one of the simplest things we can do as librarians for each other, for our patrons, and our communities, with the potential for the greatest impact is to *know our resources* such as those related to mental health and sexual and domestic violence, both locally and nationally: What is their phone number? Where are they located? What services do they offer? It's absolutely crucial to be familiar with resources outside of the police and forced/nonconsensual institutionalization which can be violent and even deadly for marginalized communities such as disabled people, people of color, and queer and transgender folks. When someone experiencing a mental health crisis is taken by police to the hospital, they may be forcibly stripped and injected with tranquilizers, as I have been before. This can be extremely traumatizing, especially if the person you're "concerned" about is already a survivor. Aaron Rose's piece, "What To Do Instead of Calling the Police: A Guide, A Syllabus, A Conversation, A Process" is a living document of resources on alternatives to policing, which range from the theoretical to practical, including best practices and guiding questions.

As a community, we can be more intentional, authentic, and supportive of ourselves and our colleagues/comrades by centering some of these principles:

- Foster a culture of radical empathy and vulnerability, free from fear of repercussions from colleagues, supervisors and/or HR.

- Refuse to use ableist slurs and language, such as crazy, insane, crippled, dumb, etc., and interrupt others' when they slip up—and not interrupting those who are reclaiming these words. Add new words to your vocabulary.

- Create inclusive and safe workplaces by offering "quiet rooms" for staff and faculty.

- Be mindful of new colleagues' environmental needs before placing them and be willing to move folks around to accommodate any accessibility needs, if necessary.

- Know both local and national resources, such as warmlines and hotlines, crisis centers, and shelters, and especially be familiar with those that don't rely on the police[3].

It can feel like ableism, saneism, and other structural forms of violence and oppression are unstoppable, impenetrable forces. However, when we come together as a community to create collective change, we can make a big difference. And even those "little" differences we create can be HUGE for the folks affected by them. Use this chapter as a starting point—but don't stop there. Continue to interrogate the ways in which ableism and saneism are normative in our field and how we can disrupt them on a daily basis.

## Conclusion

As I finish writing this chapter, I am faced with the upcoming anniversary of my rape—or as I call it, my traumaversary. It's been eight years now and while it has gotten easier to cope with, it's still a difficult time of year for me. My body remembers, even if I can't always. Writing about this is hard, so I pulled a tarot card to help me bring this chapter to a close. I drew the "Justice" card, a card encouraging me to speak my truth so I can find relief, find peace, find healing. I hope by sharing my experiences with you in the spirit of radical vulnerability will help me find relief, peace, and healing, and perhaps, it will help you find yours too.

---

3   Aaron Rose, "What To Do Instead of Calling the Police—Aaron Rose," Personal Website, Conscious Culture & Life Design, 2019, http://www.aaronxrose.com/blog/alternatives-to-police.

## Glossary

*Ableism*
A set of practices and beliefs that often originate with the idea that disabled people must be "fixed" or "cured" in one form or another, resulting in systemic and structural violence against disabled people. One manifestation of ableism is **saneism,** which is the systemic and structural oppression of mad, crazy, and mentally ill folks.

*Borderline personality disorder (BPD)*
A mental illness that often affects trauma survivors, resulting in symptoms such as an intense fear of abandonment (real or perceived) impulsive and risky behavior, suicidal behavior and/or self-injury, rapid changes in self-image and self-identity, stress-related paranoia, ongoing feelings of emptiness, wide mood swings (ranging from hours to days,) and intense anger. BPD is a highly stigmatized mental illness, resulting in widespread fear, misunderstanding, and hatred of those suffering from it.

*Post-traumatic stress disorder (PTSD)*
A mental illness that can occur in people who have experienced or witnessed a traumatic event, such as sexual violence, a serious accident, war or combat, abuse, and many other events. Everyone reacts to trauma differently but symptoms of PTSD may include intrusive thoughts (nightmares and flashbacks,) negative thoughts and feelings (feeling detached and estranged from others, ongoing fear, anger, shame, etc., and ongoing and distorted beliefs about oneself and others,) arousal and reactive symptoms (angry outbursts, behaving self-destructively, and hypervigilance,) and avoidance (avoiding reminders of the traumatic event such as avoiding people, places, activities, objects and situations that bring on distressing memories, avoiding remembering or thinking about the traumatic event, and avoiding talking about what happened or how they feel about it.)

*Radical vulnerability*
A praxis, practice, and strategy of sharing openly about experiences, identities, and stories that have been stigmatized and weaponized against us, in order to keep us quiet, small, and powerless, in order to normalize them, turning them from sources of shame to sites of growth and transformation, including opportunities for connection, solidarity, and community-building.

*Traumaversary*
The anniversary of a traumatic event.

## Acknowledgements

I want to extend my deep gratitude to Celia, for your radical empathy, loving encouragement, and care. I wouldn't be here, writing my first book chapter, without your help; to Laura, for your knowledge of resources and amazing recommendations, commitment to harm reduction, and non-judgmental, compassionate care; to Fatima, for believing me and in me when I couldn't believe in myself and for the radical work you've done to help so many survivors; and finally, to Asher for being a true friend and companion to me throughout these long years and for providing the solid support, stability, and love I needed to move from surviving to thriving as I worked towards healing.

---

## *Bibliography*

Brown, Lydia X. Z. (2018, December 17) "Abelism/Language." Retrieved from: https://www.autistichoya.com/p/ableist-words-and-terms-to-avoid.html.

Grandey, A. A. (2003). When "the show must go on": Surface acting and deep acting as determinants of emotional exhaustion and peer-rated service delivery. *Academy of Management Journal*, 46(1), 86–96.

Matteson, M. L., and Miller, S. S. (2013) A study of emotional labor in librarianship. *Library and Information Science Research* 35 (1), 54–62.

Rose, Aaron (2018 July 15) "What To Do Instead of Calling the Police: A Guide, A Syllabus, A Conversation, A Process." Retrieved from: http://www.aaronxrose.com/blog/alternatives-to-police.

# Diversity Scholar with the Trifecta of Mental Disorders: OCD, Generalized Anxiety Disorder, and Major Depression

**Marisol Moreno Ortiz**

*Content Warning*   Narrative throughout contains difficult and sensitive information that may be triggering for some. Please read with caution.

When you look at me you see a 5'4" young woman with whiskey colored eyes, brown hair, and a dimpled smile. What you don't see is that I have the great trifecta of mental disorders: Obsessive-Compulsive Disorder (OCD), Generalized Anxiety disorder, and Major Depression. Having a mind that misbehaves constantly and disturbs the peace makes working around people sometimes very difficult, even in a position that I am as passionate about as being a librarian.

As I move forward in this narrative of mine, I will talk about how my mental disorders have impacted the beginning of my journey into librarianship from conferences to applying for jobs and even writing this chapter. I will also refer to and will continue to refer to my mental difficulties as mental disorders and not mental illness. I hate the phrase, mental illness, because I am not sick, my brain is just different. My brain lacks the level of serotonin that would allow me to let go of unpleasant thoughts. I am still working on finding a better term that doesn't make me feel wary of my mental disorders.

My introduction into the academic library field was disrupted by my mental disorders. I went into the worst depression episode of my life in November 2017. By the time I began my appointment as the first Diversity Scholar in the Diversity Scholars Program (DSP) at Oregon State University Libraries and Press (OSULP) in January 2018, my emotions of enjoying and being happy doing things were just beginning to return. This depression episode was an unexpected event and one that provided me with a lot of growth, both personally and professionally, along a tough road filled with doubt and anxiety. When I have a high anxiety level the thought that causes anxiety gets stuck in my head and runs through my head repeatedly where I focus on it and fight it to decrease the anxiety. I am placed in a state of "something is wrong, and I need to fix it." But, in truth there is nothing to fix, I am fine and it's just my OCD brain. I need to constantly remind myself that it's just my OCD brain. This is a way of accepting that my brain is not perfect but that is okay, and I still can live my life and do what I enjoy doing as a librarian.

In the first week as Diversity Scholar I was close to giving up and quitting because I had a moment of agonizing anxiety where I could not focus, my body trembled, and I wanted to cry. I don't remember the exact day, maybe it was the second or third day, but my anxiety was so intense that I began to feel that I couldn't participate in the program and be a full-time Master of Library and Information Science (MLIS) student. This forced me to go to the office of DSP's lead librarian to ask her if we could talk because I was panicking. During our conversation, one of the things that I won't forget is that she told me the program was there to help me and not the other way around. We talked about reducing my work hours. After this conversation I felt supported and not alone on my journey as I started to learn the profession that I wanted to be part of. It also helped relieve the pressure I felt because the program was a great opportunity and one that I didn't want to lose because of my mental disorders. I didn't want another regret on my list.

But what caused this depression episode when things were fitting into place? Well, the answer is not so simple and one must understand that it was a series of events that led to this. I finished my term of service with AmeriCorps and went straight into my online MLIS in August 2017. This was my first time taking online courses and I was not expecting how isolating it could be. In my previous years in academia when the new term would start, I would often feel uncertain and uncomfortable which would cause my anxiety to intensify for about a week, but once I found my routine the anxiety would subside. But this time it didn't. It intensified until it was impossible for me to stop repeating OCD rituals because they decrease my anxiety. At this point, I started to berate myself for letting my brain control me. I was in a state of distress and was getting tension migraines. The outcome led to a rapid downhill where I wound up in the ER because a suicidal depression surfaced and it scared me. I wanted it to stop. But I think that this episode was unavoidable due to my antidepressant no longer keeping my serotonin at a normal level. To get better I needed to get out, move, and do things that I enjoyed doing, but this was hard to do because I was without motivation, energy, care, and was crying all the time. I was also very afraid that I would have to leave my MLIS program and DSP. I didn't want to quit because I saw my MLIS and DSP as the means for me to begin my career right away after finishing my degree. I felt like I was about to lose everything if I didn't do something about my feelings of lethargy and sadness.

I needed help, so I went and asked for it at Albany's ER in November 2017, but this ER didn't help me as I hoped it would. I was treated with more kindness by the nurse than the ER doctor. The nurse gave me a hug and let me cry on her shoulder and the ER doctor was unable to provide assurance or support that I was going to be okay. He didn't give me any useful options that gave me hope. After this disappointing encounter my mom and I decided to go to another ER close by that had better resources for people having a mental health crisis, there a mental health specialist came and evaluated my mental state. Through having a conversation with me he determined that I was not a threat to myself or others and helped me develop a plan of action to take a step forward into getting better. Getting better by taking back control was not easy. In the beginning, I spent a lot of my time watching funny videos on *YouTube* and rewatching *Psych* under the covers of my favorite fluffy light blue blanket.

The next step involved returning to therapy, calling the licensed clinical social worker (LCSW), whom I had worked with for many years before that had experience working with OCD. Unfortunately, she was only able to meet with me if I was in her Dialectical Behavior Therapy (DBT) class, which she thought would be a good idea for me to try. I met with her and she talked with me and my family about the class and after some thinking on my part I decided to apply to the class to see if I qualified. I was accepted and my treatment consisted of DBT group, a new medication that I think now, "why wasn't I prescribed this medication years ago?," one-on-one therapy with the LCSW, my coursework, and DSP. I took small steps in each of these parts of my life, kept my goals in my mind to push myself towards getting well, and I made it to taking back control. It took a couple of months, but I did it. I had to make the decision to face my OCD thoughts head on, which would be facing my thoughts every day and not fearing the anxiety they might cause. I began to enjoy doing things again, which was weird, because I was numb with sadness for so many weeks that I had to get to know the feeling of happiness again.

Unfortunately, before reaching this point and within a couple of months of starting the DBT class it was cancelled. Thanks to DSP, I had healthcare coverage that allowed me to find a new therapist who specialized in OCD and anxiety. In June 2018 I started working with a licensed psychologist and worked with her for a year. With my psychologist and my work with Exposure Response Prevention (ERP), I have come a long way and I am better than ever. I have come to control my OCD and anxiety to the point that I am enjoying everyday activities more fully instead of just going through the motions like a robot. I have reached the point of recovery with my mental disorders, which is the reason I can write this chapter. OCD, anxiety, and depression are chronic and will forever be part of myself and so during this time I was learning how to manage the mental disorders that pestered my brain while being the Diversity Scholar. I was able to find what worked for me in these new experiences that involved preparing mentally for them through imaginary exposure and doing what my OCD brain would tell me not to do because it would put me in danger.

A big and important part of my recovery is to do the things that I want to do both in my personal and library life which includes stepping out of my comfort zone and taking risks. OCD makes my library profession a real adventure where I must constantly adjust and be unafraid to take on new tasks, projects, or responsibilities, like accepting a nomination to be co-chair of the Awards Committee when I had never co-chaired anything before. When my colleague on the committee nominated me for co-chair, it caused the fuse of my anxiety to ignite and I wanted to run and hide. But knowing both other people on the committee, and that the other co-chair was someone I enjoyed working with helped. After calming down and reflecting, I realized that I needed and wanted this experience and I needed to at least try. I am glad I tried because I even got to nominate a person that deserved to be recognized for the work she did behind the scenes of the library. This approach of doing things I am afraid to do, where I question my ability to do them, has been eye opening because by learning new library skills through experiences I came to see that the fears and anxieties produced by OCD is not that scary and will fade when I face them, and my supportive work environment was a huge part of that realization.

In the beginning of DSP my anxiety surfaced a lot, especially the first ten weeks of the program because I was adjusting to the culture of the library and I met with a lot of my colleagues to talk about their careers and any advice they had for me regarding my MLIS and future career. This was hard because I was going into an environment that was just becoming part of my routine and it felt like I had no control but the more I interacted with my colleagues the more I learned and the better I felt. This increased the momentum of getting used to my new environment and helped motivate me to start projects that would help me learn about library work, especially library instruction.

The first information literacy session that I gave was for international students. The librarian that worked with these students asked me if I was interested in giving the sessions and I said that I was but as I began to prepare the session, a sense of doubt about my ability to do it crept in. But I knew that I needed to do the session in order to grow as a librarian and so I prepared my presentation that included a slide about me and how English is still hard for me sometimes when speaking some words, which made the students laugh. I brought humor into the session to help the students to feel comfortable participating as they had been on campus for only a couple of weeks from their home countries and speaking English was still difficult. I was anxious, but humor helped me relax and let go of my doubts about my abilities and I was able to focus on being a good librarian. This experience helped me learn relying on humor when stressed helps me feel better, especially if anxiety is making me feel worried. I also discovered through getting better that I am a funny person.

I also came to learn that in the library unexpected things can happen, like getting to my cubicle, checking my email, and receiving a message from the University Librarian about talking to stakeholders within a couple of hours. These stakeholders were people that donated money to the library and talking to them about my experience in DSP was important to do so that they might donate more money so the program could continue. But I was anxious, I needed to reorganize my schedule and think about what I was going to say. With anxiety and OCD, I need days in advance to prepare and be comfortable with tasks or other experiences, but with this meeting I needed to figure it out quickly, so I went into the meeting and gave it my best try. With OCD and anxiety that is all I can do. It all comes down to trying.

Throughout my appointment in DSP, OCD and anxiety often led to feelings of impostor syndrome because there were moments when I felt like I was not a real librarian. But once I was able to learn to cope with my anxiety and be okay with anxiety's presence I was able to find my librarian voice and also be an advocate for my colleagues and students. I attended a meeting where my department discussed the library partnering with the graduate school and how they wanted to have a space in the library for only graduate students to use. In the meeting it was discussed that one of the options was converting the largest classroom the library had and transforming it into the graduate study space, but this would mean that this room that many librarians used for instruction and other workshops would be taken away. I was glad that collaboration and new partnerships were being developed but I found myself thinking in the meeting that another space needed to be found because the large classroom was needed by the librarians and if it was taken away where would librarians teach large classes? There are moments of inner turmoil that I go through in minutes before I get the courage to speak and this meeting was one of those times, but I had to try to express why this option for the space was not the best option. I did speak and I am glad I did because other librarians also had similar opinions. If I had not spoken, I would have regretted it later.

My treatment is about managing my mental disorders so they don't interfere with enjoying my life and doing so every day. I did this while working to learn everything I could about academic librarianship, but I didn't shy away from mentioning my mental disorders. Living with OCD, anxiety, and depression has taught me that being open about them makes it easier to control them, instead of the other way around. I learned to be open about my mental disorders in the workplace in order to help destigmatize them. This led to me including in my email signature line a message for my colleagues, "Note: Dear Library Colleagues if you are having a bad mental health day, are in the library and need a hug, email me and I will give you one. No questions asked." No one took me up on my offer, but I hope that those that need it will.

Like anything chronic, my disorders have flare ups that occur when I decide to take on new adventures and as Diversity Scholar, I was constantly pushing myself to do so. There were a couple of times where I cried in the library bathroom, but I realized that it is okay. I needed to adjust and find ways to face my anxiety and tears are a small part of that. It also helped that OSU's library culture is very friendly and welcoming. This allowed for me to feel comfortable talking about feeling anxious with colleagues. When I asked colleagues how they were doing and then they asked me how I was doing I felt comfortable replying, "Good, but my anxiety is acting up." I learned that it is important to not be isolated from my colleagues. I would check in with the librarians that I was close to by going to talk to them at their cube. I was often afraid to scare them when they were working by just showing up and they saw my head suddenly over their cube. There were funny moments for sure.

In the library department where I spent the most time working in there was the unwritten policy that if I were at work, had no more meetings, and wanted to work from home I could, as long as I emailed the department to let them know, and I was available through Slack or email and did my work. This flexibility was wonderful for librarians in the department to have, especially for me because with mental disorders I just don't know when I will have an off day and having the ability to work from home was great. I did this a couple of times, one significant time was when I was just feeling blue, sad and very tired. I needed to re-energize and feel better, so I worked from home and that helped. Not all libraries have this type of flexibility and it really depends on the type of library position and how much flexibility it has.

During my invitations for library positions with on-site interviews, one of the questions that I make sure to ask is whether the position has flexibility in scheduling like OSULP. Most often, the answer has been no. This may be something that may need to be an accommodation request, I'm not sure, but it would be helpful for people like me that have mental disorders and really, we don't know how we are going to wake up feeling. We hope we wake up feeling awesome and happy but for people with mental disorders this is sometimes unrealistic. Sometimes, it is very hard to get out of bed. Sometimes I think, "I am so tired, I don't want to go to work," but I force myself to get up and get dressed. Once I get to work, I feel better with a brighter mood, but it really is a process and takes a lot of mental energy that a lot of people don't realize. I get mentally exhausted every day.

Some of my OCD thoughts are around the theme of contamination and germs. I worry often about getting sick and being unable to do my work and meet my commitments. I put a lot of pressure on myself sometimes when it comes to my work and this can be a good thing because it gives me the focus I need to push myself to complete things but it also places extra stress on me, which makes me more anxious and my OCD that much more present. But I have come a long way thanks to my support system and experience as Diversity Scholar. Before my recovery, even a cough from a stranger would make me cringe and want to shower right away but now being around many people in public has gotten easier where I can enjoy talking to them. This has helped make using the public bathroom a less stressful experience. With my OCD, public bathrooms used to be an issue because there is no better place for germs than a public bathroom. But using airplane bathrooms remains a difficulty as they are the smallest spaces ever. There are many places that also don't have toilet seat covers and so I always carry some with me. They have saved my bladder many times, but they are not cheap. I needed to budget and use my own money.

When traveling to conferences I need extra time to prepare myself for the travel and the energy that I will be spending. If the conference is weeks away, I plan my travel with everything that I need to make my stay in the hotel easier and enjoyable, which involves having a tolerable level of anxiety. To accomplish this, I begin by purchasing toilet seat covers before I begin my travel journey. I can always do the balance, but I want to enjoy my bathroom time just like everyone else. Traveling for conferences is a big part of the academic librarian life, even more so for those on the tenure track or wanting professional development where travel for conferences and workshops becomes essential. I was unaware of this before my Diversity Scholar position. Once I started traveling, I needed to adjust and mentally prepare myself for being close to people in a close environment. Working with my psychologist and ERP made traveling a part of my treatment and over time traveling became a part of my routine and I have become more relaxed when I travel. I enjoy it now. I enjoy talking to the person next to me and seeing new places.

At conferences I stay in hotels that seem to be the cleanest but clean hotels are not cheap. Staying at hotels was hard because there was a lot of preparation that I needed to do before I was comfortable with the idea of staying in a hotel. In the middle of 2018, before I started working with my psychologist, taking showers at hotels was hard and stressful. To paint a picture for you this was my preparation for hotels: I would buy plastic bags to place my clean towels and underwear on before placing them in my suitcase, and I would also buy rubbing alcohol to clean the hotel bathroom towel rack and faucets before taking a shower. While working with my psychologist, this was one of the items on my list that I wanted to work on, and I did. With ERP and preparing to do ERP while traveling I was able to slowly stop buying plastic bags and rubbing alcohol to clean the bathroom and shower in hotels. It was tough in the beginning because my anxiety went haywire without the bags and alcohol and OCD thoughts about contamination were more present, but it became easier and staying at hotels is now more enjoyable. In order to take a shower at a hotel I still need to mentally plan and keep in mind that I am going to take a shower, but it doesn't stress me as much as it did. But I still don't use the hotel shampoo and conditioner they provide. I buy travel sized shampoo and conditioner every time I travel to a conference. Because I was taking so many things with me to manage my disorders on my trips, I usually need to pay extra for checked luggage, which adds up. There is often no funding to cover these expenses despite need, so it came out of my pocket. As Diversity Scholar I was only working half-time and receiving a stipend, which helped, but I still needed to budget more than I had before. I travelled to conferences out of state about four times and for library positions with on-site interviews. If I had not addressed my travel and germ anxiety with my treatment, I would be spending a lot more money to accommodate my OCD.

My disorders not only drain my wallet but also my energy and this was never more apparent than when I discovered that jet lag is something that I should plan for. I learned that jet lag sucks big time. I had never had jet lag after the many times I had traveled before in my life but when I returned from my first out of state conference as Diversity Scholar in Minneapolis, jet lag hit me unexpectedly. When I returned from Minneapolis, I took a day off, and when I returned to work I was fine but the day after that I was on the bus that I took every day, when I started to feel very emotional and anxious and started crying. This episode forced me to get off the bus and call my sister to come pick me up to take me to work. She came and took me to work but during the twenty-minute drive she talked to me and convinced me that it would be better to not go in to work. When we got to the OSU library I went and talked to one of my supervisors and told her how I was feeling. After I left her office, I don't remember how I got from the fourth floor to the third floor of the library. I was moving in slow motion, like a robot. I was so drained of energy that when I got home, I laid down, and fell asleep for hours. I don't remember if I returned to work the following day or the one after that, but it did take me a couple of days to return back to normal but during those days I felt off, sad, meh. I was afraid my depression would return, but it was just jet lag. This taught me that self-care is very important before and after attending a conference. That is why I now take a greater time to self-care and rest before returning to work. It takes a great amount of emotional and physical energy to go to conferences, even more for people that are dealing with mental disorders like me.

Of the conferences that I attended, the one that I needed to plan more for was the one I attended in London. As Diversity Scholar, I had the opportunity to present at the Internet Librarian International conference in October 2018. Submitting a proposal for this conference was a long shot and completely out of my comfort zone. At this point, I had never crossed an ocean and not traveled alone to another country. Nonetheless, I submitted my proposal and it was accepted, and I became part of a panel on the diverse workforce in librarianship. I was glad I knew weeks in advance about my trip to London because with my OCD I needed to begin preparing weeks in advance to decrease my anxiety by preparing my brain. I began this process by talking to my psychologist.

The trigger of new experiences causes anxiety, the level often varies, but this time it was at a medium level, and it triggered an OCD thought of, "what if I freak out while in the air in the middle of the ocean?" This led my anxiety level to rise and the solution was to do imaginary exposure, which was to image the worst-case scenario that the thought brought up, describe it aloud and record it, and over the course of a week listen to it where I would experience the anxiety level decrease every day. I did this and it did. By the time I was to travel my anxiety was at a minimal level.

Unfortunately, an unexpected event occurred within three and a half hours remaining of my flight that upset me. The lights were off as people were sleeping and I was trying to do the same. I was getting comfortable and covering my face with my scarf when I noticed that the young man sitting by the window was putting his hand down his pants. Now, I was in the aisle seat and his girlfriend was in the middle and I kept thinking whether I would be able to tolerate staying in my seat for the remainder of the flight. With germs being a trigger for my OCD, the answer was *NO*, so I got up from my seat and went to talk to a flight attendant. I walked up to a female flight attendant and requested to speak to her in private and explained what I witnessed and asked if I could change seats. Her response was that she was going to let her manager know, and keep an eye on the young man, and then she helped me find an empty seat. I asked her if she would give me a hug, which she did, and it was so nice of her. She helped me see that if I need a hug, I need to ask for one. There are kind people in the world.

After I settled down in my new seat, I shed a few tears. I needed to calm down and so focused on watching something on the small screen in front of me. Once I arrived at my hotel in London, I was concerned that this event had ruined my experience of presenting in my first conference in the profession. I was concerned that my anxiety level would be high during my time in London because of being unable to stop running the event over and over again in my mind and this would keep me from enjoying being in another country alone. Fortunately, it didn't, and I was able to make it to Shakespeare's Globe and the London Eye. This moment helped me see that no matter how much I plan to be in control, things will happen that I don't see coming. But I can handle it. Because I did handle it, miles above as I crossed an ocean with that unfortunate event in the plane and things will be okay. I will be okay.

I was in the second year of my MLIS program when I was preparing for the conference, so I asked my classmates for any advice on presenting at conferences. Some of my classmates were already working in libraries full-time and had experience with this. One of my classmates wrote to me that it only takes thirty seconds of being brave, courageous, and once momentum takes over the anxiety goes away and it's so true. I kept this in mind at the conference and it helped once it was my turn to speak. When I started speaking, I was a little bit nervous but once I started talking, I felt much better, the pressure that I feel in my chest from anxiety went away. Now when I present, do something new, do some ERP for my OCD, or go to job interviews, I think, "All I need is thirty seconds of courage," and I will be fine.

My mental disorders also caused me to stop and think when I began applying for library positions. During this time I thought about and asked my colleagues whether I should mention that I have mental disorders. And I asked, "when is it appropriate to share this information?" But there is always the question of whether I won't get the job because of this. There is the Equal Opportunity law to not be discriminated against, but people are human. For every position that I have applied for at the end of the application there has been the voluntary disability disclosure question and every time I think whether I should answer yes or no, but I am honest and I answer yes because having OCD, Anxiety, and Depression is nothing I feel like I should hide. Even though the question is for HR purposes it's still difficult answering this question. Even writing this chapter has been difficult to write because in the back of my mind there is the question of whether this will affect my ability to get a position I want. I also have anxiety of what might happen once I'm in a position how will it affect me? I mentioned to my parents that I was writing this chapter and my father asked me if this would affect my ability to get a job, and I hope it does not. Having mental disorders is part of my identity, not the part that matters. At the end of the day the library that wants me and sees my worth will make me an offer even if they somehow find out about my mental disorders. They won't care but see this as an asset.

Writing this chapter has been stressful but it has led me to reflect on these experiences more and what I learned. I hope that my experiences and what I learned can help others with mental disorders in some way and colleagues in the library field understand that even though others and I struggle, we are still fabulous librarians. I want to help destigmatize talking about and getting support with our mental disorders in our profession and this way we can also help our students that might be struggling and just beginning to manage their own mental disorders. We need to be fearless and I am taking a greater step of fearlessness with sharing my mental disorders and my library work in this chapter and hope that this will help the people reading it to feel more fearless and share their experiences to help destigmatize mental disorders in the workplace. It's not easy but we can do it, slowly but we can do it. Change does not happen without vulnerability and risk. We must be bold.

# Finding Mental Balance at the Fortunoff Archive

**Christy Bailey-Tomecek**

*Content Warning*   Suicidal ideation, self-injury

As an archivist, I am fortunate to have a successful career. I got internships and entry-level positions in my field easily, landing my first professional archives position within six months of graduating. I was hired by Yale University, first as an Archives Assistant in the Manuscripts and Archives department and later as a Project Archivist for the Fortunoff Video Archive for Holocaust Testimonies. I achieved these things partially due to chance and financial support from my parents for my degrees. But I am also proud of myself for what I have accomplished.

I have been diagnosed with bipolar disorder, marked by moderate to severe depression and hypomania, and generalized anxiety disorder. Years before I was diagnosed as bipolar at fifteen, I started experiencing moodiness, irritability, exhaustion but regular insomnia, hourslong crying jags, and excitability where I spoke and thought rapidly. At the time, it was assumed to be teen hormones. My symptoms accelerated in high school, bringing suicidal ideation and attempts, as well as self-harm. With intensive therapy, I improved markedly by the time I started college.

At nineteen, I received a generalized anxiety diagnosis, along with my first medication for both illnesses. It took four tries to find the correct medication and I finally found it with lamotrigine at twenty-six. While therapy has been mostly successful, I continue on a regular basis to manage my symptoms of depression over my conceived "problem" status, passive suicidality, and anxiety in social situations, especially at work. I have lived alone successfully as an adult, but it was a tight-rope act and everyone sighed with relief when my now-husband and I moved in together. My husband, having seen some of my worst days, comments that if I didn't have the hypomania, I'd probably be cataton-ic from the depression and anxiety and the resulting self-hatred.

It's hard to watch all of this and think I am capable. Struggling with my mental illnesses all these years while simultaneously being successful in my career has made me feel split as a person—one state of being does not seem compatible with the other. I constantly try to bury this struggle for fear of being "weak" and threatening my success. However, the worst of my symptoms improved when I started working at the For-tunoff Archive. The emotionally difficult aspects of my work exist with-in a non-judgmental environment that acknowledges how hard this work can be. The open atmosphere also frees me from feeling shame about my mental illnesses while at work, which lessens their impact on me. In turn, I can use skills that I learned to manage my mental health to tolerate the emotional impact of regularly viewing Holocaust tes-timonies of survivors and witnesses. Now that I feel this profession-al support and know how to best harness my coping mechanisms, my goal is to support the archive's student workers using the same tools.

## Background Noise

My mental health is partly why I became an archivist. It was a plan B to my plan A of becoming an academic in English literature. Rather than studying and attending classes regularly, I spent my sophomore year having trouble leaving bed, rarely eating more than once a day, trying not to agonize over my uselessness as a human, and wondering why I ever tried to live. I recovered by the start of my junior year of college, but my GPA was damaged and my advisor informed me that I wouldn't get into any funded doctoral programs from undergrad as I had hoped.

Then I visited the Downtown Collection at New York University for a queer literature class, where the librarian brought out author David Wojnarowicz's "Magic Box," a small trunk filled with toys and other ob-jects that he used as writing prompts. We had just finished reading his essay collection *Close to the Knives* in class and I found it moving and enraging. Now I was looking at the building blocks for the writing I loved. Listening to the librarian explain how they arranged and preserved their collections, I realized that I wanted a job like that. It still engaged with the literature I loved in some way but was far more marvelous than the mass-published texts.

So off I went to grad school. I graduated and stumbled on a job posting for an Archives Assistant at Yale shortly thereafter. Since then, I've been enthusiastically engaged with the projects assigned to me. Meanwhile, I spent my graduate school years doing a considerable amount of work in therapy and figured out what medications worked best for me. Things have worked out, but my success doesn't mean that my conditions have disappeared or that it doesn't impact me on a daily basis.

Over the time that I have been in the Yale University Library community, I have tried to push away my mental illnesses from my work life because I'm afraid that it will interfere with my competent archivist identity and that my judgement and reliability as a professional will be questioned. I can't always tell how obvious my mental illnesses are to my colleagues or friends. It depends on how much I telegraph my "background noise," what I call the anxiety, depression, and passive suicidality I experience on a daily basis, along with occasional, uncontrolled upswings in mood.

There isn't much logic to how it manifests. I may be in a meeting with my supervisor, explaining calmly and confidently how to best schedule projects and update our collection metadata, but later on, I'll recall something that I did that "wasn't correct" and be overwhelmed by self-hatred, muttering my disgust, perhaps with some twitching or digging nails into my skin. Sometimes I'll be perfectly focused on my work, pleased with how fast I'm making updates. Other times I will stare vacantly at my computer, unable to get myself to do much of anything. In the past I have delayed answering emails out of anxiety over possible consequences, missed deadlines because I was too depressed to properly engage, and briefly derailed meetings due to hypomania-induced tangents.

I struggle almost daily with the feeling that I am faking being sane in a room full of *actually* sane people, people who expect me to oversee and complete projects. I have to get things done, while managing varying degrees of interference from my mental illnesses. I try my best, but I'm sure my colleagues can see right through me, see that I am actually *not one of them* and should not be trusted. And there's always the panic of:

*oh God, what if they see? Can they see what my background noise is caus-*
*ing? I shouldn't be here, how have I made it this far with how broken I am?*

Perhaps my background noise is not that obvious. My one colleague that I have confided in thinks that I perceive myself as weirder than I actually am. But I am not divorced from the moods and thoughts underpinning my actual behavior when taking stock of myself. If I do seem almost wholly "normal," it may be a result of my suppression. In any case, when I arrive home, the things I have stifled can spill out. I can have even severer depressive episodes, especially if my anxiety is on high alert about what I let slip that day. It is a frustrating, self-defeating cycle that has no reward, but sometimes it feels like what I have to do to no longer be the "damaged" woman I have labeled myself as.

## The Fortunoff Archive

The Fortunoff Video Archive for Holocaust Testimonies at Yale University was founded as the Holocaust Survivors Film Project in 1979 by Dori Laub, a child survivor and psychologist, and Laurel Vlock, a local television news producer. Vlock and Laub interviewed survivors in order to learn their stories, stories that were previously silenced by sociopolitical discomfort that emerged in the immediate post-war period and distorted by pop culture interpretations of the Holocaust. Comparative literature professor Geoffrey Hartman, himself a child survivor, brought the collection to Yale in the 1980s and the Fortunoff family endowed the archive to ensure its preservation.

While I do not have any subject expertise, I was drawn to the position by the collection's activism and my professional desire to preserve the stories of people who have suffered oppression. Now I work with documentation of the most well-known and industrialized genocide that the western world has known. Sometimes I feel like a keeper of the dead and wounded but helping stop the human cost of the Holocaust from disappearing into soulless statistics is more than worth it. The Fortunoff Archive is a way to remember the individual people through those who survived a system that tens of millions did not.

I find it ironic that I work with materials focused on trauma and human rights atrocities while constantly struggling with my own internal sadness. That being said, I view my mental illnesses and their treatment as saving graces—I can effectively manage my work thanks to the very illnesses that I normally see as my weakness.

## Daily Work

My work at Fortunoff has two major prongs. The first involves management of projects related to testimony transcription. The second focuses more broadly on maintaining the archive's metadata for collection access and management. I also provide reference and outreach for the collection as needed, which includes teaching workshops, video editing testimony clips for thematic programs, and reviewing our audio productions, including our podcast. Some of this work, like cataloging, requires me to watch testimonies in their entirety. When I develop my own lesson plans for instruction or do video editing, it requires me to sift through dozens of testimonies, sometimes watching them for entire days.

My job is not a constant emotional weight. I truly enjoy the technical, analytical parts of updating and improving metadata. I feel rewarded when I provide reference or teach with materials—I want people to use the collection. It's also worth noting that the atmosphere in the office is upbeat and cheerful. I am generally not tied up in melancholy. I love going to work most days. The difficulty of the subject matter is simply an aspect of our work.

Generally, there is a hushed, sometimes awkward response when I tell people the subject of the materials I work with. I've been told by many that they couldn't do my job and have been thanked for "my work" as if I am a veteran. That doesn't mean that a workplace or the general public would ever want to mine further into the impact of such a thing—it is sad, but the Holocaust is not something that happened to you, the staff member. You are just the one who views and listens to the experiences of its survivors and witnesses.

This is not the first time I've experienced this emotional reluctance. Before joining the Fortunoff staff, I worked with several collections documenting HIV/AIDS-related advocacy organizations. I arranged and described editorials decrying lack of government assistance for research and treatment, memos informing organization members of another death on staff, and guidelines for coping with relapsing or dying clients. Back then, the possible effects of such materials were not discussed. That didn't mean that it was forbidden to talk about it and my colleagues wouldn't have sympathetically responded if I struggled. But I would not have started that conversation since there wasn't explicit space for it. My own reticence about my mental health made me even less inclined to discuss it. It could make me sad. I could handle it. In my mind, it was something to push through, lest I betray my own weakness.

At the Fortunoff Archive, however, we truly examine the difficulties of the work. When I interviewed for my position, a cataloger was honest about how her work paused at times from how mournful the testimonies are. She asked me how I planned to manage their effects, what psychologists refer to as "vicarious trauma."[1] When testimonies have upset me, I am honest about that to my supervisor and he has been kind. We speak openly about their impact; we do not recoil from our feelings. Our acceptance allows us to acclimate to what we hear and see rather than constantly repressing. This lessens the risk of being emotionally overwhelmed, as can occur in workers who screen websites for offensive and violent content.[2]

This environment has also made me more forthcoming about my mental illnesses. I don't feel the need to censor myself in the department office. If I am having bad days and need time off, I feel okay doing so. We know that we aren't incompetent if we struggle with testimony. So why would my own mental illnesses be different? The fact that I am not seen as incapable of doing my job is incredibly valuable to me, emotionally and professionally. I do not need to suppress the effects of my illnesses the way I've done so in the past for fear that I will be found out and dismissed. My baseline ability to cope is better as I can take ownership of my emotional needs.

## Coping Mechanisms from the Past

Other library and information science professionals occasionally ask about my coping mechanisms for my work. The truth is, I don't have a specific protocol. I don't know of any archives that do. The closest thing I have are notes from a panel at the 2016 Society of American Archivists annual meeting. That panel, titled "I Second that Emotion:

---

1  Ivana Maček, "Engaging Violence: Trauma, Self-Reflection, and Knowledge," in *Engaging Violence: Trauma, Memory and Representation*, ed. Ivana Maček (East Sussex: Routledge, 2014), 5. Vicarious trauma and secondary trauma are used interchangeably at times (as I've done in the past), but secondary trauma more correctly refers to trauma transmitted from family members who have experienced primary trauma, while vicarious trauma refers to primary trauma transmitted to a therapist, caretaker, or researcher.

2  Sarah T Roberts, *Behind the Screen: Content Moderation in the Shadows of Social Media*, (New Haven; London: Yale University Press, 2019). Roberts' work provides more detail on this topic.

Working with Emotionally Challenging Collections," also suggested informal, improvised methods. These include:

- Multitasking with less emotionally stressful tasks
- Reminding themselves that "it's for the donor"
- Work alongside others
- Decompress as a team by having social events
- If working with a donor, crying with the donor is permissible[3]

My starting point for coping mirrors ones suggested at the panel. Alongside open work environments, time management is important. I avoid listening to testimonies for continuous days and switch between tasks as much as necessary. At home, I follow a similar policy. I won't read, listen, or watch anything having to do with the Holocaust, even in the most anodyne contexts.

Sometimes, I am blindsided by particularly harrowing experiences, such as choices survivors were forced to make in order to live, some which harmed or killed others. More recently, world events have had frighteningly similar overtones to the experiences documented in testimonies. Listening to an interviewee express worries about rising antisemitism or using language that echoes the language of the modern-day political right (one chilling example: a liberator interviewed in 1988 saying that the Germans "yelled [Hitler] into power, thinking that Germany will be great again. "[4]), can deeply upset me. That's when my own history with treatment becomes invaluable in confronting the depression and anxiety manifesting itself in my work.

At its core, my bipolar disorder is emotional dysregulation—my moods can be extreme and it's easy to get ensnared. I compare it to being trapped in a car with a volatile driver behind the wheel. I know what I am experiencing. I realize that the ways I am behaving are not appropriate. But I'm not driving—whatever mood is driving me cackles behind the wheel and I just try to hang in there. The trick is to assert myself and find a way to get into the driver's seat. This parallels the experience of listening to testimonies and developing symptoms of depression, like exhaustion, feeling despondent, and near-zero

---

3   Stephanie Bennett et al., "I Second That Emotion: Working with Emotionally Challenging Collections" (ARCHIVES*RECORDS 2016, Atlanta, GA, 2016), https://archives2016.sched.com/event/6mYB/109-i-second-that-emotion-working-with-emotionally-challenging-collections.

4   *Leonard L. Holocaust Testimony*, .mov file, 1988, https://fortunoff.aviaryplatform.com/collections/5/collection_resources/1319/description?

motivation. In order to perform my work, I must simultaneously stay anchored in the narrative of the testimonies, the horrific experiences they relate, and the resulting emotional impact on me.

My most common tool for handling any sort of distress is mindful distraction. One of my favorite facts about the brain is that it is impossible to focus on more than one thing at any single point in time. It can feel like I am multitasking, but that's my focus shifting quickly between things. I pick up complicated knitting projects, sew, or play detailed computer games. My goal is to be immersed in what I am doing—it's not just doing the tasks, it's deeply focusing on them and the results. Being an enthusiastic knitter is useful at work too. If I am screening testimonies for a project, I often knit something too, sort of a diffusing mechanism.

Another way vicarious trauma can worm its way into my brain is guilt about feeling upset about an experience that is not my own. Popular media about the Holocaust can make one feel sad—that is its design. But when one turns off the television or closes the book, they can leave that suffering in a fictional world. Testimonies are different. The survivor's function in an interview is not to make the viewer feel moved in a romanticized way, but to bear witness to atrocities. As a result, it can feel narcissistic to be so impacted—since it was never the viewer's suffering, how on earth could their reaction be valid when compared to someone who directly experienced starvation, disease, and casual, calculated murder?

I recognize this train of thought, however. It's similar to the background noise of my anxiety and depression colliding, where I experience guilt and anger about feeling horrible when my life is actually in a good place. I feel bad when I *should* feel good, therefore I am valueless. This causes me to withdraw further and pushes me away from seeking any sort of help or relief, because who would find my pain legitimate?

In order to emerge from the guilt, I need to verbalize my thoughts, cheerlead their validity. I try to tell others what I am feeling, or if I can't do that at the time, I record my feelings in a voice memo or a journal. It especially helps when I start viewing the experience of the survivor through the lens of witnessing—I am sharing it in the manner that I can. It is one of the most important reasons for my job.

Addressing my emotional responses also means not trying to fight or stop them from happening. As simplistic as it sounds, I'm used to being sad and scared and having to deal with those feelings as best as I can. I work to halt any self-destructive *actions* that could occur, but I'm also a regular hand at my mood disorders. It's not going to stop. It will be managed, but this is the condition as is. After so many years, I view episodes like fevers. I feel like hell, but they are temporary and I ride it out. The same is true of responses to testimonies. They are upsetting. I can acknowledge how they make me feel. But it's not judgement. It's waiting for the feeling to break, and bringing myself closer to baseline.

## Student Workers and Their Tasks

As I've mentioned before, I oversee transcription-related projects, which involves managing four to eight student workers each semester. Their work is more directly involved with testimonies than my own—they generally spend their entire shifts listening to testimonies.

Before Fortunoff started full transcription, students watched testimonies from start to finish and indexed the testimonies by creating segments with brief summaries of events. After the testimonies were digitized, we started time synchronizing these indexes with the videos, again utilizing student labor. Students do not have to listen to testimonies in their entirety and generally spending thirty minutes synchronizing every hour of testimony. In 2017, Fortunoff accumulated enough funding to begin transcription of our testimonies. Student workers must examine any unclear content marked by the transcription service and make corrections if possible. Again, the students are not expected to listen to entire testimonies.

Our job postings are aimed at both undergraduate and graduate students.[5] We get as many undergraduate as graduate students applying for positions. Many have some interest in the subject area, but graduate students are more likely to study history and/or Holocaust-related disciplines. Enthusiasm for social justice is also prevalent.

When I interviewed for my position, I asked if it was common for students to have difficulty working with the collection and if so, what the protocol was for assisting them. I was told that the student workers rarely

---

5   I do want to acknowledge that some may find it questionable for us to hire student workers to work with these materials when they are possibly taking the job solely for financial reasons. This is especially difficult given Yale's work study policy where students must contribute part of their wages to the university, making those students incredibly vulnerable to these pressures. That being said, many workers apply for the job over other ones due to interest in the topic area and we have equal amounts of work study students as not.

complained and no protocol was in place. However, since students almost entirely work with testimonies, I wanted to have a plan for managing vicarious trauma that was clearly stated to them. So, I make use of Fortunoff's open environment and the coping techniques learned in therapy.

It begins in the job interview. I describe the amount of time spent listening to testimonies and ask applicants how they would plan on handling the subject matter. Their answer is important and I use it as an opportunity for me to inform them that the archive does not punish student workers for reacting emotionally to the testimonies—we consider emotional reactions to be reasonable, not inappropriate. I strongly advise candidates to watch a testimony if they haven't already so that they can decide if they would feel comfortable working in the archive.

After the students are hired, I address these guidelines again at the beginning of their first shift. I reiterate that I know the emotional difficulties of the collection and that we will work with students accordingly. I outline that students should take breaks during their shifts if they want or need to; that unplanned days off are okay and their employment is not at risk if they take advantage of this; and that we can temporarily reassign students to administrative projects if they are struggling but do not want to miss shifts.

Establishing the archive's work environment takes over from there. All of the professional staff discuss what we are working on and ask for assistance from each other. Most of our concerns are on a practical level, but we do not hide when they are emotional. While I do not discuss my mental illnesses in detail, I do not hide their existence, including that I regularly go to therapy. I want the students to know that none of us will judge them or question their commitment to the work. I want to make clear that they will not be penalized and made to feel like their mental health should deny them a place at Yale, especially with the more punitive policies that the university may enforce.[6]

I don't minutely monitor the students, but I make sure to regularly check in. If they are visibly reacting, such as sighing while taking

---

6   Rachel Williams, "'We Just Can't Have You Here,'" *Yale News*, January 24, 2014, https://yaledailynews.com/blog/2014/01/24/we-just-cant-have-you-here/; Esmé Weijun Wang, "Yale Will Not Save You," in *The Collected Schizophrenias : Essays* (Minneapolis, MN: Graywolf Press, 2019). Both of these pieces document Yale University's strict policies on student leave for mental health issues, including involuntary withdrawal and mandatory evaluation by university psychiatric staff to be readmitted. Readmittance is often denied if there were issues of suicidality and parasuicidality, regardless of current treatment and mental health status.

off headphones or getting up quickly to leave the office, I note that. When we have a private moment, I will ask if they are okay. If I notice that their pace has slowed appreciably when checking work, I speak to the student to verify that they are keeping on task and to make sure that they are alright. If the student tells me that they are struggling, I again offer them time off or another work arrangement. I will also give them space to tell me about the testimony and how it impacted them if they wish to. I make clear that they do not have to feel guilty for being upset—much as I work to remind myself of the validity of my own feelings, I want to remind student workers of their own validity. I also respect if they do not have the same coping mechanisms as I do. Obviously, it is not my place to tell them what is correct or not.

I struggle with this ad hoc policy sometimes as I do not have any formal training on the topic. I want the students to feel supported by me, but I have to be mindful of the limitations on my own energy. Since I spend so much time in the dark places in my head, I relate heavily to other people's emotional duress and want to help. But it is not my responsibility to "fix" the students, much as I don't expect others to treat me besides my therapist and psychiatrist. To strike a balance between this empathy and a need for boundaries, I am slowly brainstorming towards a more formal protocol of care for our student workers, one where I am not the only maintainer.

As students work with me longer, they have been more forthcoming with their feedback. Students have disclosed responses like nightmares and asked me for coping strategies for testimonies that are difficult for them. I've gotten requests for days off to decompress. While it could be that I've been at the archive longer to have conversations like these, I wonder how often this was brewing before. It could have been like my experiences with the HIV/AIDS collections and more broadly with my mental illnesses, where they chose to quash their reactions so as to not threaten their jobs or look "weak." If it is the latter, I am gratified that we make them feel comfortable enough to speak about these issues. I take some strength in seeing my medical history as less of a burden and more of a learning experience that I can pass on.

## The Whole Person

I celebrated my fifth anniversary at Yale University Libraries in November 2019. That milestone is sometimes bewildering. Seeing my arc going from "mentally ill person at regular risk of paralyzing depression and self-harm" to "competent professional with well-managed bipolar and anxiety disorders" is too much like an idealized coming-of-age story for me to always accept as reality. But it is something I've achieved, in part due to my work at Fortunoff.

My identity is no longer as focused on me being a broken person who is succeeding despite the things that are "wrong" with me. Not feeling pressured to be emotionally detached from our collection materials in order to "be competent" means that I can better handle my own disorders, which in turn makes me a more engaged professional. I am starting to comfortably view my knowledge of regulation as part of my archival skillset—I am suited to the needs of these collections and guiding others with working with them.

I am still not at ease with myself—there's faulty biochemistry and years of poor conditioning to contend with. Those flashpoints do not go away overnight and the nature of my illnesses means I will always have these episodes to cycle through. But I can serve the needs of my archive, its staff, and the people whose stories we document. The context of the Fortunoff Archive allows me to live and work as a whole person. In turn, I can assist our students through the challenges of our materials since I don't have to be afraid of acknowledging what I know how to do.

## Acknowledgments

The author would like to thank Ruth Kitchin Tillman and Rosemary K. J. Davis for their insightful editing of this piece. The author would also like to thank Stephen Naron and the staff at the Fortunoff Archive for their professional guidance and support, and Ernest Bailey-Tomecek for his loving, personal support.

---

### Bibliography

Bennett, Stephanie, Stephanie Bayless, Chrystal Carpenter, Stacey Flores Chandler, and Krista Ferrante. "I Second That Emotion: Working with Emotionally Challenging Collections." Atlanta, GA, 2016. https://archives2016.sched.com/event/6mYB/109-i-second-that-emotion-working-with-emotionally-challenging-collections.

*Leonard L. Holocaust Testimony.* .Mov file, 1988. https://fortunoff.aviaryplatform.
com/collections/5/collection_resources/1319/description?

Maček, Ivana. "Engaging Violence: Trauma, Self-Reflection, and Knowledge." In
*Engaging Violence: Trauma, Memory and Representation,* edited by Ivana
Maček. East Sussex: Routledge, 2016.

Roberts, Sarah T. *Behind the Screen: Content Moderation in the Shadows of Social
Media.* New Haven; London: Yale University Press2019.

Wang, Esmé Weijun. "Yale Will Not Save You." In *The Collected Schizophrenias:
Essays.* Minneapolis, MN: Graywolf Press, 2019.

Williams, Rachel. "'We Just Can't Have You Here.'" *Yale News.* January 24, 2014.
https://yaledailynews.com/blog/2014/01/24/we-just-cant-have-you-here/.

# The Downward Spiral

## Nina Clements

It manifests physically as fogginess, as paralysis, as lead in the stomach or the head. I lay in bed, unable to move, terrified. Depression and anxiety have always been entangled with my life—vines around my goals, ambitions, and dreams—but they've grown stronger as I've grown older, squeezing the air out of me, an angry parasite. And then suddenly, I'm going down, down, down, into myself, into the tunnel. So many are in this struggle, and it looks different for each of us. What many of us share is the muted silence surrounding our depression and anxiety.

I am a depressed person, but I am also an academic librarian. How do the two intersect and interact? Does librarianship or academia more broadly attract depressive personalities? How do its various manifestations complicate our lives as librarians and as human beings? I want to focus on *disclosure*, the decision to share (or not to share) my diagnosis with colleagues and supervisors specifically, and how this disclosure can make work feel like a prison thanks to the pervasive and thriving stigma surrounding mental illness.

This essay is a kind of coming-out story, a kind of claiming. It is a narrative that keeps moving, without an ending. Of course, I can only speak to my experience with depression in Library Land. A friend who read an earlier draft suggested that this decision of disclosure is more universal than librarianship. Yes. But how does librarianship respond? Shouldn't we respond, as educated and compassionate helpers, with *more* than the usual stigma that we find in the general population?

***

Overall, mental illness in librarianship has not been studied. Erin Burns and Kristen E.C. Green began to unearth this subject in their *College & Research Libraries* article, "Academic Librarians' Experiences and Perceptions on Mental Illness Stigma and the Workplace." They conducted a review of the extant literature as well as a survey of librarians' perceptions of mental illness stigma. They defined stigma as "a set of prejudices that draw their basis from the stereotypes that use some social cues to signal perceived social categorization and elicit emotionally driven responses, usually negative, toward people who exhibit these cues."[1] Stigma still has teeth, according to the study. It concludes that "if librarians genuinely strive to create environments of inclusion within their libraries, an allowance for disclosure of mental illness without the fear of stigmatization would not only help members of our local academic communities but librarians as well."[2] Yes, but how do we get there? Spoiler alert: I don't have an answer.

My fear of stigma from others, as well as my experience of it, has influenced my decision to share the fact of my depression with colleagues and supervisors. It's not always necessary to share the diagnosis—depression is *invisible* and does not physically mark the body. This is something that I've thought about a great deal—the way in which it hides inside one, with no evidence of manifestation—there is no bruised or broken skin, no proof of illness or healing. In my first professional librarian position, I did not need to share this diagnosis. Depression lurked, much as it did in my adolescence and even childhood, beneath the veneer of high-achieving behavior. In other positions, though, I needed to make this decision of disclosure, and I still wonder if I made the right calls. My first unhidden depressive episode took place in 2015, and it was a full-fledged, incapacitating breakdown.

What happened? It's hard to identify all the tendrils that constricted me into silence and suffering. There was a catalyst, certainly. But it's not worth mentioning. For no reason at all, the depression got stronger; its power over my movements increased exponentially during that episode, and it has not lessened its grip. To be clear, the episode passed eventually, after a few months, but episodes are now harder

---

1   Erin Burns and Kristin E.C. Green, "Academic Librarians' Experiences and Perceptions on Mental Illness Stigma and the Workplace," *College & Research Libraries* 80, no. 5 (2019): 639.

2   Burns and Green, "Academic Librarians' Experiences and Perceptions," 655.

to work through than they were in my youth. This episode passed after a few months of not caring for myself, of not speaking out loud, of not working.

My partner at the time took me to therapy, took me to the psychiatrist's office, to the pharmacy for the new pills that eventually pulled me out of the fog. He cared for me as though I were a child. I felt like a burden to him. He begged me to go to work, but I was anxious about facing my supervisor and colleagues after such a long absence, and this anxiety was paralyzing.

I disclosed my depression to my supervisor all of a sudden while hunched over the phone in the dark of my car one night after therapy. My position at the time was a faculty position, and it came with unlimited sick time. This probably saved me from official scrutiny or reprimand, but it greatly inconvenienced the other library workers in my small library. I have reason to believe that my supervisor shared my diagnosis with my other two colleagues. One colleague, whether because of my diagnosis or my constant absences, refused to speak to me. At the time, I was convinced that it was the stigma of my depression that had caused what proved to be an irrevocable rift. That rift, however, that the silent colleague, who would not so much as say hello to me when we passed each other in the hallway, kept me from sharing my depression at other places and to other supervisors and colleagues. This greatly altered my future approaches to disclosure.

What did my depression/disclosure look like at my last position? It wasn't the full-fledged incapacitation of 2015, but it was also unhidden It manifested as panic, as an inability to leave my apartment and the comfort of my cats. It meant that I missed reference desk shifts and instruction sessions, often at the last possible moment. I tried to force myself to go to the library, but I often could not and that resulted in many last minute notifications to my supervisor and colleagues. After previous experiences of stigma surrounding depression, I felt strongly that I could not disclose my diagnosis to my supervisor, though I did share it with several colleagues who carried on, pretending that I had not shared it. My depression was invisible to them, and I felt like I was slowly disappearing.

While I did not diagnose the fact of my depression to my colleagues, I did disclose that I had a *chronic health condition* to my chair, my supervisor, and the dean of the library, all while eating lunch in the cafeteria. The place of meeting had not been my choice. I felt exposed there, but I shared that my illness required a month-long intensive outpatient treatment. I never said the word *depression*. We worked to change my schedule to accommodate the treatment without losing my salary.

This position was a tenure-track faculty position, and I came into it with a year of service credit. This meant that after only one year of work, I was up for my three-year review, which was a retention review. I had hoped to manage my depression with my allotted sick and vacation time, which I did not exceed. However, I had no such luck, and my unwillingness to disclose my illness seemingly served as my undoing. With every sick day, every late or missed reference desk shift, every missed or rescheduled instruction session, I gave the tenure committee (composed of three tenured members of the library) more rope and eventually, they tied me up with it. My peer evaluator clearly wrote out of frustration: "Time and attendance remain an issue and it is noted in the four weeks beginning the Fall semester, there have been three Monday opening shifts available. . . Of those three, Ms. Clements has required a substitute to fill two of those shifts and arrived minutes before the start of the third." If I had officially disclosed my mental illness, would this language still have appeared in my review? The irony is that the writer of the review knew I had depression but pretended he did not. Also, it's clear that being on time was not enough—that there was some kind of group anxiety about my ability to be where I need to be and being on time was no longer adequate. What was really being said there is: *She is sick too much and is unreliable. She is not a good colleague.* Was this true? Had my illness prevented me from being a reliable colleague? The truth was that my acute episodes of depression came on quickly and unpredictably—it was difficult to give much notice, and it was impossible to work from home during episodes, which my colleagues also seemed to expect. While the committee voted not to retain me, the dean and the university's tenure committee (composed largely of teaching faculty outside the library) overturned that decision. I was safe, for now.

\*\*\*

Depression has made me an itinerant library worker, a wanderer, a nomad. I left two positions before things reached the level of formal reprimand or critique, but I was forced out of my last position as a result of my depression and its intersection with the tenure process. Somehow, during the initial drafting of this essay, I found the ability to apply to another job in a different state, pinging myself once more across the country. Throughout the interview process, I wondered if I should disclose my mental illness, but decided against it. We have the right to protect ourselves, at least initially, it would seem. I love the allure of the fresh start, the blank slate, where everything I do is new and without fault.

It felt like I had no choice but to keep leaving positions, hoping each time that a fresh start would be the answer. I felt like I was in danger of disappearing from librarianship and from the world, that I would need to seek in-patient hospitalization or government disability. My mother unhelpfully predicted that I was not far from homelessness. Somehow, though, I didn't disappear. During the writing of this essay, I did manage, with the help of intensive therapy and an adjustment in my medication, to pull myself together and apply for a new job in another state, where I am now.

When I first began writing the essay, I was still at my small state university in California, whose campus was a former mental hospital. The buildings were beautiful, mission-style architecture and grassy courtyards. The courtyards were meant to keep people contained, though. There was no easy way in or out of them.

I'm still not brave. Here in my new position in the Midwest, I've suffered through some small depressive episodes, but I used old strategies of hiding behind sick and vacation time. I haven't yet found the courage to disclose my depression to my supervisor. There can be no ending to this story: I will disclose, or I will not disclose. Even when I disclose, I will still have depression. There is no way to resolve that. It is a struggle without end.

The writing and rewriting of this essay have helped me to realize that this struggle needs to be less private, more public, that it needs to be shared with others so that we understand how to respond to depression and mental illness with compassion. People suffering silently with anxiety and depression must understand that they are not alone. I wish there were a network of LIS professionals with depression to call upon when we need guidance, support, compassion, to make us feel seen in our libraries. The writing and rewriting of this essay have also been risky—it is a risk to come out and claim a mental illness so openly. I have a new job; I am new here, and undoubtedly, my colleagues will make a judgement or series of judgments about me for writing this essay. I hope that their judgment has nothing to do with my librarianship, or the qualities I possess that make me a good librarian. I hope they think I'm a real human being.

It's difficult for me to imagine a compassionate workplace, but I wish supervisors could better understand how depression and anxiety shape our work and sometimes take it from us. Disclosure may be one way to afford ourselves some measure of protection or job security, but it is not an easy choice, is not a panacea. To return to the idea of an inclusive workplace, it takes work to disclose a mental illness, and it takes work to receive that disclosure. Colleagues and supervisors may or may not respond with compassion and understanding, with flexibility or further rigidity. And it seems that for now, our network of support will likely be *outside* of libraries, in therapy, support groups, friendships. I hope that my colleagues from *within* libraries will be open and supportive. This is not the end, but the invisible has now been rendered visible, is now seen.

## Acknowledgments

I'd like to thank Kate Joranson, Jacob Duffy, and Stacy Russo for reading and commenting on previous versions of this draft.

*Bibliography*

Burns, Erin and Kristin E. C. Green. "Academic Librarians' Experiences and Perceptions on Mental Illness Stigma and the Workplace." *College & Research Libraries* 80, no. 5 (2019): 638–57.

# If You're Happy & You Know It, Tell Me How

**Chelsea Tarwater**

*Content Warning*   Discussion of suicidal ideation, depressive and manic episodes, and self-harm

There's a unique cognitive dissonance to singing "If You're Happy & You Know It" while you're suicidal. I play the ukulele for storytime, so I wasn't lying to the kids by clapping my hands, but I had spent the last two nights prior to this wide awake and sobbing in bed, making plans to hurt myself or to be hurt or to potentially enact one of the several options from the Google search, "least painful suicide methods."

I didn't know exactly what was happening in my head, but I knew I wasn't happy. It didn't matter that I loved my job or that I loved these kids who came every week to see me and who referred to me as the storytime lady because they connected me with something important to them. Nothing could distract me from the sunken feeling in my stomach.

I was twenty-five and I was tired of trying so hard.

I was twenty-five and I didn't know what happy felt like.

## Living Past Eighteen

My childhood memories are blurry but there is one constant: I felt wrong.

Part of it was being a lot too gay for rural Tennessee, but I know now that I was anxious—I was anxious *all* of the time. My constant resting state was mild terror for as long as I could remember, punctuated by the constant recurring dark cloud that started following me around when I was twelve and thought about dying for the first time like it could save me from myself.

Sometimes, all I can remember from high school is how much time I spent in bed with the lights off, how many times I dug something sharp into my skin, how many friends I pushed aside because I didn't believe they wanted me. I *couldn't* believe they wanted me when even *I* would prefer if I wasn't around.

When I graduated from high school, I hit a surreal point in my life.

There are three things that felt like waking up in the next year: turning nineteen when I had convinced myself I wouldn't live past eighteen. Telling a pretty girl in a parked car I wanted to kiss that I might have *depression or something like that*. Trying to ask for help for the first time and failing—making an appointment with the campus counselor and never showing up—but *trying*.

It took about five years from that missed appointment to finally show up.

## Asking For Help

After that storytime, when I smiled and sang and felt like I was about to shatter into a hundred different pieces, I went to my biweekly appointment with my therapist and told her everything that had been happening: how I poured out all my pills and held them in my hands, how I thought about chasing the lightning streaks in my head and doing the stupidest things I could think of. I've never felt darker or more honest, when I confessed the truths I wouldn't tell anyone else—when the answer to why I didn't call her before this was that I'm used to powering through.

Throughout my life, I've made an art out of not asking for help, of swallowing things down, of keeping quiet. Getting into therapy was one of the hardest things I've ever done, and I still hate every second of it, but the fact that I still go every two weeks shows how much I need it. And I know that if I didn't make that change, if I didn't speak up and ask for what I needed and learn what was happening in my brain, I wouldn't be here today.

I didn't know it at the time, but I was having a mixed-state manic episode that night before storytime: the intersection of manic and depressed, the perfect mix of states that leads to suicidal ideation because your brain is on fire and you can't think of any other way to put it out. Once I was able to describe it, it was easy to identify it because I was already tentatively being treated for Bipolar II—something that was strongly confirmed when I was prescribed Lithium after this incident and quickly felt like I was in control of my body again.

As an extremely introverted introvert, Bipolar II was a difficult diagnosis to deal with. There are definitely people who don't believe it when I tell them, partially because I learned a long time ago how to smile through anything and partially because I have so much anxiety that I rarely make good on the compulsive thoughts. I *have* them, though. I have those dangerous urges and that frantic energy that bites at my skin and makes me do things like try to make a database of my own books at 3:00AM when I have work the next morning (I am, at the very least, always on brand) and that pitched, dramatic despair that makes me feel like a teenager again.

The fact that I don't go out and do something intentionally dangerous doesn't mean that I didn't spend all day planning on doing it.

The fact that I don't get in my car and drive until I run out of gas doesn't mean that I don't frequently get *really damn close*.

## Crashing Down to Earth

My instinct is to pretend like my mental illness doesn't define me, but it's shaped my experiences and my viewpoints in so many ways that this might not be true. It defines me the same way other parts of my personality define me: introversion, competitiveness, humor—all those things mixed up with my dysfunctional brain chemicals to make me the singular, strange human-like person that I currently am.

It's important to note that defining the mental illness itself made all the difference in understanding myself and what I was going through, though. I started getting treatment assuming I had Major Depressive Disorder because major seemed like the most accurate description of my depression. When I first started taking antidepressants for it, it felt like waking up for the first time. I had this energy that seemed to border on superhuman. I hardly needed to sleep and I honestly thought that this was what I was like when I wasn't depressed. Against all odds, all the garbage inside of me was hiding someone who actually *did* the things on her Pinterest board.

I agreed to do my first presentation at a library conference during a manic episode. Future depressed me wasn't amused by this, although it ultimately opened up a lot of doors that have allowed me to present at the ALA annual conference and take other leadership roles, making me more comfortable in my skin and in this profession. Imposter syndrome essentially doesn't exist to me when I'm operating on all cylinders like that but it's very real and very strong when my brain crashes down to Earth again.

And after weeks of barely sleeping and making promises to do things I'd regret agreeing to later and unnecessarily organizing everything in the Children's Department storage room by color and size, I crashed. Hard. I wasn't aware of this at the time, but certain antidepressants can cause mania for people with bipolar disorder which meant my apparent superpowers were short-lived and artificial.

I'm in a pretty good place with my medication now so I haven't been manic in a long time, but I occasionally miss the heart-pounding intensity that made me want to clean the whole library and read all the shelves and keep moving to keep up with the rapid fire drumbeat of my brain. I lapse into depression more often, so I romanticize mania. Not needing to sleep sounds great when I'm dealing with insomnia and my grad school course load. Compulsive organizing sounds *amazing* when it's summer and the rush of kids have torn our shelves apart. And I would love to have the energy and the drive to sort ten thousand beads by color family right now even though there's absolutely no reason for it.

In the end, though, I always talk myself back into reality and think about where it's led me before.

Mania's great until it isn't, until the inevitable crash when I realize I'm not that super, until it makes me do something dangerous.

Or maybe just until I have an existential crisis during the middle of a children's song, between a Mo Willems book and an Eric Litwin book. To be fair, though, Pete the Cat is an *excellent* companion to an existential crisis.

## A Cloudy Day at Best

I've been dealing with depression for so long that I never think it's impacting my job performance, typically because it isn't. It's mainly impacting my ability to tenuously hold onto what I can only refer to as my general okayness. My depressive episodes are typically defined by hating the concept of other people even acknowledging my existence, which means working a job where I talk and perform and constantly interact with other people frays my nerves drastically. I can manage to get through a workday when I'm like this, but by the end of it, I feel like I've been gritting my teeth for nine hours.

As I've said, I've learned to smile my way through most things even when I'm gritting my teeth, due not only to a long history of repressing my feelings but to years working in customer service. From a lengthy time working in retail to my work in public libraries now, I have perfected the affectation of being okay even when I'm having an internal meltdown. Occasionally, patrons will even stop and tell me that they always see me smiling, which provokes a mixed bag of feelings. It feels satisfying that I'm dealing so well but pretending like I'm okay isn't actually dealing. It's neat that I can trick people, but it would be way neater if I didn't need to.

Talking about the role that introversion plays in a lot of public facing librarians' lives is a fascinating topic but adding depression and anxiety makes it even more so. Adding Youth Services on top of that might warrant a field study. I'm good at my job, but I'm nowhere near the picture that I assume that people who work with kids should be. It's entirely possible that, because of this, I should really be observed in my unnatural habitat.

For my undergraduate degree, I earned my secondary teacher licensure to teach English and took classes with a lot of future elementary school teachers. Primarily women, they were a blur of perfectly curled hair and shiny smiles and positivity. I started my job, where I currently work leading our early literacy program for mainly preschool and under, with some trepidation. I am not that person. I have never and will never be described as perky. I can maintain a four-year-old's energy level for about an hour before I need to go hide for a while and recover. I frequently forget to brush my hair and I don't do Zumba.

(I have no evidence that people like this do Zumba but it just feels true.)

On a baseline personality level, I'm often uncomfortable that I'm doing what I'm doing, and it feels exhausting when I'm depressed because—god, I'm the *storytime lady*. I feel like I have an obligation to channel some sort of sunniness or I'm going to make them hate reading somehow, which I can recognize is ridiculous. I can also recognize that a brain like mine is a brain that thinks I'm always on the brink of ruining anything and everything. Because of that, I often have to make a conscious effort to smile—because I'm supposed to be smiling. I try to be full of sunshine because I'm *supposed* to be full of sunshine. That's what it feels like, at least, and that's why it's exhausting: when I'm doing okay, I often feel like a cloudy day at best. And, on my worst days, I feel like a natural disaster—a hurricane, a flood, a *sinkhole*. Something that could swallow me and everyone around me up if I'm not careful.

While I'm not perky, I try to be tentatively optimistic because I know that, even if I don't fit the picture that I think I should fit, being a creature made mostly of sarcasm and mild trauma and cognitive behavioral therapy means that I can be a role model to kids who also occasionally feel like sinkholes.

## Starting A Conversation

Despite the fact that I live in a small conservative town, it's easier to reach out to queer kids than kids struggling with mental illness. A rainbow sticker goes a long way and so many kids with a mental illness—and their parents, as well—don't even realize what they're struggling with. We can court controversy with pride displays and show the queer kids in our town that they're welcome and safe in their library. It's a conversation that we're already having.

It's difficult to start up a conversation about mental health for younger kids but it's necessary. There have been several youth suicides in the past few years in our county and not enough is being done to address it—and that includes my library and me. I'm still figuring out how to use my platform for this conversation when I'm not even sure how to start it, so I do what I can: we talk about our feelings in storytime. We put bookmarks out for teens with call numbers for books about difficult topics that they might not want to address with a librarian, like suicide and sexual assault.

We try to create an environment where they'll come to us for help anyway.

I worry sometimes that kids will notice the scars on my forearm and ask about them, that parents will see them and know what I've done, but I also wonder if it would be so bad if people knew. It seems like a backwards way to be a role model, but—my scars are healed. I'm still alive. The way I hurt myself makes me a living art display of recovery and I don't know how to be proud of it yet but, at the very least, they spell out that I understand.

I don't know if I'm the adult that I needed in my life when I was a kid, but I'm still pretty surprised that I'm an adult, so I'm a work in process. It couldn't have hurt, though, to have had an awkward, messy, radically caring queer adult in my life who could tell me everything would be okay if I just asked for help—that they were where I am and are still fighting. That it's worth the fight.

I want to be a lot of things but being a person that lets kids realize how important they are to the world is the most important one.

## I'm Still Here

I'm twenty-seven and I kind of know what happiness feels like now. I feel human about 65% of the time. I can take deep breaths (breathe in for a count of four, hold for a count of seven, exhale for a count of eight) to get through a program or a patron interaction on a difficult day. I keep rubber bands on my wrists at all times to snap if I'm feeling like hurting myself. I go to therapy and I take my meds and I drink *so much water.* And when I take a mental health day, my manager and coworkers know that I'm being literal—that it's a day where being an extant, visible human seems insurmountable—and I'm incredibly lucky to be working in an environment that allows me to be literal about it and that has supported me on this extremely bumpy path to recovery. This is a privilege and perhaps even a rarity and I intend to make the most of it by treating myself well and by being unashamedly, borderline annoyingly open about mental health both for myself and for those who can't.

I've always been a chronic oversharer on social media, but in the last several years it's become a minor way to enact social change. If I talk about therapy and medication and suicidal ideation, not only do I get the external validation that I need to function but I also do my part to normalize the issues I'm facing. I get messages from people occasionally telling me that I've helped them feel more comfortable with what they're going through just by posting statuses about my own attempts to achieve that general okayness. I try to be proud of that.

I don't exactly know how to do something similar at my library, but I think that kind of openness and honesty is what's going to at least start the conversation.

And, in the meantime—I'm still figuring out happy, but I'm still here.

So. . . if you're struggling and you know it.

If you're trying and you know it.

If you're growing and you know it—I can clap for that.

# On Surviving

## Allison Rand

*Content Warning*  Mentions of violence and guns, trauma, and a brief mention of drug addiction.

I was nineteen years old when I became the survivor of a terrorist attack. It has taken me over six years to be able to admit that to myself or anyone else. I wanted desperately to be unaffected by what happened; I was plagued with guilt and anger over any acknowledgement or question about it, and I have avoided any discussion of my experience in the six years since it happened. I knew there were people out there who had it worse than me, people who saw worse things than I did, and I refused to put a name on my feelings because of it. But post-traumatic stress disorder (PTSD) is messy and opportunistic, and it doesn't care who you are or what you saw. It strikes at night when you're alone, and in crowds when you're not, and it taunts you to feed its hunger until it is satisfied and you are starved.

On April 15th, 2013, I received a text message from a friend. "Stay where you are," it said. "Generator explosion at the finish line." Then another message minutes later: "Not a generator. Bombs. Get inside." I lived just blocks from the finish line of the Boston Marathon, where two pressure cooker bombs were detonated, killing three people and seriously wounding more than a hundred. In Boston, the city shuts down for the marathon, it's a state holiday, in fact, and I'd left my dorm an hour earlier to go to the finish line. I'd made it halfway there before a friend realized she'd forgotten her keys in her room. We went back for them, waiting for her roommate to unlock the door. It was during the 20 minutes we waited that the bombing happened.

The following hours and days are seared into my brain. If I close my eyes, I can see exactly how the week played out from violent start to dramatic finish. I can reenact the three phone calls I was able to make before the cell towers were overloaded; one to my parents and two to my closest friends outside of the city. Six years have passed, but I can remember exactly the note I scribbled to my roommate in the early morning hours during the shootout at MIT and subsequent manhunt across the city. The sight of armed guards at airports still throws me back to when the National Guard stood outside my dorm room, checking the IDs of every person who entered with one hand and clutching a rifle with the other.

For the next several years, I avoided the topic. I kept my head down when the topic of the Marathon Bombings was brought up. Watching the news of mass shooting after mass shooting numbed me; I had no reason to be traumatized, I convinced myself. I hadn't been at the scene. I didn't see the carnage. All of these people had it worse than me, so I was fine. I skated through the rest of college by putting a glaze over it in my mind. If I slicked it over enough, any notion of a thought or memory would slip without sticking. By the time graduate school rolled around, I hadn't dwelled on the bombings in years. The slip-n-slide inside my mind allowed those thoughts to pass without consideration. I would blink and they would be gone.

In library school, I landed a job as a graduate assistant, which meant nearly a week of intensive training before the semester began. We were drilled reference and customer service and supervision duties, until it was time for our safety training. Nearly fifty graduate students crowded into a basement lecture hall in the library. I sat in the middle-front, with a clear view of an exit to my left, because that's how my brain now operated. We were greeted by a campus police officer, young and enthusiastic, who briefed us on fire safety, de-escalation guidelines, and "run, hide, fight" training.

"We really just want to instill these ideas in you," the officer said, "rather than practical training. You just can't know how you'll react in a high pressure situation ahead of time, so we can only train you on these concepts. When you go into survival mode, you might not react how you think you will." Another graduate assistant leaned forward from the row behind me, their hand raised.

"At my undergrad, we did trainings with officers shooting blanks," they said. The officer on stage nodded.

"Well, that's good. Then you know what it's like," he said. A feeling of guilt and anger shot through my chest. They didn't know what it was like. I knew. On that day in April, I had leapt into action, scrambling to make phone calls and find my friends and get them to safety. I knew that my survival mode put me into action, and I had a clear idea of what it would be like in an active shooter scenario. The knowledge that my rational mind would take over in place of fear was a deep knot of dread in my stomach. I wanted to be the person who fled, or hid, but I'd proven that I wasn't, and it terrified me.

After that session, I pored through the safety manual. I mentally mapped out routes from the reference desk to the nearest exits or the safest place to hide every time I was on shift. I tested how fast I might be able to lock my office door when no one else was around. At the same time, I was being told in my classes and in my work that the library was a safe space. Safe for me, safe for everyone. The narrative of the library was one of acceptance; the library was the place to go after class, to spend late nights, and to exercise the mind. No matter how many times I was told it was safe, I couldn't shake the feeling that my work was a deathtrap. I had my friends and my allies in the library in the form of people I worked with closely, or people whom I'd otherwise formed relationships with, but anyone else was a potential threat. While we discussed "problem patrons" who lingered too long or made inappropriate comments towards librarians, I was far more concerned about the patrons who seemed too curious about schedules and directions.

I lived like that for the two years I was in grad school, always on edge. My graduate school assistantship was my first time working with the general public since the bombing, and my first time ever being a supervisor for undergrad workers, and it compounded the stress and fear I'd put so much work into burying. I didn't share my experience with nearly anyone, which surely didn't help. My peers poked fun at me for being over prepared in most situations, from timing my bus rides to and from campus to finding an escape plan for a Tinder date. I think, or I hope, it came off as quirky rather than paranoid. I couldn't *not* think about the possibility of another incident. To me, it seemed inevitable.

I spoke to no one about my constant feelings of dread and terror until late into my second year of grad school, when I began to see a therapist for the compounding stress of my job hunt. I'd known, even without a diagnosis, that I had anxiety. That much was clear to me and everyone else. After my first hour-long session with my therapist, wherein I sobbed for most of the hour, she looked me up and down and said: "It's clear that you have PTSD, and I think you're also in denial about being depressed." The words hit me in the chest; they felt like a judgement or an insult, but as she spoke I also felt something click into place. Of course I had PTSD. It was so clear, so obvious that I had not actually escaped that day unscathed, and that I had carried the trauma of it close to me for years. My habits of overpreparation and avoidance were not normal, they were symptoms, and they'd multiplied under the stress of my job search.

I was four months into my job search, and another four months from graduation, and I was burnt out. I rarely slept. I consumed true crime podcasts like they were food. I thought that maybe if I listened to enough of them, I would become invincible. Maybe nothing else bad would happen to me if I knew enough about past grisly murders. Instead, it compounded and made me vigilant. I spent the rest of my waking hours applying for jobs and preparing for interviews, putting myself into a spiral of anxiety every time I interviewed and was rejected (which was a lot).

I realize now, in hindsight, that the same compulsive symptoms of PTSD I'd been indulging for years were manifesting in my job hunting habits. I overprepared, and over-researched. I asked questions to my interviewers about office spaces and privacy that were thinly veiled attempts to see how many escape routes I might have out of a future office or classroom. Perhaps the biggest failure of my job interviews was my inability to make small talk with potential future colleagues, and it wasn't because I didn't care or wasn't interested, but rather, I was afraid of getting invested in something I might lose. I didn't consciously think that anyone was at risk of physical harm, but the same feeling of uncertainty I'd felt about not knowing whether my friends were alive or dead was manifesting in the form of refusing to create attachments, even superficial ones, to something I might lose. In this case, it was the loss of the job that led to the loss of the person, but the crushing feeling of guilt and desertion was the same.

I made one exception, and let myself fall in love with the idea of one job in particular. It was the type of job I wanted, working with underserved first year students, in a location I loved that was close to family.

I felt qualified for the job, and when I arrived for my campus interview, I was confident. I connected with the students and staff that I met, and I imagined what my life might be like if that was my job. The search committee warned me it would be a slow turnaround, which I expected, but the longer I waited, the more I spiraled. The rejection came nearly six weeks after my interview, and it destroyed me. I didn't leave my apartment for days. The rejection felt personal, like someone there had looked into my eyes and seen the damage I carried with me. For all of the interview preparation workshops I'd attended on cover letter writing, salary negotiation, and interviewing, nothing had prepared me for this feeling. Everyone told me it "just wasn't the job for me," or "there are other jobs, you have other interviews," but their words couldn't pull me out of the depression I was in, and no one offered anything but words.

On paper, my graduate program offered tons of resources for job hunting. There were workshops and consultations and resume reviews, but no one prepared us for the emotional toll of it all. The competition between my graduating cohort was brutal, even if we wouldn't admit it. Every time someone announced they'd signed a contract, it was accompanied by a smug glance and a sigh of relief that they were finally off the playing field. I sank deeper into my depression, letting my PTSD compulsions run my life, because I didn't know how to cope any other way and nobody seemed to notice.

Eventually, I got a job and channeled my nervous energy into preparing to move and start over. I got a dog, which helped with my admittedly irrational fear of someone breaking into my apartment to murder me, and gave an outlet to my need for control. Dogs can't make their own decisions, after all. My PTSD has ups and downs, and my job hunt was the nadir. It was the time in my life where I felt like I was walking on hot coals all day every day, while everyone around me roasted marshmallows and told me it wasn't that bad.

As a librarian, I am assigned a lot of roles. In the eyes of my patrons, I am a keeper of knowledge, a finder of books, and a keeper of peace (and that's just what falls under "other duties" in my job description). Everyone expects me to stay calm and collected and answer every question that I can with poise and understanding. And at times, I like that about my job. But there's more to librarianship than books and knowledge and customer service. But then there's feeling terrified in your office when a patron tells you they're strung out on meth and need more. There's the patron who knows your schedule and checks for your car in the parking lot. There's the faculty member whose notorious temper leaves you terrified and sobbing. There are handfuls of names for these people: problem patron, difficult student, challenging interaction. Regardless of what we call them, fear is at the root of it. If I say the wrong thing, is this patron going to try to wait for me after my shift? Fear is the name I give to the feeling in the pit of my stomach when I have to walk across a dark parking lot after a closing shift. It's the name I give to the usually-friendly-but-sometimes-too-friendly regular. As a librarian, I must come to terms with the notion that I am largely unprotected from the dangers that come with my job, and that go unacknowledged by the people in charge. There's a deeply patriarchal history to librarianship, which is seen in the budget cuts and the expectations for librarians to bend over backwards to help someone who has previously verbally abused us. I don't need a man to protect me, but I'd like for the men in charge to recognize and acknowledge the danger our jobs create. My job leaves me fulfilled, but it will also always leave me fearful.

When I think of my mental health and my job, they exist in separate spaces. Work is work, and everything else is unrelated. But the reality is that those spaces have collided at full force, like two snow globes smashed together until shattering. The contents, which were once pristine still-lifes, are now mingled and messy and dangerous. The part of my mind that was once designated for work is inextricable from the part that looks over my shoulder for the nearest exit. They'll never again be separate, but maybe being separate was never right. Once the mess is cleaned up and I look at the contents again, they belong to the same scene. Fear and caution come with the job, and taking care of my mental health cannot be relegated to just my time outside of the library. As I start to reconstruct the vision of myself, my mental health, and my job, they begin to converge. There is no simple fix, no magic button to resolve the anxiety I feel at work or the guilt I feel at home, but six years ago I became a survivor, and I am still one now.

# Critical Perspectives and Narratives

# Full Disclosure? Issues around Disclosing Mental Illness in an Academic Library Workplace

**Alice Bennett**

*Content Warning*   Mental illness, discrimination

In recent years there has been an increase in campaigns encouraging greater openness about mental health experiences. But for those living with long-term mental illness, the decision to talk can be difficult, particularly in the workplace. Encouraging openness about mental illness is laudable, but until individuals feel safe to disclose, many will maintain secrecy about their health to avoid stigma. This chapter considers mental illness disclosure in the context of western academic libraries in Higher Education institutions, drawing on a variety of studies conducted in the United Kingdom and Europe, the United States, Canada and Australia.

## The Decision to Disclose

The dilemma of disclosure is peculiar to invisible illness and disability[1]. In one sense having to make decisions around disclosure is a privileged

---

1   A note about terminology—an invisible illness or disability is one which is not immediately apparent—such as a mental illness, diabetes or epilepsy. Regarding mental illness, this chapter considers the issue of disclosure overall, with the condition identified as an invisible illness or an invisible disability. Individuals with mental illnesses may identify as disabled or as having a chronic illness—how they identify is not the focus of this chapter, but what the barriers are to disclosing an invisible disability, chronic or mental illness in the academic library workplace.

position. An individual with an invisible disability may choose to disclose, whereas visible conditions automatically constitute part of an individual's public identity. Although invisibility can give an individual greater choice about making their condition publicly known, they can also face greater stigma or prejudice about their condition, as invisible disabilities, particularly mental illness, may not be regarded as valid as visible disabilities. Essentially the social stigma of a psychiatric diagnosis and the relative concealability of such give rise to this specific dilemma.[2] While disclosure is an issue for any invisible disability, it is generally recognized as particularly problematic for those diagnosed with mental illness.[3]

This dilemma exists across invisible illness and disability, but this chapter will focus on the disclosure of mental illness. There are potential complications around disclosure of mental illness, as the diagnosed individual may identify as having a chronic illness rather than as disabled (and in some cases may not identify as either chronically ill or disabled)[4]. Some may reject medical diagnosis, either as they do not want their experiences medicalized or they may struggle to accept a psychiatric diagnosis as part of their identity. However, it should be noted that receiving a diagnosis is not necessarily a negative experience. For some, it may explain and validate symptoms and experiences which an individual has lived with for some time. For others, it may simply name an experience or characteristic that they do not perceive as a problem.[5] But regardless of how an individual incorporates their diagnosis into their social identity, the dilemma of disclosure in the workplace remains. Even if an individual does not find their diagnosis problematic, this does not mean that they are oblivious to the potential risks and stigma of disclosure.

The nature of disclosure varies as to whether an individual identifies as disabled and how confident they are with this identity. Identifying

---

2   Annie Venville, Annette Street and Ellie Fossey, "Student Perspectives on Disclosure of Mental Illness in Post-Compulsory Education: Displacing Doxa," *Disability & Society*, 29, no. 5 (2014): 793.

3   Katharina Vornholt et al. "Disability and Employment—Overview and Highlights", *European Journal of Work and Organizational Psychology*, 27, no. 1 (2018): 48; Bos et al, "Mental Illness Stigma and Disclosure: Consequences of Coming out of the Closet", *Issues in Mental Health Nursing*, 30, no. 8 (2009): 510.

4   This chapter uses person first language in describing medical conditions and disability.

5   Annie Irvine, "Something to Declare? The Disclosure of Common Mental Health Problems at Work." *Disability & Society* 26, no. 2 (2011): 182.

as disabled can take a degree of confidence or acceptance, particularly if the condition or its diagnosis—and thus this identity—are relatively new.[6] An individual may still be coming to terms with the diagnosis of a condition and may struggle to know how to disclose as they learn to accept this as part of their identity.

## Wellbeing at Work and Disclosure

Studies of wellbeing schemes at work have primarily examined the efficacy of these programs in preventing ill-health or helping staff back into work after sickness or injury, rather than assessing any impact on those managing a disability or chronic illness unrelated to their employment and predating it.[7] Examinations of mental health and employment have tended to focus on workplace stress but pre-existing or non-work related conditions receive little attention.[8] While the prevention and reduction of workplace stress is important, this fails to acknowledge that many people are in employment with pre-existing mental illnesses or those that develop mental illnesses unrelated to workplace stress.[9]

This is also true of studies addressing mental health of staff in library workplaces—these too center on work-related stress.[10] Those with lifelong or pre-existing mental illnesses entering the library workplace are largely ignored. Studies have tended to focus on rehabilitating those who have developed a mental illness whilst employed, typically as they return to work, either from a period of leave or as they re-enter the workplace having undergone a period of worklessness.[11]

---

6    Nicole Brown and Jennifer Leigh. "Ableism in Academia: Where are the Disabled and Ill Academics?",*Disability & Society*, 33, no. 6 (2018): 986–87.

7    Fehmidah Munir,"Working for Longer: Self-Management of Chronic Health Problems in the Workplace."In *Work, Health and Wellbeing: The Challenges of Managing Health at work.* Ed.: Sarah Vickerstaff, Chris Phillipson, Ross Wilkie. (Bristol: Bristol University Press, Policy Press, 2012). 216–17.

8    Munir, "Working for Longer," 217–18.

9    It is important to distinguish between "mental health"—which is experienced by us all, fluctuating between better and worse periods—and a "mental health condition" or "mental illness", medically recognized conditions, which are experienced as chronic illness and/or disability by many individuals. Many schemes have been launched to support "mental health", including in the higher education sector. Most are designed to promote good mental health, but few are aimed at supporting those with chronic mental illnesses. Additionally, sometimes the phrase "mental health" may be used as a euphemism for mental illness.

10   Ellen I. Shupe. Stephanie K. Wambaugh and Reed J. Bramble, "Role-related Stress Experienced by Academic Librarians". *The Journal of Academic Librarianship*, 41, no. 3 (2015): 264–69.

11   Irvine, "Something to Declare?": 181.

Far less attention is paid to those who remain in employment while managing chronic conditions without taking any form of extended leave. There appears to be an assumption that those living with long term or lifelong mental illness will not have managed to remain in consistent employment and therefore those in this category are commonly excluded from studies. These are individuals who may have an ambivalent attitude to disclosure in the workplace, as those living with long term conditions or disabilities are more likely to have encountered varied reactions to their diagnosis, including in disclosure scenarios. Previous experiences will inform decisions around workplace disclosure and experience of negative responses is common. In a 2017 Australian study of post-secondary students, all those surveyed reported previous negative experiences of disclosure[12] and similarly all participants in a 2019 study of US students reported previous negative experiences of disclosure.[13] Staff living with a chronic illness or disability will enter the workplace with previous experience of disclosure which will inform if, how and to whom they disclose. If staff are expected to or encouraged to disclose, there is a need to create an environment in which staff feel safe to do so—discomfort around disclosure from past experience may make this particularly difficult for some individuals.

The drive to retain employment while living with a chronic condition or disability is central to the dilemma of disclosing an invisible illness. Maintaining a socially engaged life, including employment, is recognized as beneficial to overall wellbeing. In order to successfully manage a mental illness while employed, an individual may require workplace adjustments and therefore need to disclose their diagnosis in order to request these. However, revealing a mental illness is widely perceived as a decision which will jeopardize work prospects.[14] This presents the options of disclosing to access the required adjustments, while risking stigmatization and possible negative reactions, or deciding against disclosure to avoid potential stigma but then facing the pressure of maintaining employment without workplace support.

---

12    Venville, Street and Fossey, "Student Perspectives on Disclosure of Mental Illness": 797.

13    Heather D. Evans, "'Trial by Fire': Forms of Impairment Disclosure and Implications for Disability Identity," *Disability & Society* 34, no. 5 (May 28, 2019): 726–46, https://doi.org/10.1080/09687599.2019.1580187.

14    Venville, Street and Fossey, "Student Perspectives on Disclosure of Mental Illness": 802.

Fears surrounding negative consequences in disclosing a mental ill-ness to a prospective employer are demonstrated by a 2017 study con-ducted in the US. This study asked 570 adults (from across the US) whether they would disclose a mental illness diagnosis in four dif-ferent scenarios—in accessing healthcare, applying for education or training, applying for employment and in applying for a background check.[15] Rates of disclosure varied across the scenarios, with the high-est rate being 57%, in the education application scenario.[16] The low-est disclosure rate was in the employment application scenarios, with over two-thirds answering that they would not disclose either on a written application or at an interview.[17] Similarly in the follow up ques-tions, the employment scenario showed the highest levels of fear of discrimination.[18] In higher education, there is also fear amongst aca-demics and students of appearing less employable.[19] Even when stud-ies of disclosure were undertaken in an educational context, in part student decisions not to disclose mental illness diagnoses were for fear of negative impact on employment prospects.[20]

These fears are not without basis. Even with legislation against disabil-ity discrimination, unemployment rates for disabled people in more economically developed countries with civil rights law covering disabil-ity are around twice that of the general population. It is thought to be far higher in countries without legislation covering disability rights.[21] Regarding mental illness specifically, studies have shown that employ-ers will rate prospective employees disclosing a psychiatric diagnosis as less employable than those disclosing a physical disability, regard-less of the nature and extent of their disclosure about their condition.[22]

15  Colleen Donnelly, "Public attitudes toward disclosing mental health conditions", *Social Work in Mental Health*, 15, no. 5 (2017): 588–99.

16  Donnelly, "Public attitudes toward disclosing mental health conditions": 591.

17  Donnelly, "Public attitudes toward disclosing mental health conditions": 593.

18  Donnelly, "Public attitudes toward disclosing mental health conditions":

19  Brown and Leigh, "Ableism in academia": 987.

20  Venville, Street and Fossey, "Student perspectives on disclosure of mental illness": 800.

21  Vornholt et al, "Disability and employment—overview and highlights": 46.

22  Rebecca Spirito Dalgin and James Bellini, "Invisible Disability Disclosure in an Employment Interview Impact on Employers' Hiring Decisions and Views of Employability", *Rehabilitation Counselling Bulletin*, 52, no. 1 (2008): 12.

Popular perceptions of those with mental illnesses as being potentially dangerous or aggressive can create fear and mistrust amongst co-workers. Misunderstandings about mental illness as well as the invisibility of such conditions can lead to resentment around and unwillingness to make workplace accommodations. Due to the fear and stigma surrounding mental illnesses, those living with these conditions are more likely to suffer from discrimination than those living with other chronic illnesses or disabilities.[23]

Given the fear of being stigmatized, the decision to disclose in the workplace is typically practical rather than ideological and also typically stems from fear. Fear of personal judgment—of the number of sick days taken, of medical appointments needed or of overall performance—means that individual's desire to explain and contextualize their behavior and performance at work can outweigh fears of negative reaction and stigma. Fear of judgment is a primary motivator for disclosure in the workplace.[24]

In this way, disclosure can be a means of managing expectations of managers and colleagues. Disclosing an underlying condition explains potential relapses or flare-ups, or problems with certain aspects of a job role, as well as enabling an individual to access any provision of workplace adjustments. In her study of disability disclosure, Heather Evans distinguishes between disclosures made to access adjustments and disclosures made to prevent judgment, terming these pragmatic and confessional. There is a tendency for invisible disabilities to be disclosed in a more confessional context, which can exacerbate issues of stigma.[25]

Disclosure is rarely, if ever, a single decision and event. Rather, it is a series of decisions as to when and how to disclose, as well as to whom.[26] Even within the context of workplace, disclosure is unlikely to be a single event. Disclosure may be to one, some or all colleagues; it may be to occupational health or may be to management. There are also decisions around how much to disclose.

---

23  Vornholt et al, "Disability and Employment—Overview and Highlights": 46–47.

24  Evans, "'Trial by Fire'": 7–10.

25  Ibid., 7–8.

26  Irvine, "Something to declare? ": 183.

## Disclosure in Higher Education

A study of US students and their choices around disclosing disability at college found forms of partial disclosure were employed by several of those who participated. One form of partial disclosure used is generic disclosure—disclosing a disability but without giving any details as to the nature of the condition. A participating student used this form of disclosure to navigate college studies, enabling access to disability services while avoiding specifying the bipolar diagnosis where possible that she has a diagnosis of bipolar disorder, for fear of pre-judgments of about the condition and being treated differently.[27]

This form of generic disclosure may be successful for students with mental illnesses or other invisible disabilities, depending on how their course is structured. The organizational structure of disability support for students can vary considerably between institutions. If support is accessed via a central disability service rather than through departmental administration, this generic disclosure would be a workable strategy. If they are accessing a study support plan and other forms of adjustment through the university disability services, it is only to disability services that they need to disclose their condition; they are able to access support and adjustments without disclosure to their tutors and fellow students. While a potentially successful disclosure strategy for students in higher education, it may not be so for support or academic staff.

Although there is little work in this field specific to academic library staff, there are studies which address the problem of disclosure in higher education. The circumstances and experiences of academic staff or students with mental illnesses or other invisible disabilities in higher education will differ from those of academic library staff, but studies looking at these groups do at least give some indication of the wider culture in higher education around disclosure.

The literature considering student and academic mental health on campus suggests that the higher education environment is less conducive to openness around mental illness than has been assumed. Typically perceived as more socially liberal communities, studies suggest that higher education is a competitive environment for both students

---

27   Tara Wood. "Rhetorical Disclosures: The Stakes of Disability Identity in Higher Education", in *Negotiating Disability: Disclosure and Higher Education*. Ed. Stephanie L. Kerschbaum, Laura T. Eisenman and James M. Jones. (Michigan,:University of Michigan Press, 2017).

and academic staff, where fear of stigma is still strong. For students in higher education, disclosure is a prerequisite for student support plans and institutional accommodation, giving a greater incentive to disclose than in other social scenarios—there is a clear benefit to disclosing, as it enables support.[28] Despite this inducement, studies in both the US and Australia report low rates of disclosure, with students choosing not to disclose for fear of negative reactions from teaching staff, as well as wider stigma.[29] This suggests that despite institutional efforts to encourage disclosure and improve take up of accessibility provisions, the stigma attached to mental illnesses and other invisible disabilities persists in higher education.

The persisting stigma surrounding mental illnesses in higher education is illustrated by the willingness to disclose other invisible disabilities over mental health disabilities, even in cases of comorbidity. A significant finding from an Australian study of post-secondary students was a willingness to disclose invisible medical conditions such as hearing impairment or chronic fatigue syndrome, but not anxiety and depressive disorders. There was fear that disclosing a mental illness would be stigmatizing, as well as a belief that physical conditions would be accepted as legitimate, while mental illnesses would not.[30]

The belief that physical conditions would be accepted but mental conditions would not was also found in a US college study.[31] Two student veterans who participated in the study of disability disclosure amongst college students had chosen to disclose what one termed "physical impairments" but not mental disabilities. This decision was in part informed by both students feeling the popular perception of military veterans with PTSD meant their disclosure of any mental illness would receive a negative reaction. Although the veteran experience is very different from the experience of many individuals with mental illnesses, this nevertheless demonstrates a greater willingness to disclose physical disabilities and a fear of judgment preventing the disclosure of mental illness. This is borne out by other students who participated in the study also being more comfortable revealing visible disabilities

---

28  Venville, Street and Fossey, "Student Perspectives on Disclosure of Mental Illness": 794.

29  Venville, Street and Fossey, "Student Perspectives on Disclosure of Mental Illness."

30  Venville, Street and Fossey, "Student Perspectives on Disclosure of Mental Illness": 797–98.

31  Woods, "Rhetorical Disclosure": 80.

or Specific Learning Difficulties.[32] Rates of mental illness disclosure amongst students are higher than amongst staff and faculty in academia but these studies suggest a persistent discomfort around disclosing psychiatric conditions beyond other invisible disabilities.[33]

Belief that mental illnesses are impairments which block constructive or original thought creates a specific stigma for an academic environment. Students and staff are in the academic institution to study, to teach, to research or to support these activities. Intellectual capability is the key to the existence of academic institutions and is the primary reason for the presence there of students and staff. For both students and staff, intellectual capability may be a central part of their identity, professionally and personally. When the mind is valued so highly, mental illness becomes something to be feared. Given that intellectual promise is the justification for being in academia, any suggestion that this could be disrupted by an ongoing medical condition is a potential threat to the individual's position. While this holds true for all students, Ellen Samuels suggests that any discomfort for undergraduate students revealing mental illnesses is magnified for graduates and faculty, for whom "it clearly remains a highly risky endeavour to reveal any form of mental or cognitive difference or vulnerability: our minds, our justifications for being here, must run like steely machinery, always reliable, always stable."[34]

Many assessments of mental illness and disability in Higher Education exclude support staff. However, extant studies give a sense of an atmosphere in which mental illnesses are understood as vulnerabilities. For professional staff supporting the study, teaching and research of an academic institution, the need to be seen as reliable and stable is also important; they too must be perceived as capable in their professional networks and would be working in an environment in which disclosure of mental illness could be interpreted by others as a weakness. Competitive workplace culture pervades higher education and is

---

32   Woods, "Rhetorical Disclosure": 89.

33   Brown and Leigh, "Ableism in Academia": 988.

34   Ellen Samuels, "Passing, Coming Out, and Other Magical Acts", in *Negotiating Disability: Disclosure and Higher Education*. Ed. Stephanie L. Kerschbaum, Laura T. Eisenman, and James M. Jones. (Michigan: University of Michigan Press, 2017): 19.

problematic for library staff negotiating disability, particularly in cases of invisible disability.[35]

## Disclosure in the Library Workplace

Microaggressions have been recorded in library workplaces based on mental health status as well as based on race, gender identity and sexuality.[36] Studies of microaggressions in librarianship have focused on race and sexuality but these marginalizing behaviors also occur around disability, including mental illnesses.[37] In society more widely, microaggressions against people with mental illness are common.[38] Unlike other areas of microaggression, these frequently center on shame, often implying or even directly telling the individual that they should not disclose mental illness in certain circumstances or even at all.[39] In other cases a variety of negative consequences were experienced after disclosure, ranging from being patronized by colleagues, assumed to be incompetent, or even discriminated against openly.[40] Negative workplace consequences covered both the professional—as with being assumed to be less competent—and the personal, with being avoided socially and following disclosure being minimized—that the condition cannot be serious as the individual is working, doesn't appear mentally ill, or doesn't conform to the appearance of someone experiencing mental illness that their colleague has known or expects.[41] Those with invisible disabilities can be subjected to more microaggressions, as having an invisible condition their experience is perceived by many as less valid than that of those with visible conditions.[42] Student experience indicates that these attitudes exist in

35   Oud, "Systematic Workplace Barriers": 179.

36   Simon P. Funge et al, "Dropped in Without a Parachute: Library Managers' Supervision Experiences", *Journal of Library Administration*, 57, no. 7 (2017): 725.

37   Oud, "Systematic Workplace Barriers": 177–81.

38   Lauren Gonzales et al. "Microaggressions Experienced by Persons With Mental Illnesses: An Exploratory Study", Psychiatric *Rehabilitation Journal*, 38, no. 3 (2015): 238.

39   Lauren Gonzales et al. "Microaggressions Experienced by Persons With Mental Illnesses

40   Gonzales et al, "Microaggressions Experienced by Persons With Mental Illnesses": 236–39.

41   Ibid., 236–37.

42   Samantha Cook and Kristina Clement, "Navigating the hidden void: The unique challenges of accommodating library employees with invisible disabilities". *The Journal of Academic Librarianship*, 2019: https://doi.org/10.1016/j.acalib.2019.02.010:2.

Higher Education institutions; students with invisible disabilities reported staff challenges to the validity of disability status and reluctance to put in place accommodations.[43] Similar problems have been reported by academic library staff with invisible disabilities, as they too reported a reluctance of managers and colleagues to recognize invisible disabilities as disabilities.[44] There was also the additional problem of the assumption that because there were no staff with visible disabilities in the workplace, there were no staff with disabilities employed there at all.[45] Because their disabilities were not immediately apparent, staff experienced an erasure of their disabled identity and experience.[46]

Whether considered as a chronic condition or an invisible disability, library staff experience and disclosure of mental illness by academic library staff has received little attention. Typically, considerations of disability and mental illness in libraries have focused on users, not staff. This is not peculiar to disability or mental illness. Regarding diversity as a whole, most literature has considered the library user rather than the staff member. Work has been undertaken to start to address the need to make the profession more inclusive, but action and research has tended to neglect disability. For example, a 2017 study of library management in the US examined relationships between supervisor and supervisee with regard to support and microaggressions in the workplace.[47] The study considered personal characteristics of race, age, gender and sexuality, but personal identity and experience of disability, mental illness or chronic illness were not asked about.[48] Although this did not address these issues or relationships in the context of disability, mental illness or chronic illness, the study does suggest that support for managers in managing minority identities may be lacking.

---

43  Laura Mullins and Michèle Preyde, "The lived experience of students with an invisible disability at a Canadian university". *Disability & Society* 28, no. 2 (2013): 154–56.

44  Oud, "Systematic Workplace Barriers": 177–78.

45  Ibid.

46  Ibid.

47  Funge et al, "Dropped in Without a Parachute": 729–30.

48  Ibid.

Where disability awareness training and guidance is provided for library staff, this looks primarily, sometimes solely, at library patrons, rather than colleagues or employees. In an academic library context, disability training for library staff is typically designed to support students. As the main user group of the library, the focus on students is natural, but excluding university staff from consideration perpetuates the underrepresentation of academic and information professionals with disabilities. For example, a 2017 case study on providing staff training to support disability in libraries states *"that active and continuing staff training can improve interactions between library staff and people with disabilities"*.[49] This makes assumptions about the library workforce being entirely abled, whereas library staff themselves may have disabilities, visible or invisible.

Wellbeing elements are increasingly being incorporated into academic library services, often as an extension of increasing attention to wellbeing across university campuses. The focus is almost exclusively on student welfare. Strategically this may be part of the diversification of academic libraries, enabling them to add another service to their portfolio, as well as build relationships with other departments.[50] The increasing use of libraries in the provision of wellbeing services on campus is also practical, as libraries are often open long hours and are already a familiar and trusted spaced for many students.[51] This creates a potentially strange situation for library staff experiencing mental illness, as it creates a work environment advertising support and inclusion, but with no provision for them.

Staff with disabilities working in academic libraries may also struggle to get the workplace accommodations they need. In countries without universal health care, especially where health insurance is tied to employment, this is even more problematic, as the cost of obtaining evidence for accommodations can be prohibitive. Although institutional promotion of welfare across campus is increasingly common, the practical adjustments needed to support and include those with disabilities working and studying in Higher Education are typically

49 Michelle H. Brannen, Steven Milewski and Thura Mack, "Providing Staff Training and Programming to Support People with Disabilities: An Academic Library Case Study", *Public Services Quarterly*, 13, no. 2 (2017):73.

50 Graham Walton, "Supporting Student Wellbeing in the University Library: A Core Service or a Distraction?", *New Review of Academic Librarianship*, 24, no. 2 (2018): 122–23.

51 Ibid.

lagging behind these campaigns. Accommodations are leveling the playing field, not showing favoritism or giving unfair advantage. Discomfort around this, including academics criticizing accommodations made for students with invisible disabilities is still prevalent, suggesting that making necessary adjustments for disabilities, particularly for invisible disabilities, is not necessarily supported in Higher Education institutions.[52]

Invisible disabilities are less familiar than visible disabilities and do not necessarily fit with the popular perception of disability.[53] Studies of the experience of library staff with invisible disabilities suggest a lack of knowledge about invisible disabilities (including mental illness), among supervisors, as well as a lack of knowledge about rights to workplace adjustment.[54] There is discomfort as to how to manage and support individuals with disabilities, particularly mental illness, for which workplace adjustments may be less obvious.[55] With regard to mental illnesses, persistent stigma around mental illness may have also influenced lack of workplace accommodations.[56]

Some managers may be willing to create a supportive workplace for their staff, but many still feel discomfort in managing individuals with disabilities.[57] In part, this can stem from feeling inadequately prepared and supported to manage staff with disabilities and to handle any issues arising around disability with other staff, reflecting a need for better training and disability awareness for management and staff.[58] A 2019 American study of library employees with invisible disabilities found that while more training and guidance was needed overall, this was particularly regarding invisible disabilities, as guidance from organizations like the ALA focused on visible disabilities.[59] A 2011 UK

---

52  Mullins and Preyde, "The lived experience of students with an invisible disability":154–56.

53  Anne-Marie O'Neill, and Christine Urquhart. "Accommodating Employees with Disabilities: Perceptions of Irish Academic Library Managers". *New Review of Academic Librarianship* 17, no. 2 (2011): 249–51.

54  Oud, "Systemic Workplace Barriers": 177–79.

55  Oud, "Systemic Workplace Barriers": 179–82.

56  Ibid.

57  O'Neill and Urquhart, "Accommodating Employees with Disabilities": 249–50.

58  Ibid.

59  Cook and Clement, "Navigating the hidden void": 2.

study of common mental health problems in the workplace suggests that schemes such as Mental Health First Aid can offer useful guidance for employers and managers to support employees through periods of poor mental health, as can initiatives aimed at the general public.[60]

Perhaps the most important element in improving disability disclosure is trust.[61] The individual disclosing needs to trust that they will be believed and respected, that their condition and experiences will not be minimized. They need to trust that disclosing will not impact their career or future treatment by managers or colleagues. They need to trust that having disclosed, accommodations can be made. An environment of trust is fundamental to facilitating workplace disclosure and without it, employment legislation and institutional policy will do little, if anything, to reduce stigma and improve workplace inclusion.[62]

## Why disclose?: The Potential Benefits of Workplace Disclosure

Why encourage workplace disclosure? Firstly, disclosure is typically helpful for the individual disclosing—those who are open about their condition have better self-esteem and lower rates of self-stigma.[63] Disclosure in the workplace (provided it is not met with stigmatization) can make work life less tiring for those with invisible conditions; it is no longer imperative to mask symptoms, it removes the need to lie to colleagues and necessary adjustments can be made.

Secondly, disclosure is not just of potential benefit to the individual disclosing—in an academic library context there are wider benefits for both colleagues and library users. Research indicates that contact with individuals with psychiatric disabilities is more effective in reducing stigma than awareness training.[64] An Australian study of academic teaching staff found that those most likely to be comfortable in assisting a student presenting with mental health difficulties and those with the lowest stigmatizing behaviors had experience of mental illnesses

---

60   Irvine, "Something to Declare": 188.

61   Cook and Clement, "Navigating the hidden void": 2–3.

62   Vornholt et al, "Disability and employment—overview and highlights": 49.

63   Corrigan et al, "Mental illness stigma and disclosure in college students": 224.

64   Vornholt et al, "Disability and employment—overview and highlights": 47.

(either personally or with individuals with mental illness), with reliance primarily on personal experiences rather than any training.[65]

This is true not only of invisible disabilities as a whole, but also specifically of mental illnesses. Mental illness is often othered—it is popularly depicted as frightening and many people have preconceived ideas about what people with mental illnesses are like. One of the key ways in which this can be challenged is by supporting contact with people who have and are open about their mental illness.[66] In this case, familiarity does not breed contempt—rather contact with individuals with mental illnesses reduces prejudices about mental illness. These attitude changes are lasting and prompt changes in behavior.[67] Those with little or less belief in disability stereotypes behave more inclusively. Working to eradicate stigma and stereotyping around disabilities in the workplace in turn makes more inclusive behavior likely, creating a supportive environment for disabled staff.[68]

Increased openness of staff with disabilities would not only have the potential to reduce stigma amongst colleagues, it would benefit library users as well. The benefit of de-stigmatization in creating a more inclusive environment has significance in supporting the recruitment and retention goals of Higher Education institutions. There is pressure in the UK and Ireland to improve not just the recruitment but also the retention of underrepresented student groups, including students with disabilities.[69] The employment of staff with disabilities within a culture where they are able to disclose and be open may assist the retention of students with disabilities, as it places the university as a supportive and inclusive environment.[70]

---

65  Amelia Gulliver et al, "University staff mental health literacy, stigma and their experience of students with mental health problems", *Journal of Further and Higher Education*, 43. no. 3 (2019): 439–40.

66  Patrick Corrigan and Alicia Matthews, "Stigma and disclosure: Implications for coming out of the closet", *Journal of Mental Health*, 12, no. 3 (2003): 235.

67  Corrigan and Matthews, "Stigma and disclosure": 236.

68  Philippe T.J.H. Nelissen et al, "How and when stereotypes relate to inclusive behavior toward people with disabilities", *The International Journal of Human Resource Management*, 27, no. 14 (2016): 1620–21.

69  Elaine Chapman and Sarah-Anne Kennedy. "Nothing About Us Without Us: The benefits of hiring staff with a disability in libraries". (Conference paper NoWAL Conference: NoWAL 2019: Exploring & supporting diversity in academic libraries, University of Liverpool, Liverpool 28th June 2019).

70  Ibid.

As such, staff openness about mental illnesses could create an upward spiral in changing a workplace culture. If staff disclose mental illness to their colleagues, this contact could reduce stigma. Other staff could develop less prejudicial attitudes in dealing with colleagues and library users, whether students or staff. The employment of disabled staff and creating an environment in which they feel able to disclose is of benefit to the workplace, and society, as a whole.

## Acknowledgements

With thanks to my brother, Hugh, for his help with proofreading.

---

### *Bibliography*

Bos, Arjan E. R., Daphne Kanner, Peter Muris, Birgit Janssen and Birgit Mayer. "Mental Illness Stigma and Disclosure: Consequences of Coming out of the Closet". *Issues in Mental Health Nursing* 30, no. 8 (2009): 509–13.

Brannen, Michelle H., Steven Milewski and Thura Mack. "Providing Staff Training and Programming to Support People with Disabilities: An Academic Library Case Study". *Public Services Quarterly* 13, no. 2 (2017): 61–77.

Brown, Mary E. "Invisible Debility: Attitudes toward the Underrepresented in Library Workplaces". *Public Library Quarterly* 34, no. 2 (2015): 124–33.

Brown, Nicole and Jennifer Leigh. "Ableism in academia: where are the disabled and ill academics?". *Disability & Society* 33, no. 6 (2018): 985–89.

Chapman, Elaine and Sarah-Anne Kennedy. "Nothing About Us Without Us: The benefits of hiring staff with a disability in libraries". Paper presented at NoWAL Conference: NoWAL 2019: Exploring & supporting diversity in academic libraries. University of Liverpool, Liverpool 28th June 2019.

Cook, Samantha and Kristina Clement. "Navigating the hidden void: The unique challenges of accommodating library employees with invisible disabilities". *The Journal of Academic Librarianship*, 2019. Pre print early online publication. Accessed on 25th April 2019: https://doi.org/10.1016/j.acalib.2019.02.010

Corrigan, Patrick, and Alicia Matthews. "Stigma and disclosure: Implications for coming out of the closet". *Journal of Mental Health* 12, no. 3 (2003): 235–48.

Corrigan, Patrick W., Kristin A. Kosyluk, Fred Markowitz, Robyn Lewis Brown, Bridget Conlon, Jo Rees, Jessica Rosenberg, Sarah Ellefson and Maya Al-Khouja. "Mental illness stigma and disclosure in college students". *Journal of Mental Health* 25, no. 3 (2016): 224–30.

Davis Kendrick, Kaetrena."The Low Morale Experience of Academic Librarians: A Phenomenological Study". *Journal of Library Administration* 57, no. 8 (2017): 846–78.

Donnelly, Colleen. "Public attitudes toward disclosing mental health conditions". *Social Work in Mental Health* 15, no. 5 (2017): 588–99.

Evans, Heather D. (2019) "'Trial by fire': forms of impairment disclosure and implications for disability identity". Disability & Society. Published online 12th March 2019. Accessed on 22nd April 2019: https://doi.org/10.1080/096 87599.2019.1580187

Funge, Simon P., Audrey Robinson-Nkongola, Laura DeLancey & Austin Griffiths. "Dropped in Without a Parachute: Library Managers' Supervision Experiences", *Journal of Library Administration*, 57, no. 7 (2017): 723–41.

Gonzales, Lauren, Davidoff, Kristin C., Nadal, Kevin L. and Yanos, Philip T. "Microaggressions Experienced by Persons With Mental Illnesses: An Exploratory Study". *Psychiatric Rehabilitation Journal* 38, no. 3 (2015): 234–41.

Grimes, Susan, Erica Southgate Jill Scevak & Rachel Buchanan. "University student perspectives on institutional non-disclosure of disability and learning challenges: reasons for staying invisible". *International Journal of Inclusive Education*, 23, no. 6 (2018): 639–55.

Gulliver, Amelia, Louise Farrer, Kylie Bennett and Kathleen M Griffiths. "University staff mental health literacy, stigma and their experience of students with mental health problems". *Journal of Further and Higher Education*, 43, no. 3 (2019): 434–42.

Gulliver, Amelia, Louise Farrer, Kylie Bennett, Kathina Ali, Annika Hellsing, Natasha Katruss and Kathleen M. Griffiths. "University staff experiences of students with mental health problems and their perceptions of staff training needs". *Journal of Mental Health*, 27, no. 3 (2018): 247–56.

Irvine, Annie. "Something to declare? The disclosure of common mental health problems at work". *Disability & Society* 26, no. 2 (2011): 179–92.

———. "Common mental health problems and work" In *Work, health and wellbeing: The challenges of managing health at work*. Ed. Sarah Vickerstaff, Chris Phillipson, Ross Wilkie. (Bristol: Bristol University Press, Policy Press, 2012)

Johnstone, Jodi. "Employment of disabled persons in the academic library environment". *The Australian Library Journal* 54, no. 2 (2005): 156–63.

Juniper, Bridget, Pat Bellamy and Nicola White. "Evaluating the well-being of public library workers". *Journal of Librarianship and Information Science* 44, no. 2 (2011): 108–117.

Korsbek, Lisa. "Disclosure: What is the point and for whom?". *Journal of Mental Health*, 22, no. 3 (2013): 283–90.

Lyndon, Amy E., Allison Crowe, Karl L. Wuensch, Susan L. McCammon and Karen B. Davis. "College students' stigmatization of people with mental illness: familiarity, implicit person theory, and attribution". *Journal of Mental Health* 28, no. 3 (2019): 255–59.

Mullins, Laura and Michèle Preyde. "The lived experience of students with an invisible disability at a Canadian university". *Disability & Society* 28, no. 2 (2013):147–60.

Munir, Fehmidah. "Working for longer: self-management of chronic health problems in the workplace". In *Work, health and wellbeing: The challenges of managing health at work*. Eds:Sarah Vickerstaff, Chris Phillipson, Ross Wilkie. Bristol:Bristol University Press, Policy Press., 2012.

Nelissen, Philippe T.J.H., Ute R. Hülsheger, Gemma M.C. van Ruitenbeek and Fred R.H. Zijlstra. "How and when stereotypes relate to inclusive behavior toward people with disabilities". *The International Journal of Human Resource Management* 27, no. 14 (2016): 1610–25.

O'Neill, Anne-Marie, and Christine Urquhart. "Accommodating Employees with Disabilities: Perceptions of Irish Academic Library Managers". *New Review of Academic Librarianship* 17, no. 2 (2011): 234–58.

Oud, Joanne. "Systemic Workplace Barriers for Academic Librarians with Disabilities" *College and research libraries*, 80, no. 2 (2019): 169–94.

Ramsey, Elizabeth and Mary C. Aagard. "Academic libraries as active contributors to student wellness". *College & Undergraduate Libraries* 25 no. 4 (2018): 328–34.

Samuels, Ellen. "Passing, Coming Out, and Other Magical Acts", in *Negotiating Disability: Disclosure and Higher Education*. Ed: Stephanie L. Kerschbaum, Laura T. Eisenman, James M. Jones. Michigan: University of Michigan Press, 2017.

Shupe, Ellen I., Stephanie K. Wambaugh and Reed J. Bramble, "Role-related Stress Experienced by Academic Librarians". *The Journal of Academic Librarianship*, 41, no. 3 (2015): 264–69

Spirito Dalgin, Rebecca, and James Bellini. "Invisible Disability Disclosure in an Employment Interview Impact on Employers' Hiring Decisions and Views of Employability". *Rehabilitation Counseling Bulletin* 52, no. 1, (2008): 6–15.

Venville, Annie, Annette Street and Ellie Fossey. "Student perspectives on disclosure of mental illness in post-compulsory education: displacing doxa". *Disability & Society* 29, no. 5 (2014): 792–806.

Vornholt, Katharina, Patrizia Villotti, Beate Muschalla, Jana Bauer, Adrienne Colella, Fred Zijlstra, Gemma Van Ruitenbeek, Sjir Uitdewilligen and Marc Corbière. "Disability and employment—overview and highlights". *European Journal of Work and Organizational Psychology* 27, no. 1 (2018): 40–55.

Walton, Graham. "Supporting Student Wellbeing in the University Library: A Core Service or a Distraction?". *New Review of Academic Librarianship* 24 no. 2 (2018): 121–23.

Wood, Tara. "Rhetorical Disclosures: The Stakes of Disability Identity in Higher Education". In *Negotiating Disability: Disclosure and Higher Education*. Ed: Stephanie L. Kerschbaum, Laura T. Eisenman, James M. Jones. Michigan: University of Michigan Press, 2017.

# Words Matter: Examining the Language Used to Describe Mental Health Conditions in the Library of Congress Subject Headings (LCSH)

**Carolyn Hansen**

*Content Warning*  This chapter contains outdated and offensive terminology that has been used in library cataloging to name and describe mental health conditions and people with such conditions.

## Introduction

Controlled vocabularies present an interesting paradox; although choosing "preferred" language to describe a subject provides consistent access points that can be used to identify and locate materials in a catalog or index, controlled vocabularies also create language hierarchies in which one word or phrase becomes favored over others. This process necessarily reduces dynamic and fluid language to a fixed point, which is problematic for complex subjects such as race, gender, and disability. Although controlled vocabularies are updated in an effort to remain current, these procedures can be complicated and slow, making it difficult to keep pace with the natural evolution of language. As a result, controlled vocabularies often contain outdated and offensive language that may alienate, anger, or hurt library users. Over the last twenty years, scholarly critiques have uncovered inappropriate headings in multiple controlled vocabularies, including the Library of Congress Subject Headings (LCSH) and the National Library's Medical Subject Headings (MeSH); similar critiques of classification systems such as Library of Congress Classification (LCC), and Dewey Decimal Classification (DDC) have also been made.[1] These critiques have encouraged a movement among librarians to advocate for and participate in the revision of headings through individual action and cooperative cataloging programs.

To date, there have been no examinations of language related to mental health conditions in any controlled vocabulary. The purpose of this chapter is to begin a discussion of how controlled vocabularies categorize and represent both mental health conditions and the individuals who live with those conditions; this will be accomplished by analyzing subject headings in the LCSH related to mental health, including illness. It is the author's hope and intention that this examination will highlight problematic headings in the LCSH so that they will be revised. These types of revisions will increase the inclusiveness of the LCSH, improve user experiences of people with mental health conditions who are using the vocabulary, and reduce inaccurate or stigmatizing perceptions of mental health conditions.

## Methodology

### *The Language of "Mental Illness"*

Throughout this chapter, the term "mental health conditions" will be used as opposed to "mental illness" to describe medical conditions impacting mental health, since the word "illness" implies a medical problem that is a deviance from the body's "normal" physical and/or mental operation. For example, as of 2018 the American Psychiatric Association (APA) defined mental illness as a term that "refers collectively to all diagnosable mental disorders—health conditions involving: significant changes in thinking, emotion and/or behavior; [and]

---

1   For example, see: Hope A. Olson, *The Power to Name: Locating the Limits of Subject Representation* (Dordrecht, Netherlands: Kluwer Academic, 2002) and Emily Drabinski, "Queering the Catalog: Queer Theory and the Politics of Correction," *The Library Quarterly: Information, Community, Policy* 83, no. 2 (April 2013).

distress and/or problems functioning in social, work or family activities."[2] This definition emphasizes the diagnostic aspect of the condition, placing it in the context of a medical narrative that codifies the condition as a negative "disorder" requiring treatment or management. In contrast, "mental health conditions," as defined by the National Alliance on Mental Illness (NAMI), is a more neutral concept; according to NAMI, a mental health condition is "a condition that affects a person's thinking, feeling or mood. Such conditions may affect someone's ability to relate to others and function each day."[3] While the author chooses to use the term "mental health conditions" in this chapter when speaking in the abstract about a collective group of people, many individuals identify with the term "mental illness" and do not associate it with the negative connotations discussed above.

It is important to note that the word "disorder" will be used in this article when discussing conditions where the word is part of the official name of the condition as presented in the *Diagnostic and Statistical Manual of Mental Disorders (DSM-5)* or if the word "disorder" is part of an LCSH subject heading or authority record. Although this word can be problematic, it is difficult to discuss these conditions without referring to them by their current official names; the author apologizes for any discomfort that use of this word causes. Additionally, due to the large number of mental health conditions, this article will not present an inclusive analysis of all mental health conditions in the LCSH but will attempt instead to provide a representative sample. The omission or inclusion of a mental health condition in the LCSH analysis does not reflect any intentional value judgement or statement on the part of the author.

## Mental Health Conditions in the LCSH

### The LCSH and the Evolution of Disability Language

Although created in 1898, the first edition of the LCSH was published in 1909. At this time, the prevalent attitudes toward mental health conditions were based on the moral and medical models of disability; both models viewed disability negatively and used descriptive language

---

2   American Psychiatric Association, "What is Mental Illness?" last modified August 2018, https://www.psychiatry.org/patients-families/what-is-mental-illness.

3   National Alliance on Mental Illness, "Mental Health Conditions," accessed October 2019, https://www.nami.org/learn-more/mental-health-conditions.

that is now considered offensive. For example, according to the moral model, disability was "believed to be the result of sin" and defined as "an inferior and pitiful state."[4] Examples of the moral model in the 1909 version of the LCSH regarding mental health conditions include: "Incurables," "Imbecility," and "Inefficiency, Intellectual." In contrast to the moral model, the medical model viewed disability as a medical problem and "defined groups and individuals solely based on their impairments."[5] Examples of the medical model in the 1909 publication of the LCSH include: "Feeble-minded," and "Insane—care and treatment." Additionally, mental health conditions were presented as diseases of the brain and the nervous system, under the following hierarchy:

Brain.

—*Diseases*

*See Also* Amnesia; Aphasia; Apoplexy; Fatigue, Mental; Hydrocephalus; Insanity; Nervous system—Diseases; Psychology, Pathological; Thrombosis.

It is significant to note that the medical model is still prevalent in the American medical community (particularly through the use of medical shorthand) and appears in multiple contemporary headings in the LCSH.[6]

In the 1970s and 1980s, the social model of disability emerged as an alternative to the moral and medical models. According to scholars Dana S. Dunn and Erin E. Andrews, "the social model of disability presents disability as a neutral characteristic or attribute, not a medical problem requiring a cure, and not a presentation of moral failing."[7] The social model was later used by the social psychologist Beatrice A. Wright to argue that language should "never equate people with impairment," which Wright contended could be prevented by emphasizing

---

4    Dana S. Dunn and Erin E. Andrews, "Person-First and Identity-First Language: Developing Psychologists' Cultural Competence Using Disability Language, *American Psychologist* 70, no. 3 (April 2015): 258, doi.org/10.1037/a0038636.

5    Dunn and Andrews, "Person-First and Identity-First Language," 258.

6    Dunn and Andrews, "Person-First and Identity-First Language," 258.

7    Dunn and Andrews, "Person-First and Identity-First Language," 258.

the person before their disability.[8] As a result, person-first language (e.g. "person with disabilities" instead of "disabled person" for individuals; "people with disabilities" instead of "the disabled" for groups of people) became the preferred structure of disability language. This change was formally reflected in the LCSH in 2002, when the term "Handicapped" was changed to "Person with disabilities," citing the *American Heritage Dictionary*, the *American Disabilities Act,* and the Illinois attorney general's *Manual of Style for Depicting People with Disabilities* as "literary warrant."[9] [10] At the time, the Library of Congress's Barbara Tillet stated that the change was "in accord with ...the principle of 'putting people first,' which is advocated by most organizations and individuals with an interest in disability issues."[11] As further evidence of the widespread adoption of person-first language as applied to mental health conditions, the APA mandated in its *Publication Manual* in 2010 that scientists and professional practitioners use person-first language.[12]

Although person-first language became standard in the early 2000s, some disability scholars and advocates criticized its use in favor of identity-first language (e.g. "disabled person" instead of "person with disabilities"). Based on the minority model of disability, this approach views disability in a neutral or positive light, defining disability as "a distinct cultural and sociopolitical experience and identity."[13] In this interpretation, disability is a form of diversity, similar to "other demographic characteristics such as race and sexual orientation."[14] The mi-

---

8   Dunn and Andrews, "Person-First and Identity-First Language," 258.

9   Note: "Literary warrant" refers to using a resource as a citation in an authority record to justify the creation of a record or a change to a record. For example, if creating a name authority record for "Hansen, Carolyn" this article could be cited as the literary warrant that justifies the creation of the name authority record as well as the content of the name based on how it appears on the piece (ex. No middle name or initial in the authority record because none appears on the title page of this article). Citation information appears in name and subject authority records in separate instances of the 670 field.

10  Melissa Adler, Jeffrey T. Huber, and A. Tyler Nix, "Stigmatizing Disability: Library Classifications and the Marking and Marginalization of Books about People with Disabilities," *The Library Quarterly* 87, no. 2 (April 2017): 128, doi.org/10.1086/690734.

11  Barbara B. Tillet, "Library of Congress Liaison Report to ALA/ALCTS/CCS/CC:DA, Annual Meeting, January 2002," last modified July 10, 2010, paragraph 25, http://www.libraries.psu.edu/tas/jca/ccda/lc0201.html.

12  Dunn and Andrews, "Person-First and Identity-First Language," 256.

13  Dunn and Andrews, "Person-First and Identity-First Language," 259.

14  Dunn and Andrews, "Person-First and Identity-First Language," 259.

nority model argues that by separating a person from their disability through the language "person *with* …", person-first language is ableist and prevents individuals and groups from claiming disability as part of their identity.[15]

Since disability language continues to evolve and there is debate about whether person-first or identity-first language should be used, it is difficult to determine a universal standard to be applied to headings related to mental health conditions in the LCSH. Since the creation of new headings and modification of existing headings in the LCSH must be justified by literary warrant, applying a universal standard would require significant investment in both time and labor to find evidence to justify changes at the individual record level. It is significant to note that at this time, there has been little, if any, research analyzing user behavior of people with mental health conditions to provide evidence in support of a preference for person-first or identity-first language. In research conducted in 2013, the scholar Amelia Koford conducted interviews with nine participants working in various academic fields with research focused on disability, though not specifically focused on mental health conditions.[16] In these interviews, only two participants discussed person-first and identity-first language; interestingly, the participants disagreed on which format they preferred.[17] More research is needed on user behavior regarding mental health conditions and disability; ideally, larger studies incorporating persons outside of academia and including individuals with mental health conditions would be conducted.

## Inconsistent Use of Person-First and Identity-First Language

Examining headings related to mental health conditions in the LCSH reveals mixed use of person-first and identity-first language.[18] For example, person-first language is used in the broader headings "People with disabilities" and "People with mental disabilities." However, headings referring to people with more specific conditions are

---

15  Dunn and Andrews, "Person-First and Identity-First Language," 259.

16  Amelia Koford, "How Disability Studies Scholars Interact with Subject Headings," *Cataloging & Classification Quarterly* 52, no. 4 (2014): 394, doi.org/10.1080/01639374.2014.891288.

17  Koford, "How Disability Studies Scholars Interact with Subject Headings," 399–400.

18  Note: All quoted subject headings from the modern LCSH from: Library of Congress, "Library of Congress Authorities," last modified September 15, 2019, http://authorities.loc.gov.

constructed with identity-first language, including: "Depressed persons," "Manic-depressive persons," and "Autistic people." The reasons for this inconsistency are unclear, although there are also some headings in the LCSH that fall somewhere between person-first and identity-first language, particularly when referring to children and teenagers with mental health conditions. These headings include: "Depression in children" (as opposed to "Children with depression" or "Depressed children"), "Depression in adolescence," "Borderline personality disorder in children," and "Borderline personality disorder in adolescence." For mental health conditions that do not have an authorized heading for a person with that specific condition, the LCSH provides the option of using the topical subdivision "Patients" after the name of the condition (the scope note for the record "Patients" actually indicates that the subdivision should be used "under individual diseases and types of diseases"). Following these instructions, an individual or group of people with Obsessive-Compulsive Disorder would be described in the LCSH as "Obsessive-Compulsive disorder—Patients." By associating mental health conditions with the term "Patients," the LCSH continues to reinforce the medical model of disability, which presents individuals with mental health conditions as "sick" or in need of treatment.

## Mental Health Conditions and Objectifying Language

As discussed earlier, the medical model of disability refers to individuals and groups solely by their physical and/or mental disability (ex. "Disabled" instead of "Disabled person" or "People with disabilities"). This approach, according to Dunn and Andrews, "promotes essentialism" toward people with disabilities because "their personalities, abilities, interests, and other personal qualities are subordinated by a condition that is perceived to be a dominant trait."[19] There are multiple examples in the LCSH that refer to individuals with mental health conditions in this way, including: "Mentally ill," "Narcissists," Neurotics," Psychopaths," and "Schizophrenics." These headings are offensive and require review; at minimum, revisions should be considered using person-first or identity-first language (ex. "People with schizophrenia" or "Schizophrenic person" instead of "Schizophrenics"). Also, it is significant to note that none of the authority records for these

---

19   Dunn and Andrews, "Person-First and Identity-First Language," 259.

headings contain detailed scope notes that would contextualize or explain the language being used.

Examination of the authority record for the heading "Mentally ill" reveals troubling cross-references in addition to the objectifying language in the heading itself; for example, cross-references (field 450) include "Insane" and "Mentally disordered" as well as the broader term (field 550) "Sick." There are also several narrower terms for "Mentally ill" that continue the use of objectifying language, such as "Children of the mentally ill," "Discrimination against the mentally ill," "Libraries and the mentally ill," etc. Interestingly, similar headings exist that use person-first language in regard to disability ("Discrimination against people with disabilities" and "Libraries and people with disabilities"). The reasons why some mental health conditions are described in the LCSH using outdated language models are unclear; literary warrant may explain some of these differences, however, many authority records for headings relating to mental health conditions are minimal with limited information in the records' source data/citations field (field 670) that would explain how literary warrant justified the use of specific language.

## Outdated or Offensive Language

Many headings in the LCSH related to mental health conditions contain outdated or offensive language in the main heading or cross-references in the authority record. For example, headings exist for mental health conditions that are no longer used in formal medical diagnosis; a scope note in the authority record for the heading "Hysteria" even states that it is "An out moded [sic] term...Hysteria is no longer recognized as a separate clinical entity without qualification." It is significant to note that the mental health condition "Hysterical neurosis" (a 450 reference in the LCSH authority for "Hysteria") has a long association with sexist conceptions of women and it was deleted from the *DSM-III* in 1980.[20] Similarly, a LCSH heading exists for "Neuroses," which as a mental health condition was also removed from the *DSM-III*.[21] Lastly,

---

20   Cecilia Tasca, Mariangela Rapetti, Mauro Giovanni Carta, and Biana Fadda, "Women and Hysteria in the History of Mental Health," *Clinical Practice and Epidemiology in Mental Health* 8 (2012): 110, doi.org/10.2174/1745017901208010110.

21   S. Torgersen, "Neurotic Depression and DSM-III," *Acta Psychiatrica Scandinavica* 73, no. s328 (1986): 31, doi.org/10.1111/j.1600-0447.1986.tb10521.x.

the LCSH contains a heading for "Psychology, Pathological," which is identical to a heading from the vocabulary's first publication in 1909; the more current terminology is "Psychopathology." If the LCSH is intending to follow the medical model to describe mental health conditions—which is in itself problematic—it is failing to even remain current with accepted medical language.

Some headings in the LCSH contain offensive language that perpetuates stereotypes about people with mental health conditions. For example, the heading "Dangerously mentally ill" seems to refer to people with mental health conditions who are hospitalized and could be physically violent. References in the authority record for this heading include "Dangerous mental patients" and "Insane, Criminal and dangerous." In addition to the objectifying language of referring to people with mental health conditions as "mentally ill," the authority links mental health conditions with danger, insanity, and criminality. This language is unnecessarily negative and value-laden; in contrast, a heading in the LCSH referring to women who commit violent acts is constructed as "Violence in women."

Another problematic heading in the LCSH related to mental health conditions is "Ex-mental patients," whose authority record contains cross-references (field 450) for "Ex-mentally ill," "Former [sic] mentally ill," and "Mentally restored." These cross-references ignore the chronic nature of some mental health conditions and deny that a mental health condition could be a neutral or even positive part of an individual's personal or group identity. Additionally, the record cites the following pattern as justification for the heading's structure: "LC pattern: Ex-convicts; Ex-nuns; Ex-monks." This pattern again links mental health conditions with criminality ("Ex-convicts"), which is inappropriate and offensive. Oddly, it also links mental health conditions to leaving religious vocations ("Ex-nuns" and "Ex-monks"), which has little in common with having a mental health condition or being treated for that condition in inpatient or outpatient facilities. Since headings exist for "Psychiatric hospitals" and "Psychotherapy patients," the choice of referring to individuals in treatment as "Mental patients" is at best strange and inconsistent with other related authorized headings using the LC pattern described above. The reoccurrence of the concept of "patient hood" in regard to individuals with mental health conditions is also troubling; in addition to the topical subdivision "Patients" that was previously discussed, the example "Ex-mental patients" places patient hood in the primary portion of a topical heading. This word choice continues to reinforce the medical model of disability by emphasizing an individual's status as a patient, which places them in a medical narrative of diagnosis, treatment, and recovery. This narrative may not reflect the lived experience of an individual with a mental health condition—again, their condition may be chronic and not fit a linear narrative or they may view the condition as a neutral or positive component of their identity that should not only be seen in the context of treatment.

## Inappropriate or Questionable Hierarchy

In addition to problematic headings and cross-references in authority records, the hierarchy of some subject headings in the LCSH related to mental health conditions contain inappropriate and/or questionable hierarchies. For example, the heading for Major Depression is "Depression, Mental," which contains the parent headings "Neuroses" and "Psychology, Pathological." Additional headings with these parent headings include: "Anxiety disorders," "Panic disorders," "Agoraphobia," "Post-traumatic stress disorder," and "Rape trauma syndrome." By categorizing these mental health conditions as forms of "Neuroses," a term which is no longer used in the psychiatric community, the LCSH perpetuates inaccurate beliefs about these conditions and contributes to existing stigma. Furthermore, the categorization of almost all mental health conditions under the broad parent heading "Psychology, Pathological," presents these conditions in the context of being abnormal or as "Mental diseases" (this last term is listed as a cross-reference in the authority record for Psychology, Pathological). All mental health conditions under the term "Psychology, Pathological" and under the narrower term "Neuroses" in particular, deserve review to determine if these categorizations are still appropriate.

## Conclusion

As stated in the introduction, this chapter marks the beginning of a discussion into how mental health conditions and people who live with those conditions are categorized and represented in controlled vocabularies. The purpose of this discussion is to encourage heading revision in the LCSH as well as to spark more research into related headings or terms in other controlled vocabularies. While it is impossible to create controlled vocabularies with completely neutral language, there is much that can be done to improve the LCSH in regard to headings about mental health and illness. This includes the review and revision of mixed-use person-first and identity-first language, modification of objectifying, outdated, or offensive language, and research into the language that people with mental health conditions identify with and prefer to use. Libraries take great care to make their physical spaces welcoming and inclusive; we should extend that philosophy to our digital spaces (including online catalogs, digital collections, finding aid portals, and associated metadata) as well. No one wants to be referred to as a "Psychopath," "Ex-mental patient," or "Dangerously mentally ill"—this language is alienating and hurtful to librarians and patrons living with mental health conditions. So, let's get to work.[22]

## Acknowledgements

The author would like to acknowledge the earlier work of librarians studying the language of cataloging and its relationship to power structures and personal agency, including Emily Drabinski, Hope Olson, Melissa Adler, and Violet Fox.

---

### *Bibliography*

Adler, Melissa, Huber, Jeffrey T. and A. Tyler Nix. "Stigmatizing Disability: Library Classifications and the Marking and Marginalization of Books about People with Disabilities." *The Library Quarterly* 87: no. 2 (April 2017): 117–35. doi.org/10.1086/690734.

American Psychiatric Association (APA). "What is Mental Illness?" Last modified August 2018. https://www.psychiatry.org/patients-families/what-is-mental-illness.

Dunn, Dana S., and Andrews, Erin E. "Person-First and Identity-First Language: Developing Psychologists' Cultural Competence Using Disability Language." *American Psychologist* 70, no. 3 (April 2015): 255–64. doi.org/10.1037/a0038636.

---

22  Proposing new headings or requesting changes to the LCSH requires a membership in the Subject Authority Cooperative Program (SACO). If your library is a SACO member, your Cataloging Department can submit proposals to LC for review. This is the most direct approach. Alternately, you can contact a SACO Funnel, which is a group of individuals from multiple institutions who are authorized to request subject headings changes related to a particular topic (see: loc.gov/aba/pcc/saco/funnels.html). There is also a crowd-sourced platform called The Cataloging Lab where anyone can create a proposal to be submitted to LC by a cataloger with SACO authorization (see: cataloginglab.org/kbtopic/subjects/)

Koford, Amelia. "How Disability Studies Scholars Interact with Subject Headings." *Cataloging & Classification Quarterly* 52, no. 4 (2014): 388–411. doi.org/10.1 080/01639374.2014.891288.

Library of Congress. "Library of Congress Authorities." Last modified September 15, 2019. http://authorities.loc.gov.

Library of Congress. Catalog Division. *Subject Headings Used in the Dictionary Catalogues of the Library of Congress*. Washington: G.P.O., Library Branch, 1909. Volume 1. https://hdl.handle.net/2027/coo.31924050327042

Library of Congress. Catalog Division. *Subject Headings Used in the Dictionary Catalogues of the Library of Congress*. Washington: G.P.O., Library Branch, 1909. Volume 2. https://hdl.handle.net/2027/coo.31924050327059

National Alliance on Mental Illness (NAMI). "Mental Health Conditions." Accessed October 29, 2019. https://www.nami.org/learn-more/ mental-health-conditions.

Tasca, Cecilia, Rapetti, Mariangela, Carta, Mauro Giovanni, and Biana Fadda. "Women and Hysteria in the History of Mental Health." *Clinical Practice and Epidemiology in Mental Health* 8 (2012): 110–119. doi.org/10.2174/17450 17901208010110.

Tillett, Barbara B. "Library of Congress Liaison Report to ALA/ALCTS/CCS/CC:DA, Annual Meeting, January 2002." Last modified July 10, 2010. http://www. libraries.psu.edu/tas/jca/ccda/lc0201.html.

Torgersen, S. "Neurotic Depression and DSM-III." *Acta Psychiatrica Scandinavica* 73, no. s328 (1986): 31–34. doi.org/10.1111/j.1600-0447.1986.tb10521.x.

# Neoliberalism, Mental Health, and Labor in the Library Workplace

**Michelle Ashley Gohr and Andrew Barber**

*Content Warning*   This paper contains discussions of mental health, mental illness, and workplace trauma.

## Introduction

Current literature on the mental health of library workers in the United States focuses predominantly on librarians and burnout. While this is a serious issue that sheds light on the high-stress/low-support working environment of librarians, paraprofessional and support staff remain largely overlooked in discussions of mental health in the Library and Information Science (LIS) professions. Broadening our perspective and focusing on paraprofessional staff (i.e., support workers, MLIS students, interns, student workers, etc.) may help reveal the unique stressors and systemic failures that impact workers with mental health issues.

It's crucial to acknowledge that the term "paraprofessional" is problematic on its own, suggesting that unskilled laborers work beside or in conjunction with librarians and administrators. The truth is, academic library paraprofessionals are skilled laborers. Minimum qualifications for these positions typically include a bachelor's degree and previous academic library experience. While there is significant overlap in the responsibilities of librarians and staff, the MLIS as symbolic capital creates a social and professional rift between these workers.

In an attempt to address and rectify concerning trends in LIS surrounding class and alienation of library paraprofessionals, this article uses critical theories—such as disability, feminist, and queer studies— and Marxist philosophy to theoretically and critically analyze an increase in depression and anxiety among LIS staff, as linked to the larger reproduction of systems of oppression and a trend towards neoliberalism in the library as an institution. Largely a class issue, paraprofessional workers have the least control over their work schedules and are often assigned shift work that entails late evening, overnight, and weekend hours. Research has linked these routines to increased risk of depression and other mental health issues.[1] Given that paraprofessionals often exist in a psychologically and physically hostile working environment, a rise in diagnoses of mental illnesses, including depression and anxiety may be the consequence of a variety of factors including neoliberal gaslighting in the form of poor organizational climate and occupational stress.

Abstracting beyond the library, neoliberalism is a political, economic, and social project critically understood to foster an environment of increasingly efficient capital accumulation and reestablish, or create, a powerful economic elite.[2] Evidence of this is found in the financial crisis of 2008, the wealth gap disparity, the increasingly polarized political ideologies and far right turn in global and domestic politics, the deregulation of industry and consequence-free poisoning of rivers and sources of drinking water in marginalized communities, the dismantling of unions resulting in endangerment of workers, and more.

To accomplish this, the neoliberal state operates along a series of contradictions (presenting free-market ideology yet actively legislating a pro-business economy, balancing democratic principles with economic authoritarianism, valuing individual autonomy but increasing

---

1  Aeyoung Lee et al., "Night Shift Work and Risk of Depression: Meta-Analysis of Observational Studies," *Journal of Korean Medical Science* 32, no. 7 (July 1, 2017): 1091–96, https://doi.org/10.3346/jkms.2017.32.7.1091; Bengt B. Arnetz, Todd Lucas, and Judith E. Arnetz, "Organizational Climate, Occupational Stress, and Employee Mental Health: Mediating Effects of Organizational Efficiency," *Journal of Occupational and Environmental Medicine* 53, no. 1 (January 2011): 34, https://doi.org/10.1097/JOM.0b013e3181ffo5b; Brice Faraut, Virginie Bayon, and Damien Léger, "Neuroendocrine, Immune and Oxidative Stress in Shift Workers," *Sleep Medicine Reviews* 17, no. 6 (December 1, 2013): 433–44, https://doi.org/10.1016/j.smrv.2012.12.006.

2  David Harvey, *A Brief History of Neoliberalism*, Reprinted (Oxford: Oxford Univ. Press, 2011).

surveillance and police power to disrupt voluntary efforts to unionize, etc.) to the point that this state apparatus appears unsustainable and temporary. This ultimately resulted in the "restoration of class power."[3] It is our position that these class antagonisms are recreated and perpetuated within the library workplace, resulting in corollary anxieties (including mental illness) within the library worker.

Since the American Library Association (ALA) last conducted a paraprofessional and support worker survey in 1997,[4] there exists a significant gap in current information on the morale and health of academic library support workers. This outdated information exists alongside a bleak backdrop in mental health research, which suggests that depression and anxiety are on the rise, especially among younger and marginalized populations.[5] The lack of literature specifically focusing on paraprofessional/support workers obscures what is unique about the library as a workplace and its relationship to issues of both mental health—or the emotional and social well-being in the workplace—and mental illness—or how workers develop or cope with pre-existing illnesses in the form of anxiety disorders, trauma-related disorders, etc.. This prevents us from understanding how and why libraries[6] are reproducing larger systems of oppression, but more importantly how (and if) they are willing to address these issues. By bringing these workers into an academic investigation and critical discourse, we hope to both theorize on and build a dialogue around these valid, intersectional, and impactful mental health issues.

## Statistics

According to the World Health Organization (WHO), "Depression is the leading cause of disability worldwide, and is a major contributor to the

---

3  Harvey, *A Brief History of Neoliberalism*,79.

4  http://www.ala.org/rt/sites/ala.org.rt/files/content/lssirtstratplan/issuessurvey/Results.pdf

5  A. H. Weinberger et al., "Trends in Depression Prevalence in the USA from 2005 to 2015: Widening Disparities in Vulnerable Groups," *Psychological Medicine* 48, no. 8 (2018): 1308–15, https://doi.org/10.1017/S0033291717002781.

6  Both authors are employed in academic libraries and may frame discussions based on our personal experiences but wish to acknowledge and address to the best of our ability the unique issues faced in all library types.

overall global burden of disease."[7] Additionally, not only does depression affect roughly 4.4% of the world's population (322 million people), but both depression and anxiety disorders have seen a significant and steady increase since 2005.[8] By 2030, depression is expected to be the leading cause of burden of disease in high-income countries and the second leading cause in the world.[9]

In a 2017 US Department of Health and Human Services survey responses indicated that 7.1% (~17.3 million) of U.S. adults have suffered from a major depressive episode, and young adults experienced a rate nearly double that (13.1%).[10] As noted above, although these results are already high, the prevalence of depression in the United States is on the rise across the board demographically, with those aged 12-17 years old experiencing the most rapid increase in depression, followed by those aged 18-25. [11]

These brief statistics paint a grim portrait regarding the societal and global state of mental health, but they are only made more concerning when factoring in intersecting and marginalized identities, which, when taken together, constitute a crisis affecting the most vulnerable within libraries.

## Workplace Environments

While it's been widely cited that common contributors to changes in global mental health may include negative economic developments (globalization, falling wages, etc.),[12] social climate (increased

---

7    World Health Organization, "Depression," World Health Organization, accessed June 25, 2019, https://www.who.int/news-room/fact-sheets/detail/depression.

8    M. J. Friedrich, "Depression Is the Leading Cause of Disability Around the World," *JAMA* 317, no. 15 (April 18, 2017): 1517–1517, https://doi.org/10.1001/jama.2017.3826.

9    Colin D. Mathers and Dejan Loncar, "Projections of Global Mortality and Burden of Disease from 2002 to 2030," *PLoS Medicine* 3, no. 11 (2006): 2011–30, https://doi.org/10.1371/journal. pmed.0030442.

10   Substance Abuse and Mental Health Services (SAMHSA)Administration, "National Survey on Drug Use and Health" (U.S. Department of Health and Human Services, 2017), https://www. samhsa.gov/data/report/2017-nsduh-detailed-tables.

11   Weinberger et al., "Trends in Depression Prevalence in the USA from 2005 to 2015."

12   J. K. Burns, "Poverty, Inequality and a Political Economy of Mental Health," *Epidemiology and Psychiatric Sciences* 24, no. 2 (April 2015): 107–13, https://doi.org/10.1017/S2045796015000086.

nationalism, hate crimes, inequality, etc.),[13] and national politics/policies (passing of discriminatory policies, polarization, neoliberalism, etc.),[14] these systems are also couched in deeper institutionalized ideologies and systems that function invisibly. While we can attempt to use data to "prove" a decline in mental health based on an observable measurement of economy, in reality, the causes of declining mental health are far more complex; we are perceiving a change in the way we live and are treated and it's making us unhappy. One such change is the stratification of labor across class lines.

Library workers may often perform within rigid environments, where they lose their ability to direct their own actions or determine their work. Instead, they are placed in an exploited class that is solely responsible for the mechanistic labor that keeps the library functioning behind the scenes while offering the workers little gratification. Compare these working conditions of library employees to Marx's theory of alienation, which posits that under a capitalist mode of production, workers become alienated from their labor when deprived of the right to think and direct their own actions and are therefore stripped of the right to choose and direct their own schedule, work, and, by extension, life and destiny. Although library workers aren't manufacturing a tangible product, the commodity produced within libraries is (emotional) care and knowledge. While library workers are facing physical devaluation (lower wages, etc.) described by Marx, they are also simultaneously being emotionally and cognitively devalued.

Library workers, which include MLIS unpaid interns and student workers, are overwhelmingly responsible for material processing, shelving, sorting, scanning and digitizing, answering directional and technical questions, building security, and other rote tasks that seldom leave room for creativity or autonomy. Given this reality, research which has found that risk of common mental disorders, such as mild to moderate anxiety and depressive disorders, are associated with "low decision authority, low decision latitude, high job demands, low occupational

---

13  David R. Williams, "Stress and the Mental Health of Populations of Color: Advancing Our Understanding of Race-Related Stressors," *Journal of Health and Social Behavior* 59, no. 4 (December 1, 2018): 466–85, https://doi.org/10.1177/0022146518814251.

14  "The Lancet Countdown on Health and Climate Change: From 25 Years of Inaction to a Global Transformation for Public Health,–*The Lancet*," accessed August 3, 2019, https://www.thelancet.com/journals/lancet/article/PIIS0140-6736(17)32464-9/fulltext?elsca1=tlpr.

social support, and job insecurity."[15] Furthermore, changes to systems or processes are often if not always made without input from those library workers who are exclusively affected by such changes, which signals both their position as the proletariat within the system and is a greater ideological signaling of their worth within the library system. While this work is essential, assigning the responsibility of this work to part-time, underpaid laborers serves to socially and monetarily devalue this significant work and stratify the labor across class lines.[16]

## Class Structure

When issues of mental health are discussed in library literature they tend to focus on burnout, depression, anxiety, and/or PTSD experienced by credentialed librarians or those in professional positions.[17] Unfortunately, this often comes at the expense of a broader look into the systemic mechanisms behind these issues, all of which likely have a disproportionate impact on library workers without professional degrees. This is further complicated— even for professional degree holders—by recession dynamics, bloated employment markets, shrinking opportunities which offer adequate (or any) compensation, and institutional cost cutting.

As Bird and Cannon highlight, librarians do not typically identify as workers.[18] Because they may belong to the ALA and have completed a graduate degree program, librarians instead identify as "professionals." Such an identity is fostered and encouraged by library schools and the ALA. Even though librarians must report to administrators, who often times are not librarians, this professional education and identity compels librarians to identify more with management than

---

15  Stephen Stansfeld and Bridget Candy, "Psychosocial Work Environment and Mental Health–A Meta-Analytic Review," *Scandinavian Journal of Work, Environment & Health* 32, no. 6 (December 2006): 443–62.

16  Samuel B. Harvey et al., "Can Work Make You Mentally Ill? A Systematic Meta-Review of Work-Related Risk Factors for Common Mental Health Problems," *Occupational and Environmental Medicine* 74, no. 4 (April 1, 2017): 301–10, https://doi.org/10.1136/oemed-2016-104015.

17  Kaetrena Davis Kendrick, "The Low Morale Experience of Academic Librarians: A Phenomenological Study," *Journal of Library Administration* 57, no. 8 (November 17, 2017): 846–78, https://doi.org/10.1080/01930826.2017.1368325.

18  Amanda Bird and Braden Cannon, "From Steam Engines to Search Engines: Class Struggle in an Information Economy," in *Class and Librarianship: Essays at the Intersection of Information, Labor and Capital*, ed. Erik Estep and Nathaniel F. Enright (Sacramento, CA: Library Juice Press, 2016), 49–72.

with workers, and paraprofessionals view librarians as authority fig-ures instead of workers.[19][20]

The ideological stance of the LIS profession can be defined and imag-ined through paraprofessional labor, which sees broader systematic ideologies of social class being reproduced in the hierarchy and divi-sion of labor in the library. This is evidenced through the growing eco-nomic precarity of paraprofessionals (i.e., greater experience require-ments for less pay/undercompensation, inflexible schedules, growing trend/reliance on contingent work broadly within the field) and the flexploitation[21] of paraprofessionals and MLIS students (e.g., normal-ization of insecure work, unpaid labor, lack of bargaining power). In turn, these exploitative labor practices, as rooted in the neoliberal history of the institution, are having an immense impact on the mate-rial and psychological welfare of library workers/laborers.

Flexploitation pressures "workers into accepting neoliberalism through this constant threat of insecurity, of losing their jobs."[22] This is partic-ularly true in "right-to-work" states, where labor laws protect an em-ployer's right to terminate, effectively instilling permanent anxiety re-garding one's job security. Additionally, according to Bourdieu, "job insecurity robs people not only of a future, but of a belief in the future that can impel one to change it, of a capacity to 'project themselves into the future.'"[23] This frames work, and access to work, as a privilege and commodity, which creates rifts among staff and librarians and compe-tition within LIS in order to dissuade coalition building and discussion.

This anxiety disproportionately affects student workers who are con-sistently assigned mechanistic labor. Their duties are likely to ac-cumulate without fair increase in compensation throughout their

19  Bird and Cannon, "From Steam Engines to Search Engines," 55–56.

20  For further recommended critiques on the classed nature of librarianship and unionization read RM Harris "Librarianship: the erosion of a woman's profession"

21  A specific form of exploitation under neoliberalism in which workers are employed in inher-ently insecure or impermanent positions and under constant threat of job loss

22  Philippe Lynes, "Flexibility I–Bourdieu and Flexploitation," Obsercation Du Discours Financier En Traduction (blog), 2016, http://odft.nt2.ca/blogue/flexibility-i-bourdieu-and-flexploitation.

23  Lynes, " Flexibility I–Bourdieu and Flexploitation."

employment. Being the lowest paid library staff[24] and having the least decision latitude of all workers, student workers are acutely aware of their position in the hierarchy. After all, why don't we refer to student workers as coworkers? They report feelings of inferiority and second-class citizenship, while recognizing a "disproportionate labor-to-pay exchange" throughout the field.[25]

While many (but not all) credentialed librarians may enjoy typical or flexible work hours, paraprofessionals and students often have little control over their own work and must also work undesirable shifts, often without pay differential. Conflicts between one's nonwork/personal life and work responsibilities resulting from working alternative shifts significantly contribute to poor mental health. Additionally, the presence or absence of social support both from coworkers and outside of work has a critical impact on the mental health and "resilience" of library shift workers. While it's encouraging that supportive supervisors in the workplace have been shown to significantly reduce the negative psychological impacts of working nights, rarely are other intentional mechanisms put in place to safeguard and support the mental health of both supervisors and shift workers working in an isolated environment.[26]

The lack of emotional and physical support and consideration for shift work in libraries is evidenced by high turnover. Research by Shields shows that fewer than 12% of shift workers continued this working schedule the following year.[27] The same study shows that this work routinely puts workers at a higher risk of an increase in psychological distress as well as development of a chronic condition, such as diabetes, heart disease, or high blood pressure in the near future.

## Happiness Industry

Despite overwhelming personal and statistical evidence that there is a historically unacknowledged and problematic culture of emotional

---

24   In Arizona we have 3 public universities: Arizona State University, University of Arizona, and Northern Arizona University. Of the three public universities, University of Arizona is the only one that pays student workers the state minimum wage of $12 an hour. All others pay less than the minimum wage due to a temporary worker exemption in Arizona's minimum wage law.

25   Elliott Kuecker, "Ideology and Rhetoric of Undergraduate Student Workers in Academic Libraries," *Progressive Librarian*, no. 46 (2017): 53–55.

26   Philip Bohle and Andrew J. Tilley, "The Impact of Night Work On Psychological Well-Being," *Ergonomics* 32, no. 9 (September 1989): 1089–99, https://doi.org/10.1080/00140138908966876.

27   Margot Shields, "Shift Work and Health," *Health Reports* 13, no. 4 (July 2002): 11–33.

and physical exploitation in libraries that results in widespread depression and chronic illness among workers,[28] new neoliberal trends to "address" a crisis of mental health in the workplace have been increasingly adopted by libraries (as larger parts of the institutions to which they belong). "As positive psychology and happiness measurement have permeated our political and economic culture since the 1990s, there has been a growing unease with the way in which notions of happiness and well-being have been adopted by policy makers and managers."[29] Rather than addressing the exploitative conditions that give rise to psychological distress and illness, which may require incursion of greater financial costs to the employer (via better access to healthcare, increased pay, time off, etc.), positive psychology prioritizes financial benefit over individual health by manufacturing a sense of employee happiness through "objective" measurements.

Consider the unironic trend in opinion polling towards placing monetary values on emotional and mental health to show impacts on productivity and the economy. Companies often address mental health not because the health of workers is important, but because "mental health and substance abuse cost US businesses between $80 and $100 billion annually."[30] The solution? Incorporate workplace meditation and yoga, because "prioritizing the mental and emotional wellbeing of employees will increase profit."[31]

Additionally, research has shown that "happier" employees are more productive (up to 12%), work harder, take less sick time and leave, are more committed, and so on.[32] Corporate obsession with combating workplace depression and anxiety as a guise to maintain/boost profit

---

28  Abigail L. Phillips, "Mental Health Behind the Desk," *Library Journal* 144, no. 5 (June 2019): 51–51; Liz Farler and Judith Broady-Preston, "Workplace Stress in Libraries: A Case Study," *Aslib Proceedings* 64, no. 3 (2012): 225–40.

29  William Davies, *The Happiness Industry : How the Government and Big Business Sold Us Well-Being* (Verso Books, 2015), 10.

30  Carley Sime, "The Cost Of Ignoring Mental Health In The Workplace," Forbes, April 17, 2019, https://www.forbes.com/sites/carleysime/2019/04/17/the-cost-of-ignoring-mental-health-in-the-workplace/.

31  Matthew Jones, "How Mental Health Can Save Businesses $225 Billion Each Year," Inc., 2016, https://www.inc.com/matthew-jones/how-mental-health-can-save-businesses-225-billion-each-year.html.

32  Andrew J. Oswald, Eugenio Proto, and Daniel Sgroi, "Happiness and Productivity," *Journal of Labor Economics* 33, no. 4 (October 1, 2015): 789–822, https://doi.org/10.1086/681096.

manifests through the growing trends of employing "chief happiness officers."

This increasing concern for workplace happiness is typically focused on thinly veiled "techniques" for overall wellness which ultimately serve to extend our ability to work rather than making us happy. For example, taking microbreaks (so that we can concentrate longer), stretching (so that we have more energy), offering privacy screens (to feel less surveilled), and more puts workers in a position where if they don't "care for themselves" properly through meditation, working at standing desks, or stretching every 15 minutes, then they are the sole cause of their own suffering and, therefore, aren't fit to continue producing for the company/organization.

While library workers are suffering from rising rates of depression and anxiety, libraries as institutions are being used as a tool in the happiness regime to provide free services and care for the mental health of their communities. While this is noble, library workers are placed in a position of caring for their communities while not receiving care from their institutions, thus amplifying the possibility of developing mental and chronic health conditions.

## Corporatization and Surveillance

Increasingly, libraries are being discussed and run as businesses rather than public institutions.[33] As a result, integration of neoliberal ideologies has led to the development of corporate managerialism as the basis for library administrational structure. Library administrations focus on strategic planning, branding, professional training, and responsiveness to stakeholders, while those at the bottom of the workplace hierarchy remain largely unconsidered. This discourse and trend has led to an increase in control over workers (emotionally and physically), an increase in surveillance, a decrease in trust, and a general restructuring of the library in the image of corporate organizations (corporatization).

Although surveillance serves a broad number of purposes, it is justified in this context as a benevolent tool to monitor and maximize worker well-being and happiness. Functionally, that tool optimizes a

---

33   Karen Antell et al., "Should Libraries Be Run Like Businesses?," *Reference & User Services Quarterly* 52, no. 3 (March 22, 2013): 182–85, https://doi.org/10.5860/rusq.52.3.3326.

workforce based on measurable data in order to increase and ensure productivity and efficiency. Infrastructures of measurement and surveillance are tools of the corporate happiness industry.

Neoliberalised healthcare systems and mindfulness rhetoric shift the burden of responsibility onto individuals to take responsibility for their state or symptoms via mechanisms of self-surveillance. This prevailing neoliberal shift in the broader society then manifests in libraries in various ableist ways, such as the insistence that employees with disabilities self-identify in order to receive "reasonable" (meaning any) accommodation in the workplace.[34] Such self-identification of disability and/or mental illness potentially exposes the worker to increased scrutiny or surveillance by management. Since confidentiality is not guaranteed, this scrutiny may extend to coworkers, forming a network of surveillance and actively thwarting the potential for coalition building.

## Internal Organization and Division of Labor

Spatial and temporal organization of academic working environments in which staff and librarians are kept separate is another key aspect of the division of LIS labor, potentially contributing to declining mental health. Compare this with the linguistic organization/structure of an academic library in which titles and rank (i.e., academic professional vs. paraprofessional) serve the function of maintaining not only the organizational and spatial hierarchy, but also legitimizing Althusser's concept of the library as an ideological state apparatus that functions to maintain order and internally reproduce capitalist relations of production.

As Bales argues, the academic library operates as an Ideological State Apparatus (ISA). ISA's are structures, or institutions, that function to condition people through ideology by presenting people with their material circumstances "in a form shaped by society's conventions and put forth as authentic and unalienable [...]. The academic library

---

34    Robert Wilton and Stephanie Schuer, "Towards Socio-Spatial Inclusion? Disabled People, Neo-liberalism and the Contemporary Labour Market," *Area* 38, no. 2 (June 1, 2006): 186–95, https://doi.org/10.1111/j.1475-4762.2006.00668.x; Margaret Price et al., "Disclosure of Mental Disability by College and University Faculty: The Negotiation of Accommodations, Supports, and Barriers," *Disability Studies Quarterly* 37, no. 2 (June 1, 2017), https://doi.org/10.18061/dsq.v37i2.5487.

[...] imposes a hierarchy upon itself and its inhabitants that is compatible with and allied to the capitalism in which it has survived."[35]

The very existence of a gap in the literature, which essentially erases the experiences of paraprofessionals, is indicative of the devaluation of this specific work as "unskilled/unintellectual" labor in relation to the labor of librarians or academic professionals. This division is evidenced by a variety of tangible and intangible mechanisms of assessment, including merit in the form of an MLIS, workspace real estate, intellectual vs. manual labor, and so on. Thus, the LIS profession reproduces capitalist labor valuation, resulting in commodification of the LIS worker and subsequent justification of inequitable pay, accommodations, and insecure work.

## Compensation and flexibility

Minimal and unguaranteed opportunities for career advancement, in addition to tuition reduction benefits, influence workers to take undesirable evening and overnight shifts. Late shift staffing shortages, which may be intentional—as evidenced by library administration leaning into positive corporate "lean staffing" rhetoric and related exploitative cost cutting techniques—[36] create a sense that the worker is obligated to work through symptoms of both physical and mental illness. Issues of race, gender, and sexual orientation intersect with confused job roles, sleep deprivation, lack of exposure to sunlight, and social isolation to compound feelings of loneliness and sadness in depressed workers.

By being required to work outside of the typical workday, paraprofessionals function in opposition to the "natural rhythms" of the American workday. The mental illness of overnight workers may then be understood as a correlative symptom of the conflicts they experience between the economic pressures to be a consumptive civic/social agent

35   Stephen E. Bales, "The Academic Library as Crypto-Temple: A Marxian Analysis," in *Class and Librarianship: Essays at the Intersection of Information, Labor and Capital*, ed. Erik Estep and Nathaniel F. Enright (Sacramento, CA: Library Juice Press, 2016), 14–15.

36   Anne Linton, "Staffing the Modern Library: A How-To-Do-It-Manual," *Journal of the Medical Library Association* 94, no. 4 (October 2006): 472–73; Mark Bieraugel, "Managing Library Innovation Using the Lean Startup Method," *Library Management* 36, no. 4/5 (January 1, 2015): 351–61, https://doi.org/10.1108/LM-10-2014-0131; Gerald Beasley and Trish Rosseel, "Leaning into Sustainability at University of Alberta Libraries," *Library Management* 37, no. 3 (January 1, 2016): 136–48, https://doi.org/10.1108/LM-04-2016-0023.

during the typical 9-5 business day and a productive economic agent during the late night. In conflict with the "natural hegemonies" of American capitalism, the health issues arising from such a work schedule are pathologized by the medical professions as consequences for adopting an unnatural sleep schedule.[37] In other words, the overnight worker's mental and physiological health issues are medically conceptualized in natural terms inextricably linked to the rhythms of American capitalism. Ultimately, "this science ends up blaming-and medicating- individuals for their own misery and ignores the context that has contributed to it."[38]

## Conclusion

Mental health has declined and will continue to decline if immediate and critically reflective action isn't taken within the LIS profession. Unless libraries completely divorce themselves from aspects of neoliberalism such as happiness metrics, corporatization, organizational hierarchies/social stratification, etc., libraries as an institution will not improve and the primary victims will be those with the least social capital.

Happiness is commodified in a neoliberal society as a marker of success, wealth, and balanced health, and thus is codified as desirable under this hegemonic project. Therefore, societies' "obsession with medicalization and the tendency to treat 'mental illness' as a problem within the individual continues to be supported within the prevailing neoliberal logic that downplays the social realm, treats individuals as self-contained agents, and pathologizes thoughts and behaviors that deviate from what the market defines as functional, productive, or desirable."[39] Within libraries, this interacts with the paraprofessionals lack of autonomy and potential status as a marginalized worker. Library workers are initially placed in a system which deprives them of autonomy and creativity, which then punishes them for unproductiveness or not finding happiness in their work.

---

37 Matthew Wolf-Meyer, "Natural Hegemonies: Sleep and the Rhythms of American Capitalism," *Current Anthropology* 52, no. 6 (December 2011): 876–95, https://doi.org/10.1086/662550.

38 Davies, 6; Ryan J. Dougherty, "The Psychological Management of the Poor: Prescribing Psychoactive Drugs in the Age of Neoliberalism," *Journal of Social Issues* 75, no. 1 (2019): 217–37, https://doi.org/10.1111/josi.12313.

39 Luigi Esposito and Fernando M. Perez, "Neoliberalism and the Commodification of Mental Health," *Humanity & Society* 38, no. 4 (November 1, 2014): 414–42, https://doi.org/10.1177/0160597614544958.

We hope this exploration into the ways in which libraries mirror neo-liberal conditions in the workplace serves as a primer for future research. Many of these issues deserve a deeper inquiry than we were able to provide here. Understanding how libraries perpetuate class antagonisms in the workplace serves to inform why paraprofessional morale is so low and library workers are experiencing poor mental health. Specifically, the health of paraprofessionals needs to be investigated to the same degree the health of librarians has been studied. Beginning here, we can theorize and build a more equitable and compassionate library workplace that not only cares for workers but exists to counter the oppressive neoliberal conditions outside of the library.

## Call to Action

Because librarians are credentialed members of the ALA, a professional organization, paraprofessionals and librarians are structurally divided. As a result of this professional divide, paraprofessional workers may be inclined to organize separately, or as in many cases (e.g. Portland State University), two separate unions may already exist that are often at odds with one another. This is purely divisive and counter to establishing a united front in what is ultimately a class struggle.

Librarians and support workers experience common mental health issues that are either the result of or exacerbated by their working conditions. The struggle for better labor conditions and improved mental health is a shared struggle necessitating a united opposition wherever possible. But if it is truly the Master's degree that imposes this professional divide, then perhaps the Master's degree (and thus the structure of professionalization) must be disposed of. Unfortunately, because of the circular hierarchy imposed by the ALA requiring obtaining a library degree from ALA-accredited institutions, this issue will likely persist without significant resistance. Therefore, small intentional changes on institutional (i.e. greater representation within governing bodies) and local levels is necessary.

Furthermore, credentialed and non-credentialed library workers should embrace a model of critical community practice in order to build a critically reflective social movement to identify sources of oppression and create collective solutions.[40] Since unionizing is politically

---

40   Scotney D. Evans et al., "Critical Community Pratice: An Introduction to the Special Section," *Journal for Social Action in Counseling & Psychology* 6, no. 1 (June 1, 2014): 1–15.

and geographically limited, social mobilization can be a powerful tool for the collective. Such community building will break down or at least resist surveillance networks and hierarchical management.

The LIS profession and individuals within it should immediately break the practice of treating and discussing (especially disabled) workers from a deficit perspective,[41] or as corporeal anomalies that don't fit within the "normal" structure of a library and who are unable to do "standard," often arbitrary work (such as lift 25 lbs as outlined in job descriptions).[42] To solve this we must examine and rectify our language through the lens of critical disability theory both institutionally (such as job descriptions and hiring committees) and individually (on an interpersonal basis). We must also be constantly vigilant and wary of how language use within libraries functions as a mechanism of control to assimilate workers and normalize exploitation.

---

## Bibliography

Arnetz, Bengt B., Todd Lucas, and Judith E. Arnetz. "Organizational Climate, Occupational Stress, and Employee Mental Health: Mediating Effects of Organizational Efficiency." *Journal of Occupational and Environmental Medicine* 53, no. 1 (January 2011): 34. https://doi.org/10.1097/JOM.0b013e3181ffo5b.

Bales, Stephen E. "The Academic Library as Crypto-Temple: A Marxian Analysis." In *Class and Librarianship: Essays at the Intersection of Information, Labor and Capital*, edited by Erik Estep and Nathaniel F. Enright, 5–24. Sacramento, CA: Library Juice Press, 2016.

Beasley, Gerald, and Trish Rosseel. "Leaning into Sustainability at University of Alberta Libraries." *Library Management* 37, no. 3 (January 1, 2016): 136–48. https://doi.org/10.1108/LM-04-2016-0023.

Bieraugel, Mark. "Managing Library Innovation Using the Lean Startup Method." *Library Management* 36, no. 4/5 (January 1, 2015): 351–61. https://doi.org/10.1108/LM-10-2014-0131.

---

41  Jessica Schomberg, "Disability at Work: Libraries, Built to Exclude," in *Politics and Theory of Critical Librarianship* (Sacramento, CA: Library Juice Press, 2018), 111–23, https://cornerstone.lib.mnsu.edu/lib_services_fac_pubs/149.

42  Aimi Hamraie, "Universal Design and the Problem of 'Post-Disability' Ideology," *Design and Culture* 8, no. 3 (September 1, 2016): 285–309, https://doi.org/10.1080/17547075.2016.1218714.

Bird, Amanda, and Braden Cannon. "From Steam Engines to Search Engines: Class Struggle in an Information Economy." In *Class and Librarianship: Essays at the Intersection of Information, Labor and Capital*, edited by Erik Estep and Nathaniel F. Enright, 49–72. Sacramento, CA: Library Juice Press, 2016.

Bohle, Philip, and Andrew J. Tilley. "The Impact of Night Work On Psychological Well-Being." *Ergonomics* 32, no. 9 (September 1989): 1089–99. https://doi.org/10.1080/00140138908966876.

Burns, J. K. "Poverty, Inequality and a Political Economy of Mental Health." *Epidemiology and Psychiatric Sciences* 24, no. 2 (April 2015): 107–13. https://doi.org/10.1017/S2045796015000086.

Davies, William. *The Happiness Industry : How the Government and Big Business Sold Us Well-Being*. Verso Books, 2015.

Esposito, Luigi, and Fernando M. Perez. "Neoliberalism and the Commodification of Mental Health." *Humanity & Society* 38, no. 4 (November 1, 2014): 414–42. https://doi.org/10.1177/0160597614544958.

Evans, Scotney D., Natalie Kivell, Miryam Haarlammert, Krithika Malhotra, and Adam Rosen. "Critical Community Pratice: An Introduction to the Special Section." *Journal for Social Action in Counseling & Psychology* 6, no. 1 (June 1, 2014): 1–15.

Faraut, Brice, Virginie Bayon, and Damien Léger. "Neuroendocrine, Immune and Oxidative Stress in Shift Workers." *Sleep Medicine Reviews* 17, no. 6 (December 1, 2013): 433–44. https://doi.org/10.1016/j.smrv.2012.12.006.

Farler, Liz, and Judith Broady-Preston. "Workplace Stress in Libraries: A Case Study." *Aslib Proceedings* 64, no. 3 (2012): 225–40.

Friedrich, M. J. "Depression Is the Leading Cause of Disability Around the World." *JAMA* 317, no. 15 (April 18, 2017): 1517–1517. https://doi.org/10.1001/jama.2017.3826.

Hamraie, Aimi. "Universal Design and the Problem of 'Post-Disability' Ideology." *Design and Culture* 8, no. 3 (September 1, 2016): 285–309. https://doi.org/10.1080/17547075.2016.1218714.

Harvard Medical School. "National Comorbidity Survey (NCS)," August 21, 2017. https://www.hcp.med.harvard.edu/ncs/ftpdir/table_ncsr_12monthprevgenderxage.pdf.

Harvey, David. *A Brief History of Neoliberalism*. Reprinted. Oxford: Oxford Univ. Press, 2011.

Harvey, Samuel B., Matthew Modini, Sadhbh Joyce, Josie S. Milligan-Saville, Leona Tan, Arnstein Mykletun, Richard A. Bryant, Helen Christensen, and Philip B. Mitchell. "Can Work Make You Mentally Ill? A Systematic Meta-Review of Work-Related Risk Factors for Common Mental Health Problems." *Occupational and Environmental Medicine* 74, no. 4 (April 1, 2017): 301–10. https://doi.org/10.1136/oemed-2016-104015.

Jones, Matthew. "How Mental Health Can Save Businesses $225 Billion Each Year." Inc., 2016. https://www.inc.com/matthew-jones/how-mental-health-can-save-businesses-225-billion-each-year.html.

Kendrick, Kaetrena Davis. "The Low Morale Experience of Academic Librarians: A Phenomenological Study." *Journal of Library Administration* 57, no. 8 (November 17, 2017): 846–78. https://doi.org/10.1080/01930826.2 017.1368325.

Kuecker, Elliott. "Ideology and Rhetoric of Undergraduate Student Workers in Academic Libraries." *Progressive Librarian*, no. 46 (2017): 13.

Lee, Aeyoung, Seung-Kwon Myung, Jung Jin Cho, Yu-Jin Jung, Jong Lull Yoon, and Mee Young Kim. "Night Shift Work and Risk of Depression: Meta-Analysis of Observational Studies." *Journal of Korean Medical Science* 32, no. 7 (July 1, 2017): 1091–96. https://doi.org/10.3346/jkms.2017.32.7.1091.

Linton, Anne. "Staffing the Modern Library: A How-To-Do-It-Manual." *Journal of the Medical Library Association* 94, no. 4 (October 2006): 472–73.

Mathers, Colin D., and Dejan Loncar. "Projections of Global Mortality and Burden of Disease from 2002 to 2030." *PLoS Medicine* 3, no. 11 (2006): 2011–30. https://doi.org/10.1371/journal.pmed.0030442.

Oswald, Andrew J., Eugenio Proto, and Daniel Sgroi. "Happiness and Productivity." *Journal of Labor Economics* 33, no. 4 (October 1, 2015): 789–822. https:// doi.org/10.1086/681096.

Phillips, Abigail L. "Mental Health Behind the Desk." *Library Journal* 144, no. 5 (June 2019): 51–51.

Schomberg, Jessica. "Disability at Work: Libraries, Built to Exclude." In *Politics and Theory of Critical Librarianship*, 111–23. Sacramento, CA: Library Juice Press, 2018. https://cornerstone.lib.mnsu.edu/lib_services_fac_pubs/149.

Shields, Margot. "Shift Work and Health." *Health Reports* 13, no. 4 (July 2002): 11–33.

Sime, Carley. "The Cost Of Ignoring Mental Health In The Workplace." Forbes, April 17, 2019. https://www.forbes.com/sites/carleysime/2019/04/17/ the-cost-of-ignoring-mental-health-in-the-workplace/.

Stansfeld, Stephen, and Bridget Candy. "Psychosocial Work Environment and Mental Health–A Meta-Analytic Review." *Scandinavian Journal of Work, Environment & Health* 32, no. 6 (December 2006): 443–62.

Substance Abuse and Mental Health Services (SAMHSA)Administration. "National Survey on Drug Use and Health." U.S. Department of Health and Human Services, 2017. https://www.samhsa.gov/data/sites/default/files/cbhsq-reports/NSDUHDetailedTabs2017/NSDUHDetailedTabs2017.htm#tab8-56B.

"The Lancet Countdown on Health and Climate Change: From 25 Years of Inaction to a Global Transformation for Public Health–The Lancet." Accessed August 3, 2019. https://www.thelancet.com/journals/lancet/article/ PIIS0140-6736(17)32464-9/fulltext?elsca1=tlpr.

Weinberger, A. H., M. Gbedemah, A. M. Martinez, D. Nash, S. Galea, and R. D. Goodwin. "Trends in Depression Prevalence in the USA from 2005 to 2015: Widening Disparities in Vulnerable Groups." *Psychological Medicine* 48, no. 8 (2018): 1308–15. https://doi.org/10.1017/S0033291717002781.

Williams, David R. "Stress and the Mental Health of Populations of Color: Advancing Our Understanding of Race-Related Stressors." *Journal of Health and Social Behavior* 59, no. 4 (December 1, 2018): 466–85. https://doi.org/10.1177/0022146518814251.

Wolf-Meyer, Matthew. "Natural Hegemonies: Sleep and the Rhythms of American Capitalism." *Current Anthropology* 52, no. 6 (December 2011): 876–95. https://doi.org/10.1086/662550.

World Health Organization. "Depression." World Health Organization. Accessed June 25, 2019. https://www.who.int/news-room/fact-sheets/detail/depression.

# Defusing Stereotypes Through Humor: A Social Media Analysis

## Pamela Andrews and Melissa Freiley

If one is a library worker, they have probably encountered a misrepresentation of their job by some less-knowledgeable person. Someone might ask if they have shushed anyone today. Another person might make a comment that it must be nice to get paid for reading. Library workers are no strangers to the prevailing librarian stereotypes that include the stern librarian with a low tolerance for noise, the lazy librarian who is able to sit and read all day, and the superhero librarian. Those who are also familiar with mental health conditions know that these library stereotypes can also be used to further stigmatize those who experience mental health conditions, penalizing workers who struggle with organization, energy levels, emotional labor, boundaries, and other issues that manifest in the workplace as part of their symptoms. In this chapter, we explore the use of humor and social media as a means to intervene in stigmatization and facilitate communication across the gap that exists between stereotypical images and the lived experiences of library workers. We also use the term mental health conditions over mental illness as it emphasizes health over illness and uses person-first language.

The difficulty in talking about stereotypical images is that they are not universally viewed as harmful. Arthur Asa Berger claims that stereotypes are general assumptions about a particular group of people that can be positive, negative, neutral, or mixed.[1] Depending upon

---

1   Arthur Asa Berger, "A Frenchman, an Englishman, and a German... Stereotypes in Humorous Texts," in *Psychology of Stereotypes*, ed. Eleanor L. Simon (Hauppauge, NY: Nova Science Publishers, 2011), 329–33.

the person, their image of the community, and their relationship to it, stereotypes can work in many different ways. For those who find stereotypical images trivial or humorous, these can serve as a way of connecting with the community. For those who find stereotypical images alienating or exclusionary, stereotypes can discourage them from pursuing or moving further in the profession. Annie Pho and Turner Masland describe stereotypes as creating a norm against which others can be measured and found wanting.[2] Specifically discussing librarian stereotypes, Beth Posner describes how traditional and contemporary stereotypes fall into binaries, in which librarians are discussed as one of two extreme poles of a characteristic, often as very traditional or very heroic.[3] Gr Keer and Andrew Carlos chart the root of these stereotypes to the evolution of the profession and the "negotiation of gender, race, class, and sexuality within library organizations."[4] Looking at media and stereotypical depictions of librarians, the images are primarily of white women.[5] These enduring stereotypes aid in patrons inaccurately describing both what a librarian should behave like—very good or very awful—and who can be identified as a librarian—white women and men—feeding into a toxic cycle that reinforces how the profession views itself.[6] This reality is reflected in a 2012 American Library Association survey reporting that 88% of credentialed librarians are white, a fact that often obscures longstanding contributions by non-white librarians to the profession.[7] In addition,

---

2    Annie Pho and Turner Masland, "The Revolution Will Not Be Stereotyped: Changing Perceptions Through Diversity," in *The Librarian Stereotype: Deconstructing Perceptions and Presentations of Information Work*, ed. Nicole Pagowsky and Miriam Rigby (Chicago, IL: Association of College & Research Libraries, 2014), 257–82.

3    Beth Posner, "The Use of Psychological Defense Mechanisms–By Librarians and the Public–In Response to Traditional and Binary Librarian Stereotypes," in *The Psychology of Librarianship*, ed. H. Stephen Wright, Lynn Gullickson Spencer, and Leanne VandeCreek (Sacramento, CA: Library Juice Press, 2015), 215–52.

4    Gr Keer and Andrew Carlos, "The Stereotype Stereotype: Our Obsession with Librarian Representation," in *The Librarian Stereotype: Deconstructing Perceptions and Presentations of Information Work*, ed. Nicole Pagowsky and Miriam Rigby (Chicago, IL: Association of College & Research Libraries, 2014), 63–83.

5    Keer and Carlos, "The Stereotype Stereotype," 63–83; Margaret J. Gibson, "Dismiss the Stereotype! Combating Racism and Continuing Our Progress," in *The 21st-Century Black Librarian in America: Issues and Challenges*, ed. Andrew P. Jackson, Julius C. Jefferson Jr., and Akilah S. Nosakhere (Lanham, NC: The Scarecrow Press, Inc., 2012), 229–32.

6    Posner, "Use of Psychological Defense Mechanisms," 215–52.

7    "Diversity Counts 2009-2010 Update," American Library Association Office for Research and Statistics, 2012, http://www.ala.org/aboutala/offices/diversity/diversitycounts/2009-2010update; Caitlin M.J. Pollock and Shelley P. Haley, "'When I Enter': Black Women and Disruption of the White, Heteronormative Narrative of Librarianship," in *Pushing the Margins: Women of Color and Intersectionality in LIS*, ed. Rose L. Chou and Annie Pho (Sacramento, CA: Library Juice Press, 2018), 15–59.

non-white librarians face challenges from other stereotypes associated with their ethnicity.[8] Changing the basis of these stereotypes requires further evolution of the profession, in which we restructure the current power structures to include and build with non-white librarians in meaningful ways.[9]

Returning to mental health conditions, Annie Pho and Turner Masland advocate for consideration of invisible differences—including sexual orientation, socioeconomic background, neurodiversity, and mental health conditions—and how these differences intersect to shape one's lived experiences.[10] Each aspect comes with its own stereotypes, creating a minefield of expectations and responses as individuals navigate the different associated social and physical realms. Erin Burns and Kristin E.C. Green's study of mental health conditions stigma emphasizes how the visible and invisible cues contribute to misunderstandings of mental health conditions and how these misunderstandings can contribute to negative stereotypes.[11] Burns and Green reference Satorius and Schulze's four dimensions through which stigma can manifest: "interpersonal interaction, public imagery of mental illness, structural discrimination, and access to social roles."[12] In light of these dimensions, Burns and Green argue that librarians with mental health conditions have "increased exposure to the other two dimensions of stigma, public imagery of mental illness and structural discrimination."[13] Public imagery of mental illness often takes the form of stereotypical images, and when coupled with colleagues who may react positively or negatively to these images, one's own self-perception can be influenced in both positive and negative ways.

---

8    Pho and Masland, "The Revolution Will Not Be Stereotyped," 257–82.

9    Rosalinda Hernandez Linares and Sojourna J. Cunningham, "Small Brown Faces in Large White Spaces," in *Pushing the Margins: Women of Color and Intersectionality in LIS*, ed. Rose L. Chou and Annie Pho (Sacramento, CA: Library Juice Press, 2018), 253–71; Pho and Masland, "The Revolution Will Not Be Stereotyped," 257–82.

10   Pho and Masland, "The Revolution Will Not Be Stereotyped," 257–82.

11   Erin Burns and Kristin E.C. Green, "Academic Librarians' Experiences and Perceptions on Mental Illness Stigma and the Workplace," *College & Research Libraries* 80, no. 5 (July 2019): 638–57.

12   Norman Satorius and Hugh Schulze, "Conclusions and Recommendations," in *Reducing the Stigma of Mental Illness: A Report from a Global Programme of the World Psychiatric Association*, (Cambridge, UK: Cambridge University Press, 2005), 152–71, quoted in Burns and Green, "Experiences and Perceptions on Mental Illness Stigma," 641.

13   Burns and Green, "Experiences and Perceptions on Mental Illness Stigma," 641.

## Stereotypical Depictions

To further explore Posner's description of binary library stereotypes, we wanted to look at recent depictions of each extreme. The traditional librarian image is one of the most pervasive, having persisted from the early 1900s: a stern, bespectacled librarian, hair in a tight bun, wearing neutral colors and telling patrons to be quiet. This stereotypical traditional librarian craves order and balks when that order is disrupted, even as users are using library resources.[14] Recently, in a July 17, 2019 story called "Your Local Library May Have A New Offering In Stock: A Resident Social Worker," Colin Dwyer with National Public Radio (NPR) stated that "Libraries have always had far more on their plate than the stereotype of the silence-obsessed introvert who cares only for reordering the fiction section."[15] While this is true, by continuing to invoke the traditional stereotype, we keep it in the public consciousness. The invocation of introversion, obsession, extreme order, and an aggressive posture in keeping that order unite to form an unhealthy image of repression.

This negative stereotype stands in direct opposition to the positive, but still problematic, librarian stereotype that we call the "flamekeeper of civilization," which elicits an image of the librarian wisely caring for civilization's treasured resources and allowing and guiding ignorant patrons to access such resources. Without the flamekeeper, people would be lost—less-civilized and unenlightened. In the movies, this stereotype can be seen in the 2004 movie *The Librarian: Quest for the Spear*. Starring Noah Wyle as a perpetual student/bookworm-turned-librarian who eventually saves the world, he becomes a "liberated librarian" in the process, complete with more masculine confidence, assertiveness, and a new wardrobe.[16] This example also points to the gender roles typically associated with each depiction; rarely will you see a male example of the traditional "shusher." However, the valorization of librarians bleeds into reality through other sensationalism. Numerous news headlines proclaim the exalted

14   Marie L. Radford, and Gary P. Radford. "Librarians and Party Girls: Cultural Studies and the Meaning of the Librarian," *Library Quarterly* 73, no. 1 (January 2003): 54–69.

15   Colin Dwyer, "Your Local Library May Have A New Offering In Stock: A Resident Social Worker," NPR, July 17, 2019, https://www.npr.org/2019/07/17/730286523/your-local-library-may-have-a-new-offering-in-stock-a-resident-social-worker.

16   Jennifer Snoek-Brown, "'Quest for the' Liberated Librarian," *Reel Librarians* (blog), November 11, 2015, https://reel-librarians.com/2015/11/11/quest-for-the-liberated-librarian/.

position of the librarian, from "The 'Rock Star' Librarians Who Choose What Your Kids Read" to "This Heroic Librarian Created a Free 'Fashion Library' For Job Seekers In Need" to "On 'Jeopardy!', It Took a Librarian to Beat a Gambler."

While female librarians may be held as heroic as well, they are more likely to be valorized through nurturing adjectives which resonate with the flamekeeper as a caretaker of civilization. Gina Schlessel-man-Tarango traces the evolution of this trope through what she calls the "Lady Bountiful" in which this message of enlightenment carries threads of patriarchy, white supremacy, and ideal femininity to contin-ue a message of colonialism.[17] In parallel to Fobazi Ettarh's concept of "vocational awe" in which the "ideas, values, and assumptions librar-ians have about themselves and the profession...result in beliefs that libraries as institutions are inherently good and sacred, and therefore beyond critique," the flamekeeper stereotype can easily set itself upon the pedestal of the morally good in contrast to the outdated, restrict-ed traditional librarian image.[18] Not only does this image place a heavy burden on library workers, it also lends to the notion that library work-ers are infallible warriors of information and community, inseparable from their important jobs. These perceptions of infallibility and the job as total identity are especially harmful to those library workers with mental health conditions, who may resist showing fallibility (being in-authentic) or experience microaggressions if they do show fallibility, particularly as symptoms of mental health conditions still carry stig-ma in the workplace and may place their employment in jeopardy.[19]

Looking at these two images as binary positions, the following paral-lels can be extracted from the traits they embody: If the flamekeep-er is the untiring, excited educator, the traditional librarian (in all of her perceived frumpiness) is the tired, unexcited gatekeeper who be-lieves those who are not serious about libraries perhaps do not be-long. One is the welcoming caretaker, the other the inflexible overseer. One is positive, one is negative; the flamekeeper librarian succeeds in educating the masses, the traditional librarian fails in reaching most

---

17   Gina Schlesselman-Tarango, "The Legacy of Lady Bountiful: White Women in the Library," *Library Trends* 64, no. 4 (2016): 667–86.

18   Fobazi Ettarh, "Vocational Awe and Librarianship: The Lies We Tell Ourselves," *In the Library with the Lead Pipe*, January 10, 2018, http://www.inthelibrarywiththeleadpipe.org/2018/voca-tional-awe/.

19   Burns and Green, "Experiences and Perceptions on Mental Illness Stigma," 638–57.

community members. Locating mental health conditions within these binaries places librarians in a precarious position in which they have to locate their own identity along this spectrum while still reconciling it with both ends. Disclosure is risky, yet communication is necessary for building understanding between these groups.

## Humorous Interventions through Social Media

Often a coping mechanism in itself, humor can be used to create breathing space in which librarians can draw attention to the paradoxes and inconsistencies between these images, the behaviors these images influence, and the reality of their lived experiences. In doing so, it can also point out the ridiculous nature of pigeonholing professionals into one of the binary stereotypes. However, Rod A. Martin cautions that research has found only possible short-term psychological benefits to humor and laughter—not long-term.[20] While humor may function as a way to intervene in stereotypes for the short-term, long-term relief requires a prolonged, critical look at how institutions perpetuate these stereotypes as professional norms. The nature of humor as a way to play with norms and expectations can also help bring together those who feel othered, to make visible the gaps between "normalcy" and their reality.[21] When those with mental health conditions joke about their conditions, it can be a way of reclaiming it and representing the condition in a less-draining way than the norm of always being serious about it.[22] However, it can be overdone, i.e. someone who constantly jokes about their condition, and this humor saturation can lend to the perception of trivialization and normalized behaviors and the avoidance of one's problems. Too much humor can actually inhibit positive growth. So, like in many of life's activities, moderation and thought are key.

Unfortunately, librarian stereotypes rarely portray them as having good senses of humor. As the summary on the back of the book *The Laughing Librarian: A History of American Library Humor* states, "despite the stodgy stereotypes, libraries and librarians themselves can

---

20  Rod A. Martin, *The Psychology of Humor: An Integrative Approach* (Amsterdam: Elsevier Academic Press, 2007).

21  Martin, *The Psychology of Humor*, 115.

22  Bailey Calfee, "The Complicated Benefits of Mental Illness Memes," *Nylon*, September 10, 2018, https://nylon.com/articles/mental-illness-memes.

be quite funny."[23] From what we authors have witnessed on social media, we'd have to agree! The #LibraryLife hashtag, for example, contains at least a few humorous anecdotes in any given week. Although Twitter is only one form of communication, and by no means is considered a standard, the number of librarians who do use it have built a meaningful community through which they can exchange observations from their lived experiences. A similar example exists in Emily Wills's and Andre Fecteau's 2016 study of the short-lived, humorous 2012 Twitter hashtag #muslimcandyheartrejects; they found that humor can be a means of connecting with others with similar stories, easing tension, and building community.[24]

To specifically examine mental health issues among library workers, we wanted to take advantage of the #LISMentalHealthWeek campaign to understand how those who are part of both the library community and who experience mental health conditions communicate about the professional and personal issues they must navigate. Started by Kelly McElroy and Cecily Walker in 2016, #LISMentalHealthWeek is a specific moment in which participants have a focused, week-long discussion on mental health topics. To announce the campaign, organizers created a Google Document of Resources, with the dates, how to participate, and information on three other, related initiatives: 1) The Twitter account @mindfulinlis, encouraged followers to complete an act of mindfulness for 30 days; 2) This very book solicited chapter proposals during that time and advertised using the #LISMentalHealthWeek campaign; 3) The second issue of the LIS Mental Health Zine, *Reserve and Renew: It Came from the Brain*, began delivery to recipients. As the editors, Kelly McElroy, Abigail Phillips, Kate Deibel, Marisol Moreno Ortiz, Violet Fox, Annie Pho, and Nicole Gustavsen were involved in the origin of #LISMentalHealthWeek, many of the zine submissions and Twitter conversations related.

Although the 2019 week ran from February 17 to 24, 2019, we scraped tweets using the #LISMentalHealthWeek hashtag from February 16 to February 23, 2019. Due to the nature of this conversation, this dataset will not be made openly available. The February 16-23, 2019 capture

---

23   Jeanette C. Smith, *The Laughing Librarian: A History of American Library Humor* (Jefferson, NC: McFarland, 2012).

24   Emily Regan Wills and Andre Fecteau, "Humor and Identity on Twitter: #muslimcandyheartrejects as a Digital Space for Identity Construction," *Journal of Muslim Minority Affairs* 36, no. 1 (March 2016): 32–45.

resulted in a collection of 1,019 tweets. After removing retweets and tweets that were deleted after the campaign, we found that 499 tweets provided original text, or added additional text in reply or as a quote tweet. Table 1 lists the number of tweets found by type. These 499 unduplicated tweets originated from 150 unique Twitter accounts. These tweets received an average of 10 likes, with a max of 303 likes and a median of six likes.

| Tweet Type | Number of Tweets |
|------------|------------------|
| Original | 313 |
| Reply | 145 |
| Quote | 41 |

**Table 1**   Number of Tweets By Type

Of these tweets, 11 originated from a Twitter account associated with #LISMentalHealthWeek, @mindfulinlis, which promotes Mindfulness for Librarians and other Library and Information Science practitioners. Another 34 tweets came from the account @LISMH_anon. This account allowed for anonymous participation, with tweets generated through anonymous form submissions set up through the #LISMentalHealthWeek Resources Google Document. Although other hashtags were used during the Twitter campaign, the most frequent additional hashtag used was #POCinLIS, noting how racism and discrimination feed into mental health issues for people of color in libraries. While none of these tweets specifically cited stereotypical images, themes of unprofessional conduct and conceptions of professionalism were prominent throughout the dataset.

Although the dedicated, hour-long #LISMentalHealthWeek Twitter chat on February 19, 2019, asked specific questions of participants, many of the tweets discussed systemic issues faced by graduate students in Library and Information Science programs, librarians, and library paraprofessionals. Many participants signaled appreciation for stories shared, and the majority of tweets provided a serious, honest reflection of the obstacles they faced. Although no one tweet stayed within one content area, we looked at the major function of each tweet and used these themes to broadly categorize the conversations involved. Across the data set we grouped tweets into the following themes:

- Reference to Library Position: tweets describing issues faced in the workplace or as a result of their professional position, including introductory tweets that specified the user's position.

- Statements of Advocacy: tweets about a position that extended beyond the scope of an individual workplace to discuss systemic issues, or to provide outward facing advice to show care to others.

- Resources: tweets containing links to specific resources that promote mental health awareness.

- Gratitude: tweets containing statements of gratitude for the #LISMentalHealth week conversations and participants.

- Lived Experiences: tweets describing the realities faced by those with mental health conditions.

- Discussion of Treatment and Self-Care: tweets containing descriptions of treatments or self-care strategies, including offering comfort to others.

We coded each of the 499 tweets as relating to the theme which most strongly resonated with its message, rather than allowing multiple themes to apply to a single tweet. Table 2 contains the frequency in which these themes appeared, including the total count of tweets found to resonate most strongly with each theme.

| Content | Number of Tweets |
| --- | --- |
| Reference to Library Position | 78 |
| Statement of Advocacy | 89 |
| Resources | 47 |
| Gratitude | 50 |
| Lived Experiences | 134 |
| Discussion of Treatment and Self-Care | 101 |

**Table 2**   Tweets by Content Type

The majority of tweets, then, described participants' lived experiences, closely followed by messages in support of or describing treatments and self-care strategies. The prominence of lived experiences and messages describing treatment and self-care point toward the need for more realistic discussions of what it is to live with mental health conditions within the library profession, and how that quality of life can be improved. In looking at how these messages are communicated, we wanted to investigate specific uses of humor to communicate within this intersection of libraries and mental health.

## Humorous Communications

Reviewing the set of 499 tweets, we identified 33 as containing explicit instances of humorous language or references. This is not to say that the other tweets are devoid of humor, but rather that those exchanges carried a serious, less or non-humorous, undertone appropriate to the content related. Of the more humorous tweets, we found that they ranged across three themes from the previous content analysis, as detailed in Table 3.

| Content Type | Number of Humorous Tweets |
|---|---|
| Reference to Library Position | 2 |
| Statement of Advocacy | 1 |
| Resources | 0 |
| Gratitude | 0 |
| Lived Experiences | 9 |
| Discussion of Treatment and Self-Care | 21 |

**Table 3**  Tweets with Explicit Humor Per Content Type

After identifying a subset of tweets as humorous, we wanted to look at what kinds of humor they involved. In itself, humor is a complex, multifaceted concept with many manifestations. Drawing from research on psychology and communication, we relied on the Humor Styles Questionnaire, a self-report inventory based on responses to questions about how humor is used by the individual.[25] This questionnaire then

---

25  Rod A. Martin et al., "Individual Differences in Uses of Humor and Their Relation to Psychological Well-Being: Development of the Humor Styles Questionnaire." *Journal of Research in Personality* 37, no. 1 (2003): 48–75.

graphs the use of humor within one of four style quadrants, depending on whether the humor is benevolent or detrimental, and whether it reflects one's relationship to themselves or to others. The four style quadrants are described as:

- Affiliative: humor that is benevolent and focused on others;
- Self-enhancing: humor that is benevolent, and focused on the self;
- Aggressive: humor that is detrimental, and focused on others; or
- Self-defeating: humor that is detrimental, and focused on self.

Although the Humor Styles Questionnaire is designed to be answered by the speaker, we felt it was appropriate to use this framework to categorize our interpretation of each message as these tweets were written specifically to connect with the imagined audience and communicate the user's experiences. In this respect, we used the framework to understand how these uses of humor might demonstrate someone's positive or negative experiences in navigating the professional world as someone with a mental health condition. Table 4 contains the frequency of tweet per style of humor.

| Style of Humor | Number of Tweets |
|----------------|------------------|
| Affiliative | 15 |
| Self-enhancing | 7 |
| Aggressive | 2 |
| Self-defeating | 9 |

**Table 4**   Tweets Per Style of Humor

Within the humorous tweet subset, we found that the majority of tweets used a style of affiliative humor. As #LISMentalHealthWeek was designed to create and support a community for those in library science with mental health conditions, this finding was not surprising. The almost even split between self-enhancing and self-defeating humor also speaks to individual trends toward optimism and pessimism, but continue to relate to the group. Equally expectant was a low number of aggressive instances, although these were used primarily to call out systemic inequities and discrimination.

#LISMentalHealthWeek is an important and valuable campaign to highlight inconsistencies between the perceptions of librarianship and mental health against the realities of library professionals with mental health conditions. While this community explicitly encourages conversation between these professionals, we also wanted to look at messages dealing with mental health conditions from the broader library professional community outside of this specific campaign. As many of these humorous messages took the form of visual memes, we wanted to examine the visual rhetoric and compare it to our findings from our #LISMentalHealthWeek dataset.

## Explicit Humor and Memes

The term "meme," comes from biologist Richard Dawkins, but the concept of cultural evolution—"die Mneme," or memory—originated in the 1870s with Austrian sociologist Ewald Hering. In a discussion of memes, Shifman states that "while memes are seemingly trivial and mundane artifacts, they actually reflect deep social and cultural structures."[26] The increase of images as touchstones for discussing human behavior provides us with alternatives to stereotypical images that still have common elements depicted in media, but allow librarians to exist along a fuller spectrum by including not just the cultural touchstone but also the subverted text that better reflects reality. Looking into the rhetoric involved in memes surrounding mental health, we gathered six specific instances of humor referencing mental health in librarianship, shared by other librarians the authors follow and collected during the same month as #LISMentalHealthWeek. Within these six instances of humor, we collected two image-based memes, and four text-based memes as following:

Tweet 1    tweet introducing the linked image as a "Current Mood." The linked image was a screenshot from the Britney Spears music video "...Baby One More Time." In this screenshot, the lyric "My Loneliness is Killing Me" is sub-titled, with "Loneliness" crossed out and replaced with the text "My extremely unrealistic expectation of where my life should be at this point knowing I've put very little effort so far."

---

26    Limor Shifman, *Memes in Digital Culture* (Cambridge, MA: The MIT Press, 2014), 15.

Tweet 2    tweet introducing the linked image as a "Current Mood." The linked image contained a screenshot of the man from *The Brave Fighter of Sun Fighbird* anime TV series gesturing to a butterfly with the subtitled text "Is this a pigeon?" In this meme, the butterfly is labelled as "alcohol" and the word "pigeon" is crossed out and replaced with "anxiety medication."

Tweet 3    tweet telling a story of requesting an emotional support animal, but requesting a non-traditional service animal such as a family member's ferret, followed by an image of a ferret being placed in a mailbox.

Tweet 4    Quote tweet detailing a scripted dialogue exchange in which a therapist claims that their patient uses humor to deflect trauma. The patient appreciatively retorts, "What I'm hearing is you think I'm funny"

Tweet 5    Quoted Tweet referencing a fact that the funniest people are the most depressed with a response that humor as a primary coping mechanism is their superpower.

Tweet 6    tweet in reply to a Horoscope, presenting their own horoscope constructed out of how the user feels about their anxiety.

Reviewing these tweets, we then categorized them into the four style quadrants of humor as detailed in Table 5.

| Tweet | Style of Humor |
| --- | --- |
| Tweet 1 | Self-defeating |
| Tweet 2 | Self-enhancing |
| Tweet 3 | Self-enhancing |
| Tweet 4 | Self-enhancing |
| Tweet 5 | Self-enhancing |
| Tweet 6 | Self-defeating |

**Table** 5    Meme tweets per style of humor

While this is a very small sample set, all of these images worked primarily in relation to the user's self rather than the group. As memes are intended for greater circulation, it is not possible to know exactly who might identify with its message. It can be, and was found, in a way that circulates between members of the library profession and members with mental health conditions. However, as this is done outside the mission of sharing lived experiences of mental health conditions, these memes discuss mental health without explicitly disclosing a condition. In doing so, users are able to communicate feelings associated with mental health conditions in a way that can translate those experiences into a perspective that elides stigmatization. Both the visual and text-based memes operate in a way that takes the originating material and subverts it to demonstrate not only the experiences and symptoms of mental health issues, but to also demonstrate distance between the symptomatic and normalcy. In each of these, the delivery or alteration creates a space between the user and reader. For conditions with invisible symptoms, this space may be crucial for highlighting the fact that, even if the user does not wish to fully disclose their health, there is a difference to be expressed.

## The Conversations We Need

As demonstrated through both sets of tweets, humor can be used to show connection and to validate one's membership in the group, but isn't as necessary to understand the perspective communicated. Jason Crabtree et al. found that "identification with a stigmatized group can buffer individuals from the adverse effects of stigma."[27] While identifying with a stigmatized group is not a net positive act, the group can provide stress-buffering mechanisms.[28] This effect is demonstrated within the tweets as the majority of messages carried experiences showing membership in the group and messages of treatment and coping mechanisms for others to learn from.

Communicating with librarians who are not known to have mental health conditions can often prompt librarians with mental health conditions to describe symptoms and ways of being in ways less associated with mental health conditions. Memes and humor are influential and contagious. They connect people, and though they may be simple, the limit is the creator's imagination. We can then use humor and memes to further promote communication between those with and

---

27    Jason W. Crabtree, S. Alexander Haslam, Tom Postmes, and Catherine Haslam, "Mental Health Support Groups, Stigma, and Self-Esteem: Positive and Negative Implications of Group Identification," *Journal of Social Issues* 66, no. 3 (September 2010): 553.

28    Crabtree, Haslam, Postmes, and Haslam. "Mental Health Support Groups," 553–69.

those without mental health conditions and dismantle the stereotypical characteristics that reinforce the more extreme examples of the profession. Humor's power to connect and memes' power to permeate make them excellent methods for bridging the gap between those who have mental health conditions and those who do not. By specifically meme-ifying stereotypical images of librarians, librarians can use these images to demonstrate the space between the image and reality.

As the dismantling of stereotypes requires further advocacy within the profession, humor is not the only tool or a single tool for enacting change. However, advocacy can still be promoted through humor. Both the National Alliance on Mental Illness (@NAMICommunicate) and The Trevor Project (@TrevorProject) occasionally tweet memes, such as NAMI's tweet on May 8, 2019, asking to hear from any women of a certain age who identified a little too well with the meme of SpongeBob nervously biting off both hands' fingernails. This meme, while showing subtle humor, manages to engage virtual audiences through likes and retweets and project empathy and community for those struggling while validating their lived experiences and making them relatable to others. Calling attention to these experiences, and generating empathy, is part of the process. As an augment to other forms of advocacy, humor and memes perhaps can serve the important role of connecting and validating experiences and feelings. We can choose to reinforce or defy stereotypes in the memes and humor that we create and share.

To demonstrate how we want to reframe identity through these images, we asked Amanda Sexton of University of Arkansas-Fort Smith to help us with creating our own meme for how we view ourselves. Figure 1 contains original artwork by Amanda Sexton depicting one of the authors as a traditional librarian and reframing the negative stereotype into a positive one that more accurately reflects how the authors would fit along this spectrum of librarian images.[29]

In this meme, the user is depicted as a traditional, shushing librarian cat lady, one foot securely bolstered by a stack of books, and the other guarding her cat companion. The other side posits the left as false and reasserts the right as the truer side. While this invites a binary comparison, the use of "sometimes" and not "all the time," shifts the meme from a sense of the absolute to a sense of temporality. The librarian is

---

29  Amanda Sexton, *Librarian Meme,* 2019.

**What society THINKS I do  vs  What I actually SOMETIMES do**

**Figure 1**  Alternative Librarian Meme

shown in a relaxed pose, peacefully coexisting among multiple cat companions, reading a book and listening to music. The music and reading may be moments of self-care to help relax from mental health condition symptoms. This is not a librarian at work, this is a librarian at rest.

This meme is able to speak against the traditional stereotype, not by presenting an opposite view but rather a more natural view. By including this image, we want to encourage library professionals with and without mental health conditions to build spaces and images where humanity is emphasized over the sensational. We also want to highlight that communities such as #LISMentalHealthWeek, where more natural and realistic portrayals are communicated, do exist and provide alternative spaces where the profession is critiqued and engaged with in a manner that helps professionals with mental health conditions feel validated. And for the rest of the year, humor can also be used to translate those experiences to others without necessarily disclosing mental health conditions. When doing so, however, it may be helpful to think critically about how this humor is reaching others and how its style of humor may reinforce or disrupt negative and stereotypical images.

Will a meme or humor change the greater than a century-long stereotype of the traditional shushing librarian? Or save us from our vocational awe? Or lead to systemic changes in our workplaces and colleagues' mindsets? Highly unlikely. What it can do is connect us, give us breathing room to cope with the stress of mental health conditions and serious advocacy work, and help slowly build that mountain of positive change.

## Acknowledgements

The authors wish to thank Amanda Sexton at University of Arkansas—Fort Smith for lending her artistic talents. Thank you also to the individuals who created and who participated in the #LISMentalHealth conversation. Your words inspire and sustain.

---

## *Bibliography*

Berger, Arthur Asa. "A Frenchman, an Englishman, and a German… Stereotypes in Humorous Texts." In *Psychology of Stereotypes*, edited by Eleanor L. Simon, 329–33. Hauppauge, NY: Nova Science Publishers, 2011.

Burns, Erin and Kristin E.C. Green. "Academic Librarians' Experiences and Perceptions on Mental Illness Stigma and the Workplace." *College & Research Libraries* 80, no. 5 (2019), 638–57.

Calfee, Bailey. "The Complicated Benefits of Mental Illness Memes." *Nylon*, September 10, 2018. Accessed June 3, 2019. https://nylon.com/articles/mental-illness-memes.

Crabtree, Jason W., S. Alexander Haslam, Tom Postmes, and Catherine Haslam. "Mental Health Support Groups, Stigma, and Self-Esteem: Positive and Negative Implications of Group Identification." *Journal of Social Issues* 66, no. 3 (2010): 553–69.

"Diversity Counts 2009–2010 Update." *American Library Association Office for Research and Statistics*, September 18, 2012. http://www.ala.org/aboutala/offices/diversity/diversitycounts/2009-2010update.

Dwyer, Colin. "Your Local Library May Have A New Offering In Stock: A Resident Social Worker." *NPR*. July 17, 2019. https://www.npr.org/2019/07/17/730286523/your-local-library-may-have-a-new-offering-in-stock-a-resident-social-worker.

Ettarh, Fobazi. "Vocational Awe and Librarianship: The Lies We Tell Ourselves." *In the Library With the Lead Pipe*. January 10, 2018. http://www.inthelibrarywiththeleadpipe.org/2018/vocational-awe/.

Gibson, Margaret J. "Dismiss the Stereotype! Combating Racism and Continuing Our Progress." In *The 21st-Century Black Librarian in America: Issues and Challenges*, edited by Andrew P. Jackson, Julius C. Jefferson Jr., and Akilah S. Nosakhere, 229–32. Lanham, NC: The Scarecrow Press, Inc., 2012.

Keer, Gr, and Andrew Carlos. "The Stereotype Stereotype: Our Obsession with Librarian Representation." In *The Librarian Stereotype: Deconstructing Perceptions and Presentations of Information Work*, edited by Nicole Pagowsky and Miriam Rigby, 63–83. Chicago, IL: Association of College & Research Libraries, 2014.

Linares, Rosalinda Hernandez, and Sojourna J. Cunningham. "Small Brown Faces in Large White Spaces." In *Pushing the Margins: Women of Color and Intersectionality in LIS*, edited by Rose L. Chou and Annie Pho, 253–71. Sacramento, CA: Library Juice Press, 2018.

Martin, Rod A. *The Psychology of Humor: An Integrative Approach*. Amsterdam: Elsevier Academic Press, 2007.

Martin, Rod A., Patricia Puhlik-Doris, Gwen Larsen, Jeanette Gray, and Kelly Weir. "Individual Differences in Uses of Humor and Their Relation to Psychological Well-Being: Development of the Humor Styles Questionnaire." *Journal of Research in Personality* 37, no. 1 (2003): 48–75.

Pho, Annie, and Turner Masland. "The Revolution Will Not Be Stereotyped: Changing Perceptions Through Diversity." In *The Librarian Stereotype: Deconstructing Perceptions and Presentations of Information Work*, edited by Nicole Pagowsky and Miriam Rigby, 257–82. Chicago, IL: Association of College & Research Libraries, 2014.

Pollock, Caitlin M. J., and Shelley P. Haley. "'When I Enter': Black Women and Disruption of the White, Heteronormative Narrative of Librarianship." In *Pushing the Margins: Women of Color and Intersectionality in LIS*, edited by Rose L. Chou and Annie Pho, 15–59. Sacramento, CA: Library Juice Press, 2018.

Posner, Beth. "The Use of Psychological Defense Mechanisms–By Librarians and the Public–In Response to Traditional and Binary Librarian Stereotypes." In *The Psychology of Librarianship*, edited by H. Stephen Wright, Lynn Gullickson Spencer, and Leanne VandeCreek, 215–52. Sacramento, CA: Library Juice Press, 2015.

Radford, Marie L., and Gary P. Radford. "Librarians and Party Girls: Cultural Studies and the Meaning of the Librarian." *Library Quarterly* 73, no. 1 (2003): 54–69.

Sexton, Amanda. *Librarian Meme*. 2019.

Snoek-Brown, Jennifer. "'Quest for the' Liberated Librarian." Reel Librarians (blog), November 11, 2015. https://reel-librarians.com/2015/11/11/quest-for-the-liberated-librarian/.

Schlesselman-Tarango, Gina. "The Legacy of Lady Bountiful: White Women in the Library." *Library Trends* 64, no. 4 (2016): 667–86.

Schneider, Martha, Martin Voracek, and Ulrich S. Tran. "A Joke a Day Keeps the Doctor Away? Meta-Analytical Evidence of Differential Associations of Habitual Humor Styles with Mental Health." *Scandinavian Journal of Psychology* 59, no. 3 (2018): 289–300.

Shifman, Limor. *Memes in Digital Culture*. MIT Press Essential Knowledge Series. Cambridge, MA: The MIT Press, 2014.

Smith, Jeanette C. *The Laughing Librarian: A History of American Library Humor*. Jefferson, NC: McFarland, 2012.

Wills, Emily Regan, and Andre Fecteau. "Humor and Identity on Twitter: #muslimcandyheartrejects as a Digital Space for Identity Construction." *Journal of Muslim Minority Affairs* 36, no. 1 (2016): 32–45.

# The Perils of Public Service: Emotional Labor and Mental Illness in Library Employees

**Sara Harrington**

## Introduction—Mental Illness in the US

According to the Substance Abuse and Mental Health Services Administration (SAMHSA), approximately 46.6 million adults in the United States—just under 1 in 5—will grapple with mental illness in a given year.[1] Anxiety and depression are especially prevalent. 7.1% of U.S. adults reported having had a major depressive episode in the past year, 64% of whom experienced severe impairment due to their depression.[2] Meanwhile, research indicates that while "only" 19.1% of U.S. adults have experienced any anxiety disorder (including General Anxiety Disorder, Obsessive-Compulsive disorder, Post-Traumatic Stress disorder, and other disorders generally categorized under the umbrella of anxiety disorders) in the past year, a whopping 31.1% will deal with an anxiety disorder at some point in their lives.[3]

---

1   Center for Behavioral Health Statistics and Quality et al., "Results from the 2017 National Survey on Drug Use and Health: Detailed Tables" (Rockville, MD: Substance Abuse and Mental Health Services Administration (SAMHSA), 2018), https://www.samhsa.gov/data/report/2017-nsduh-detailed-tables.

2   Center for Behavioral Health Statistics and Quality et al, "Results from the 2017 National Survey on Drug Use and Health: Detailed Tables" Table 8.57A-B,

3   National Institute of Mental Health, "NIMH » Anxiety Disorders," Anxiety Disorders, 2018, https://www.nimh.nih.gov/health/topics/anxiety-disorders/index.shtml.

With these staggering figures taken into consideration, it is no surprise that mental illness is a hot topic within the field of Library and Information Science (LIS). With frontline librarians dealing with the public on a day-to-day basis, training and research on how to deal with patrons experiencing mental illness– from providing mental health resources to crisis intervention tips and techniques on how to best serve neurodivergent individuals—is not difficult to find. Less available, however, is information regarding mental illness behind the service desk—a surprising fact, given the prevalence of mental illness in the general population, of which surely librarians are a part. Nonetheless, there has been a movement in recent years toward raising awareness of mental illness among LIS workers. Those in the field have sparked conversations online in myriad ways, perhaps most notably with the inception of #LISMentalHealth week in 2016, a campaign organized in order to shine a spotlight on the issue, as well as to provide an avenue for discussion among library and archives workers.[4]

Still, there seems to be a dearth of research on the subject, with only a precious few scholarly articles addressing the specific topic of mental illness in the library workforce. One such study, conducted by Erin Burns and Kristin Green, surveyed 549 academic librarians about their experiences with mental illness; more than half reported having been formally diagnosed with a mental illness at some point in their life. When given the option to elaborate, 40% of those who chose to divulge their specific diagnoses reported "that they have or have had both depression and anxiety."[5] Some respondents also reported that their symptoms were exacerbated by work-related stress,[6] which reflects psychoneuroimmunology findings that "chronic stress can lead to or exacerbate mood disorders."[7] This connection between chronic stress and poor mental health is not surprising, given the

---

4   Maura Smale, "Academic Libraries and Mental Health: LIS Mental Health Week," *ACRLog* (blog), January 16, 2016, https://acrlog.org/2016/01/18/academic-libraries-and-mental-health-lis-mental-health-week/.

5   Erin Burns and Kristin E. C. Green, "Academic Librarians' Experiences and Perceptions on Mental Illness Stigma and the Workplace," *College & Research Libraries* 80, no. 5 (July 2019): 638–57, https://doi.org/10.5860/crl.80.5.638.

6   Burns and Green, , "Academic Librarians' Experiences and Perceptions on Mental Illness Stigma and the Workplace."

7   "Mental and Emotional Impact of Stress," MentalHelp.net, accessed May 27, 2020, https://www.mentalhelp.net/stress/emotional-impact/.

well-established negative effects of stress on both the body and the brain.[8] But what are some of the unique stressors of library work that can have a deleterious impact on library workers, particularly those that are already struggling with mental illness? In addition to heavier workloads, rapid technological and organizational changes, and ever-pervasive budget cuts, one of the biggest potential sources of stress for library staff is the demand for emotional labor that is such an inextricable part of the job.

In this chapter, I will discuss the extent to which emotional labor is expected from frontline staff in the environment of a public library, and how this particular aspect of the job can compound the problems of employees with mental illness. In addition, I will explore the intersection of these factors with gender, examining the ways in which women—who make up the vast majority of frontline librarians—[9] are especially impacted by these detrimental circumstances. Although my focus will be primarily on employees of public libraries, much of what I will cover can also be applied to frontline workers in other library and information science positions.

## Emotional Labor in Libraries

The concept of "emotional labor" was developed by sociologist Arlie Hochschild in her seminal 1983 book, *The Managed Heart: Commercialization of Human Feeling*. Hochschild defines emotional labor as "the management of feeling to create a publicly observable facial and bodily display" within the context of a person's role as an employee of an organization; it is done with the intention to create a certain impression or feeling in others.[10] In customer service roles, clients are usually the center of most of the employee's emotional labor. The employee is expected to hide any fatigue or irritation they may be experiencing at any given time, divorcing themselves from their own inner workings,

---

8    Marissa Maldonado, "How Stress Affects Mental Health," *PsychCentral* (blog), February 25, 2014, //psychcentral.com/blog/how-stress-affects-mental-health/; Rebecca Bernstein, "The Mind and Mental Health: How Stress Affects the Brain," *Touro University Worldwide* (blog), July 26, 2016, https://www.tuw.edu/health/how-stress-affects-the-brain/.

9    "Library Professionals: Facts, Figures, and Union Membership," Department for Professional Employees, AFL-CIO, 2020, https://www.dpeaflcio.org/factsheets/library-professionals-facts-and-figures.No Reference

10    Arlie Russell Hochschild, "Exploring the Managed Heart," in *The Managed Heart: Commercialization of Human Feeling*, 1st ed. (University of California Press, 2012).

and produce a uniformly pleasant experience for the customer, regardless of the disposition or behavior of said client.

In public libraries, most emotional labor demands come from the public librarian's work with patrons. This emotional labor is inextricably linked with job performance expectations; it is indeed codified into the professional guidelines established by no less a professional authority than the American Library Association (ALA). According to Emmelhainz, Pappas, and Seale, a closer reading of the "Guidelines for Behavioral Performance of Reference and Information Service Providers" set forth by the Reference & User Services Association (RUSA) reveals that "librarian behavior is repeatedly articulated and evaluated in terms of attending to the *emotional* state of the patron."[11] Analyzing the guidelines for explicit or implicit emotional labor expectations falling within nine separate categories, the authors found that approximately 70% of the RUSA guidelines reflect some degree of expectation of emotional labor.[12] By repeatedly centering the comfort and ease of the patron as the first priority of the reference transaction, they contend, the RUSA guidelines effectively make the patron's emotional state–not just their informational request–the responsibility of the librarian.

The RUSA guidelines reflect the modern image of the librarian as a passionate, service-driven jack-of-all trades who is motivated not by career goals or remuneration, but by their selfless desire to serve and guide the public. This librarian is more than a competent information professional; she is a source of comfort and healing to her community and is always willing to go above and beyond to make sure that the patron not only finds what they need, but feels good about themselves in the process. Linda Christian styles this image as the "New Librarian"; Linda Fried Foster refers to it as "The Mommy Model" of librarianship.[13]

---

11  Celia Emmelhainz, Erin Pappas, and Maura Seale, "Behavioral Expectations for the Mommy Librarian: The Successful Reference Transaction as Emotional Labor," in *The Feminist Reference Desk: Concepts, Critiques, and Conversations* (Sacramento, California: Library Juice Press, 2017), https://escholarship.org/uc/item/2mq851m0.

12  The categories used were "Being Approachable", "Comforting and Encouraging", "Working on [Patron] Timing", "Full Focus on [the Patron]", "Embodied Friendliness", "A Service Orientation", "Referring and Follow-Up", "Meeting [Patron] Needs", and "General Emotional Labor"; Emmelhainz, Pappas, and Seale, "Behavorial Expectations for the Mommy Librarian," 33.

13  Linda Christian, "A Passion Deficit: Occupational Burnout and the New Librarian: A Recommendation Report," *The Southeastern Librarian* 62, no. 4 (January 2, 2015), https://digitalcommons.kennesaw.edu/seln/vol62/iss4/2.

Regardless of what one chooses to call it, conforming to this model relies heavily on the performance of emotional labor. The New Librarian can't be tired, or sad; she can't be angry at the unhappy patron who called her an insulting name, or bored when explaining how to use the copier for the 50th time of the day. She is endlessly enthusiastic, and absolutely fascinated by every reference request. Most of all, she never complains about her job or her patrons, because to her it is more than a job: it is a calling. Fobazi Ettarh argues that this "vocational awe", exemplified by media images of librarians as unwavering community activists and saviors, "set[s] the expectation that the fulfillment of job duties requires sacrifice [...] and only through such dramatic sacrifice can librarians accomplish something "bigger than themselves"."[14]

The sacrifice that Ettarh speaks of is, primarily, emotional and psychological. To meet the lofty ideal described above, the employee must continuously put their own emotional needs and self-care to the side; the smiling mask of the unflappable public servant must remain intact, despite the emotional dissonance this may invoke. This process would take a toll on anyone, but for those already struggling with mental illness, this level of emotional labor can be a pernicious burden on an already fragile psyche.

## The Toll of Emotional Labor

In order to explore the toll of emotional labor on those living with mental illness, it is first necessary to examine how emotional labor is enacted at the ground level. As has already been established, emotional labor consists of an employee's efforts to manage their emotions in order to conform to the (spoken or unspoken) professional expectations of their job. There is, however, more than one way for an employee to undertake this emotion management. According to Hochschild, emotion management attempts generally fall into one of two categories: either *surface acting* or *deep acting*.

*Surface acting*, as the name implies, is the attempt to mask existing emotions on the surface level by, for example, projecting a smiling, happy front when one is actually experiencing fatigue, anxiety,

---

14    Fobazi Ettarh, "Vocational Awe and Librarianship: The Lies We Tell Ourselves," *In the Library with the Lead Pipe* (2018) http://www.inthelibrarywiththeleadpipe.org/2018/vocational-awe/.

or frustration. When engaging in surface acting, only the outer self is changed, not one's experience of the situation. *Deep acting*, on the other hand, is analogous to "method acting"—rather than changing one's expression of emotion, it seeks to change the emotion on the experiential level, often (but not always) by mentally reframing the situation in such a way that a perceived negative condition is transformed into a neutral or positive condition.[15] An example of this might be the librarian who, when faced with an irate customer, attempts to see the situation from the patron's point of view, perhaps imagining that the person might be having a bad day or has had previously negative experiences with the library. In this way, the librarian's negative emotional response is, by conscious effort, mitigated to a certain degree.

Psychologically speaking, surface acting and deep acting are both types of emotional regulation strategies. Surface acting is a response-focused strategy of emotional regulation—performed once the emotion has already taken root–while deep acting can be classified as an antecedent-focused strategy—enacted at the beginning of the emotion generation process in an attempt to stop negative feelings in their tracks.[16] More specifically, surface acting and deep acting can be compared to two of the most common and often-researched types of emotion regulation techniques: suppression and reappraisal. Suppression, like surface acting, is response-focused, and involves inhibiting expression of one's emotional state, whereas cognitive reappraisal is an antecedent-focused strategy that seeks to shape one's emotional state by re-interpreting the emotional stimulus.[17]

Although there is evidence that emotional regulation may not be as straightforward as previously thought, most researchers tend to agree that reappraisal is a generally *adaptive* strategy, while suppression is generally *maladaptive*. The use of suppression and other response-focused emotional regulation strategies has been linked with an increase in the experience of the emotion in question rather than its decrease. In other words, attempts at regulating emotions using

---

15  Arlie Russell Hochschild, "Managing Feeling," in *The Managed Heart: Commercialization of Human Feeling*, 1st ed. (University of California Press, 2012).

16  Afsoon Eftekhari, Lori A. Zoellner, and Shree A. Vigil, "Patterns of Emotion Regulation and Psychopathology," *Anxiety, Stress, and Coping* 22, no. 5 (October 2009): 571–86, https://doi.org/10.1080/10615800802179860.

17  JE Arndt and E Fujiwara, "Interactions between Emotion Regulation and Mental Health," *Austin Journal of Psychiatry and Behavioral Sciences* 1, no. 5 (2014): 1–8.

suppression—and its emotional labor counterpart, surface acting—are likely to actually make a person experiencing depression or anxiety *more* depressed or anxious.[18] Studies have shown that this strategy can cause "poor recall of information [...] and increased levels of anxiety and negative affect;" in contrast, reappraisal can cause "improved memory [...] and decreased anxiety and depression."[19]

Unfortunately, the more an employee struggling with mental illness tries to live up to the emotional labor expectations of their job, the harder it may be for them to do so. Research suggests that people with mood disorders are statistically more likely to use maladaptive regulation strategies and less likely to use adaptive regulation strategies[20]—in fact, some findings suggest that "inappropriate or ineffective emotion regulation is a critical component in the development and maintenance of depression and anxiety disorders."[21] In other words, difficulty regulating negative emotions in a healthy and effective way is a symptom of many common mental illnesses. The result is that employees with mental illnesses are more likely to use strategies of emotional regulation that will only worsen their psychological symptoms, further depleting their mental and emotional resources and leading to a self-perpetuating cycle. When coupled with the aforementioned vocational awe that leads many public librarians to ignore their own self-care and emotional needs, librarians with mental illnesses are at increased risk for job burnout, as well as potentially serious psychological ramifications.

## Intersection with Gender

As previously mentioned, women make up the vast majority of library workers; 79-84%, in fact.[22] With men in LIS disproportionately found in administrative roles, frontline library staff members are

---

18 Ananda Amstadter, "Emotion Regulation and Anxiety Disorders," *Journal of Anxiety Disorders* 22, no. 2 (January 1, 2008): 211–21, https://doi.org/10.1016/j.janxdis.2007.02.004.

19 Eftekhari, Zoellner, and Vigil, "Patterns of Emotion Regulation and Psychopathology,"573.

20 Arndt and Fujiwara, "Interactions between Emotion Regulation and Mental Health," 2

21 Angelo Compare et al., "Emotional Regulation and Depression: A Potential Mediator between Heart and Mind," Review Article, Cardiovascular Psychiatry and Neurology (Hindawi, June 22, 2014), https://doi.org/10.1155/2014/324374.

22 "Library Professionals: Facts, Figures, and Union Membership," Department for Professional Employees.

overwhelmingly female.[23] Public work, in general, is often stratified along gender lines; according to a study of state employment in Florida, entry and mid-level positions are by and large filled by women, while the highest levels of government work are populated by men.[24] Similarly, the Women in Public Service project reports that while women make up 43.2% of the civil service workforce, they account for only 34.4% of the decision-making roles.[25]

This vertical stratification should not be surprising. Jobs requiring assertiveness, decisiveness, and technical expertise—such as high-level administrative jobs—are often perceived to be best suited to men, while jobs requiring geniality, emotional intelligence, and relationship management are often seen as "women's work". In fact, job segregation by gender is often used to explain (at least in part) the pay gap in the U.S.; men tend to work in high-paying leadership roles, while women are more often found in lower-paying support roles. Guy and Newman argue that this disparity boils down to a simple explanation: emotional labor. Their analysis suggests that emotional labor is often invisible and uncompensated, particularly when it is performed by women, because caring is thought to be a natural trait of women. Thus, jobs that, at their core, revolve around emotional labor—such as frontline library work—are perceived to require fewer skills, and are paid accordingly. [26]

Gendered perceptions of "men's work" and "women's work" doesn't only affect which jobs women have or how they are paid; it also often impacts the way they are treated while on the job. Because women are generally viewed as more nurturing than men, a higher degree of emotional labor is often expected of them. Patrons and employers alike expect women in such roles to be naturally warm, friendly, and caring, and therefore any deviation from this expectation is perceived in a negative light compared to the perception of a man behaving similarly

23 American Library Association, "Library Directors: Gender and Salary," 2007, http://www.ala. org/tools/research/librarystaffstats/diversity/libdirectors.

24 Mary Ellen Guy and Meredith A. Newman, "Women's Jobs, Men's Jobs: Sex Segregation and Emotional Labor," *Public Administration Review* 64, no. 3 (2004): 289–98, https://doi. org/10.1111/j.1540-6210.2004.00373.x.

25 UNDP Gender Equality in Public Administration, "Data: Women in Public Service," The Women in Public Service Project, 2018, https://web.archive.org/web/20191118053310/http://data.50x50movement.org/data/view/58c07c8f9cd5d61100f399fa.

26 Guy and Newman, "Women's Jobs, Men's Jobs."

in the same role. For example, if a male library worker responds to a reference request in a polite but business-like manner, he is often seen as knowledgeable and authoritative; a female library worker who responds in the same manner is more likely to be seen as cold or unfriendly. Correspondingly, female library workers are often seen by patrons as less capable than their male counterparts and are more likely to face challenges to their authority. As Marcia Bellas puts it in her study of university professors' emotional labor, "women [...] appear to face a double bind. [They] are expected to be nice and accommodating, but if they are too nice, they are not respected."[27]

The balancing act between asserting authority and fulfilling the gendered expectation of maintaining a warm, nurturing demeanor clearly demands an increase in the emotional labor performed by female library staff. Unfortunately, not only are women expected to perform higher levels of emotional labor, but they are also more likely to struggle with depression and anxiety disorders than men are.[28] Furthermore, while those with mental illnesses are, in general, statistically more likely to use maladaptive emotional regulation techniques, it has been found that women with mental illness are more likely than their male counterparts to find it difficult to effectively regulate and repair negative emotions.[29] This means that women not only bear a heavier load when it comes to emotional labor, but they may also find it more difficult to recover from the effects of this burden. This leaves women in library and information science particularly vulnerable to the detrimental impact of stress caused by intensive daily emotional labor—especially those already struggling with mental illness.

## Conclusion

It is abundantly clear that the intense level of emotional labor involved in library work can have a significant impact on the psychological

---

27 Marcia L. Bellas, "Emotional Labor in Academia: The Case of Professors," *The ANNALS of the American Academy of Political and Social Science*, September 8, 2016, https://doi.org/10.1177/000271629956100107.

28 Center for Behavioral Health Statistics and Quality et al., "Results from the 2017 National Survey on Drug Use and Health: Detailed Tables"; National Institute of Mental Health, "NIMH » Anxiety Disorders."

29 Julian F. Thayer et al., "Gender Differences in the Relationship between Emotional Regulation and Depressive Symptoms," *Cognitive Therapy and Research* 27, no. 3 (June 1, 2003): 349–64, https://doi.org/10.1023/A:1023922618287.

well-being of employees living with mental illness. What is less clear, however, is how to go about mitigating this impact. With so little research done on the subject to this point, an evidence-based, concrete course of action is difficult to assess. However, there are a few steps that library employers and employees alike can take to create an environment conducive to mental health and well-being.

The first step, it seems, is to acknowledge and define the role that emotional labor plays in library work. By recognizing the ubiquity of emotional labor, as well as the toll it can take on an employee's mental health, a space can be created for tools and resources to address it. Training in emotional intelligence and regulation, whether offered by the employer or attended independently by the employee, can make it easier for library workers to understand their emotions and how to effectively manage them. Appreciating the draining effect of emotional labor also further validates the need for regular time away from the service desk, whether in the form of regular work breaks, or time spent working behind the scenes. Finally, recognizing emotional labor allows for it to be valued and compensated fairly as a necessary skill of the job.

Additionally, employers and employees both must be aware of mental illness and its impact on one's work. As common as depression, anxiety disorders, and other mental illnesses are, employees with mental illness continue to be underserved by their employers. One significant reason for this disparity is the stigma attached to mental illness, which is often viewed as less "real" than other, more visible, disabilities. According to one survey, approximately 31% of U.S. adults either agreed or strongly agreed that people with mental illnesses are often "simply making excuses."[30] For this reason, many employees are hesitant to reveal their mental illness to their employers or coworkers. For example, more than half of the academic librarians surveyed by Burns and Green agreed or strongly agreed that "other people's reactions to mental illness keeps them from disclosing their own mental illness to others"; one respondent commented that they "don't advertise [their] depression because [they] believe it would be seen by some

---

30   Peter Moore, "One-Third Think Many with Mental Illness 'Making Excuses,'" YouGov, May 30, 2018, https://today.yougov.com/topics/health/articles-reports/2018/05/30/one-third-think-many-mental-illness-making-excuses.

as a weakness and would be held against [them]."[31] Further efforts to educate and raise awareness about mental illness in general, and in the library workforce in particular, are necessary to combat this pervasive and harmful stigma.

The purpose of this analysis was to connect the dots between disparate realms of study to highlight the negative impact of emotional labor on library workers experiencing mental illness. This review of the literature on the topic has made it clear that there is much research left to be done. Although there are a few studies of emotional labor in library work environments, nearly none address the topic of emotional labor in conjunction with mental illness. Future studies should focus on the relationship between the two, and ways in which to alleviate the resultant psychological strain. In addition, although the mediating factor of gender was briefly touched on here, there is much more to study through the intersectional effects of race, gender, age, and physical disability with both mental illness and emotional labor. For example, it has been established that librarians of color often face challenges to their authority and competency by library patrons, much as female librarians do, which as we have seen can increase the amount of emotional labor required to meet job expectations.[32] Additionally, research suggests that the relationship between surface acting and increased stress may be mediated by the race, culture, and personality traits of individual workers. A comprehensive and intersectional examination is required to reach a true understanding of the impact of emotional labor on the mental health of library employees.

## Acknowledgements

I would like to thank the editors of this book for their tireless efforts and constructive feedback, as well as the friends, family, and loved ones that have supported me both personally and professionally during the writing of this piece.

---

31  Burns and Green, "Academic Librarians' Experiences and Perceptions on Mental Illness Stigma and the Workplace."

32  Juleah Swanson, Azusa Tanaka, and Isabel Gonzalez-Smith, "Lived Experience of Academic Librarians of Color," *College & Research Libraries* 79, no. 7 (2018), https://doi.org/10.5860/crl.79.7.876.

## *Bibliography*

American Library Association. "Library Directors: Gender and Salary," 2007. http://www.ala.org/tools/research/librarystaffstats/diversity/libdirectors.

Amstadter, Ananda. "Emotion Regulation and Anxiety Disorders." *Journal of Anxiety Disorders* 22, no. 2 (January 1, 2008): 211–21. https://doi.org/10.1016/j.janxdis.2007.02.004.

Arndt, JE, and E Fujiwara. "Interactions between Emotion Regulation and Mental Health." *Austin Journal of Psychiatry and Behavioral Sciences* 1, no. 5 (2014): 1–8.

Bellas, Marcia L. "Emotional Labor in Academia: The Case of Professors:" *The ANNALS of the American Academy of Political and Social Science,* September 8, 2016. https://doi.org/10.1177/000271629956100107.

Burns, Erin, and Kristin E. C. Green. "Academic Librarians' Experiences and Perceptions on Mental Illness Stigma and the Workplace." *College & Research Libraries* 80, no. 5 (July 2019): 638–57. https://doi.org/10.5860/crl.80.5.638.

Center for Behavioral Health Statistics and Quality, Substance Abuse and Mental Health Services Administration, .S. Department of Health and Human Services, and RTI International. "Results from the 2017 National Survey on Drug Use and Health: Detailed Tables." Rockville, MD: Substance Abuse and Mental Health Services Administration (SAMHSA), 2018. https://www.samhsa.gov/data/report/2017-nsduh-detailed-tables.

Christian, Linda. "A Passion Deficit: Occupational Burnout and the New Librarian: A Recommendation Report." *The Southeastern Librarian* 62, no. 4 (January 2, 2015). https://digitalcommons.kennesaw.edu/seln/vol62/iss4/2.

Compare, Angelo, Cristina Zarbo, Edo Shonin, William Van Gordon, and Chiara Marconi. "Emotional Regulation and Depression: A Potential Mediator between Heart and Mind." Review Article. Cardiovascular Psychiatry and Neurology. Hindawi, June 22, 2014. https://doi.org/10.1155/2014/324374.

Eftekhari, Afsoon, Lori A. Zoellner, and Shree A. Vigil. "Patterns of Emotion Regulation and Psychopathology." *Anxiety, Stress, and Coping* 22, no. 5 (October 2009): 571–86. https://doi.org/10.1080/10615800802179860.

Emmelhainz, Celia, Erin Pappas, and Maura Seale. "Behavioral Expectations for the Mommy Librarian: The Successful Reference Transaction as Emotional Labor." In *The Feminist Reference Desk: Concepts, Critiques, and Conversations.* Sacramento, California: Library Juice Press, 2017. https://escholarship.org/uc/item/2mq851m0.

Ettarh, Fobazi. "Vocational Awe and Librarianship: The Lies We Tell Ourselves." *In the Library with the Lead Pipe,* 2018. http://www.inthelibrarywiththeleadpipe.org/2018/vocational-awe/.

Guy, Mary Ellen, and Meredith A. Newman. "Women's Jobs, Men's Jobs: Sex Segregation and Emotional Labor." *Public Administration Review* 64, no. 3 (2004): 289–98. https://doi.org/10.1111/j.1540-6210.2004.00373.x.

Hochschild, Arlie Russell. "Exploring the Managed Heart." In *The Managed Heart: Commercialization of Human Feeling*, 1st ed. University of California Press, 2012.

———. "Managing Feeling." In *The Managed Heart: Commercialization of Human Feeling*, 1st ed. University of California Press, 2012.

Department for Professional Employees, AFL-CIO. "Library Professionals: Facts, Figures, and Union Membership," 2020. https://www.dpeaflcio.org/factsheets/library-professionals-facts-and-figures.

Maldonado, Marissa. "How Stress Affects Mental Health." *PsychCentral* (blog), February 25, 2014. //psychcentral.com/blog/how-stress-affects-mental-health/.

MentalHelp.net. "Mental and Emotional Impact of Stress." Accessed May 27, 2020. https://www.mentalhelp.net/stress/emotional-impact/.

Moore, Peter. "One-Third Think Many with Mental Illness 'Making Excuses.'" YouGov, May 30, 2018. https://today.yougov.com/topics/health/articles-reports/2018/05/30one-third-think-many-mental-illness-making-excuses.

National Institute of Mental Health. "NIMH » Anxiety Disorders." Anxiety Disorders, 2018. https://www.nimh.nih.gov/health/topics/anxiety-disorders/index.shtml.

Rebecca Bernstein. "The Mind and Mental Health: How Stress Affects the Brain." *Touro University Worldwide* (blog), July 26, 2016. https://www.tuw.edu/health/how-stress-affects-the-brain/.

Smale, Maura. "Academic Libraries and Mental Health: LIS Mental Health Week." *ACRLog* (blog), January 16, 2016. https://acrlog.org/2016/01/18/academic-libraries-and-mental-health-lis-mental-health-week/.

Swanson, Juleah, Azusa Tanaka, and Isabel Gonzalez-Smith. "Lived Experience of Academic Librarians of Color." *College & Research Libraries* 79, no. 7 (2018). https://doi.org/10.5860/crl.79.7.876.

Thayer, Julian F., Lynn A. Rossy, Elisabeth Ruiz-Padial, and Bjorn Helge Johnsen. "Gender Differences in the Relationship between Emotional Regulation and Depressive Symptoms." *Cognitive Therapy and Research* 27, no. 3 (June 1, 2003): 349–64. https://doi.org/10.1023/A:1023922618287.

UNDP Gender Equality in Public Administration. "Data: Women in Public Service." The Women in Public Service Project, 2018. https://web.archive.org/web/20191118053310/http://data.50x50movement.org/data/view/58c07c8f9cd5d61100f399fa.

# The Language of Libraries: What Does It All Mean?

**Brady Lund**

Language is often envisioned as a concrete construct: if people call an object a "dog," then it IS a dog and should be universally understood in that way. There are, according to this perspective, attributes of this object, called "dog," that distinguish it from another object called "cat." Perhaps, in the case of cats and dogs, that is true. What about more abstract concepts with less clear distinctions, though? Are there universally accepted differences between "instructional librarian" and "student learning librarian" that make it necessary to use these two different words in our literature and job descriptions? If one were to read "student learning librarian" with only familiarity with the word "instructional librarian," would they still be able to understand what is meant, or would they be fooled into thinking a "cat" is a "dog"?

Often, people figure out the language as they go. These people may never have thought about the language used in job descriptions because they are fortunate enough to not have it cause them any difficulties. Many individuals, however, are either completely unable or experience extreme mental distress when faced with unclear language. There are individuals who struggle with language even when it is written or spoken in the most articulate manner possible. They certainly find no reprieve when confronted with the inanely complex and incoherent language often used in the library profession. This chapter focuses on these individuals and how their experiences may inform a more coherent vocabulary for describing the profession of librarianship.

## Communication Disorders and How They Relate to Mental Illness

A communication disorder is a physiological or neurological difference that significantly limits an individual's ability to communicate effectively, either in spoken or written word (or both).[1] Many communication disorders, arguably, are not in themselves mental illnesses; however, a sizeable portion of individuals with communication disorders do develop mental illnesses like anxiety and depression as a consequence of the social isolation they often experience. Several communication disorders (e.g., Autism), however, are themselves considered by some professionals as mental illnesses and several others co-occur with mental illnesses like Attention Deficit Hyperactivity Disorder, Obsessive Compulsive Disorder, and Dementia due to the physiological/neurological nature of the disorders. Communication and mental illness are intimately intertwined and so it is important to include this topic in any discussion of mental illness and, particularly, to identify how the nature of language used in libraries can provoke greater intensity of anxiety and other mental health conditions as a result of unnecessary ambiguity and poor word choice.

The following sub-sections of this chapter provide descriptions of just a few of the dozens of communication disorders that exist. According to at least one estimate, nearly 8% of children have a communication disorder[2], which is consistent with the University of New Hampshire's 2017 report on the percentage of adults with hearing or cognitive disorders.[3] Communication disorders are experienced by large numbers of the United States' population (30 million plus) and manifest in hundreds of unique ways. However, the linguistic and communication causes of mental distress among individuals with communication disorders are often shared and the solutions share much in common, with the potential to help all library employees, not just those with a communication disorder.

1   Owens, Metz, and Haas, *Introduction to Communication Disorders : A Life Span Perspective*, (Boston; Toronto: Allyn and Bacon, 2000).

2   Black, Vahratian, and Hoffman, "Communication Disorders and Use of Intervention Services Among Children Aged 3–17 Years," *NCHS Data Brief*, no. 205 (June 2015): 1–8.

3   Kraus et al., *2017 Disability Statistics Annual Report. A Publication of the Rehabilitation Research and Training Center on Disability Statistics and Demographics*, (Institute on Disability, University of New Hampshire, 2018), https://eric.ed.gov/?id=ED583258.

## Autism Spectrum Disorders

Autism Spectrum Disorder (ASD) is a developmental disorder that affects an individual's ability to perceive communication intents (spoken/written/signaled messages) and socialize with others.[4] Approximately 1/45-1/58 people (depending on the source) are diagnosed with ASD, making the total incidence in the United States 5-10 million and 150-200 million worldwide (which would make individuals with autism the eighth largest country by population worldwide). [5] Severity of ASD can range from low-functioning (co-morbidity with intellectual disorder and other mental health/behavioral conditions) to high-functioning (no comorbidity with other conditions, average-to-above-average intelligence, mild social-communication differences/delays). Some common symptoms of ASD are poor eye contact/non-verbals, delayed speech, poor understanding of figurative/ambiguous language and concepts, repetitive behaviors, and high sensitivity to sensory input (such as touch). Often, individuals with ASD can develop strong social anxiety as a result of their inability to communicate effectively. While some individuals with low-functioning autism may not be able to attain regular employment, individuals with high-functioning ASD are capable of attaining full-time employment with appropriate organizational supports—including in libraries.[6]

## Aphasia

Aphasia is a communication disorder that results from damage to part of the brain—specifically, the language centers of the brain, Wernicke's and Broca's area, most commonly from a stroke.[7] As such, Aphasia most frequently affects adults, many of whom may already be employed. Aphasia affects the ability to understand and use language. Aphasia can cause severe anxiety and depression for individuals who have lost an ability they once had. Individuals with aphasia may be able to work after sufficient recovery and therapy.

---

4   Frith, *Autism : Explaining the Enigma / Uta Frith*, 2nd ed. (Malden, MA: Blackwell, 2003).

5   Jon Baio et al., "Prevalence of Autism Spectrum Disorder Among Children Aged 8 Years - Autism and Developmental Disabilities Monitoring Network, 11 Sites, United States, 2014," Morbidity and Mortality Weekly Report. Surveillance Summaries (Washington, D.C.: 2002) 67, no. 6 (April 27, 2018): 1–23, https://doi.org/10.15585/mmwr.ss6706a1.

6   Strub and Stewart, "Case Study: Shelving and the Autistic Employee,". *Journal of Access Services* 7, no. 4 (September 20, 2010): 262–68. https://doi.org/10.1080/15367967.2010.508369.

7   David Howard and Frances M. Hatfield, Aphasia Therapy: Historical and Contemporary Issues (London: Routledge, 2018).

## Disfluency

Disfluency, more commonly called stuttering, is a speech-communication disorder that results in frequent interruptions of speech, called blocks.[8] About 1 in 100 people stutter. While stuttering often occurs early in life, with its severity tapering over time, in some adults it can continue with high severity. Stuttering is commonly associated with anxiety disorder. Not being able to communicate ideas verbally as developed in the mind can cause severe emotional distress. While stuttering affects communication, it does not affect intelligence or the ability to perform meaningful work in any way. Many accomplished, influential figures stutter, including many professors and elected government officials. These individuals, however, can still benefit immensely from a supportive workplace culture (as everyone can).

## Hearing Loss/Deafness

Individuals with hearing loss or deafness would likely object to having this condition described as a disorder, preferring rather to characterize it as a difference (physiologically speaking it is a disorder of the hearing mechanism, but socially it is often not perceive as something that limits the individual). Regardless, clear written communication is vitally important for individuals with deafness, as this is the primary medium through which they perceive information, not being able to gather supplemental information from audio input.[9] Individuals with hearing loss/deafness do not inherently have a mental illness, but ostracism by members of society can cause extreme distress and narrowing of social groups.[10]

## Why has Problematic Language Emerged in Librarianship?

Library and information science (LIS) is a discipline rife with half-baked paradigms and social cliques. There are so many voices in the room, so to speak, within LIS that having consistency in the language we use is virtually impossible. The voices come from a variety of backgrounds

---

8   Ward, "Stuttering and Cluttering (Second Edition) : Frameworks for Understanding and Treatment."

9   Fellinger, Holzinger, and Pollard, "Mental Health of Deaf People," *Lancet* 379, no. 9820 (March 17, 2012): 1037–44, https://doi.org/10.1016/S0140-6736(11)61143-4.

10   Fellinger, Holzinger, and Pollard, "Mental Health of Deaf People."

and have a variety of ambitions and intents. They bring unique lexicons from their backgrounds, fracturing the terminology we use to refer to—for instance—ontology, knowledge organization, cataloging and classification. There are people who want to contribute new theory and philosophy to the discipline and profession and people who are primarily focused on practical change. Paradigms clash—paradigms that are often not well formulated in the first place. Before long, the profession has come to have over 100 different terms to refer to reference services and no agreement as to which is most appropriate.

To be clear, this is not merely a problem in LIS. It is global across virtually all professions.[11] LIS, however, in addition to being the focus of this book, is also somewhat of a surprising offender given the strong service orientation that it always touts. Library and information science is generally considered a social science, as such it should ultimately focus on people, but it is not always the case. Here are just a few "problems," or considerations as to why our language in LIS has become so problematic.

### Library and Information Science Paradigms

There is a clash between library science and information science. We often refer to the two together ("library and information science") but rarely do we do so correctly. Most MLS students have very little conception of what information science is—that it describes the theoretical and generalizable (outside libraries) aspects of the discipline, things like information seeking behavior, information needs, information exchange, information organization, and information administration.[12] These are areas in which libraries work—yes, engaging in a reference interview or information literacy class is exchanging or diffusing information—but rarely do librarians speak in these terms or apply these theories in their everyday work. What one person might call organization of information, another might call bibliographic control. The split is that the first person would be talking about the broad theoretical concept of organizing information—which librarians do, but

---

11  Duff, "Language Socialization, Higher Education, and Work," In *Language Socialization*, ed. Patricia A. Duff and Stephen May, 1–18, Encyclopedia of Language and Education., (Cham: Springer International Publishing, 2017), https://doi.org/10.1007/978-3-319-02327-4_19-1.

12  Bates, "The Information Professions: Knowledge, Memory, Heritage," *Information Research* 20, no. 1 (March 2015): 248–62.

also biologists, chemists, computer scientists, and many others—and the second would be talking about the specific task they are performing—assigning metadata based on the attributes of the physical book they have in their hands. So, both individuals refer to the same thing but use different vocabulary. Now imagine a recent LIS graduate, who has little experience in a library, and has learned from LIS instructors or the work environment about "information organization" but not "bibliographic control." They have never heard of such a term before. When a job description says "experience with bibliographic control," the potential applicant may assume it is a job they are unable to perform—though this may not actually be the case.

## Cultural Differences

The word "culture" is used loosely here to refer to the functioning of the library itself. A culture might vary from one library to the next. The way that librarians refer about objects, tasks, and ideas can frequently vary within a small geographic area—let alone the entire United States or world. The language used reflects the area in which the employees were raised, their educational background, and prior life and work experiences. They will refer to things based on what they know and what they feel best communicates a message. It is not unlike moving from one part of a country to another: there are shared aspects of the culture, but enough variation that it can cause discomfort or confusion. In the case of library operations, these cultural differences are almost always unnecessary, but have evolved because library employees have not been made to realize the value of a consistent, supportive communicative culture—one that does not diminish personality or freedom but rather one that is cognizant and reflexive to the prospective needs of current and future employees and applicants.

## The Nature of the English Language

The United States is wealthier and produces more research than any other country in the world.[13] For this reason, the U.S. holds considerable power over the world's knowledge. Yet, the United States is heterogeneous and has one of the most complex languages and largest

---

13   SJR–International Science Ranking, "Country Ranking." Commercial Academic, accessed January 4, 2020. https://www.scimagojr.com/countryrank.php.

number of dialectical variations in the world.[14] It is the nature of the English language to be horrendously complex—and growing more complex all the time. It is the nature of the United States to choose the best ideas and assimilate these ideas and their associated terminology from around the world—but it is also the nature of the United States for certain ideas to diffuse to the general population at different rates.[15] So, while certain libraries may be tuned into the idea of universal design, others may never have heard of it. Wide disparities in funding, geography, and politics in one of the world's largest countries also influences how ideas and language is diffused, resulting in broadly different vocabulary from place to place. There is no quick fix to this problem (replacing the English language is impractical, I would say). Rather, one must accept that there will also be some ambiguity and problematic language no matter how much we plan for what we want to communicate.

## What is the Problem?

Problematic language in any context is an information problem, because language conveys information. The letter *a* is kind of like a subject heading in the collections of one's mind to find all concepts whose names start with a, and neurological research indicates that humans' process of thinking about language in this way is very similar to using a computer system to find a resource.[16] Information experts should be concerned with the ways in which information can be conveyed as clearly and helpfully as possible. This is important for everyone, not just those with mental illness or disabilities. How can librarians curate words—like they would with a collection—to be meaningful and useful to the person with whom they are speaking? If it is possible for a library to create a glossary of terms that are not common sense that are used by the organization, this might be a good start as a resource to include as an appendix to job descriptions and policies. Even terms that may under certain light seem commonplace but are referred to by many different names in other settings should be included in such a glossary. Using this controlled vocabulary when creating new policy

---

14 Lippi-Green, *English with an Accent,* (Routledge, 2013)

15 Wagner, "Remarks on the Geography of Language," *Geographical Review* 48, no. 1 (1958): 86–97, https://doi.org/10.2307/211703.

16 Benson, *The Neurology of Thinking / D. Frank Benson,* (New York: Oxford University Press, 1994).

and position announcements will help assure new issues do not arise and that everything remains consistent; as a result all employees/applicants know what you mean when you use a certain word, because it is always used in the same way.[17]

Outside of written job descriptions and policy, it is important to keep in mind that humans are always communicating. Whether a person is speaking or not, messages are conveyed by their nonverbal behavior. Improving the clarity of communication also involves checking what our nonverbal behavior is communicating. Facial expression, posture and gesture can all convey that what is being said is not what is actually felt (regardless of reality). The idea that individuals with mental illness or disability would not be able to pick up on these cues is deeply mistaken. The nonverbal behaviors of individuals in charge will affect the perceptions and emotions others have towards those individuals.

Something to think deeply about as for organizational decision-makers is consistency in language between the job description and the actions of the organization. One way to quickly erode confidence and trust is to state that one set of duties will be required for a job and then introduce a completely new set of duties for a new employee. The duties may also be thought, by the employer, to be consistent with the description, yet seem inconsistent to new employees given their unfamiliarity with the specific library. This type of unintentional ambiguity—where the employer believes they are not being ambiguous, but employees do experience a feeling of ambiguity—could be easily combatted by simply elaborating on what library terms mean within the specific context of a given library. Employees should have the right to be confident that they are able to perform the duties required of them and employers should want to make sure this is the case as well. That cannot happen if the duties are not clearly communicated from the start and cemented in the actual work the employee performs. Unclear communication leads to far too many opportunities for trust to be broken on both the side of the individual with mental illness or disability and the employer.

Additionally, the stigma attributed to mental illness and disability, particularly in employment settings, is misguided. The simple fact is that many individuals with anxiety, depression, autism, sight and

---

17   Aitchison, *Thesaurus Construction and Use : A Practical Manual* / Jean Aitchison, Alan Gilchrist, David Bawden. 4th edition. (London: Aslib IMI, 2000).

hearing loss are perfectly capable of performing meaningful work. It is only the belief that they cannot perform meaningful work that stands in their way. It reinforces discriminatory hiring practices and convinces individuals that language use should be "our way or the highway."

## Next Steps

There is no one perfect solution to "fix" how language is used in LIS—short of erasing everyone's dictionary and starting from scratch—but there are some strategies that when used together can certainly improve conditions for everyone. The most fundamental step that may be taken is simply including stakeholders with disabilities or mental illness in the library management processes. This may include having disability services at a university look over job descriptions to ensure they are written in a way that individuals with communication disorders can understand. It may also involve including students and instructors with disabilities and/or mental illness on the planning committee for new library policy or strategic directions. Rather than assume what these individuals want, ask them!

Libraries should also consider using internally controlled vocabularies. We may not be able to fix the language used by all of librarianship, but we can at least begin to fix the language we use in our own library. Hiring committees can define ambiguous terms in job descriptions in order to make them easier to understand. Here is an example:

> "The Information Services librarian will spend approximately half of their time fulfilling students' and faculty research requests."

> Information Services may be known as reference services, user services, patron search assistance, reference and instructional services at other libraries. It describes duties pertaining to assisting individuals in finding the information they need.

> Approximately means *on average*. Some weeks, when special events are occurring or during finals when the library is busy, the number of hours spent may be higher or lower than this average.

> Fulfilling may also be called *satisfying* or *completing*. Essentially, it means making sure the user is happy with the information you find for them.

Research requests or search assistance is the information need of the user and the process you, as the librarian, take to help find the information for them.

This process should also include the identification and removal of language that has multiple meanings or is written at a reading level higher than what is necessary for the position. For instance:

"The librarian is responsible for building relationships with a variety of clients."

A qualifier should be included to specify what type of relationship. Being able to communicate needs is one thing, becoming friends and making sales pitches is another and requires a different kind of person.

"The librarian is responsible for building professional working relationships with a variety of clients to help them satisfy their information needs."

Also,

"Engages in reflexive evaluation of pedagogical methods using quantitative and qualitative strategies."

Could be stated as,

"The librarians should be able and willing to regularly assess the quality of their instruction and teaching style using quantitative and qualitative feedback from students, peers, and administrators."

Job descriptions are not novels. Nor are they instructions. They are descriptions.

If a library does not want to define their own terms, a reference source, like the *Dictionary for Library and Information Science,* could be used.[18] Dictionaries are imperfect because they express how the authors/editors of the dictionary use a certain word, not necessarily how the general public or a specific library uses it. No one has agreed that

---

18    Reitz, *Dictionary for Library and Information Science / Joan M. Reitz,* (Westport, Conn.: Libraries Unlimited, 2004).

the dictionary is the definitive source for how language should be used in the profession. Additionally, dictionaries are not always written for clarity (also see: *vagueness*). Nonetheless, a dictionary could be used as a resource from which to create the index for your library. However, your library must determine that the definition provided by the dictionary does indeed describe the function performed for your library. For instance, the *Dictionary for Library and Information Science* defines *Adult Services* as "Materials, services, and programs intended to meet the needs of adult users of a public library, as opposed to those designed for children and young adults."[19] Perhaps your library uses the term specifically to mean "specialized adult education classes offered by the library," in which case the definition from Dictionary for LIS above is not adequate.

With policies, specificity is more important than brevity. There is no room for ambiguity in communicating to employees what an employer expects of them. Not only should libraries specify what behaviors are and are not permitted, but they should do so while also specifying the contexts in which the behaviors are/are not appropriate and any exceptions that might exist. This is important for individuals who may interpret policies too literally. For instance, if there is a library policy pertaining to time limits for public computer usage, but during the summer these computers are never full, it may make sense to relax the policy during this time. However, if this exception to the policy is left unwritten, it disadvantages those who interpret rules very literally. Thus, the policy should be revised to state that "there will be time limits on computer usage when all computers are occupied, but during times when the library is less busy these restrictions may be relaxed or removed. Patrons should check with the circulation desk to be sure of what time limit is currently in place." This verbiage allows an enforceable policy to be in place while allowing flexibility and understanding among patrons. Policies tend to already be quite lengthy but making sure they are clear to all users and employees is crucial for promoting an equitable environment.

Library administrators should always listen in the same way that they want to be heard. It's a variation of the Golden Rule: Think about the listening attention and receptivity you want others to give and make sure to give the same to them. This means active listening most likely,

---

19    Reitz, *Dictionary for Library and Information Science* / Joan M. Reitz.

but also listening—and discussion—that matches the level of communication that the communication partner is able to handle. If personal space or sustained eye-contact clearly causes anxiety for the communication partner, it is important to recognize this fact and back off. Learn effective code-switching and be malleable to each individual with whom you interact.

## Conclusion

Language and communication can prove to be a significant barrier to a supportive work environment and employment for individuals with disabilities and/or mental illness. With effort to consider deeply how language is used and to clarify terms, the work environment within libraries can be improved. By involving community stakeholders and employees familiar with disabilities in hiring and policy change meetings, inclusion may be built directly into how a library is run. While such changes will undoubtedly benefit individuals with disabilities and mental illness, they will also benefit all employees and library visitors. Greater clarity in communication harms no one.

---

### *Bibliography*

Aitchison, Jean. *Thesaurus Construction and Use : A Practical Manual / Jean Aitchison, Alan Gilchrist, David Bawden.* Fourth edition. London: Aslib IMI, 2000.

Baio, Jon, Lisa Wiggins, Deborah L. Christensen, Matthew J. Maenner, Julie Daniels, Zachary Warren, Margaret Kurzius-Spencer, et al. "Prevalence of Autism Spectrum Disorder Among Children Aged 8 Years - Autism and Developmental Disabilities Monitoring Network, 11 Sites, United States, 2014." *Morbidity and Mortality Weekly Report. Surveillance Summaries* (Washington, D.C.: 2002) 67, no. 6 (April 27, 2018): 1–23. https://doi.org/10.15585/mmwr.ss6706a1.

Bates, Marcia. "The Information Professions: Knowledge, Memory, Heritage." *Information Research* 20, no. 1 (March 2015): 248–62.

Benson, D. Frank (David Frank). *The Neurology of Thinking / D. Frank Benson.* New York: Oxford University Press, 1994.

Black, Lindsey I., Anjel Vahratian, and Howard J. Hoffman. "Communication Disorders and Use of Intervention Services Among Children Aged 3–17 Years: United States, 2012." *NCHS Data Brief*, no. 205 (June 2015): 1–8.

SJR–International Science Ranking. "Country Ranking." Commercial Academic. Accessed January 4, 2020. https://www.scimagojr.com/countryrank.php.

Duff, Patricia A. "Language Socialization, Higher Education, and Work." In *Language Socialization*, edited by Patricia A. Duff and Stephen May, 1–18. Encyclopedia of Language and Education. Cham: Springer International Publishing, 2017. https://doi.org/10.1007/978-3-319-02327-4_19-1.

Fellinger, Johannes, Daniel Holzinger, and Robert Pollard. "Mental Health of Deaf People." *Lancet (London, England)* 379, no. 9820 (March 17, 2012): 1037–44. https://doi.org/10.1016/S0140-6736(11)61143-4.

Frith, Uta. *Autism : Explaining the Enigma / Uta Frith.* Second edition. Malden, MA: Blackwell, 2003.

Howard, David. *Aphasia Therapy Historical and Contemporary Issues.* Routledge, 2018.

Kraus, L., E. Lauer, R. Coleman, and A. Houtenville. *2017 Disability Statistics Annual Report. A Publication of the Rehabilitation Research and Training Center on Disability Statistics and Demographics.* Institute on Disability, University of New Hampshire, 2018. https://eric.ed.gov/?id=ED583258.

Lippi-Green, Rosina. *English with an Accent.* Routledge, 2013.

Owens, Robert E., Dale Evan. Metz, and Adelaide. Haas. *Introduction to Communication Disorders : A Life Span Perspective.* Boston; Toronto: Allyn and Bacon, 2000.

Reitz, Joan M. *Dictionary for Library and Information Science / Joan M. Reitz.* Westport, Conn.: Libraries Unlimited, 2004.

Strub, Maurini R., and Louann Stewart. "Case Study: Shelving and the Autistic Employee." *Journal of Access Services* 7, no. 4 (September 20, 2010): 262–68. https://doi.org/10.1080/15367967.2010.508369.

Wagner, Philip L. "Remarks on the Geography of Language." *Geographical Review* 48, no. 1 (1958): 86–97. https://doi.org/10.2307/211703.

Ward, David. "Stuttering and Cluttering (Second Edition) : Frameworks for Understanding and Treatment," 2017. https://www.taylorfrancis.com/books/e/9781315727073.

# Stuck in the Filter: Health, Anxiety, and Feeding the Fear

**Stacey Astill**

*Content Warning*   Please be aware that this chapter will discuss anxiety, depression, negative thoughts around food, it will also touch on bereavement, and there is one mention of drinking as a coping strategy.

Sensationalized health information is not a new phenomenon, but its impact is amplified by use of the internet and the ability of anyone to reach a large audience. When this is combined with the need for 'click bait' headlines to draw in advertising revenue the results aren't usually well researched, health promoting articles—instead, this week alone, I have read about how yoga, oral sex, and wine can kill you (stroke, stroke, cancer risk equivalent to smoking 10 cigarettes). The information doesn't stop with the news articles–shares and regurgitation of information continue the spread. This has led to discussion of how health professionals can work more effectively with journalists to ensure robust reporting; and the United Kingdom's National Health Service (NHS) creating the Behind the Headlines service to provide a breakdown of the sensationalized stories of the week and tackle the misinformation—demonstrating the significant impact news reporting can have on the population as a whole.[1]

---

1   Julie Leask, Claire Hooker, and Catherine King, "Media Coverage of Health Issues and how to Work More Effectively with Journalists: A Qualitative Study," *BMC Public Health* 10, (Sep 08, 2010): 535. doi:10.1186/1471-2458-10-535; NHS. "Behind the Headlines." Accessed Jul 31, 2019. https://www.nhs.uk/news/.

Scare mongering around treatments (immunization[2]), diagnosis, or specific medications (statins[3], anti-depressants[4], HRT[5]) has impacted patient care and choices.[6] As health library staff it is important for us to ensure the quality of the information we provide to our colleagues in health and social care disciplines, however library workers fall into a liminal space between patient and medical professional. Health library professionals are not specifically medically trained but do have to make evidence-based decisions regarding health information on a daily basis. Library staff act as a filter for this information—assessing evidence basis, the quality of research, and digging down to find the truth in the sensation. Largely, the role is research, yet library staff are not necessarily seen in the same light or supported in the same way as researchers studying emotionally difficult topics.

More consideration needs to be made of the impact of a constant barrage of health information—specifically for people with anxiety. Library staff who also experience mental health conditions are vulnerable to the duality—knowing reasonably that the scaremongering news is inherently incorrect, yet still experiencing nervousness around specific foods, treatments, weight, or any number of other triggers which could impact them due to mental health or personal experiences (such as bereavement, severe illness, or other lived experiences). Invasive thoughts, anxiety responses, and other difficulties need to be acknowledged as a reasonable reaction to the repeated exposure to difficult stimulus—library staff should not be expected to cope with this phenomenon alone or feel unable to seek support in developing resilience and other strategies to help with the constant barrage of sensationalized health information. Understanding the demands of this work would be beneficial to those with any mental health conditions who work in medical library fields.

---

2   NYC Health. "Measles." https://www1.nyc.gov/site/doh/health/health-topics/measles.page, Accessed, Sep 19, 2019.

3   NHS Behind the Headlines, "Statins 'may Not Help' Over-75s without Diabetes," accessed Oct 24, 2019. https://www.nhs.uk/news/older-people/statins-may-not-help-over-75s-without-diabetes/.

4   Sam Blanchard, "NHS Dished Out More Prescriptions than EVER before in 2018," Needs a month and day and name of publication 2019, https://www.dailymail.co.uk/health/article-6859589/A-nation-pill-poppers-NHS-dishes-prescriptions-before.html.

5   Sarah Knapton. "HRT may Raise the Risk of Developing Alzheimer's Disease, New Study Suggests." *Telegraph.Co.Uk*, Mar 7, 2019, https://search.proquest.com/docview/2188817603.

6   Jessica Fishman, Thomas Ten Have, David Casarett, "Cancer and the Media: How does the News Report on Treatment and Outcomes?" *Archives of Internal Medicine* 170, no. 6 (Mar 22, 2010): 515–18, 517.

**Stuck in the Filter Health, Anxiety, and Feeding the Fear**

This chapter will consider the impact of health news on library staff who act as filters for it and experience anxiety. The discussion will be framed within the wider topic of health news and the ways in which it is reported on. I will write from the perspective of a clinically anxious library staff member who currently holds sole responsibility for a news bulletin targeted at health and social care staff on the Isle of Man. The news bulletin is a current awareness service sent out weekly and curated by our library; creating it involves monitoring health news from a range of sources throughout the week and collating the stories which are relevant and useful into the current awareness bulletin. Throughout the chapter I will add italicised personal anecdotes to frame the discussion around my experiences of writing this bulletin as someone who is prone to anxiety and disordered eating.

I would like to preface the main body of this work by specifying that I am very lucky to have supportive colleagues who will always take over or help out if I need a break from this role, however I think it is important to consider the impact the regular expose to health information has and the amount of staff who perform these tasks daily without recognition for the deeper impact it may have on them.

**The Liminal Space**

We are aware that research can cause damage to the researcher. This is formalized in guidelines such as those of the Social Research Association,[7] and acknowledged in literature such as Hubbard, Backett-Millburn, and Kemmer's work on emotional research, suggesting strategies to allow research teams to better equip themselves for coping with emotion effectively during their research.[8] These concerns are especially true of areas in which the research would be obviously considered distressing—child abuse, domestic violence, the Holocaust—however it is less commented on in areas which may not be immediately

---

7  Note: This resource has between removed between the first and second drafts of this chapter, but can be viewed via the Wayback machine. Social Research Association, "A Code of Practice for the Safety of Social Researchers," accessed 1/07/19, https://web.archive.org/web/20190214113246/http://the-sra.org.uk/wp-content/uploads/safety_code_of_practice.pdf.

8  Gill Hubbard, Kathryn Backett-Milburn, and Debbie Kemmer. "Working with Emotion: Issues for the Researcher in Fieldwork and Teamwork," *International Journal of Social Research Methodology* 4, no. 2 (2001): 119–37.

perceived as difficult and distressing for the researcher. There are also guidelines by various organizations including the UK government.[9] Even though these are formalized guidelines, or policy-based advice, they are still fairly vague on how researchers should go about protecting themselves. The UK guidelines somewhat problematically suggest decompression time either at the pub, or home "on the sofa", offering a choice between a social space (with no acknowledgement of the drinking culture and related difficulties which accompany it), or solitary reflection. The advice which is offered about safeguarding researcher mental health relies on the researcher themselves to assess whether they will be able to listen to testimony or read resources without causing themselves distress.[10] This places the onus on the researcher themselves, and relies on them knowing what will and won't be triggering to their emotions. These guides are fairly unclear, however about those taking part in less formalized research, such as the role of library staff working in health and social care sectors have even less acknowledgement. The work library staff do when compiling news bulletins and combing through large amounts of health news is still research, in my case actively seeking out information on a daily basis, however as it is not formalized as a research project. Therefore, staff undertaking work similar to mine fall into a liminal space.

## Health News

As a need for advertising revenue and site visits increase competition to drive traffic to websites, the need for clickbait headlines increases. Discussion regarding the disconnect between headlines and the studies which they attempt to convey are not a new phenomenon, nor are baseless headlines which are not at all reflected in the data. In an article from 2000 a simple dissonance between headlines in Vancouver papers (detailing ward closures of 30% of acute care beds in British Columbia between 1991 and 1996) and the data around patient care, the evidence showed no change in death rates or hospital admissions, yet headlines claimed otherwise.[11] Lay people are much more likely to

---

9   Ria Jesrani, "Making Research Safer for Everyone Involved—User Research in Government," accessed Aug 19, 2019. https://userresearch.blog.gov.uk/2018/11/20/making-research-safer-for-everyone-involved/.

10   Jesrani, "Making Research Safe For Everyone Involved."

11   Noralou P Roos, "The Disconnect between the Data and the Headlines," *CMAJ* 163, no. 4 (2000): 411–12., 411

have seen the newspaper headlines than the academic studies, therefore fears are stoked by the media and often not allayed.

The factors driving misinformation in the media are various: unqualified spokespeople, poor provision of context, inexperienced reporters, and purposeful bias intended to either sell or discredit products or services, promote specific agendas.[12]

A discussion of credibility when reporting on health news considers a hierarchy of factors which add to the reliability of a story–however this is information provided to the scientific community often in a paywalled journal, and not provided to members of the public. Despite assertions that single source stories have poor reliability this doesn't prevent newspapers from publishing these reports, or the public from believing them.[13] In an assessment of reporting on health information in Turkish news undertaken in 2018 59.6% of articles listed the source for their information, however, there was no guarantee that readers would be able to access them–sometimes these sources were also other newspaper articles, demonstrating the way in which information can begin to circulate without a credible basis. As well as this only 5.3% of stories listed an author, and only 2% provided other perspectives. This demonstrates a lack of accountability as the majority of articles cannot be linked to their author, as well as only providing a perspective by a single journalist who may not have the medical knowledge required to synthesize the article for laypeople.

This knowledge does not prevent the anxious mind from ruminating on health information, despite knowing that there is a chance the news stories are likely sensationalized, over exaggerated, or provide misunderstandings. Rumination and repetitive thoughts are a symptom of anxiety and can cause great distress, although they can range in content and be totally random in some cases, they can also be triggered by circumstances. If a person with anxiety reads large amounts of health information, especially sensationalized information, then this can, in turn, trigger intrusive thoughts.[14] There is no way to deal with intrusive thoughts other than changing the way in which the

---

12  Capli, Bulent, Sule Karatas Ozaydin, and Serife Ozturk, "Ethical Issues in Health Communication: Health-Related News Sourcing Practices," *Nutrition* 55, (2018): S14–S15. , S14.

13  Capli, Bulent, Ozaydin, Ozturk, "Ethical Issues in Health Communication," S14.

14  Martin Seif, Sally Winston,"Unwanted Intrusive Thoughts," accessed Oct 29, 2019. https://adaa.org/learn-from-us/from-the-experts/blog-posts/consumer/unwanted-intrusive-thoughts.

person having them interacts with them, however this is a long and difficult process. When being exposed to stimuli regularly, a constant level of resilience is required to cope with the information being processed, particularly stressful periods or worsening of mental health can impact resilience and reduce coping mechanisms. Health information is an already difficult topic filled with misinformation, providing a constant filter for that can be mentally draining.

## Morality

As well as the issues described above, health reporting often also ascribes morality to its stories. Fat is bad, thinness is good; anorexia is an illness, binge eating disorder is a lack of self-control; exercise is good, not exercising is bad. These assertions exclude fat people, people with mobility issues, and people with recognized illnesses deemed less significant by the moral compass of society such as lung cancer patients who smoke or fat people with heart disease. One of the ways in which this is exemplified, is the air of *you deserved it* directed towards the aforementioned groups as opposed to the shock when traditionally 'fit' and 'healthy' people become ill.[15] The process of stigmatizing groups for various reasons is described as the reduction "...from a whole and usual person to a tainted, discounted one".[16] When you are being repeatedly informed that you are a tainted person it can be difficult to remain mentally robust—instead, the belief in the socially engineered stigma (e.g. weight, smoking) devalues your self-worth and can begin to permeate your consciousness.[17]

This type or reporting is evident in *Cancer Research's* controversial obesity campaign,[18] despite evidence that shaming people about their weight does not lead to weight loss, and can, in fact, lead to weight gain they still ran an aggressive, shaming campaign.[19] Morality is as-

---

15  Abigail C. Saguy, and Kjerstin Gruys, "Morality and Health: News Media Constructions of Overweight and Eating Disorders." *Social Problems* 57, no. 2 (2010): 231–50., 232.

16  Erving Goffman,*Stigma: Notes on the Management of Spoiled Identity* Simon and Schuster, 1963. 3.

17  Lawrence Hsin Yang , Arthur Kleinman, Bruce G. Link, Jo C. Phelan, Sing Lee, and Byron Good, "Culture and Stigma: Adding Moral Experience to Stigma Theory," *Social Science & Medicine* 64, no. 7 (2007): 1524–35, 1525.

18  Natasha Devon. "Cancer Research's Obesity Campaign Isn't just Misguided—it's Dangerous," Oct 24, 2019,https://metro.co.uk/2019/07/03/cancer-researchs-obesity-campaign-isnt-just-misguided-its-dangerous-10108310/

19  Sikorski, Claudia, Melanie Luppa, Tobias Luck, and Steffi G. Riedel-Heller, "Weight Stigma "gets Under the Skin"-Evidence for an Adapted Psychological Mediation Framework-a Systematic Review," *Obesity* 23, no. 2 (Feb, 2015): 266–76. doi:10.1002/oby.20952., 266.

signed and enforced on certain physical attributes or patterns of behavior, and this can in turn exacerbate or trigger disordered eating or anxiety around food and eating. Because of controversy, such campaigns are repeatedly discussed in the media, being advertised, debated, and defended. This cycle leads to perpetuated exposure to potentially harmful campaigns in the media, alongside the physical signs and basic advertising campaigns which were already in place.

The morality of food and eating is one of the most regular items I find in the health news, moralising over what is *good* and *bad* is a common occurrence, with many stories about miracle good foods which can cure and save you (e.g. blueberries); contrasted with bad foods which are killing you (e.g. sugary and processed foods). What I also find however, is that the good and bad foods change just as regularly as they appear, and can sometimes cross the boundaries between good and bad. Alcohol is a key example of this type of transient classification, week to week it can change from being good for your heart, to causing strokes. Despite being aware that there is very little truth in the sensational headlines some can be impactful when they play into pre-existing anxiety, or particularly emotional periods in our professional lives.

* * *

*Two weeks after my Dad died unexpectedly from a simultaneous stroke and heart attack I returned to work. I went straight back to providing the health bulletin. I remember vividly that within the first two days I read two articles about food. One focused on foods that could prevent heart disease and heart attacks, the other one was about things that could cause them. I had made my father some of those 'bad' foods over the years and in an already emotional and anxious state, I zeroed in on this and suffered from repetitive thoughts about it—blaming myself. I knew this was irrational, but that didn't prevent negative patterns of thought or anxious reactions to it.*

*I cried at my desk each time I read these stories. It had not even crossed my mind that such an ordinary part of my job would become so emotionally draining. I began to worry about the food the rest of my family was eating, tried to work out how to include heart attack preventatives in my diet (blueberries featured heavily), and generally just played the events over and over in my head repeatedly considering what had happened to my Dad and whether I could have done anything to change this.*

*I knew my behavior was not rational, but this was part of my job which needed to be done, and something I had not considered the impact of. These articles stuck in my mind and it was very difficult to shake the cycle of anxiety and self-flagellation they caused.*

## How does This Relate to Library Staff?

Library staff fall into a liminal space between laypeople and medically trained professionals, however many of us view health information on a regular basis. One of the areas that crops up time and time again especially in tabloid and health news is food and nutrition—as discussed earlier in the chapter.

Diet culture is highly persistent in much of Western society and this is evident in the news cycle. In a 2003 analysis of a sample of health information, only 17% of stories mentioned research or specific studies.[20] Diet was one of the major categories reported on (23%) compared to topics such as physical activity (8%).[21]

When this is coupled with Generalised Anxiety Disorder (GAD), or other mental illnesses which could cause difficult patterns of thought around food and eating the difficulty of filtering through this information every day can be impactful. Stigma has been discussed previously in this chapter, but it is important to clarify that there is also a stigma around seeking mental health support. Despite the fact many people will be impacted by health news and information, there is also further stigmatization which then prevents them from seeking help for the resulting illness, even if it is particularly serious or a flare up of an existing condition.[22]

\* \* \*

*I had not considered the impact that reading the health news daily would have on my anxiety in relation to food. I found that I was reading daily articles about the horrors of being fat (which I am), the benefits of extremely restrictive diets (such as Keto, eating once a day, multi-day*

20  Caburnay et al, "The News on Health Behavior: Coverage of Diet, Activity, and Tobacco in Local Newspapers," *Health Education & Behavior* 30, no. 6 (2003): 709–22 , 716.

21  Caburnay et al., "The News on Health Behavior," 715.

22  Patrick W. Corrigan, Benjamin G. Druss, and Deborah A. Perlick, "The Impact of Mental Illness Stigma on Seeking and Participating in Mental Health Care." *Psychological Science in the Public Interest* 15, no. 2 (2014), 37.

*fasting), and the various foods which could kill you or save you (crisps vs blueberries). I started to find that some of these articles would stick with me, I became more intensely worried about and focused on my weight, and had more concerns about what I was eating—I began to associate guilt and morality with certain foods. This was not healthy behaviour for me (or for anyone), and I began to worry or feel anxious about my health when eating certain things. I worked hard to employ techniques I had learned to cope with these intrusive and persistent thoughts, but it was still difficult to accept that I would have to continue to see these headlines. One of the main strategies I employ to cope with intrusive thoughts is to examine the thought and deconstruct it to prove the worry it caused was baseless. Because so much health news told me that fat people will die of various health complications it was much more complex to deal with. The majority of these stories would never make it to the bulletin as I was acting as the filter, but I had to keep reading them to discount them.*

## Stress and Health News Reporting

Reporting on health stories is often sensationalized or poorly translated from the initial study. This difficulty is acknowledged by some health reporters themselves, a survey of reporters in five Midwestern states showed that although over half found it nearly always easy, or usually easy to find reliable health information less than 20% of the same reporters felt able to understand the key health issues that they were reporting on. In terms of the reporting itself, 20% found it often or nearly always difficult to put health news in context. Overall, the majority felt their reporting and interpreting was sometimes easy and sometimes difficult.[23] Reporters are able to identify this issue, but it does not prevent the need for health news to be shared and reported on.

These facts become even more significant when paired with views such as those expressed in an overview of health and media which discredits the reliability of health news, yet simultaneously uses language which gives parallel credence to health information reported in the media and medical experts. Confusing statements such as "...as ordinary people we must decide to trust or distrust media messages in much the same way we decide to trust or distrust medical advice

---

23  Voss, Melinda, "Checking the Pulse: Midwestern Reporters' Opinions on their Ability to Report Health Care News," *American Journal of Public Health* 92, no. 7 (Jul, 2002): 1158–60,doi:10.2105/ajph.92.7.1158., 1159.

or other expertise"[24] do not help clarify how to avoid misinformation. This statement does not provide clarity, instead it affirms that news in the media is likely to be shades of the truth and therefore to use personal judgement, yet at the same time including medical professionals in this analogy implies that both are equally as reliable, which is not the case.

Although this chapter focuses specifically on health and social care news, the media's impact on members of the public is addressed most regularly in terms of terrorism. Studies consider the increases in anxiety caused by coverage of terror related incidents, or the impact it will have on children. In a more general study about life stressors in 2017, 56% of respondents to the survey who regularly followed the news said it caused them stress. Despite 72% of respondents stating their belief that the media over exaggerates stories, there is still an overlap of those who believe this but are still stressed. Similarly, library staff in medical and social care settings who are aware that stories are both overblown and often based on small facts from surveys can still find that the information impacts them. Knowledge of the unreliable nature of the reporting is not always enough to protect from the impact of the news, which can cycle as intrusive thoughts.[25]

Information about the impact of health news on anxiety was recognized as a little-studied area by McNaughton-Cassill in 2001, however a body of scholarly work did not build around this observation. This work draws together multiple strands: the fact that the media is often unduly negative in coverage of stories, that prominent stories are most likely to influence public attitudes, and that this leads to those consuming news having an inflated concept of danger and life stress.[26] People with anxiety are likely to see information on topics they are anxious about. This behavior then perpetuates a cycle–the anxious person finds more negative and sensationalized reports, so is more anxious, and seeks out further information. Working in health libraries not only provides the search skills to access a range of health

---

24 Clive Seale, "Health and Media: An Overview," *Sociology of Health & Illness* 25, no. 6 (2003): 513–31., 514.

25 American Psychological Association, "APA Stress in America™ Survey: US at 'Lowest Point we can Remember,' Future of Nation most Commonly Reported Source of Stress," APA, https://www.apa.org/news/press/releases/2017/11/lowest-point.

26 Mary E McNaughton-Cassill,"The News Media and Psychological Distress," *Anxiety, Stress and Coping* 14, no. 2 (2001): 193–211., 194.

information, but can also mean this is a requirement of the role. If an anxious library staff member is seeking to interrupt the negative cycle, they still have to undertake research as part of this role.

* * *

*I am fat. Not a little bit fat. A lot fat. I exercise regularly, I eat a lot of healthy foods, but I'm fat, and I have spent a long time coming to terms with that. Obviously, health news focuses very regularly on obesity, and seeing regular information about all the ways in which I'm more likely to die because I'm fat eventually takes a toll. Not necessarily the one which was intended—I certainly haven't lost weight, but I do now worry fairly consistently about dropping dead from a heart attack, having a stroke, or any number of other things depending on what the news is shouting most about at the time. Symptoms of anxiety including chest pains, palpitations, shortness of breath, are similar to those of the illnesses mentioned in many health news articles about obesity related conditions. Therefore, my anxiety response feeds into the cycle—read health story, feel anxious about it, look it up more, experience similar symptoms, feel more anxious about it, look up more about it. I have learned to rely on information such as that provided on NHS evidence, or patient.info, but it's very easy to find sensationalist information online. Especially information dressed up as concern in health news.*

Because of the regularity of sensationalized health news the British Nutrition Foundation and NHS Evidence have gone so far as to designate web pages specifically to tackle the false or misleading health information which appears, using their sites to discuss the headlines and provide framing and context (however one wonders how accessible these websites are to members of the public unless they specifically know to look for them).[27] Even though I am privileged enough to be aware of and have easy access to these resources, I still find it difficult to be unaffected by the information I am filtering.

## Support in Libraries

An unofficial survey of library staff conducted via Twitter and an email circular for UK Health library staff revealed that the majority of

---

27   British Nutrition Foundation, "Facts Behind the Headlines," accessed January 7th, 2019,https://www.nutrition.org.uk/nutritioninthenews/headlines.html. ; NHS Behind the Headlines.

services whose staff replied had no formal policies in place for staff wellbeing when exposed to large volumes of health news, or to distressing literature search topics. Multiple staff spoke about informal policies and understanding managers—the bulk of these involved staff being offered a chance to talk about the content of what they had viewed. There was also mention of being given a chance to do craft projects or break for a cup of tea instead of continuing to view the information.

One of the key things this exercise highlighted was that most staff perceived the phrasing of "health news" to refer to literature searching, a more formalized process than that of assessing health news daily. Staff described how difficult they found running certain literature searches, and stressed that immersing themselves in topics such as domestic violence for 8 hours a day could be mentally exhausting and negatively impactful. Although this chapter does not focus on this line of enquiry, it is an area which would benefit from future research.

## Conclusion

The risk of large doses of health news doesn't appear to be something formally considered by many, if any, UK health libraries. Despite evidence that health news is often poorly represented and sensationalised, evidence that news can cause anxious responses in those consuming it, and the requirement for many health library staff to regularly read health news as part of their roles, there is very little written about the impact this could have on mental health. From informal queries colleagues do not seem to identify this as a concern, but some do have informal solutions in place—such as passing on specific tasks which are distressing to the researching staff member.

When library staff with anxiety are required to act as filters for health information there is a propensity for added stress responses—more than the neurotypical distress which has been disclosed during the aforementioned informal survey. Filtering and managing health information can impact all staff, however those with anxiety and other mental health complexities may find it more difficult and require more coping mechanisms and support to allow them to perform their role safely.

## Acknowledgements

Acknowledgements: I would like to thank my wonderful colleagues for their ongoing support, the UK medical library networks (LHINN and NULJ) for their thoughtful answers to my queries about existing support, and Miranda and Carrie for making this collection possible.

---

## *Bibliography*

American Psychological Association. "APA Stress in America™ Survey: US at 'Lowest Point we can Remember;' Future of Nation most Commonly Reported Source of Stress." APA. https://www.apa.org/news/press/releases/2017/11/lowest-point.

Blanchard, Sam. "NHS Dished Out More Prescriptions than EVER before in 2018.". Accessed Oct 24, 2019. https://www.dailymail.co.uk/health/article-6859589/A-nation-pill-poppers-NHS-dishes-prescriptions-before.html.

British Nutrition Foundation. "Facts Behind the Headlines." Accessed January 31, 2019. https://www.nutrition.org.uk/nutritioninthenews/headlines.html.

Caburnay, Charlene A., Matthew W. Kreuter, Douglas A. Luke, Robert A. Logan, Heather A. Jacobsen, Vinay C. Reddy, Anitha R. Vempaty, and Hythem R. Zayed. "The News on Health Behavior: Coverage of Diet, Activity, and Tobacco in Local Newspapers." *Health Education & Behavior* 30, no. 6 (2003): 709-722.

Capli, Bulent, Sule Karatas Ozaydin, and Serife Ozturk. "Ethical Issues in Health Communication: Health-Related News Sourcing Practices." *Nutrition* 55, (2018): S14-S15.

Corrigan, Patrick W., Benjamin G. Druss, and Deborah A. Perlick. "The Impact of Mental Illness Stigma on Seeking and Participating in Mental Health Care." Psychological Science in the Public Interest 15, no. 2 (2014): 37-70.

Devon, Natasha. "Cancer Research's Obesity Campaign Isn't Just Misguided–it's Dangerous.". Accessed Oct 24, 2019. https://metro.co.uk/2019/07/03/cancer-researchs-obesity-campaign-isnt-just-misguided-its-dangerous-10108310/.

Fishman, Jessica, Thomas Ten Have, and David Casarett. "Cancer and the Media: How does the News Report on Treatment and Outcomes?" *Archives of Internal Medicine* 170, no. 6 (Mar 22, 2010): 515-518. doi:10.1001/archinternmed.2010.11.

Goffman, Erving. *Stigma: Notes on the Management of Spoiled Identity* Simon and Schuster, 1986.

Hubbard, Gill, Kathryn Backett-Milburn, and Debbie Kemmer. "Working with Emotion: Issues for the Researcher in Fieldwork and Teamwork." *International Journal of Social Research Methodology* 4, no. 2 (2001): 119-137.

Jesrani, Ria. "Making Research Safer for Everyone Involved–User Research in Government." . Accessed Aug 19, 2019. https://userresearch.blog.gov. uk/2018/11/20/making-research-safer-for-everyone-involved/.

Knapton, Sarah. "HRT may Raise the Risk of Developing Alzheimer's Disease, New Study Suggests." *Telegraph.Co.Uk*, Mar 7, 2019. https://search.proquest. com/docview/2188817603.

Leask, Julie, Claire Hooker, and Catherine King. "Media Coverage of Health Issues and how to Work More Effectively with Journalists: A Qualitative Study." *BMC Public Health* 10, (Sep 08, 2010): 535. doi:10.1186/1471-2458-10-535.

McNaughton-cassill, Mary E. "The News Media and Psychological Distress." *Anxiety, Stress and Coping* 14, no. 2 (2001): 193-211.

NHS. "Behind the Headlines." Accessed Jul 31, 2019. https://www.nhs.uk/news/.

NHS Behind the Headlines. "Statins 'may Not Help' Over-75s without Diabetes." . Accessed Oct 24, 2019. https://www.nhs.uk/news/older-people/ statins-may-not-help-over-75s-without-diabetes/.

NYC Health. "Measles." Accessed September 24, 2019, . https://www1.nyc.gov/site/ doh/health/health-topics/measles.page.

Roos, Noralou P. "The Disconnect between the Data and the Headlines." *Cmaj* 163, no. 4 (2000): 411-412.

Saguy, Abigail C. and Kjerstin Gruys. "Morality and Health: News Media Constructions of Overweight and Eating Disorders." *Social Problems* 57, no. 2 (2010): 231-250.

Seale, Clive. "Health and Media: An Overview." *Sociology of Health & Illness* 25, no. 6 (2003): 513-531. doi:10.1111/1467-9566.t01-1-00356.

Seif, Martin and Sally Winston. "Unwanted Intrusive Thoughts." Accessed Oct 29, 2019. https://adaa.org/learn-from-us/from-the-experts/blog-posts/ consumer/unwanted-intrusive-thoughts

Sikorski, Claudia, Melanie Luppa, Tobias Luck, and Steffi G. Riedel-Heller. "Weight Stigma "gets Under the Skin"-Evidence for an Adapted Psychological Mediation Framework-a Systematic Review." *Obesity* 23, no. 2 (Feb, 2015): 266-276. doi:10.1002/oby.20952.

Social Research Association. "A Code of Practice for the Safety of Social Researchers." Accessed January 7, 2019. https://web.archive.org/ web/20190214113246/http://the-sra.org.uk/wp-content/uploads/safety_ code_of_practice.pdf.

Voss, Melinda. "Checking the Pulse: Midwestern Reporters' Opinions on their Ability to Report Health Care News." *American Journal of Public Health* 92, no. 7 (Jul, 2002): 1158-1160. doi:10.2105/ajph.92.7.1158.

Yang, Lawrence Hsin, Arthur Kleinman, Bruce G. Link, Jo C. Phelan, Sing Lee, and Byron Good. "Culture and Stigma: Adding Moral Experience to Stigma Theory." *Social Science & Medicine* 64, no. 7 (2007): 1524-1535.

# Mental Illness and the In-Person Interview

**Ian Ross Hughes**

## Introduction

"In studies mostly performed in the United States, employer attitudes toward employment of individuals with psychiatric disabilities tended to be more negative than attitudes toward individuals with other disabilities"[1] People with "psychiatric disabilities," or mental illness as I will refer to it in this chapter, fear the idea of employers or potential employers finding out about their condition. Personally and professionally dealing with mental illness is tough. As a librarian, I have had to deal with it in every aspect of my life from graduate school, to finding my first job in the profession, to working in the field, and trying to move up into better opportunities.

Every aspect of having mental illness can be tough on a person and is something that those in the library field should be conscious of from the workplace to conferences. One area that can be draining for librarians with mental illness is the day or two of the second interview. Most of the library research gives advice and prepares the job seeker for that big day but there doesn't seem to be much written to remind the hiring institution about what the interviewee is going through, much less how much more difficult it is when that person has a mental illness.

---

1   Ozawa, Akihiko, Emiko Kikuchi, and Jun Yaeda. "Causal Analysis of Employer Attitude Formation toward Employing Individuals with Psychiatric Disabilities," *Journal of Vocational Rehabilitation* 44, no. 2 (2016): 201. doi:10.3233/JVR-150791.

The second interview, or on-campus interview, is meant to gauge the fit of the candidate as well as sell the interviewee on why they should choose that institution. It's questionable whether the rigors of the day accurately display the candidate's qualifications for the position or their fit at the institution. This chapter will break down the day, expectations, and how they may impede someone struggling with mental illness. It will follow up with some simple solutions to make the day a little more digestible for someone with mental illness while possibly improving the process for everyone.

I write this chapter as someone who has been through the process. I have been diagnosed with rapid cycle Cyclothymia, a minor form of bi-polar disorder, and ADHD along with some other lesser impacting issues. The most important thing to know about my Cyclothymia as it relates to my own experiences is that my mood fluctuates several times in a day between hypomania, a minor depression, and back to balanced.

## Mental Illness

The National Alliance on Mental Illness (NAMI) says of mental illness, "A mental illness is a condition that affects a person's thinking, feeling or mood. Such conditions may affect someone's ability to relate to others and function each day. Each person will have different experiences, even people with the same diagnosis."[2] The list of conditions on the NAMI site includes ADHD, Anxiety Disorders, Bipolar Disorder, Depression, Obsessive-compulsive Disorder, and Schizophrenia, in addition to many others. Each of these conditions, as well as all conditions that fall under mental illness, create problems and barriers to overcome.

The NAMI website lists several symptoms such as mania, depression, severe anxiety, obsession, compulsions, mood swings, and the possibility of setting off posttraumatic stress. It's important that interviewers remember that the interviewees may be experiencing symptoms during the course of the day. Members of the search committee do not need to be trained in spotting these symptoms, they should just be aware that it is possible that a candidate may be experiencing one or more mental illness symptoms.

---

2  "Mental Health Conditions," NAMI, accessed June 4, 2019, https://www.nami.org/Learn-More/Mental-Health-Conditions.

What can make the mental illness more unnerving for the candidate is the fear of the social stigmas surrounding their illness. The candidate may fear that their issues will reflect poorly on them as a candidate or the thought that the potential employer might not understand the symptoms they are experiencing. The stigma and fear of judgement are stressors that compound the mental illness symptoms and make them more difficult to deal with in the moment.

Research supports the claim that candidates fear both the stigma of having mental health issues and that future employers will judge them based on their diagnosis. In a study done by Colleen Donnelly, 570 adults were asked whether they would disclose mental illness in various situations, including job interviews, 190 of 352 participants who indicated they would not share their mental illness issues in a face to face interview, cited "Concerns about repercussions and discrimination" as the reason they would not share.[3]

Though I make it clear upfront, no later than the second interview, that I have bipolar, I can relate with the stigmatization fear. I once had a negative experience interviewing at a major research institution in the Midwest during a snowy January day. In the winter I wear a professional knee length coat. The first person who interviewed me cited the coat and that I looked "crazy," as the reason to ask, "you're not going to come in here and shoot the place up are you?" I had not disclosed my mental illness yet and was shaken by the question and the reasoning.

## Groups and Departments

Before the listing of the groups and departments a candidate has to meet, there is matter of travel to a location. If the candidate is lucky, and they desire to stay close to their current location, then it is a short drive or trip via public transportation. But many candidates have to travel great distances to get to the interview. Even if the candidate gets in the night before, there is still exhaustion and stress tied to the next day. The interview eve could consist of getting from the airport to the hotel, maybe locating food, practicing a presentation, and perhaps checking out the surrounding area. The schedule before the interview happens can be stressful.

---

3   Colleen Donnelly, "Public Attitudes toward Disclosing Mental Health Conditions," *Social Work in Mental Health* 15 no. 5 (2017): 591. doi:10.1080/15332985.2017.1302039.

In addition to the possibility of travel, the candidate has to potentially meet several different groups in the library and outside. Daniel
Barkley refers to it as meeting the library family.[4] However, as the article "A Cohort Study of Entry Level Librarians and the Academic Job
Search" details, in addition to meeting groups within the library there
is the potential to meet several outside groups.[5] Though Reed, Carroll,
and Jahre highlight the experiences of entry level librarians, many of
these groups could sit in or have their time with a candidate for most
librarian interviews. Some of the meeting groups listed in the article include, the search committee, librarians in similar roles, Human
Resources, a Direct Supervisor, non-library administrator, non-library
faculty, and an informal meet and greet.[6] Then the candidates also
have to partake in activities like a library tour, campus tour, and meals
or at least lunch with library personnel.[7] This also includes some sort
of presentation.

The combination of presentation, different forms of meeting the listed groups, food and possibly several tours leads to a packed day that
doesn't allow for much rest. That lack of rest, in addition to the stress
can lead to the onset of symptoms, or exacerbate symptoms that
might already be present. If the day is not well planned, or clear objectives are not set, the day can be further complicated.

I was at one second interview where it got 15 to 20 minutes behind
schedule and they were rushing me to every meeting with little time
to stop. It didn't seem like much was getting accomplished, several of
the stops covered similar information to the previous meetings, and
near the end of the night my bipolar had cycled so often I was exhausted. The last meeting and dinner with a couple members of the
search committee were difficult to manage. On a separate occasion, I
was at a second interview that gave several breaks between meetings
and had me meet with very specific groups for the job. They used my
presentation as a way to also meet the staff, and it made for a more

---

4   Daniel Barkley, "Live and In-Person: Get Ready to Meet the Entire Library Family," in *How to Stay Afloat in the Academic Library Job Pool,* ed. Teresa Y. Neely (Chicago: American Library Association, 2011), 83.

5   Jason B. Reed, Alexander J. Carroll, and Benjamin Jahre, "A Cohort Study of Entry Level Librarians and the Academic Job Search," *Endnotes* 6, no. 1 (2015): 13–14, OmniFile Full Text Mega.

6   Reed, Carroll, and Jahre, "A Cohort Study," 13–14.

7   Reed, Carroll, and Jahre, "A Cohort Study," 13–14.

manageable experience. I felt like I was able to better show how I could manage the tasks of the job and relate to coworkers as opposed to worrying about the process.

## Expectations

In an article that polled libraries that have interviewed entry level librarians, Hodge and Spoor asked for the three most important character traits they sought out in candidates. Intelligence, enthusiasm, cooperativeness, responsibility, and friendliness ranked highest in their survey.[8]

Other literature on job interviews often suggest the interviewee needs to have confidence but that can be difficult to do with the anxiety, pressure, and stress of everything that needs to happen in the day. Young, Behnke, and Mann have even connected the level of anxiety during an interview to the level of anxiety a person feels leading up to doing public speaking.[9] Carrying that high level of anxiousness makes some advice difficult to follow. For example, in Barkley's book chapter, "Interview Don'ts" he offers well-intentioned advice such as "Don't be lazy in your speech," "Don't disregard your body language," and "Don't cross your arms, jam your hands into your pockets, or use any other signs to tell your interviewers that you don't want them to get to know you." that various mental illness conditions may affect an individual's ability to consistently do.[10] There are mental illness conditions that may impact any of these factors, while in general they may be good to be aware of, and no blame to Barkley for mentioning them, but speech patterns and body language may be the cause of multiple things. I sometimes need to move when my bipolar begins to cycle, if I cannot get up and walk, my knee shakes to release energy. This could easily fall under body language or be interpreted as me not wanting to be there.

Research regarding non-verbal and verbal cues in the interview process done by De Groot and Gooty probed how interviewers judge

---

8   Megan Hodge, and Nicole Spoor, "Congratulations! You've Landed an Interview: What Do Hiring Committees Really Want?" *New Library World* 113 no. 3/4 (2012): 150. doi:10.1108/03074801211218534.

9   Young, Melissa J., Ralph R. Behnke, and Yvonne M. Mann, "Anxiety Patterns in Employment Interviews," *Communication Reports* 17, no. 1 (2004): 49–57.

10   Barkley, "Live and In-Person:," 89–90.

interviewees personality traits among other things.[11] Their end conclusion, however, illustrates that at the very least, interviewers should be aware that they are judging cues.

"The data reported in this paper show practitioners that no matter how much an interview is structured, nonverbal cues cause interviewers to make attributions about candidates. If we face this fact, rather than consider information from cues as bias that should be ignored, interviewers can do a better job of focusing on job-related behavior and information in the interview, while realizing that the cues are providing information that must be attended to or it could result in error in the process."[12]

After the long day that was detailed in the "Groups and Departments" section of this chapter and reading what could possibly constitute mental illness, a connection can be made to why someone with mental illness goes in fearing the stigma of what they have or how they will be judged while interviewing. Expectations should solely focus on how a candidate can perform at their job, and even then, something as little as a question can be overdone. I was once in a second interview for a tenured position and was asked several times whether I thought I could publish. Between my bipolar, ADHD, and exhaustion, the answer got less confident throughout the day. Of course I feel I can publish, but the repeated question throughout the day wore me down to where I no longer felt well answering it confidently.

## Recommendations

Often in articles for jobs or for job seekers, advice is given on how to be more successful. In an article by Lonergan, an extreme case is given for how not to run the in-person interview.[13] In this section, I will give ideas on how to improve a search to be more inclusive of those with mental illness or make the process less hectic in general.

---

11   De Groot, Timothy, and Janaki Gooty. "Can Nonverbal Cues Be Used to Make Meaningful Personality Attributions in Employment Interviews?" *Journal of Business and Psychology* 24, no2(2009): 179–92,

12   De Groot and Gooty, "Can Nonverbal," 190.

13   Lonergan, David. "How to Run a Bad Personnel Search, Part Two," *Community & Junior College Libraries* 15 no. 1 (2009): 51–54. doi:10.1080/02763910802665052.

Do not judge body language, try to keep your assessment of the candidate on their presentation and on their merits for the position. Someone with mental illness may be dealing with extra stressors in addition to the anxiety of the day.

If a candidate seems to lack confidence in a particular area, find out why. That lack of confidence may not be real and you may be dealing with someone who does know what they are doing but are struggling to express it in that moment or they may not be in a position that replicates the job conditions.

Be clear, internally, on your objectives for assessing the candidate. If you have a short amount of time with the interviewee, prioritize the most important goals and create a flexible schedule that doesn't put the candidate and yourself in a time crunch. Being specific about what you want to accomplish can help you develop a day that allows the candidate to succeed.

The interviewee is gauging the institution as much as the institution is gauging the interviewee, so it's nice to allow them to see as much on campus as possible, but don't sacrifice the important aspects of the time you have together to show them things that are lower on the priority list.

Give the interviewee a couple of moments between major meetings to rest and refresh.

Allow the candidate the opportunity to eat alone. This could be a nice stretch of time for them to regroup. It also can allow for someone with an eating disorder the opportunity to not feel judged.

## Conclusion

By keeping in mind the issues that the candidate could be facing, in addition to the stressful nature of the day, the interviewer should be more flexible with their schedule and mindful of how to successfully navigate the on-campus interview. The search committee should be clear on what the job will entail and the objectives they want to achieve in the process and stick to fulfilling the top goals on the priority list of the in-person interview. The candidate has a lot to face on the day and should be ready to show that they are a good fit for the position, but the institution needs to put future employees as well as current employees in the position to succeed. Remaining cognizant that the day is stressful, and oftentimes too full to achieve that success, as well as keeping in mind potential mental illness issues which the candidate should not feel they have to fear, the search committee can allow themselves and their candidates a better opportunity to see if the position is a fit. Eliminating superficial barriers and hiring the best candidate should be the ultimate goal.

---

## Bibliography

Barkley, Daniel. "Live and In-Person: Get Ready to Meet the Entire Library Family," in *How to Stay Afloat in the Academic Library Job Pool*, ed. Teresa Y. Neely, 83-96. Chicago: American Library Association, 2011.

De Groot, Timothy, and Janaki Gooty. "Can Nonverbal Cues Be Used to Make Meaningful Personality Attributions in Employment Interviews?" *Journal of Business and Psychology* 24, no2(2009): 179–92. doi:10.1007/s10869-009-9098-0.

Donnelly, Colleen. "Public Attitudes toward Disclosing Mental Health Conditions." *Social Work in Mental Health* 15, no. 5 (2017): 588–99. doi:10.1080/15332985.2017.1302039.

Hodge, Megan, and Nicole Spoor. "Congratulations! You've Landed an Interview: What Do Hiring Committees Really Want?" *New Library World* 113 no. 3/4 (2012): 139–61. doi:10.1108/03074801211218534.

Lonergan, David. "How to Run a Bad Personnel Search, Part Two." *Community & Junior College Libraries* 15, no. 1 (2009): 51–54. doi:10.1080/02763910802665052

"Mental Health Conditions." NAMI. accessed June 4, 2019. https://www.nami.org/Learn-More/Mental-Health-Conditions.

Ozawa, Akihiko, Emiko Kikuchi, and Jun Yaeda. "Causal Analysis of Employer Attitude Formation toward Employing Individuals with Psychiatric Disabilities." *Journal of Vocational Rehabilitation* 44, no. 2 (2016): 201–12. doi:10.3233/JVR-150791.

Reed, Jason B., Alexander J. Carroll, and Benjamin Jahre. "A Cohort Study of Entry Level Librarians and the Academic Job Search." *Endnotes* 6, no. 1 (2015): 1–22. OmniFile Full Text Mega.

Young, Melissa J., Ralph R. Behnke, and Yvonne M. Mann. "Anxiety Patterns in Employment Interviews." *Communication Reports* 17, no 1 (2004): 49–57. doi:10.1080/08934210409389373.

# Caring Work:
# Reflections on Care and Librarianship

## Stephanie S. Rosen

*Content Warning*   This chapter briefly mentions police violence
against and murder of people of color, and suicide.

## I. Academic Depression

On 05/13/16, ssrosen wrote, "I am out sick today and unfortunately will
have to miss our meeting."

On 9/13/16, ssrosen wrote, "I'm leaving early, not feeling well…"

On 10/10/16, 11/14/16, 1/16/17, 1/30/17, 2/1/17, 3/6/17, 4/7/17, 4/18/17,
7/9/17, 8/1/17, and 9/6/17, ssrosen wrote "I will be out sick" or "I need
to take a sick day."

On 10/17/17, ssrosen wrote, "I have to leave early to help my partner
who is having health problems."

In response, msitar wrote, "feel better" or, "feel better soon" or, "if
there's anything I can do to help, just let me know."

These snippets of text are small exchanges from the archive of my second year as a librarian. And they are traces of a culture that made it possible for me to work. Before these, I had never written an email to take a
sick day. When I was an academic—that is, when I was simultaneously a
scholar conducting research, an instructor teaching college, and a graduate student completing a doctoral degree—there was not a "day" to take

off. Work filled every corner of my day, and evening, and weekend. And while I was an academic, I almost always felt bad—regularly depressed, periodically immobilized—but that didn't stop me from working.

In fact, I had become a passable academic because I was constantly terrified that I could not prove, on demand, my self-worth with the enumeration of a bibliography, the archeology of a keyword, or a thought I had had that no one else had written. In retrospect, I notice that I didn't have a sense of self-worth but had found a system in which I could generate it, just by reading enough and thinking enough. Of course, under that system, nothing was ever enough, and the anxiety fueled both my work and my depression in a self-perpetuating cycle, interrupted occasionally by the rush and numbness of drinking or getting high.

As it turned out, my graduate advisor wrote a book about this, which came out in print while I was working with her.

Academia breeds particular forms of panic and anxiety leading to what gets called depression—the fear that you have nothing to say, or that you can't say what you want to say, or that you have something to say but it's not important enough or smart enough. In this particular enclave of the professional managerial class, there is an epidemic of anxiety-induced depression that is widely acknowledged informally but not always shared publicly or seen as worthy of investigation.[1]

Ann Cvetkovich's *Depression: A Public Feeling*, published in 2012, looks at academic depression and more broadly at "how, for many of us … everyday life produces feelings of despair and anxiety, sometimes extreme, sometimes throbbing along at a low level, and hence barely discernible from just the way things are, feelings that get internalized and named, for better or worse, as depression."[2] Departing from popular and professional discourses that explain depression as the result of biochemical disorders or traumatic pasts, or both—she provides an "analysis of why and how its feelings are produced by social forces."[3] An example of the Public Feelings approach to affect theory,[4] the book

---

1 Ann Cvetkovich, *Depression: A Public Feeling* (Durham, NC: Duke University Press, 2012). 18.

2 Cvetkovich, *Depression*. 14

3 Cvetkovich, *Depression*. 14

4 See Cvetkovich, *Depression*. 1–10. For a readable introduction to the field, see also Hua Hsu, "Affect Theory and the New Age of Anxiety," The New Yorker, March 18, 2019, https://www.newyorker.com/magazine/2019/03/25/affect-theory-and-the-new-age-of-anxiety.

sets out to describe how depression feels, how it is culturally produced, and how it can be a resource for alternative political action.

Since then, the conversation linking academia to depression—and to anxiety, abuse, and addiction—has only grown. "Quit Lit," a popular genre of personal essay linking the labor conditions of higher education to the lived, affective experience of surviving inside exploitative and manipulative contexts, has flourished in the years since I finished my PhD. These essays, which vary in tone and focus, all testify that the ways we feel bad as academics—which are real and biochemical and take up residence in the body and mind—are not just "in here." They are also "out there" in institutions that deny sustainable conditions for many of us, and actually deny life for some of us.[5]

As depression and anxiety have become keywords for academia and the professoriate, *care* is becoming a keyword for librarianship and library workers. Recent library and information science scholarship is concerned with both care and maintenance, to borrow a phrase from Shannon Mattern's influential 2018 article.[6] Maintenance—the stewardship of resources, preservation of materials, cleaning of data—has taken on new interest as a kind of care, following developments in science and technology studies.[7] And care—the affective and educative dimension of our interpersonal work—has come into clearer

5  Rebecca Schuman embraces the anger of realizing that graduate school, for most, structurally cannot lead to tenure track employment, in the often cited example, "Thesis Hatement," *Slate*, April 5, 2013, http://www.slate.com/articles/life/culturebox/2013/04/there_are_no_academic_jobs_and_getting_a_ph_d_will_make_you_into_a_horrible.html. Erin Bartram explores the grief of being "left behind" in the limbo of adjunct employment and ultimately leaving academia behind in "The Sublimated Grief of the Left Behind," Erin Bartram (blog), February 11, 2018, http://erinbartram.com/uncategorized/the-sublimated-grief-of-the-left-behind/. Herb Childress describes the abusive dynamic of contingent academic employment in "This Is How You Kill a Profession," The Chronicle Review, March 27, 2019, https://www.chronicle.com/interactives/2019-03-27-childress . And, in an essay that predates what is often categorized as "quit lit," Alexis Pauline Gumbs contextualizes her decision to turn down tenure-track job offers and provides archival evidence of the ways in which academic institutions denied life-saving leaves or accommodations to Black Feminist scholars (including Audre Lorde and June Jordan) before their deaths. Alexis Pauline Gumbs, "The Shape of My Impact," *Feminist Wire*, October 29, 2012, https://thefeministwire.com/2012/10/the-shape-of-my-impact/.

6  Shannon Mattern, "Maintenance and Care," *Places Journal*, November 20, 2018, https://doi.org/10.22269/181120.

7  See for example María Puig de la Bellacasa, *Matters of Care: Speculative Ethics in More than Human Worlds*, Posthumanities 41 (Minneapolis: University of Minnesota Press, 2017); Aryn Martin, Natasha Myers, and Ana Viseu, "The Politics of Care in Technoscience," *Social Studies of Science* 45, no. 5 (October 2015): 625–41, https://doi.org/10.1177/0306312715602073; Steven J. Jackson, "Rethinking Repair," in *Media Technologies*, ed. Tarleton Gillespie, Pablo J. Boczkowski, and Kirsten A. Foot (Cambridge: MIT Press, 2014), 221–40; and Andy Russell, Jessica Meyerson, and Lee Vinsel, The Maintainers, n.d., http://themaintainers.org/.

historical focus following important critical studies by scholars like Gina Schlesselman-Tarango and Fobazi Ettarh.[8] They show that our professional performance of caring is overdetermined by a history of white saviorism that not only prefigures the demographics of our profession but also prevents adequate attention to our own working conditions. The professional history of the librarian is such that we are always the caretaker, never the cared for.

This essay is a personal and professional reckoning with being in that position, and especially with being on the giving end of care that isn't helping, and actually has the potential to cause harm. The kind of care that those of us socialized to be nice white ladies are most likely to have learned, and most need to unlearn; the kind of care that has been historically enrolled in the project of librarianship, and which our profession must broadly examine and dismantle. If we are to create cultures in which we all can work, that care for our own needs—through illness, mental illness, changing caregiving obligations, shifting interdependencies, and differential access to life-sustaining conditions—we might begin by examining the ways we embody care.

## II. Caregiving

For me, becoming a librarian coincided with becoming a caregiver. Both were unplanned. My path to librarianship was through a PhD in English, specializing in disability studies, and years of experience applying accessibility standards to digital humanities scholarship and teaching. In my final doctoral year, as I dutifully applied to professorships and cycled through the grief and panic of the academic job market, a librarian position for which I was qualified appeared. The hope this position offered—as a way out of, but not wholly away from, the parts of academic life that fueled my anxiety and depression—was so absolute and so counter to my previous reality that I could only hold to the superstition that it was not real, until the acts of moving to a new state and going to work every day eventually wore that belief down.

At the same time that this new reality—with its financial stability, job security, and supportive community of coworkers—afforded my

---

8   Gina Schlesselman-Tarango, "The Legacy of Lady Bountiful: White Women in the Library," *Library Trends* 64, no. 4 (Spring 2016): 667–86; Fobazi Ettarh, "Vocational Awe and Librarianship: The Lies We Tell Ourselves," *In the Library with the Lead Pipe*, January 10, 2018, http://www.inthelibrarywiththeleadpipe.org/2018/vocational-awe/#identifier_19_8690.

mental health a needed resting ground, an unexpected series of traumas began to punctuate the world that my partner and I had begun to build in our new home. Historically, 2016 was a time of rough awakening for many relatively comfortable white people like me, and a time of heightened alarm for Black and Brown people like my partner. Young Black men were murdered, again and again, in gruesome scenes that were broadcast, again and again, over social media in a stream that, by summer of that year, felt constant—from the car, on the street, in a backyard. Then, there was the campaign and election, with its waves of mob confidence and grim undercurrents.

Privately, in the social world that my partner and I inhabited, everyone was dying too. Early in 2016, an elder who was my partner's childhood protector died of natural causes. She would have been enough to mourn, but she was the first in a series of deaths that were much more troubling. There were two suicides, two women of color: one brilliant trans scholar, one teenage daughter of our closest local friends. There were two haunting, suspicious deaths, two queer-of-color academics: one gay Black man, one queer Latinx man. A frozen river and a police holding cell. And there was one young femme, keeping so many other people alive, who died of cancer. All of these people were connected to my partner, fellow travelers and kindreds, and all of them were removed, by location or by a generation. And although my partner knew them all, there was no one else (not even me), and certainly no community in our new home in a new, predominantly white city, who shared all these losses.

In this mix of loss and danger, experienced within the relative stability of our situation, my partner began to experience debilitating floods of body memories from past trauma that became increasingly disruptive to everyday life. The survival responses they had developed to cope with abuse—repeated acts of gendered and racialized violence—began suddenly surfacing in response to what seemed, to me, like minor challenges, invisible threats, or my best attempts to help. And as they adjusted their life to accommodate the new limitations imposed by these intrusions, and the physical pain and fatigue that accompanied them (medical leave from their doctoral program, giving up a new job), I struggled with how to care for them.

In the realm of depression, anxiety, PTSD, and addiction, caring can be problematic. Trauma becomes vicarious not just by way of empathy but because PTSD symptoms are unpredictable and uncontrollable. To the witness, they originate in another dimension and land squarely in the present, random and dangerous. To witness them, to dodge them as they come without warning, is traumatic. As my partner's symptoms intensified, I was witnessing and dodging, afraid and flailing, a nervous system in response to a system in distress. And yet, I had no words to say this and could not talk to anyone. My competing realities kept me confused and ashamed.

Through moments of painful clarity I recognized that, while I was trying to sustain our collective life and care for the person I loved, I was making things worse. In attempting to maintain a set of expectations that had somewhere and somehow deeply shifted, I was constantly imposing control, reacting on impulse, and ignoring my own experience. I was enacting a kind of care that I recognized from disability thinking as a problem. Disability scholars and activists have exposed the public rhetorics and private dynamics in which care (and cure) can function as a harmful narrative, a form of coercion, or a screen for real violence.[9] Indeed, a dangerous potential in caring behavior is present almost everywhere care is theorized, from feminist ethics to STS and affect theory to self-help literature.[10] I found a version of it that spoke to me in the self-help literature I discovered when I sought strategies for survival during this time.

I spent months reacting to my partner reacting to the effects of post-traumatic stress: panicking when they were choked by despair, defending when they lashed out in anger, paralyzed when they were overcome with fear. I was either on edge or depleted, needing hours or days to recover from crises. I missed work, lost memory, and felt a general sinking hopelessness unlike any prior depression. And,

---

9    Disability critiques of care and cure are present from the early independent living movement to today's disability justice activism. Many recent scholars have explored the complexities of compulsory cure narratives and the violence sometimes enacted in the name of cure and care. See Anne McGuire, *War on Autism: On the Cultural Logic of Normative Violence* (Ann Arbor: University of Michigan Press, 2016); Eunjung Kim, *Curative Violence: Rehabilitating Disability, Gender, and Sexuality in Modern Korea* (Durham, NC: Duke University Press, 2017); Eli Clare, *Brilliant Imperfection: Grappling with Cure* (Durham: Duke University Press, 2017); Leah Lakshmi Piepzna-Samarasinha, *Care Work: Dreaming Disability Justice* (Vancouver: Arsenal Pulp Press, 2018).

10   In feminist ethics, see Barbara Hillyer Davis, "Women, Disability, and Feminism: Notes toward a New Theory," *Frontiers: A Journal of Women Studies* 8, no. 1 (1984): 1–5; Susan Wendell, "Toward a Feminist Theory of Disability," *Hypatia* 4, no. 2 (Summer 1989): 104–24; Eva Feder Kittay, *Love's Labor: Essays on Women, Equality, and Dependency* (New York: Routledge, 1999). In STS, see the special issue on "The Politics of Care in Technoscience," ed. Aryn Martin, Natasha Myers, and Ana Viseu, special issue, *Social Studies of Science* 45, no. 5 (October 2015): 627, passim, https://doi.org/10.1177/0306312715602073. In affect theory, see Lauren Berlant, ed., *Compassion: The Culture and Politics of an Emotion* (New York: Routledge, 2004), 9–10, passim.

although I found numb relief by indulging in addictions that allowed me to check out and quiet my pain, I eventually suspected that sobriety might provide a better baseline from which to assess my reality. I began that path, found a recovery community, and, nervous at one of my first meetings, stumbled across the concept of codependence.

Unlike the disability studies literature on *interdependence* (which sometimes uses the term codependence to mean the same thing), self-help literature on codependence addresses problematic caring behavior as a kind of addiction. Caretaking, it teaches, can be escapist, avoidant, compulsive, a coping mechanism to get outside what is unbearable within the self. While there are limits to the usefulness of pathologizing this social script as an addiction, what resonated with me was the understanding of "the codependent"—or anyone with a dependency, chemical or behavioral—as unable to bear their own felt experience, and often unable even to access it. Through recovery, I learned practices to ground in the present, experience my feelings, and process them in a community of support. That work continues, but it got me to a place from which I could care for myself and witness my partner, allowing us, together, to develop strategies of interdependence based in love,[11] mutual aid, and self-determination.

## III. Caring Profession

When I first encountered the idea of codependence—caring for another as an attempt at self-regulation, disguised in selflessness—I recognized patterns from my own life, and I also recognized the contours of "helping," "saving," and "-splaining" behavior that have been sketched out in the writing of anti-racist and feminist writers.[12] For all of us, the histories that inform how we perform care are personal and cultural, raced and gendered, intergenerational and embodied. In Leah Lakshmi Piepzna-Samarasinha's accounts of disability justice collectives

---

11  Although my example is a romantic relationship, Mia Mingus encourages us to think about creating access and disability justice, in any context, as a form of love. Mia Mingus, "'Disability Justice' Is Simply Another Term for Love," *Leaving Evidence* (blog), November 3, 2018, https://leavingevidence.wordpress.com/2018/11/03/disability-justice-is-simply-another-term-for-love/.

12  On saving and helping, see for example Teju Cole, "The White-Savior Industrial Complex," *The Atlantic*, March 21, 2012, https://www.theatlantic.com/international/archive/2012/03/the-white-savior-industrial-complex/254843/. On explaining and mansplaining, see Rebecca Solnit, "Men Still Explain Things to Me," *The Nation*, August 20, 2012, https://www.thenation.com/article/men-still-explain-things-me/.

working to create mutual care webs outside of the state and the family, a good part of the work involved is in getting beyond what care has always meant, to the disabled people of color involved.

> Many of us had been raised as immigrants and/or women or femmes of color to always jump up and feed people first, do all the dishes, and help without being asked, while serving ourselves last. For many of us, care had been something that was forced on us—something abusive family members or teachers or health care workers did, whether we liked it or not. Or care had been something it wasn't safe to say that we needed — because there was no care out there for us, no health care, no therapist, no parent with time, no safe parent who actually cared. Maybe as disabled people, if we wanted to have any kind of independence, we had to deny that we needed any help at all...[13]

For many members of this care collective, care is complicated by the "exploitative histories of care labor experienced by Black and brown communities" and the weaponization of care against "disabled people with few resources."[14] For some, care may feel like *what we have always done*, rather than *what we deserve*. But for me, socialized to be a nice white lady, care is complicated in other ways. I have learned that someone occupying my specific intersectional identity is deserving of care and, as such, holds power to choose which others to care for. Indeed, in cultures of white womanhood we are often taught that our compassion is, in itself, a meaningful political act, and a sufficient one.[15] And we are often taught that our compassion, knowledge, or help is needed and indeed desired by certain others.

In librarianship writ large, we have a historical legacy of this particular complication. Recent scholarship has shown how our profession is built on histories of gendered and racialized dynamics that center white women in positions of relative power and protection. Schlesselman-Tarango's article on "The Legacy of Lady Bountiful: White Women in the Library," recounts how librarianship has historically been a

---

13  Piepzna-Samarasinha, *Care Work*. 56.

14  Jina B Kim, "Disability in an Age of Fascism," *American Quarterly*, forthcoming.

15  See Lauren Berlant, "Compassion (and Withholding)," in *Compassion: The Culture and Politics of an Emotion*, ed. Lauren Berlant (New York: Routledge, 2004), 1–13; and Lauren Berlant, *The Female Complaint: The Unfinished Business of Sentimentality in American Culture* (Durham: Duke University Press, 2008).

civilizing mission, and reminds us that "it was the white female subject who was considered germane for the moralizing missionary projects meant to 'civilize' early library users."[16] Tracking the figure of "Lady Bountiful," she examines the ways in which white femininity functions to exert power in librarianship, a field which "was not only birthed in but also remains engaged in both racism and sexism."[17] Lady Bountiful shows up in the British nineteenth-century popular imagination as a figure of specifically embodied charitable benevolence. White women, the story goes, were naturally suited to roles of imperial teacher, landed benefactor, and library worker, possessing "sensitivity, kindness, sympathy" and "the ability to elevate, influence, and morally and culturally uplift."[18]

This historical figure persists. Even today, "the ideal library worker … is not simply white, female, cisgender, heterosexual, able-bodied, and middle or upper class, but also subscribes to a specific type of benevolence."[19] The lasting influence of this specifically embodied benevolence manifests in the demographics of actual library workers; it shapes a harmful preconception of "those who benefit from our services" as Other or even "deficient, inherently needy, or in need of saving;"[20] and it prefigures the library-patron relationship as one of unequal power wrapped in gestures of service.

Building on this scholarship, Ettarh's influential work on "vocational awe" gathers together lines of thought that question the ways in which care work in librarianship can occlude racialized power dynamics that place librarians (figured as nice white ladies) above the "community" that they serve and ultimately save. She reviews the historical discourses linking the library to the sanctuary, and shows that these deeply rooted archetypes not only overdetermine the ways in which we engage with patrons—limiting the possibility of a "more reciprocal, respectful, and responsible relationship"[21]—but also affect the ways

---

16  Schlesselman-Tarango, "The Legacy of Lady Bountiful: White Women in the Library." 668.

17  Schlesselman-Tarango, "The Legacy of Lady Bountiful." 668.

18  Schlesselman-Tarango, "The Legacy of Lady Bountiful." 673–74.

19  Schlesselman-Tarango, "The Legacy of Lady Bountiful." 680.

20  Schlesselman-Tarango, "The Legacy of Lady Bountiful." 681.

21  Schlesselman-Tarango, "The Legacy of Lady Bountiful." 681.

we largely do not hold our institutions accountable for conditions that might better sustain our work and minds and bodies.

The result is that care work in librarianship is, in most cases, narrowly aligned with something "we" do for "our patrons," and which ultimately accrues power back to us—not with any number of other possible configurations: our institutions caring for and sustaining a diverse staff of library workers; library patrons determining what they need from their institutions; library staff engaging in mutual aid. And the suppression of these alternate practices, in service of a single narrative of the benevolent, resilient librarian, has particular consequences for library workers who are already marginalized by ableism, white supremacy, capitalism, and heteropatriarchy.[22]

Discourses of resilience, as Christine Moeller shows in her study of precarity and professionalism, reinforce a myth of individualism and independence that compounds discrimination against "those who are already oppressed, marginalized, and/or struggling in some way."[23] The resilience narrative "'disregards the system that is making people unwell' and instead focuses on an individual-deficit model," preventing mobilization for systemic change and, in particular, putting librarians with disabilities in a tight bind.[24] Disclosing disability (in order to attain needed accommodations) carries a risk when all library staff are supposed to meet a "white, heteronormative, ableist" conception of the ideal professional.[25] Meanwhile, employees who do disclose must occupy an impossible position "between 'being disabled "enough"' to make the request in the first place, but not so disabled as to be unable to perform the 'essential functions' of the position or require accommodations that might be determined to be burdensome."[26] The result is that many library workers with disabilities do not request accommodations at all, and those who have successfully arranged accommodations are less likely to pursue professional opportunities that would

22  Patty Berne, "Disability Justice—a Working Draft," (blog), Sins Invalid, June 10, 2015, http://sinsinvalid.org/blog/disability-justice-a-working-draft-by-patty-berne.

23  Christine M. Moeller, "Disability, Identity, and Professionalism: Precarity in Librarianship," *Library Trends* 67, no. 3 (2019): 455–70, https://doi.org/10.1353/lib.2019.0006. 460.

24  Kristina Diprose, "Resilience Is Futile," *Soundings* 58 (Winter 2014): 44–56, https://doi.org/10.3898/136266215814379736, cited in Moeller, "Disability, Identity, and Professionalism." 460.

25  Moeller, "Disability, Identity, and Professionalism." 461.

26  Margaret Price, *Mad at School: Rhetorics of Mental Disability and Academic Life* (Ann Arbor: University of Michigan Press, 2011), cited in Moeller, "Disability, Identity, and Professionalism." 464.

place them with another supervisor or unit, where they'd have to start all over again.[27]

In a profession that is literally built on caring, we still have much to learn about creating conditions that support the wellbeing, and care about the survival, of many of us. We have much to learn from the practices of creating access and offering care that are happening in movements of disability justice.

## IV. Care Work

In my own story, I was able to care for my partner, learn to care for myself, and learn to care for my partner again, without losing my job or disclosing much personal information or officially requesting accommodations—even though, in this story, my partner's mental illness affected mine and both affected my ability to work. The emails I shared in the opening of this essay reflect one small way this happened. My supervisor taught me how to take a sick day. She established the norm, in our work team, of writing the words "I'm out sick today" to notify folks that she would be out. This is against the usual practice of writing words like "think I'm coming down with something" or "fighting a cold, going to stay home"—scripts that leave no room and no privacy for the vagaries of disability and caregiving. This small intervention could be considered a "micropractice" of accessibility, a concept from Margaret Price that Moeller points to when considering alternatives to resilience. Another such practice, named by Price and expanded by Moeller, is asking, What do you need? Moeller writes:

> When asked of all employees, such a question no longer requires employees with disabilities to single themselves out and accept the myriad of risks associated with disclosure, but instead assumes (correctly) that all employees have a variety of needs. For example, workplace options typically offered as accommodations, such as ergonomic office furniture, flexible schedules, regular breaks throughout the workday, minimal fluorescent lighting, the ability to occasionally work from home, an office with a door, and advance

---

27  Joanne Oud, "Systemic Workplace Barriers for Academic Librarians with Disabilities," *College & Research Libraries* 80, no. 2 (March 2019): 169–94, https://doi.org/10.5860/crl.80.2.169; Alan Roulstone and Jannine Williams, "Being Disabled, Being a Manager: 'Glass Partitions' and Conditional Identities in the Contemporary Workplace," *Disability & Society* 29, no. 1 (January 2, 2014): 16–29, https://doi.org/10.1080/09687599.2013.764280.

notice of meetings and agendas, may help those with disabilities, but these workplace adaptations could also benefit many other employees, such as primary caregivers.[28]

Yes. This micropractice is a powerful example of the shifts that can be enacted by centering rather than marginalizing disabled experience. And, more than any particular practice or micropractice, the way towards more equitable practices of care in librarianship is through the ongoing work of caring critically—attending to the "often tacit moral economies that contour our … practices"[29]—and the commitment to learning alongside those already doing the work of care and repair.

In a world where "breakdown is our epistemic and experiential reality," Mattern writes, "we really need to study … how the world gets put back together."[30] And yet, the commonly used activist refrain, "the system isn't broken, it's working exactly as it's supposed to," only underscores the fact that what "works" is designed to break some of us, and that we come to this knowledge at different times. An ethic of care can be a starting ground for learning from those for whom the world is more broken, and repairing *that* world, with those who already are. For me, this means disability justice, a practice and politics based in cross-movement solidarity and leadership by the most impacted.[31] It means, as Piepzna-Samarasinha writes, "movements that know how to bring each other food and medicine and see that care work as not a sideline to 'the real work' of activism, but the real work of activism, all while building cultures where we don't shame each other for being sick or having needs."[32]

Piepzna-Samarasinha's words, imported from the sphere of activism to that of the workplace, sound even more radical. And yet, they describe a world we can work towards. For all of its historical connections

---

28  Moeller, "Disability, Identity, and Professionalism." 467.

29  Martin, Myers, and Viseu, "The Politics of Care in Technoscience."

30  Mattern, "Maintenance and Care."

31  Berne, "Disability Justice—a Working Draft."

32  Leah Lakshmi Piepzna-Samarasinha, "To Survive the Trumpocalypse, We Need Wild Disability Justice Dreams," *Truthout*, May 20, 2018, https://truthout.org/articles/to-survive-the-trumpocalypse-we-need-wild-disability-justice-dreams/.

to the sanctuary, the library will not save us. No institution will.[33] And yet, we as library workers can continue to transform the institution, to infuse it with an "intersectional feminism that can grapple with the constellations of power manifest in concatenations of capitalism, colonialism, race, class, ability, and gender."[34] And we can do this as we also create work cultures, which exceed the institution, where we care for each other. In my own work to unlearn harmful care practices and embody more liberatory ones, I've found that this path is intentional, improvisational, radical, and lifelong. It is informed by the ethic and commitment, practiced by disability justice activists, of not leaving each other behind.[35]

## Acknowledgements

Writing this essay was possible only with the support of many people. Thank you to Ann Cvetkovich for talking about mental illness and feeling bad in academic spaces. Thanks to Gretchen Phillips for talking to me about recovery. Thanks to Meghan Sitar for being that supervisor. Thanks to Megan Keene for witnessing me write honestly about myself. Thanks to Kei Kaimana for saying yes. Thanks to my editors Miranda Dube and Carrie Wade for reading multiple versions of this work.

---

### *Bibliography*

Bartram, Erin. "The Sublimated Grief of the Left Behind." *Doomed to Distraction* (blog), February 11, 2018. http://erinbartram.com/uncategorized/the-sublimated-grief-of-the-left-behind/.

Berlant, Lauren Gail. *The Female Complaint: The Unfinished Business of Sentimentality in American Culture.* Durham: Duke University Press, 2008. http://0-dx.doi.org.oasis.unisa.ac.za/10.1215/9780822389163.

---

33  This phrase is inspired by Gumbs, "The Shape of My Impact": "The university was not created to save my life. The university is not about the preservation of a bright brown body. The university will use me alive and use me dead. The university does not intend to love me. The university does not know how to love me. The university in fact, does not love me. But the universe does."

34  Martin, Myers, and Viseu, "The Politics of Care in Technoscience."

35  Berne, "Disability Justice—a Working Draft."

Berlant, Lauren. "Compassion (and Withholding)." In *Compassion: The Culture and Politics of an Emotion*, edited by Lauren Berlant, 1–13. New York: Routledge, 2004.

Berne, Patty. "Disability Justice—a Working Draft." Blog. Sins Invalid, June 10, 2015. http://sinsinvalid.org/blog/disability-justice-a-working-draft-by-patty-berne.

Childress, Herb. "This Is How You Kill a Profession." The Chronicle of Higher Education, March 27, 2019. https://www.chronicle.com/interactives/2019-03-27-childress.

Clare, Eli. *Brilliant Imperfection: Grappling with Cure.* Durham: Duke University Press, 2017.

Cole, Teju. "The White-Savior Industrial Complex." The Atlantic, March 21, 2012. https://www.theatlantic.com/international/archive/2012/03/the-white-savior-industrial-complex/254843/.

Cvetkovich, Ann. *Depression : A Public Feeling.* Durham, NC: Duke University Press, 2012.

Davis, Barbara Hillyer. "Women, Disability, and Feminism: Notes toward a New Theory." *Frontiers: A Journal of Women Studies* 8, no. 1 (1984): 1–5.

Diprose, Kristina. "Resilience Is Futile." *Soundings: A Journal of Politics and Culture* 58 (Winter 2014): 44–56. https://doi.org/10.3898/136266215814379736.

Ettarh, Fobazi. "Vocational Awe and Librarianship: The Lies We Tell Ourselves." *In the Library with the Lead Pipe*, January 10, 2018. http://www.inthelibrarywiththeleadpipe.org/2018/vocational-awe/#identifier_19_8690.

Gumbs, Alexis Pauline. "The Shape of My Impact." *Feminist Wire* (blog), October 29, 2012. https://thefeministwire.com/2012/10/the-shape-of-my-impact/.

Hsu, Hua. "Affect Theory and the New Age of Anxiety." *The New Yorker*, March 18, 2019. https://www.newyorker.com/magazine/2019/03/25/affect-theory-and-the-new-age-of-anxiety.

Jackson, Steven J. "Rethinking Repair." In *Media Technologies*, edited by Tarleton Gillespie, Pablo J. Boczkowski, and Kirsten A. Foot, 221–40. The MIT Press, 2014. https://doi.org/10.7551/mitpress/9780262525374.003.0011.

Kim, Eunjung. *Curative Violence : Rehabilitating Disability, Gender, and Sexuality in Modern Korea.* Durham: Duke University Press, 2017.

Kim, Jina B. "Disability in an Age of Fascism." *American Quarterly*, forthcoming.

Kittay, Eva Feder. *Love's Labor : Essays on Women, Equality, and Dependency.* Thinking Gender. New York: Routledge, 1999.

Mattern, Shannon. "Maintenance and Care." *Places Journal*, November 20, 2018. https://doi.org/10.22269/181120.

Martin, Aryn, Natasha Myers, and Ana Viseu. "The Politics of Care in Technoscience." *Social Studies of Science* 45, no. 5 (October 2015): 625–41. https://doi.org/10.1177/0306312715602073.

McGuire, Anne. *War on Autism : On the Cultural Logic of Normative Violence.* Ann Arbor: University of Michigan Press, 2016.

Mingus, Mia. "'Disability Justice' Is Simply Another Term for Love." *Leaving Evidence* (blog), November 3, 2018. https://leavingevidence.wordpress.com/2018/11/03/disability-justice-is-simply-another-term-for-love/.

Moeller, Christine M. "Disability, Identity, and Professionalism: Precarity in Librarianship." *Library Trends* 67, no. 3 (May 8, 2019): 455–70. https://doi.org/10.1353/lib.2019.0006.

Oud, Joanne. "Systemic Workplace Barriers for Academic Librarians with Disabilities." *College & Research Libraries* 80, no. 2 (March 2019): 169–94. https://doi.org/10.5860/crl.80.2.169.

Piepzna-Samarasinha, Leah Lakshmi. *Care Work : Dreaming Disability Justice.* Vancouver: Arsenal Pulp Press, 2018.

Piepzna-Samarasinha, Leah Lakshmi. "To Survive the Trumpocalypse, We Need Wild Disability Justice Dreams." *Truthout*, May 20, 2018. https://truthout.org/articles/to-survive-the-trumpocalypse-we-need-wild-disability-justice-dreams/.

Price, Margaret. *Mad at School: Rhetorics of Mental Disability and Academic Life.* Ann Arbor: University of Michigan Press, 2011.

Puig de la Bellacasa, María. *Matters of Care: Speculative Ethics in More than Human Worlds.* Minneapolis: University of Minnesota Press, 2017.

Roulstone, Alan, and Jannine Williams. "Being Disabled, Being a Manager: 'Glass Partitions' and Conditional Identities in the Contemporary Workplace." *Disability & Society* 29, no. 1 (January 2, 2014): 16–29. https://doi.org/10.1080/09687599.2013.764280.

Russell, Andy, Jessica Meyerson, and Lee Vinsel. The Maintainers, n.d. http://themaintainers.org/.

Schlesselman-Tarango, Gina. "The Legacy of Lady Bountiful: White Women in the Library." *Library Trends* 64, no. 4 (Spring 2016): 667–86.

Schuman, Rebecca. "Thesis Hatement." *Slate*, April 5, 2013. http://www.slate.com/articles/life/culturebox/2013/04/there_are_no_academic_jobs_and_getting_a_ph_d_will_make_you_into_a_horrible.html.

Solnit, Rebecca. "Men Still Explain Things to Me." The Nation, August 20, 2012. https://www.thenation.com/article/men-still-explain-things-me/.

Wendell, Susan. "Toward a Feminist Theory of Disability." *Hypatia* 4, no. 2 (1989): 104–124.

# Lean on Me: Support and Shared Experience in the Anxious Workplace

**Marie Campbell, Clayton Hume, Max Powers, and Ann Sen**

We are four librarians working together at a community college in the Midwestern United States; the four of us are the only full-time, non-administrative employees at our library. We are also four human beings who have significant personal experience with mental disorders, including generalized anxiety disorder, social anxiety, depression, bipolar II, and PTSD. We wanted to explore how these two realities intertwine–how our mental disorders affect our work in libraries, and vice versa. We were especially interested in how our ostensibly similar experiences differed from or corresponded with each other, and how sharing these circumstances with each other—both by experiencing them together and by discussing them together—affected how we perceived them.

## Methodology

There are four of us; all four of us were simultaneously observers and participants in a qualitative exploration of our experiences with mental disorders in the library. This process was largely informal and highly iterative. We started with unstructured personal writing, so each of us individually could start to see what we were most invested in discussing. After sharing our initial writings with each other, we drafted a list of specific questions related to our work experiences that we wanted to answer. Several rounds of writing, discussion, and re-writing occurred until we identified our most essential questions and developed robust individual responses to each. We then compared our responses to look for common themes, points of difference, and connections to the literature; a summary of those themes and differences constitutes this autoethnography.

It may be important for context to know that we are all white, cis-gendered women, we all hold an MLIS, and we all work full-time. Our experiences reflect the privileges and pitfalls that these circumstances afford.

## Management

Our collective experience with management is what brought us to examine the library work/mental disorder overlap in the first place, and has been decidedly damaging to our mental health as a whole. It was the most persistent thread we uncovered during our inquiry. A study by Harris, citing Tepper, used eleven items of a fifteen-item scale that measure abusive supervision.[1] The abusive actions we have experienced at our library are often more underhanded and not as in your face, but certainly would be measurable with the same response scale.

Abusive supervisory practices such as negligence, stonewalling, and bullying have impacted the job performance of all four of us. According to Harris, who cites Bies, examples of supervisory abuse can also include "public criticism, rudeness, breaking promises, inconsiderate actions, and the silent treatment."[2] Since all of the librarians have experienced these and additional methods of abuse, daily functions such as overall job performance have been critically impaired. Harris goes on to examine Hobfoll's COR theory (conservation of resources) which defines four ways in which job performance is interrupted due to abusive supervisory practices. These include threats of resource loss, actual resource loss, employees feeling like the work expected of them exceeds the resources available, and the idea that what employees put into their work does not equal what is returned to them. Harris also discusses the concept of "managing upwards," which is where, along with an abusive supervisor, comes the idea that employees are

---

1   Kenneth J. Harris, K. Michele Kacmar, and Suzanne Zivnuskac, "An Investigation of Abusive Supervision as a Predictor of Performance and the Meaning of Work as a Moderator of the Relationship," *The Leadership Quarterly* 18, no. 3 (June 2007): 252–63, https://doi.org/10.1016/j.leaqua.2007.03.007.

2   Harris, Kacmar, and Zivnuskac., "An Investigation of Abusive Supervision," 253.

responsible for the work of someone else (their superior) instead of or in addition to doing their own work.[3] We have all certainly been "managing upwards" to compensate for our absent and negligent boss, which is yet another toll on the emotional and mental resources we could be using to address our mental disorders.

According to an article by Marianne Ryan, emotional bullying can be described as something that can be direct or indirect and includes things like non-verbal cues. Also, people feel left out of conversations or decisions, stonewalling, or even making up the rules as they go along.[4] At our institution, some librarians get preferential treatment, some get the silent treatment. Regardless of favoritism, ideas are hijacked, people are cornered, and unnecessary measures are taken in order to avoid conflict or bullying. This has brought about feelings of being invisible or professionally inadequate among all of us.

Another way management style affects us is our director's laissez-faire way of working with us. According to Awan citing Bittel, this style of manager has little to no interaction with employees and gives no direction to others.[5] This not only increases our anxiety about what it is we should be doing with our work, it also makes us feel like the work we are doing is not worthwhile which in turn increases our depression.

## Instruction

Among the four librarians, three of us actively participate in library instruction in classroom settings. While recognizing that teaching comes in a variety of forms including in-class instruction, research appointments, and reference questions, we all differ in opinion regarding which contexts bring about the most anxiety.

One librarian reported that library instruction makes her so nervous, she cries in her office prior to sessions and has trouble breathing. Once in a classroom, her anxiety increases as she is terrified that people will think she is "stupid" or an imposter. According to Clark, Vardeman, and

---

3   Harris, Kacmar, and Zivnuskac., "An Investigation of Abusive Supervision," 253.

4   Marianne Ryan, "Besting the Workplace Bully," *Reference & User Services Quarterly* 55, no. 4 (Summer 2016): 267–69.

5   Muhammad Rafiq Awan and Khalid Mahmood, "Relationship among Leadership Style, Organizational Culture and Employee Commitment in University Libraries," *Library Management* 31, no. 4/5 (January 1, 2010): 253–66, https://doi.org/10.1108/01435121011046326.

Barba, imposter phenomenon is a noticeable anxiety which is brought on by feelings of inadequacy and involves being scared that others will recognize this and expose the con artist for who they truly are.[6] For our librarian, no amount of preparation alters this terror. She has tested a few different methods of either over-preparation or going into the classroom with not much preparation and letting the class determine where she will go, and with all methods tested, it yields the same results.

Another librarian has the opposite feelings on classroom instruction and is very comfortable in the classroom setting; her anxiety only comes into play after the instruction session. She is unable to stop obsessively ruminating about the session and it makes her feel "markedly depressed afterwards if [she feels] it didn't go well."

In addition to our differing issues within the classroom itself, management practices again contribute greatly to our experience of anxiety and depression, mostly through lack of involvement from our director. They do not supervise our teaching, and provide no guidelines or feedback on our instruction. Our director seems to have no expectations for instruction except to maintain or increase the number of sessions, but "shoots down" any ideas suggested for faculty outreach. Disagreements and misunderstandings with faculty regarding our instructional duties are left up to us to resolve individually, with no official instruction policy documents or statements to back us up—interactions that are difficult to manage when experiencing the imposter phenomenon or PTSD-related anxiety. Our director will generally not inquire about classroom instruction until information is needed regarding statistics or other instruction-related reports for their own meetings and committee work. On multiple occasions, we have been asked to give our director information regarding our instruction work, only to then have this information presented to administrators as if it were our director's accomplishment. The lack of credit we receive for our work is often depressing and limits our motivation to continue. Also, while it is stated to us that instruction sessions should be at the top priority when scheduling our time, our instructional schedule is often overlooked by our director, and additional, conflicting events they add to our calendars will then become our problem to resolve. The overall

---

6   Melanie Clark, Kimberly Vardeman, and Shelley Barba, "Perceived Inadequacy: A Study of the Imposter Phenomenon among College and Research Librarians," *College & Research Libraries* 75, no. 3 (2014), https://doi.org/10.5860/crl12-423.

lack of authentic interest and repeated self-serving behavior from our director regarding the most important of our job duties is frustrating and demoralizing.

## Reference/Public Service

We were especially interested to explore the intersection of reference work with mental disorders, since studies we reviewed from the literature, when they directly addressed anxiety of individual librarians, focused more on classroom teaching than other forms of interaction with patrons.[7] When "anxiety" at the reference desk was addressed, we found that clinical anxiety experienced by librarians was not the topic of discussion.[8]

Of the four of us, three are regularly scheduled for reference duties. This includes staffing the walk-up reference desk and pre-scheduled research appointments. Notably, one of us, who experiences significant anxiety in connection with classroom instruction sessions, did not report any similar feelings associated with the reference desk. While reference is still a form of teaching, the informality of reference interactions frees her from the hierarchical structure and public speaking aspects of the classroom and provokes no distress. For the remaining two, the reference desk is often a source of conflict due to mental disorders. The second of our reference trio reports feeling "too vulnerable" interacting on the desk with an unknown and unpredictable public, after a lifetime of abusive relationships. Reference interactions also demand a great deal of emotional caretaking from the librarian on behalf of the patron.[9] A spate of personal losses have exacerbated existing depression for this librarian and made it difficult to provide caregiving for herself, "let alone grumpy strangers." The remaining librarian with public service responsibilities finds the desk similarly stressful. In addition to the basic fear of scrutiny that accompanies social anxiety, a previous layoff due to budget cuts has led to

---

7   Kaetrena D. Davis, "The Academic Librarian as Instructor," *College & Undergraduate Libraries* 14, no. 2 (2007): 77–101, https://doi.org/10.1300/ J106v14n02_06.

8   C. Paul Vincent, "The Profession's Growing Anxiety," *Library Journal*, March 1, 1989; Anne Powers, "'Librarian's Anxiety'? How Community College Librarians Feel About Their Reference Desk Service," *Community & Junior College Libraries* 16, no. 1 (2010): 54–70.

9   Celia Emmelhainz, Erin Pappas, and Maura Seale, "Behavioral Expectations for the Mommy Librarian: The Successful Reference Transaction as Emotional Labor," in *The Feminist Reference Desk: Concepts, Critiques, and Conversations* (Sacramento: Library Juice Press, 2017).

a deep fear of again being found "redundant," which manifests as an effort to always be seen working intently on other tasks at the desk, between interactions with patrons. This anxiety and focus on other work makes it difficult to drop everything and fully shift focus to patrons when they arrive, and (similar to her coworker) leads to a struggle to serve the emotional needs of those patrons while also keeping her own anxiety under control.

These struggles disappear for the third librarian within the context of reference appointments, which are scheduled by students at least an hour in advance via an online system. Knowing exactly when and where the interaction will take place—usually in a room or office away from the very visible desk—allows for time to prepare and be fully present in the interaction. This librarian believes that her decade spent in therapy, which she would probably not have undergone if she had not had significant problems with anxiety and depression, has improved her ability to connect with students during research appointments. The clarity of communication that therapy demands seems to transfer well to these conditions. In her words, "sitting in a room and working through a problem through careful listening...is something I have a lot of experience with." In contrast, the first librarian, who finds the reference desk freeing, finds the research appointment to be slightly stultifying. This is due mostly, again, to managing patron expectations. In this librarian's experience, students who drop in often have lower expectations for the interaction which are easier to meet or exceed. In research appointments, they are often visiting the library at the behest of their instructor, and believe that they should be able to walk away "with their A in hand." In this way research appointments provoke anxiety for her due to unrealistic expectations and the frustration these often provoke in students. Her anxieties about reference desk instruction align with those discussed by Powers, who found many librarian survey respondents to be disheartened by things such as not having an adequate amount of time to assist students, and feeling like students are looking at reference services as something that will just fill a requirement for a class.[10]

The negligent tendencies of management also markedly impacts reference desk service. Our director is theoretically responsible for

---

10   Powers, "'Librarian's Anxiety'? How Community College Librarians Feel About Their Reference Desk Service."

covering a share of reference desk and research appointment shifts, just as the librarians are, but the director is also responsible for deciding the master schedule of those shifts. During the years that the four of us have been employed here, we have seen the director's shifts on the reference desk shrink steadily down to zero hours. Neither the total hours of coverage each week nor the number of librarians employed here has changed, so librarians spend more time on the desk each week as a result. That means more cumulative time spent experiencing the attendant anxieties of reference service. The director schedules themselves for research appointment shifts, but is prone to leaving early and deferring responsibility for any scheduled appointments to whichever librarian is readily visible, often as the director is walking out the door. The last-minute nature of this transfer means that the anxiety-relieving preparation time usually enjoyed by one librarian cannot be deployed by her; other librarians find themselves stressed by having to defer their other duties in order to cover appointments for the absent director.

## Technical Services

Only one of the four of us has responsibilities within technical services. Working in technical services does reduce her anxiety regarding working with the unpredictable public; dealing primarily with physical resources creates a safe environment that can seem ideal for those with social anxiety. Librarians dealing with these issues may gravitate toward this type of work. However, it does not solve the problem of working with unstable coworkers.

In the case of our library, this librarian is the only full-time employee working in technical services and therefore reports directly to the library director. Unfortunately, interactions involving this abusive individual are unpredictable and disrupt the otherwise smooth functioning of the department. This chaotic system can be very anxiety inducing and creates the desire to avoid all interactions which in turn causes the system to break down further.

While this librarian feels competent in her role in technical services, what was once an ideal working environment away from the general public has become highly anxiety-inducing to the point that she now suffers from depression "on a daily basis." Reluctantly, seeking another employment situation seems to be the only solution to remedy her current heightened struggle with her mental disorders.

## Student Workers

At our institution, all student workers (all of whom are part-time) are hired, trained, and report to the library director, and are at no point specifically instructed to report to or follow instructions from other full-time staff. However, this director, as noted previously, is chronically absent. Librarians are expected to, as part of their job descriptions, supervise the overall functioning of the combined service desk where both they and the student workers do their work, though they have no official authority. Our technical services librarian, while not scheduled to staff the desk, is the expert on our ILMS, and is often called on to instruct student workers in its functioning. Thus, student worker interactions cause increased anxiety; firstly, from being a basic social interaction, but also from the ambiguity of the relationship between the librarians and student workers. This creates an awkwardness when they need to be corrected or trained, their "official" boss is not present to do so, and therefore a librarian takes responsibility for it. The student workers question whether or not they need to listen to other staff members or just the director, and training and behavioral issues continue. Student workers also come with a variety of personalities that when thrown into the mix with these sometimes tense interactions create a number of anxiety-inducing situations.

## Campus Service/Meetings/Committees

All four librarians experience anxiety when engaging in meetings, especially those with employees of our institution from outside of the library. Our director prefers our library as an entity to remain independent and actively works to limit our involvement outside the library, so there are few people in other departments with whom we have significant professional relationships. In addition, our director is chronically absent from the running of the library, and negligent in all their duties. Because of this, our director is typically not aware of what is going on in the library yet is always physically present at meetings with those outside of the library to maintain a facade of diligence. This leaves the rest of us in the precarious position of covering for their lack of knowledge of our work when we do interface with administration and faculty, a position which causes us all a great deal of anxiety and resentment.

In addition to our shared anxiety as a result of our director's selective presence at meetings, our individual anxieties tend to manifest in

the setting of meetings as well. One of us has purposely chosen to focus on technical services to avoid interacting with the public and colleagues any more than necessary, so being required to attend meetings brings her outside of this comfort zone she has created to manage
her anxiety. Another one of us often manages her anxiety by spending a significant amount of time preparing for work duties. The unpredictable, often last-minute nature of meetings means that this coping
mechanism cannot be employed and the mere anticipation of unpredictable work situations causes a great deal of anxiety. One of us has
a fear of authority which increases when members of the upper administration at the college are present at meetings. These various circumstances that seem to converge in a meeting setting lead us to face
great difficulty in speaking up during meetings.

## Outreach

Three of our four librarians have "liaison responsibilities and library
promotion" listed in our job descriptions. Outreach to faculty and staff
is thus a shared responsibility amongst us. However, despite this mention of "liaison responsibilities," there is no formal liaison structure in
place. There is also no guidance for outreach from upper administration, a lack which we find is amplified by our director's efforts to isolate us. We found that this not only negatively impacts our outreach
efforts, but the intensity of our mental disorders as we pursue them.
Social anxiety and the imposter phenomenon are both exacerbated by
this sort of environment. Interfacing with teaching faculty, especially,
triggers imposter phenomenon-related anxiety for one of us. The prevailing advice for developing better campus relationships—cold-call-
ing people, going to campus events (often, it is implied, alone), asking
to attend or speak at departmental meetings—represent significant
challenges for people suffering from social anxiety, as well. We discovered that in the face of these challenges, we collectively practice
avoidance. Since there is no input from anyone above us about outreach goals, our avoidance goes unnoticed. Our outreach efforts are
not as robust, as a result.

## Flexibility of Schedule/Arrangement

At our academic library we are afforded a degree of flexibility in our
schedules that may not be present in other jobs in the library world.
Since we do not have a time clock and are salaried, we do not have

anyone paying attention to when we come and go. In addition to this inherent flexibility, our director is chronically absent, often only coming to work one or two days a week, so there is even less oversight than would be typical of a flexible academic position. This has its benefits, as our leave is generous and makes allowances for things like bereavement or gaps in childcare. However, there is a downside to this flexibility. With no one paying attention to our work patterns, there is no one to notice when we become chronically late or when the number of days of work that we are missing is increasing. What would be a cause for concern for supervisors in a more typical work setting goes unnoticed in our case, and when we are struggling with depression or anxiety, we are often left to manage it alone. In addition to this, the combination of a lack of structure and a director who takes egregious advantage of this flexibility makes it difficult to keep reasonable standards in perspective for the rest of us. Our director tends to enforce standards arbitrarily, based on their fondness for individual staff members or their moods, leaving us all with the anxiety of not knowing whether a behavior—such as using leave time—is acceptable from one day to another.

## Benefits

Our access to mental health treatment options is completely dependent on the benefits afforded us from our jobs. Our health insurance makes generous allowances for mental health treatment, which allows all of us to participate in therapy and, when needed, medication to manage our mental disorders. However, many aspects of our jobs exacerbate our anxiety, so it is not necessarily purely beneficial. At least one of us has had to choose between library jobs based on their coverage of mental health treatment. While there is a faculty union at our current institution, we are considered staff, and there is no staff union. Our yearly cost of living raises are designed to match those negotiated for faculty by their union, but we have no guarantee for these raises. Benefits such as parental leave have been negotiated for faculty through their union, while staff has to rely on what administration deems fair for us individually. One of us has been through a pregnancy and unpaid maternity leave during our time at our library, which is an immense financial struggle. Finances are a major anxiety trigger for at least one of us, so this lack of negotiating power and uncertainty in our pay and benefits from year to year tends to cause significant anxiety.

## Abusive relationships

While all four of us have experienced traumas in our past, two of us have experienced varying levels of abusive relationships that have affected our personal and professional lives. After discussing several things that impacted our careers in the past, we realized that we have had similar events keeping us from performing at our optimum levels. According to a study by Swanberg, victims of abuse feel "too psychologically distressed", "too depressed", or "too anxious" to be efficient at their places of employment.[11]

An area of anxiety affecting one librarian stems from her history of abuse from her father and former spouse. Her history prevented her from being able to initiate conversations with employers. Additionally, it caused her anxiety to increase at work specifically when working with the public and experiencing feelings of vulnerability. Another librarian reported her personal experiences with abuse stating "the idea of shame was my main reason for never discussing it at the workplace. I did not want anyone to know that the events were happening because I was morbidly embarrassed and ashamed that I had allowed this to happen…. and not just once, but multiple times!" Swanberg also states that shame is among the three reasons women did not share their home environment with their co-workers, the other two including the fear of losing their position, and having the desire to be able to cope with their life on their own terms. Swanberg also stated that in a study by Riger, 85% of women had ended up missing work due to their abuse at home.[12] From everything we have discussed among the two of us who have experienced abuse, we have both missed work due to abuse for one reason or another.

## Grief

Several of us have had to deal with significant grief while working at the library, with losses ranging from beloved pets to parents. While we are allowed bereavement leave, the effects of grief far outlast the few days off to deal with the immediate aftermath of a loss. Returning to

---

11   Jennifer E. Swanberg and T. K. Logan, "Domestic Violence and Employment: A Qualitative Study," *Journal of Occupational Health Psychology* 10, no. 1 (January 2005): 3–17, https://doi.org/10.1037/1076-8998.10.1.3.

12   Swanberg and Logan, "Domestic Violence and Employment," 3

work just a few short days after a monumental personal loss results in significant anxiety in itself. Add to that the nature of public-facing librarianship, which is highly focused on attending to the needs of others, and the result is emotional fatigue. Often the grief is at the forefront of the mind, and otherwise innocuous comments can trigger waves of sadness and anxiety. This can lead those of us dealing with grief to isolate and avoid interacting with colleagues and patrons. For at least one of us, the acute depression and increased anxiety that followed the death of a family member lasted nearly a year, making regular job duties difficult and taking on new responsibilities an overwhelming prospect.

## Friendship

Bonding with coworkers over a shared stressor can result in a working relationship that develops into an ongoing friendship. The four of us commiserate frequently over our current working conditions and it has been a help to us to know that we are not alone. Our discussions serve as a "tiny tap on a giant barrel of stress that [we] can let a little pour out of as needed." Stressful situations wherein it is difficult to know "which way is up" can be put into perspective, and a better understanding of the factors at play can make an untenable situation bearable. In our case, dealing with the same library director's unpredictability, although it affects us all differently and to varying degrees, has resulted in a shared comradery. The longest-employed among us has maintained friendships with several librarians previously employed at our institution and enjoys a similar comradery with them, based on their corresponding experiences working here under our director. The pervasive problem of low morale is mitigated, to at least a small extent, by having "solidarity with coworkers" around it.

We all struggled with our mental disorders before we started working in libraries, and certainly before working in this library specifically. We have many struggles that aren't directly related to our library work. And yet, our shared library workplace has become a site for sharing our experiences with those struggles as well. Our discussions about management served as a bridge to discussing our mental disorders in general, and these discussions have also been an enormous source of support for us. We understand each other's needs and are willing to "help each other and cover for each other" when any one of us needs to take time off to go to therapy or discuss something that "may not seem like a big deal" to someone who doesn't share our mental disorders. For at least one of us, this is happily not unique to this one workplace; in all previous library jobs, she has leaned on the people she deemed her "Problems Friends," or friends who "have similar struggles with anxiety and depression" and who she feels "safe" talking to. All four of us are "Problems Friends" here. We have managed to create, at least on a micro level, the "environments of inclusion" that Burns and Green suggest as a remedy for the stigma we might feel disclosing our mental disorders elsewhere.[13]

## Conclusion

The experience of writing this chapter has revealed to us the extent of the similarities in our experience of mental disorders in the work place, as well as leading us to make adjustments in our work and personal lives. We discovered that workplace triggers for symptoms of our disorders are largely the same—and are focused on interpersonal interaction, especially with the public and authority figures—while our experience of those disorders can differ in very interesting ways. The variety of ways we experience teaching and reference-related anxiety was intriguing to us, as well as the unique (among us) experience of our technical services librarian interacting with students.

While a range of situations exacerbating our mental disorders were discussed here, the common thread seems to be ineffective management. The majority of these situations were not engineered by our director, but every single one of them was made worse by abuse and an acute lack of leadership. However, this constant negative presence in the workplace has had the unexpected benefit of strengthening our bond. Without this shared challenge, we might have remained casual colleagues; with it, we are friends.

Reflecting on these phenomena has also led to changes in the way they play out for us. One librarian reports that since writing this chapter, she no longer has the same heightened amount of anxiety associated with library instruction. It has not been resolved completely by any means, but she feels "like she can cope better" and is no longer "crying in [her] office before every class." Another has turned the tide

---

13  Erin Burns and Kristin E.C. Green, "Academic Librarians' Experiences and Perceptions on Mental Illness Stigma and the Workplace," *College & Research Libraries [Online]* 80, no. 5 (July 11, 2019), https://doi.org/10.5860/crl.80.5.638.

by taking librarian concerns regarding management to a person in an appropriate leadership position, despite persistent fears of retaliation. Yet another of us, having heightened awareness of her classroom experience while working on this chapter, realized that her "comfort" in the classroom is probably actually just a temporary suppression of social anxiety symptoms, and the obsessive overthinking that follows them occurs "when [she] can no longer suppress it."

Delving into such personal matters as our histories of mental disorders, and then sharing them so plainly with each other, has been a painful and vulnerable process. We would not have attempted it if we were not all also receiving professional mental health treatment, and even with that, it remains to be seen if it will ultimately turn out to have been "a good idea." Despite the painful aspects, however, right now we view the process as a positive one. Being able to discuss these issues together has brought about a more cohesive working environment, at least for the four of us. The nascent friendships we discussed feel "solidified" through this venture. While the need for change remains with our management situation, those changes appear to be on the horizon. With continued support of each other while in this position, and while we all pursue future working endeavors, we will always have this shared experience which foremost helped us to survive, but also to grow as individuals and as information professionals.

## Bibliography

Awan, Muhammad Rafiq, and Khalid Mahmood. "Relationship among Leadership Style, Organizational Culture and Employee Commitment in University Libraries." *Library Management* 31, no. 4/5 (January 1, 2010): 253–66. https://doi.org/10.1108/01435121011046326.

Burns, Erin, and Kristin E.C. Green. "Academic Librarians' Experiences and Perceptions on Mental Illness Stigma and the Workplace." *College & Research Libraries [Online]* 80, no. 5 (July 11, 2019). https://doi.org/10.5860/crl.80.5.638.

Clark, Melanie, Kimberly Vardeman, and Shelley Barba. "Perceived Inadequacy: A Study of the Imposter Phenomenon among College and Research Librarians." *College & Research Libraries* 75, no. 3 (2014). https://doi.org/10.5860/crl12-423.

Davis, Kaetrena D. "The Academic Librarian as Instructor." *College & Undergraduate Libraries* 14, no. 2 (2007): 77–101. https://doi.org/10.1300/ J106v14n02_06.

Emmelhainz, Celia, Erin Pappas, and Maura Seale. "Behavioral Expectations for the Mommy Librarian: The Successful Reference Transaction as Emotional Labor." In *The Feminist Reference Desk: Concepts, Critiques, and Conversations.* Sacramento: Library Juice Press, 2017.

Harris, Kenneth J., K. Michele Kacmar, and Suzanne Zivnuskac. "An Investigation of Abusive Supervision as a Predictor of Performance and the Meaning of Work as a Moderator of the Relationship." *The Leadership Quarterly* 18, no. 3 (June 2007): 252–63. https://doi.org/10.1016/j.leaqua.2007.03.007.

Powers, Anne. "'Librarian's Anxiety'? How Community College Librarians Feel About Their Reference Desk Service." *Community & Junior College Libraries* 16, no. 1 (2010): 54–70.

Ryan, Marianne. "Besting the Workplace Bully." *Reference & User Services Quarterly* 55, no. 4 (Summer 2016): 267–69.

Swanberg, Jennifer E., and T. K. Logan. "Domestic Violence and Employment: A Qualitative Study." *Journal of Occupational Health Psychology* 10, no. 1 (January 2005): 3–17. https://doi.org/10.1037/1076-8998.10.1.3.

Vincent, C. Paul. "The Profession's Growing Anxiety." *Library Journal,* March 1, 1989.

## *Works Consulted*

Adebayo, Oyeronke, Chidi Deborah Segun-Adeniran, Michael Opeoluwa Fagbohun, and Odaro Osayande. "Investigating Occupational Burnout in Library Personnel." *Library Philosophy and Practice (e-Journal),* 2018.

Aluri, Rao, and Mary Reichel. "Performance Evaluation: A Deadly Disease?" *The Journal of Academic Librarianship* 20, no. 3 (June 1994): 145–55. https://doi.org/10.1016/0099-1333(94)90008-6.

Bianchi, Renzo, Irvin Sam Schofield, Pierre Vandel, and Eric Laurent. "On the Depressive Nature of the 'Burnout Syndrome': A Clarification." *European Psychiatry* 41 (2017): 109–10.

Bianchi, Renzo, Irvin Sam Schonfeld, and Eric Laurent. "Burnout–Depression Overlap: A Review." *Clinical Psychology Review* 36 (March 2015): 28–41.

Bunge, Charles. "Stress in the Library." *Library Journal* 112, no. 15 (September 15, 1987): 47–51.

Ciolacu, Mihai Valentin. "Emotional Regulation Strategies Proposed to Librarians to Reduce Emotional Burnout." *Romanian Journal of Experimental Applied Psychology* 6, no. 2 (May2015): 67–75.

Davis Kendrick, Kaetrena. "The Low Morale Experience of Academic Librarians: A Phenomenological Study." *Journal of Library Administration* 0 (2017): 1–33. https://doi.org/10.1080/01930826.2017.1368325.

Deibel, Kate, Violet Fox, Nicole Gustavsen, Kelly McElroy, Abigail Phillips, and Annie Pho, eds. *Reserve and Renew: The LIS Mental Health Zine.* Vol. 1. United States, 2018.

Ettarh, Fobazi. "Vocational Awe and Librarianship: The Lies We Tell Ourselves." *In The Library With The Lead Pipe*, January 10, 2018. http://www.inthelibrarywiththeleadpipe.org/2018/vocational-awe/.

Evans, Teresa M., Lindsay Bira, Jazmin Beltran Gastelum, L Todd Weiss, and Nathan L Vanderford. "Evidence for a Mental Health Crisis in Graduate Education." *Nature Biotechnology* 36, no. 3 (March 6, 2018): 282–84.

Gibson-Beverly, Gina, and Jonathan P. Schwartz. "Attachment, Entitlement, and the Impostor Phenomenon in Female Graduate Students." *Journal of College Counseling* 11, no. 2 (Fall 2018): 119–32.

Lacey, Sajni, and Melanie Parlette-Stewart. "Jumping into the Deep: Imposter Syndrome, Defining Success, and the New Librarian." *Partnership: The Canadian Journal of Library and Information Practice and Research* 12, no. 1 (2017): 1–15.

Matteson, Miriam L., Sharon Chittock, and David Mease. "In Their Own Words: Stories of Emotional Labor from the Library Workforce." *Library Quarterly: Information, Community, Policy* 85, no. 1 (2015): 85–105. https://doi.org/10.1086/679027.

Pho, Annie, Abigail Phillips, Marisol Moreno Ortiz, Kelly McElroy, Nicole Gustavsen, Violet Fox, and Kate Deibel, eds. *Reserve and Renew Issue 2: It Came From the Brain!* Vol. 2. United States, 2019.

Roose, Tina. "Stress at the Reference Desk." *Library Journal* 114, no. 14 (September 1, 1989): 166–67.

Ryan, Marianne. "Besting the Workplace Bully." *Reference & User Services Quarterly* 55, no. 4 (Summer 2016): 267–69.

Salyers, Michelle P., Melanie A. Watkins, Amber Painter, Eric A. Snajdr, Lauren O. Gilmer, Jennifer M. Garabrant, and Nancy H. Henry. "Predictors of Burnout in Public Library Employees." *Journal of Librarianship and Information Science* 00, no. 0 (February 21, 2018): 1–10. https://doi.org/10.1177/0961000618759415.

Sheesley, Deborah F. "Burnout and the Academic Teaching Librarian: An Examination of the Problem and Suggested Solutions." *Journal of Academic Librarianship* 27, no. 6 (2001): 447–51. https://doi.org/10.1016/S0099-1333(01)00264-6.

Shupe, Ellen I., Stephanie K. Wambaugh, and Reed J. Bramble. "Role-Related Stress Experienced by Academic Librarians." *The Journal of Academic Librarianship* 41, no. 3 (May 2015): 264–69. https://doi.org/10.1016/j.acalib.2015.03.016.

# The Situated Experience

# ILL, NOT I.L.L

## Chaundria Campos

Since I began writing this chapter, I have spent countless hours poring over books and articles to understand and try to emulate how other people talk about themselves. What way is the most effective to tell my story and how best to interest you, the reader, have been questions that I have asked myself repeatedly. After researching how to write a narrative, I came to the conclusion that the band-aid approach would be best. This will undoubtedly be a painful and uncomfortable recollection so for my sake, I will explain my experiences bluntly and without the fluff that I first thought I should include. Through reading this, I hope that you gain an understanding of mental health issues and mental illnesses as well as how deeply they pervade the perceptions of those who are affected by it. I also hope that it'll shine a light on the need for reform in how mental health is approached in society and in the profession of librarianship.

I am black and I am a woman. I served for a brief period in the armed forces and I work in an academic library. The divisiveness that my specific mental illnesses have incited within each of these communities has been both a learning opportunity and a deterrent for me on multiple occasions. The confused expressions on the faces of those that I've confided in have often left me with feelings of deep regret and disappointment. Many uncomfortable meetings and therapy sessions have left me jaded when it comes to seeking help or relief from the mental turmoil that my depression and anxiety can cause. The blank stares of former colleagues and subordinates that have seen me at my worst during a flashback or panic attack have deepened my resolve to work towards better informing those around me of the impact that mental illness can have on a person, whether it be a fellow library worker or a weary patron.

## My Experiences

My relationship with the words "we have resources for that" began after I joined the military. My disdain for *the phrase* began when it was uttered in the office of an Army behavioral health specialist. "We have resources for that," she said after I poured my heart out to her. I didn't grasp the emotions that I felt until years later. Disappointment and shame flowed through my body. Here I was telling this expressionless woman about my childhood trauma and fears, and all she could do was redirect me to another "specialist"? *The phrase* echoes in my mind whenever there is a situation that requires me to disclose my "disabilities". "Do you, sir or ma'am? Do you really have resources that will help me?" I often thought. This statement infuriated me, not only because it comes off as an attempt at distancing or redirection, but because it is so often used as a shield. Very few people acknowledge the reality of depression, anxiety, post-traumatic stress disorder (PTSD), or any other mental illness directly or without apologizing in some capacity. It's the reality of how society sees mental illness: A thing to be avoided or redirected to someone more accustomed to the grim and dirty film that clings to it.

What does it mean to wake up each morning and have to give yourself reasons to get out of bed or shower? Are other people as afraid of loud noises and quick movements as I am? How do I stop my heart from racing and my palms from sweating when anyone makes eye contact with me? How do I quell my fear of the things around me? Did my coworkers notice me blank out? My negative thoughts pervaded every action or inaction, every response to a question or attempt at small talk. Everything seemed to be happening all at once and at lightning speed. I could only ignore the urge to run away or do my best to avoid the sometimes imaginary problems that my mind created. This is the part where someone normally asks, "Have you sought help?" or "Have you tried having a more positive outlook?" Yes, and yes.

Throughout all of my attempts at a resolution or a "cure" to my mental health issues, one thing has always remained constant: There is always someone on the other side of a desk that seems to be waiting to express that there are resources for individuals in my predicament or state of mind. The flawed attempts to redirect and escape are too common and until there is a more open and realistic view established about mental health and mental illnesses in our society, I fear that these approaches will always be the norm. It's what training on this matter says to do, isn't it? Refer the troubled individual to mental health. Call a suicide hotline. Use the acronym A.C.E (ask, care, and escort). Cold and insincere redirection. This is not to say that all attempts at directing an individual to a mental health or wellbeing program are disingenuous or insincere, but many of mine seem to have been and when I compared the more sincere redirection to the former, I felt a sense of emptiness and abandonment that can only be described as, hopelessness.

## Mental Health Stigma

Sitting across from a supervisor or colleague and disclosing my diagnoses is sometimes as frustrating and ineffective as speaking to a wall. No one is expected to understand the complexity of these illnesses and be prepared to have to respond to issues related to them directly. That would be dangerous and uncomfortable. Over the years, my favorite response to my disclosure is, "From war right?". No. I have never seen war. I have never had to kill anyone and I've never had a movie moment that required me to hide behind an overturned Humvee and figure out how to drag a buddy away from crossfire. I enjoyed most of my time in the military and my anxiety is not a result of anything that occurred while I was enlisted. People have different responses to someone that is afflicted by a mental health disorder, and that's what's kept me civil in most cases. Some feel tense and uncomfortable because they "don't want to dwell on the negative." Others choose to refer you to a mental health professional because they're "not qualified to handle mental health things." Each response has its own intention and feel to it.

For every effort made to create distance away from, redirect, or minimize the "afflictions", there is an increased sense of loneliness.

## Anxiety and Blackness

As a child, I experienced a lot of loss and instability. Having learned through experience and many counseling sessions, I can reflect on these moments and acknowledge that I was troubled. The unique style of discipline in my household often resulted in anxiety attacks. I can remember my mother throwing away my artwork and my grandmother briskly walking over to comfort me as I heaved and rocked back and forth. My anxiety attacks were never called what they were. I had "bad nerves" and was "sensitive" according to my grandmother and loved ones. I never saw a therapist or psychologist and any inkling of depression was chalked up to my "dramatic" nature. In my urban, black household mental health was not something that was high on the list of priorities. Making money for bills, ensuring that the children were dressed well enough for school, and being able to occasionally have fun at the local club was though. Looking at my childhood and many of the interactions that I've had with some of my libraries' patrons and community members over the years I realize that any discussions that have been had about depression or anxiety were brushed aside or dismissed with mentions of a greater need for religion or hope in another form which in my case (and the case of my close friends affected by these issues), was not the most helpful advice. The solution was never to seek professional help. I disassociated myself and decided that joining the army could be a way to find happiness, purpose, and a sense of belonging.

Not long after I enlisted in the army a dark realization dawned on me. Any hint of mental health issues could result in my dismissal. The hushed tones that the behavioral health specialists, sergeants, and other soldiers spoke in when I answered my mental health evaluations honestly told me everything that I needed to know. I could not possibly be "army strong" if I was depressed or anxious. The hectic training environment, mass punishments, and constant need to be alert aggravated my anxiety for months. I was prescribed an antidepressant and an adult attention deficit disorder (ADHD) medication after one particularly long visit to the troop medical clinic. I was warned to "be careful with that" when my drill sergeant heard that I was to take them for the duration of my training. After many subtle warnings, I stopped taking my prescriptions and began journaling. Fighting my fears and being courageous were ingrained in me during basic training, along with following the orders of those in command and not showing weakness. Towards the middle of my brief time on active duty, I wound up sitting across from a behavioral health specialist in an office that I thought was safe and free from judgment. The many lectures I had sat through on behavioral health in the army led me to feel that I could be myself in the office of this stone-faced, monotone woman. I confided in her and told her of my childhood and the many traumatic events that peppered it. I told her of the loss I felt after my grandfather died and my waning faith in Christianity. I told her everything and she was the first one to say, "We have resources for that" and I believed her. A few weeks later, as I checked my medical record to apply for a scholarship,

I saw it. In all capital letters at the top of my lists of diagnoses was "DEPRESSION". The feeling of betrayal has yet to subside.

## Finding Hope in LIS

After two years in South Korea, I received a four-year Reserved Officers Training Program (ROTC) scholarship from the army. My depression caused a rift between me, the professor of military science, and most of my ROTC peers. She requested my medical records and a three-year battle to retain my position as an officer candidate ensued. To be short, I experienced the worst parts of the army during this time. A new professor of military science was assigned to my battalion and in her words, I was just "one of these sick soldiers that wanted to get over on the system". I fought harder after hearing the disgust in her voice during this meeting, and although I lost this battle, I was victorious in finding my passion: Libraries. I met and worked with an amazing archivist during my time with a veteran's program that was focused on archaeology and curation. Through this, I found employment with my city's main public library branch. Although I was struggling financially and mentally, I felt the happiest I had felt in years within the walls of the library. My mentors and peers accepted me as I was on my best days and my worst. I only confided in one of my coworkers, and her response to my plight gave me a deeper love for library workers and libraries in general. The reactions that the librarians and security personnel had to patron issues that ultimately were caused by mental illnesses gave me hope and a sense of comfort that no other environment has given me since. It would be two years later in the walls of one of my now sacred spaces that I would encounter *the phrase* again.

## "We have resources for that"

Post-graduation, I was fortunate enough to continue working in a library setting. All of the wonder and knowledge that fills the walls of libraries and the encouragement of my previous employer gave me an idealistic view of how my mental health concerns would be perceived within the field of library and information science. My therapist encouraged me to be more trusting after my disturbing ordeal with the army. An assault during my time as an undergraduate and many other negative experiences left a cloud hanging over me and I was to "work through it with [my] art" and try to be less guarded.

My new optimistic outlook motivated me to trust blindly so that I could cancel out my paranoia or in the words of one colleague, be more "naive" than my intelligence would convey. I do not wish to go into the details of this experience, but I am willing to share the result. In a room, surrounded by my supervisors, I disclosed my diagnosis of PTSD and the context of my mistake. I wanted desperately to trust and not be seen as paranoid or anxious. A week later *the phrase* "We have resources for that" would fill my ears once again and I would see red. The sentence was said with caution and apprehension, like a careful apology. Although it was prefaced with a disclaimer that explained that the person didn't know what post-traumatic stress disorder was like, it stung and disappointed me the same as it had before. Really?! In a building full of information professionals mental health is still uncharted waters. My mind raced as I gazed upon the worried and uncomfortable face of the person across from me. They seemed unsure and in need of an escape, but why say those words? It's always those exact words. The need to provide an appropriate response snapped me out of my fog. "Thank you. I appreciate that."

## Understanding and Sharing

To anyone on the outside looking in, there would likely be no immediate cause to assume that I have any issues with my mental health. I may occasionally jump at the sight of my own shadow and have a tendency to hide in the book stacks. Students seem to enjoy the discussions we have and think I'm "chill" as I encourage them to knock out their finals and work hard to get far. At social gatherings, there's not likely an onlooker that notices my frequent trips to the bathroom and love of the refreshment table when it's not crowded. "Food is life!" I exclaim while hoping it's not obvious that I cried in the bathroom or had a minor panic attack walking to grab a glass of wine to take the edge off. Lunch is best spent alone so that there's no need to wonder if I'm eating too loudly, scaring someone with my true-crime shows, or just being abnormal in general. I tell my peers I like to sit in my car because "I'm just a weirdo."

The reality is that on most days I'm afraid of interacting with the people around me. I wonder if they'll hurt me or if I'm being used in some capacity. I venture to the stacks to get a break from socializing. When a book drops in the stacks no one is going to run to calm me down when I crumple into a ball to the sound of what I think is a gunshot. Hopefully no one sees it or my awkward attempts at recovering from the embarrassment. While I'm at social events observing any and every movement of the people around me, there isn't a voice that intervenes to tell me that nobody is going to hurt me. I have to go to the bathroom to give myself pep talks that often end in me "happy crying" because I talked myself through it without having to call my husband or my best friend. When I sit at my desk and wonder what it's all for, I am the only one that can list the reasons why I go on to myself. "You love books and people are alright sometimes", I often tell myself. 'You'll be a librarian soon enough. Just believe". Working in an environment that is meant to be a beacon of hope and a source of knowledge for young minds is sometimes trying with depression. Smiling and encouraging young people, while I panic each time the entrance to the library is opened, is difficult. As I said, everything's happening all at once. Time moves faster, or slower, or stands still depending on where my thoughts are. I revisit the worst moments of my life during meetings and events and miss out on the joy and camaraderie that I could and should be experiencing.

I'm still a black woman. I'm still a veteran. And I still work in a library. After experiencing what it is to suffer from mental illness in all of these roles, I can say honestly and with great confidence that I know that there are resources for people like me. I'm aware that there are mindfulness techniques to help with my anxiety. I also know who to speak with about my anxiety and depression. I know. I'm aware of the on-site psychologists. I see a suicide hotline flyer posted somewhere at least once a week. I know! I know that there are resources. It's required. What's not required is individual library workers having an understanding and being informed about the impact that a mental illness has on someone, and it shows through the sometimes liability escaping policies and procedures for dealing with mental illness that I've observed in organizations ranging from federal to educational. I've attended programs that are designed to make library workers more aware of how to react to mental illness in patrons and those around them. They make a difference.

## Therapy Through Learning and Teaching

Whatever the challenges faced by those of us living with a mental illness or mental health issues, there is hope. Library and information science is a field dedicated to providing everyone, regardless of what their beliefs, sex, age, sexual orientation, disabilities, etc. are with information. Library workers are educators and facilitators working in institutions meant to provide answers and encourage inquiry. Libraries need a plan. We have to look within our organizations, our leadership and figure out how the dismissal of discussions about mental illness can be addressed. What do library workers and others need to know and understand about mental health that could prevent cold or ineffective responses to those in need of empathy and acceptance?

J. J. Pionke answers these questions best in their writing, "The Impact of Disbelief: On Being a Library Employee with a Disability."[1] They include a list of guidelines that focuses on alleviating the difficulties faced by those with invisible disabilities in libraries. The most important in my eyes being "educate all employees." Research and initiatives designed to provide "Mental Health First Aid"[2] have graced the pages of library and information science journals.[3] The positive impacts that initiatives like these can have on those that suffer from mental illnesses is immeasurable, but the effort is only worthwhile if a conversation about mental wellbeing and empathy is actually had. We can create educational pamphlets, boast about our universities' amazing A.D.A. programs, and nod our heads while an employee is venting or crying out for help, but if we don't actually put in the work to understand mental health's effects on each other, all we can offer is a polite and tactful "We have resources for that ."

## Acknowledgements

I want to thank the people in my life that have accepted me as I am. My loving and quirky family. My amazing husband and life partner, Alfredo. My supportive and devoted brother, Octavious. And every friend and acquaintance that has ever been there for me when I was at my worst. Thank you all.

*Bibliography*

Pionke, J. J. "The Impact of Disbelief: On Being a Library Employee with a Disability." *Library Trends* 67, no. 3 (May 8, 2019): 423–35. https://doi.org/10.1353/lib.2019.0004.

Throgmorton, Katilin . "Mental Health First Aid:  Training Librarians to Help Patrons in Crisis." *American Libraries Magazine*, March 1, 2017. https://americanlibrariesmagazine.org/2017/03/01/mental-health-first-aid/.

1   J. J. Pionke, "The Impact of Disbelief: On Being a Library Employee with a Disability," Library Trends 67, no. 3 (May 8, 2019): 423–35, https://doi.org/10.1353/lib.2019.0004.

2   Katilin Throgmorton, "Mental Health First Aid:  Training Librarians to Help Patrons in Crisis," American Libraries Magazine, March 1, 2017, https://americanlibrariesmagazine.org/2017/03/01/mental-health-first-aid/.

3   Throgmorton, K. (2017). Mental health first aid. *American Libraries*, 48 (3), 22–23.

# Arbitrary and Capricious: Mental Health, Library Work, and Deciding Just How Much to Talk About It All

**Jasmine Rizer**

*Content warning*   Description of a mildly traumatic encounter with a deeply insensitive mental health practitioner.

*Author's note*   In this essay, I refer to my employment at a large research university. All statements and opinions in this chapter are, of course, my own, and are not intended to represent any policies or positions of my employer.

Throughout this essay I have chosen to use phrases such as "ongoing mental health issues" to describe my history of obsessive-compulsive disorder (OCD), possible depression, and substance abuse. My intention is not to make mental illness seem like something that must be referred to euphemistically; this choice of wording reflects only the language with which I am personally most comfortable.

One of the most vindicating moments of my life occurred near the end of my first appointment with my current therapist when she told me that, for health-insurance purposes, she was going to record a diagnosis of obsessive-compulsive disorder (OCD) in my file.

"If you're comfortable with that," she emphasized, going on to explain that the diagnosis did not have to be set in stone.

Comfortable? I was ready to turn cartwheels.

*For almost my entire adult life, I had exhibited textbook OCD symptoms. Throughout my college years these symptoms didn't interfere with my life all that much. Because my obsessions did not revolve around cleanliness and order, I didn't look like what most people think an OCD sufferer looks like. From the outside, a lot of my symptoms probably looked like personality quirks. Even now there are times when I don't realize something I'm doing on a regular basis is unhealthy and strange, and has sprung from a misfire in my brain somewhere—until suddenly I do realize just that.*

This session, where I was finally diagnosed with the mental disorder I already knew I had, did not mark the first occasion of seeking professional help for it. A lot of the suffering that mental illness has caused me and a lot of what it has cost me is invisible. However, when I was about twenty-four, I reached a point where it was hard to conceal from even casual acquaintances that something was very wrong. That was when I set up an appointment with a therapist I had never seen before. I can't remember now how I found her. In all seriousness, I probably looked under "Psychotherapists" in the telephone book. When we met face-to-face, this woman, or girl as she seemed to me since she looked barely older than myself, refused to listen to my symptoms. In fact, she stopped just short of laughing in my face at the idea that I might have been able to make any kind of accurate guess as to what was going wrong with my own brain. Not only did I never go back to see that particular therapist again, it would be roughly a decade before I would be able to trust another mental health professional. "Terrified" is not too strong a word to describe how I felt about setting myself up for that kind of treatment again.

I did not survive the intervening years on my own. My mother provided more care and support to her fully-grown daughter than many parents would have been on board to give. Also a lifesaver (literally, I suspect) during this time was a book called *Brain Lock* by Dr. Jeffrey M. Schwartz, now out in a twentieth-anniversary edition, recommended to me by a kind and knowledgeable stranger on the Internet. People in my life occasionally suggested that I see a therapist, but I never forgot how I had been treated by the last therapist I had asked for help.

The thing that is hard to express, and this essay may not even really be the place to go into it, is how much suffering an anxiety disorder can cause, and how little anybody, other than the mentally ill person and those people extremely close to them, may be able to tell what a toll the illness is taking.

During my long stretch between therapists, I was already working at the library where I am still employed, and I remember one day so awful that I had to kneel down in the stacks and pound my fist against the floor before I could summon the wherewithal to walk back to my desk. Eventually, I did. I pulled myself together and I walked back to my desk. Anybody looking for an excuse to minimize the impact of mental illness on one's overall well-being could have pointed to me and said, "Well, look at her. She doesn't seem to be all that affected by this OCD thing. There she sits, working in the library database like everyone else in this room." The irony of mental illness is that the better the sufferer is at boxing up their pain and going about their business externally silent, but internally screaming in distress, the more excuse the world at large has to fold its arms and declare skeptically that the person is malingering, avoiding responsibility, and not really ill in any sense of the word and just needs to suck it up.

Every day wasn't a pounding-on-the-floor day. That was an unusually bad day. I had a lot of bad days during that time. The intensity of those bad days varied, but over the long haul things seemed to be growing more manageable. Eventually, I even made it through my MLIS program. Later I faced the daunting prospect of the all-day interview that ended up landing me my current position. All of these things were stressful and probably caused minor setbacks along the way. The entire stretch of time from my initial disastrous brush with that less-than-sensitive therapist to the time when I was offered my first post-MLIS position was roughly ten years. They were ten years best visualized as a sine wave—up and down from one day to another—but at the end of this period, there seemed to be a definite trend away from that up-and-down towards some kind of stability. Unfortunately, I would not enjoy that stability for as long as I hoped.

I'd like to pause for a moment here to explain how inextricable my OCD actually is from my life as a librarian. I am a serials cataloger, a job I happen to be very good at, and also a job that could not be better at stoking my OCD if someone had designed it for this purpose while cackling sadistically like a comic-book villain. There are a lot of rules. Not all of those rules are straightforward. Sometimes it seems like every bibliographic record I see is connected to a million other records for things it continues, or things it supplements, or things it absorbed twenty years ago, and all of them need cleanup of some kind. It is probably hard even for people without OCD to be sure of where to draw the line when it comes to understanding that one person cannot single-handedly make an entire database perfect. I also take cataloging as a public service seriously. I want people to be able to find things after I have finished my work on the bibliographic records. Here too it is hard to draw the line between an admirable dedication to public service and a sinister, counter-productive obsession with perfection.

All of these factors created the perfect position for OCD to make its move and take up more space in my work life than I could handle. If that sounds like I'm anthropomorphizing a mental illness, that's because OCD quite often feels like a person who hates me, who wants control of my life, and who is surprisingly adept at finding ways to outfox me at every turn. At the end of my first year in my first post-MLIS position, OCD got the chance to make its move. After a dreadful holiday break, over the course of which a number of ultimately fixable but nevertheless very stressful events took place, I came back to work with my mental health in the worst shambles it had been in for some time. I was fortunate beyond words in the response of my then supervisor to this turn of events, something I will discuss in greater depth later in this chapter.

Less prominent in my life but sometimes running in the background all the same is what my current therapist once referred to as "low-lying depression." It's an apt description. Anxiety shoves its face into everything, stubborn and intrusive and often downright mean. Depression, when it does happen, just sort of hovers in my life like fog. I may not be able to stop myself from crying on the way to the bus stop, but I have usually more or less pulled myself together by the time I arrive at work. To the extent that depression manifests in my work life at all, I suspect it does so as an overwhelming weariness and an ominous feeling that I cannot take on even one more thing, no matter how tiny.

The third major component of the nebulous mess on which I hang the label *my mental health issues* is also the one that I have spent the least time discussing with professionals over the years, because it is the one that has interfered the least with my functioning. It's also the hardest to define. It is perhaps something slightly greater than "history of substance abuse" and significantly lesser than "addiction disorder." In college, I definitely developed a relationship with alcohol that was too intense to be healthy. It probably had something to do with the alcoholism growing perilously close to me on my family tree, and for years after I quit drinking, I thought I was probably a recovering alcoholic. Then I started reading memoirs by *actual* recovering alcoholics, and it was clear that I did not face anything even close to their struggles in staying sober.

The best way I know how to explain it is this: I am someone who does not drink because I shouldn't. I *could* drink in moderation if I wanted to. I realize that this sounds exactly like something that an alcoholic in profound denial would say, but I have spent a great deal of time in coming to this conclusion, and in this case it happens to be true. However, trying to live with any reasonable concept of "drinking in moderation" would take up so much of my time and be such a drain on my mental resources. I would be occupied by constant thoughts and worries: How much is *too* much? How often is too often? Whose definition of "one drink" do I employ? The National Institute of Health? Wikipedia? The manufacturers of those novelty wineglasses with a bowl about the size of a small soup bowl?

Admittedly, some of these complications may have less to do with my spot on the addiction spectrum and more to do with where my history of problem drinking intersects with my OCD. One way my OCD manifests is through a sometimes almost overwhelming urge to put into place in every aspect of my life a series of complicated rules and if-then conditions. In a comic strip I once drew I tried to explain this phenomenon using the words, "The green dress goes with the black shoes because it's *Tuesday*." If OCD can make getting dressed that complicated, imagine what it could do to any attempt on my part to drink in moderation—especially when I would probably, at least sometimes, prefer to drink a *whole lot*.

The impact of all these complications on my everyday work life is minimal. Still, sometimes an invitation to a happy-hour based networking event, complete with sly wink-wink exhortations to come "enjoy a beverage" with my colleagues, sets my teeth on edge if I receive it on a bad day.

How much I discuss any of this in the workplace depends on a lot of variables. How long have I known you? How much do I care about making a good impression on you? Do you deal with any mental health issues of your own that I am aware of? With regards to my OCD, I have had very little choice but to be honest about it. There came a point fairly early in my career as a librarian at which it began to affect my work life so severely that there was simply no way to avoid speaking with my then-supervisor about what was going on. OCD affects the kind of work

I do in a very concrete way. I doubt that I am as productive in terms of volume as a less meticulous cataloger would be. At the time when I found it necessary to have this difficult conversation with my supervisor, my confidence in my own ability to do good work had reached such an exhausting low that I routinely pestered her about all manner of things that I should have been able to figure out for myself—though I don't think my supervisor would ever have put it in those terms. Sometimes I am a lot less patient with myself than others are with me.

When this conversation happened, I was incredibly lucky. My supervisor's main concern was what I needed from her in terms of support in order to handle this rough mental-health patch in the workplace.

My remarkable good fortune and privilege in enjoying an enlightened work environment was highlighted for me when I spoke with my father on the telephone later that week. He asked in a state of obvious concern whether disclosing the perilous state of my mental health to my supervisor might not jeopardize my continued employment. In theory, the answer to that question is that I am protected by the Americans with Disabilities Act from being fired for such a disclosure, but the truth is that if I'd had the spectacular bad luck to have a supervisor who wanted rid of me because they were uninformed or uncomfortable around the subject of mental illness, such a person could probably have found a way to get rid of me without openly violating the ADA.

At the time of this writing, I check in with my therapist every three or four weeks. I never make a mystery of where I am going when I take time off from work for these appointments. At first, this was less about modeling good behavior and more about not causing undue anxiety to any of my colleagues. It seemed to me that if I disappeared regularly every three or four weeks, for some event to which I referred only as "an appointment," people were going to worry about me. Trying to allay folks' possible concerns by adding, "It's nothing bad!" seemed likely to create an unnecessary amount of mystery around the whole thing. This is why I have mostly always told people, "I have a therapy appointment tomorrow."

Having gotten into this habit, I like to think that it *does* model good behavior, that it subtly reinforces the idea of needing regular mental health tune-ups as nothing to be ashamed of or discuss in a hushed voice.

I do, however, try not to be obnoxious about it.

In thinking about what would constitute being obnoxious, I recall something my best friend and I said in middle school when we felt someone was trying unsuccessfully to be casual about sharing information of perceived great importance (usually something noteworthy about the speaker themselves.) "Can't you just hear the italics in their voice?", we would say. I try hard not to be that person at work, the person in whose voice you can hear the italics when I discuss mental health. You know: "I'm going to *therapy* now."

This is something I think about quite often. The word "stigma" comes up again and again and again when reading about the general public's perception of mental illness, and I believe that it is important to push back against the idea that a person with ongoing mental health problems needs to be ashamed of those problems, or avoid discussing them for fear of making other people uncomfortable.

At the same time, I am aware that if you talk about anything *too* much—especially anything as serious as mental health—people just stop listening after a while. I look back and cringe when I consider the amount of self-congratulatory chest thumping I did after I quit drinking. Some people have told me that hearing about that whole process was enlightening for them and that I have nothing to apologize for, but I know there must also have been people who got sick of hearing about it.

Aside from the fact that others might begin to tune me out after a while, writing me off as that lady who always wants to talk about mental illness, there is also the fact that my therapist has advised me that it is not necessarily productive for me to think of myself primarily in terms of my anxiety disorder. I am inclined to agree with her. I may have to approach many (even most) situations in my life with the awareness that I have patterns of thought and behavior into which I might easily fall if I don't monitor myself closely. That said, OCD in all its unpleasantness has already eaten up enough of my life without getting to take over my identity as well.

The lines I draw with regard to how much mental health talk at work is *too* much mental health talk at work, are frankly pretty arbitrary and capricious. For instance, on the wall outside my cubicle hangs a dry-erase board where members of my section write reminders of their whereabouts: "So-and-so in meeting at 3:00," and that sort of thing. Invariably when I am out in the middle of the day for a therapist's visit, I write on this board, "Jasmine @ Dr.'s appt." To write "Jasmine @ therapy" just feels like too much.

I mention this small detail not because I imagine the contents of my markerboard that interesting in themselves, but because I think it is illustrative of just how arbitrary this kind of distinction probably is for everyone. The thought process is unique to every individual. Sometimes there's not even a thought process involved at all, just a feeling of *This is too much information* or *Nobody wants to hear about this right now*.

I am fairly certain that I don't get it right all the time. Approach me with a simple "how's it going?" at the wrong moment, and I may respond with such a glut of overshare that I can't quite look you in the eye again for some time.

I have taken on a lot of added responsibility at my job in the last few years, and I occasionally arrive suddenly and unexpectedly at the end of my tether. When this happens, I am fortunate to have a temperament more inclined towards sinking my face in my hands, or admitting bleakly, "I don't know what to do about this," than towards snapping at people. Even so, it makes people uncomfortable to see someone come apart like that. I try to take responsibility for that and apologize accordingly. I suspect that my unpredictable serotonin levels may have a lot to do with those moments, but I can't offer any definitive proof that I wouldn't fall apart even in a world where my brain functioned perfectly, so I try not to use my mental health struggles as an excuse or a mitigating circumstance. I try simply to say,, "I'm sorry I got so upset earlier. Please understand that I wasn't mad at you; I was overwhelmed by the problem you told me about," without adding anything like, "I've been really depressed this week." For another person, maybe "I've been really depressed this week" would be a completely appropriate piece of information to include. I'm coming to understand that these are very personal matters, and you simply can't tell others how they should be managing themselves.

Substance abuse and my relationship to it come up a lot less often at work than do these everyday complications I've discussed, but I do live in a college town, so it is on my mind a lot. I was once asked by a colleague, quite inoffensively and in a context in which she had every reason to ask this question, "Do you not drink?"

What I answered was, "Not anymore."

I would love to able to say that I did this in the hopes of making a problematic history with alcohol seem ordinary, normal, a thing that might easily happen to a nice lady at work. The truth is, I framed my reply as I did because I felt like not-drinking as a former problem drinker might somehow seem less scowling and judgmental than not-drinking as someone who simply chooses not to drink.

I realize that this is not a good way to think about this issue. Lots of people abstain from lots of things without passing judgment on others who enjoy those same things. However, it's surprisingly hard to remember this fact when a lovely co-worker whose feelings you don't want to hurt asks, "Do you not drink?"

The fear of seeming judgmental is one reason I generally don't talk about this issue at work, even at times when maybe I should. The other reason is that I am very leery of wearing my problematic history with alcohol like a fashionable accessory, piggybacking on an experience of marginalization and of suffering that is not really mine to claim. Sometimes I wonder what it would even look like to begin that conversation. "I'm not an alcoholic, but I seem to be the closest thing to one in this room" seems obnoxious on multiple levels.

At any rate, inclusivity for folks with a history of substance abuse is not an issue that comes up often at my workplace. The sum total of my meaningful contributions on this front has thus far consisted of submitting some anonymous comments on one survey about my workplace's annual staff party. That didn't feel particularly courageous (in fact, it felt a little obnoxious), but maybe every act of visibility doesn't have to feel courageous. Maybe every act of mental health advocacy doesn't have to be something that would play well in a Hollywood movie. Maybe it can be as small and as boring as saying, "Just so y'all know, holding the staff party in a bar year after year might make attendance problematic for some people." Even when nobody is going to know for sure who said it.

There is of course a certain amount of safety in anonymity. There is also a certain amount of safety in the many unearned layers of privilege in which I am ensconced.

I work at a large research university in what is in many ways a fairly progressive college town. My employer is a winner of multiple diversity awards, and the particular department of the Libraries in which I work is one where my ongoing mental health issues are accepted as a fact of life, both by my colleagues and by the person in charge of allowing me to have time off. I am aware there is no shortage of workplaces in which I might have to deal with a supervisor who would grant my time off for therapy grudgingly, ungraciously, or even not at all. I realize that in many workplaces, the announcement, "I'm leaving for my therapy appointment now" would be met with shocked silence and/or intrusive questions.

I didn't really do anything to deserve such an accepting workplace. I just got lucky. I also didn't do anything to deserve to be spared the extra layers of nonsense that I am spared by my status as a white, cisgender woman. The odds are awfully small that my ongoing mental health struggles or the effect of those struggles on my productivity or the time I take off from work for mental-health wellness appointments will ever be used as an object lesson to prop up tired, ugly stereotypes about my entire ethnic group, or to call into question whether I am capable of discerning my own gender identity.

However, no amount of privilege would *compel* me to say one word about the state of my mental health to anyone, at work or in any other setting, if I did not want to. I believe deeply that it is nobody's responsibility to be the poster child for mental illness in any situation. No matter how auspicious the circumstances, no one has the right to tell you that you must give up your privacy for the sake of capital-R Representation. These are decisions that a person can only make for themselves.

It has been a long journey since I first sat in my therapist's office and heard the words that confirmed so many of my suspicions about why my life had been so difficult for so many years. For as long as I continue working for my present employer, I am likely to continue the balancing act of modeling openness and lack of embarrassment about mental illness, while trying not to subject my colleagues to a never-ending stream of performative announcements about my *therapy* appointments. I will probably continue to misjudge this balance horribly at times, and I will probably continue to have to apologize to people for the occasions when I drop my face into my hands and say, "I don't know how to fix this."

I believe I was discussing the very fact of my writing this essay with my therapist when she said to me that being open about these issues "takes a lot of guts." I don't know that it makes me feel particularly courageous, but if my small efforts to keep from further stigmatizing mental illness help to make the whole subject less scary for someone in my orbit—at work or anywhere—it is well worth whatever small amount of bravery I have had to muster.

# One Among Many: Fit, Precarity, and Neurodiversity in Academic Libraries

**Evelyn E. Nalepinski[1]**

From the moment I entered grade school, I knew I was different from the other children. By the time I was eight years old, I was so aware of my own 'differences' that I became convinced I was a being of another species from a distant time/space/world. Somehow, my parents had been duped into accepting me as their own, but I felt a duty to protect them from this knowledge, so I planned to carefully keep the truth hidden until the day my people appeared on Earth to find me. At that time, I had no idea who my people were, or if they really existed, but I still hoped they were out there somewhere. As an adult, I of course recognize the fiction in this story, but I continue to long for some sense of belonging that goes beyond the solidarity shared amongst all of us 'weirdos.' Yet that belonging eludes me, and I remain an outsider.

Throughout my life, other people have reinforced my outsider status by assigning me a variety of labels that emphasize my differences. These labels include insults and negative comments, but also medical labels and diagnoses. I won't catalog the insults here, but my medical labels include PTSD, generalized anxiety disorder, struggles with

---

1   As someone in a contingent position, and as someone whose employment in a previous position was threatened after disclosing one of the conditions discussed herein, I do not feel it is safe for me to associate this writing with my own name. My hope is that by sharing my experiences and acknowledging my own precarity, I can render visible the ways in which we need to change our practices and our profession to better reflect the values that librarianship regularly claims, especially equity, diversity, and inclusion.

occasional bouts of depression, a mostly-secret history of anorexia, ADHD, plus the big one I'm never supposed to mention because people are so afraid of it: Autism. These labels or 'diagnoses' constitute so much more than a single checklist but are a complex web of overlapping and interwoven experiences. While these diagnoses play a significant role in who I am and how I interact with the world, they are also parts of me that remain unacknowledged and largely unaccepted (or unacceptable) within the profession of academic librarianship, not just for me, but for countless others who may have similar conditions. Knowing that I am not alone in these kinds of experiences, I cannot continue to remain silent.

In a system that values rigor and expertise, vulnerability and differences are tolerated only when they are seen as adding value. So, as an academic librarian, I'm not autistic, but rather a creative thinker! Doesn't that sound better? Unfortunately, that position is an immense burden for anyone like me. So, too, are conversations around mental 'health and wellness,' which further burden individuals trying to live in an ableist world. I want to unpack these burdens, examine them closely, and push this profession to be the inclusive and welcoming place that it claims to be.

## A Note on Content and Language

I am drawing inspiration from Eli Clare, who notes that "in the late 1980s and 1990s, feminists developed the practice of trigger warnings to give people a heads-up before details of violence were spoken out loud."[2] Clare also points out that "none of us can reliably predict what will trigger someone we don't know well,"[3] but I want my readers to know up front that this chapter mentions incidents and experiences that may be triggering for some. My life experiences as discussed here include bullying, ableism, domestic abuse, sexual assault and rape. I also recognize that this chapter may be triggering to readers in ways I have not anticipated, so please, dear readers, be kind to yourself as you read this chapter. As Clare explains, "trigger warnings are in essence tools for self-care and collective care."[4] Feel free to set this

---

2   Eli Clare, *Brilliant Imperfection* (Durham, NC: Duke University Press, 2017), xix.

3   Clare, *Brilliant Imperfection*, xix.

4   Clare, *Brilliant Imperfection*, xx.

piece down and come back later, or even never. Only you can decide what is best for you.

In writing this chapter, I wanted to honor the choices of the editors while speaking authentically to my own viewpoint, so I have used both the phrases 'mental illness' and 'mental disability' throughout. I chose to use 'mental disabilities' because this phrase includes mental illness and cognitive and intellectual differences of many kinds, along with medical conditions like the so-called 'brain fog' that accompanies my autoimmune conditions. While I know that some may be resistant to the inclusion of the word 'disability,' the fear that 'disability' has negative connotations reflects (and perpetuates) ableism, the idea that disability somehow renders a mind or body as 'less than.' This perspective continues to inflict prejudice, harm, and violence on people who may or may not identify as disabled (consider, for example, the eugenics movement, or the institutionalization of those deemed 'feeble-minded' or 'unfit' for society, such as women with 'hysteria'). To end this harm, we must all remember that disability and personhood are not incongruent. In a similar manner, I choose to refer to myself as autistic, a naming that is common among autism activists. While some may prefer person-first language (as in, 'a person with autism'), I reject the conception that I need to assert my personhood first, as though my autism somehow diminishes my humanity. My autism is a part of how I work in the world, and therefore I cannot be a 'person with autism' because my person cannot exist without or outside of autism. I cannot set it down like a suitcase. I am autistic, and that is how I prefer to refer to myself. Others may make different choices, and that is their prerogative.

## Who am I and where do I "fit?"

Like a fictional protagonist, my storyline involves a creation story that might serve as foreshadowing for the future events of my own life. The story begins with my mother sitting in her hospital bed waiting for labor to begin, when she realized she was getting hungry and decided to order lunch. A few minutes later, however, it became apparent that lunch would have to wait, and half an hour later I was born. As I emerged from the womb, I allegedly looked the doctor in the eye and examined him thoroughly (as you might imagine, this is beyond my recollection). The doctor was somewhat taken aback and told my mother that this was a sign that I would be a special child.

Special, indeed. I taught myself to read by the age of three. My eager-ness to unlock the power of those symbols must have seemed like the master key to knowledge, and yet neither I nor my parents knew what this simple act of meaning-making would lead to once I entered pub-lic school. Let's just say I was a bit of an anomaly in kindergarten. My parents will occasionally recount the story of my teacher calling them into school, and gravely informing them that I could read, and quite well at that. My parents, who had already thoroughly tested my read-ing capabilities themselves, were unsure why this was the subject of a parent-teacher conference. Apparently, I was quite the exception in this regard, and no one knew exactly what to do with me. The teachers and administrators had not been expecting a student like me, and thus my existence was completely unanticipated. What to do with me?!? I still don't know what the 'right' answer to that question might have been, but I do wonder if there was a possibility out there somewhere that everyone just missed, an alternate timeline where I thrived as a human being whether or not I 'fit.' My timeline, my history, was gener-ally one of desperately trying to fit in even though it was clear I never would. I kept, no, *keep*, hoping. Now here I am writing about how I *still* don't fit, so I suppose, dear reader, you can guess how that has worked out for me.

Throughout my life I have struggled with 'fitting in,' and have been continually reminded that my mind (and my body) are different and outside of the norm. My thoughts and emotions have been largely mis-understood and often disparaged. I am too sad, too emotional, too in-tense, too anxious, and altogether too weird. Because of this, I have felt 'wrong' for most of my life, and it was only recently that I began to understand that all of my mental experiences were connected to conditions that could be named, much like some of my physical con-ditions (which are beyond the scope of this particular piece). In this naming came not only understanding, but a little less shame, and a sense that maybe I wasn't the freak I had imagined myself to be. May-be (just maybe) it was okay that all my prayers to become 'normal' had remained unanswered. I am not 'too sad'–I struggle with depression. I am not 'too anxious'–I have generalized anxiety disorder. I am not 'too emotional' or 'too intense' or 'too weird'–I am empathic and process the world around me differently because I am autistic. And because I move through this world in a female body, these diagnoses, names, and understandings of my ways of being were denied to me for de-cades by the medical system.

I was told by medical professionals that maybe I had seasonal affective disorder, and I should just get more light or sunshine. I was told I just needed someone I could talk with. After I began experiencing a suddenly racing heartbeat and shortness of breath so severe that I was sent to the hospital in an ambulance, I was told that nothing was wrong with my heart or my lungs, that everything checked out fine, and maybe I just had a little low blood sugar. I eventually gave up, deciding I would just have to live with these 'inexplicable' conditions because clearly the doctors weren't going to help me. It took me *two decades* to learn that what I had experienced were panic attacks related to my anxiety disorder, that I was struggling with depression, PTSD, and anorexia, and that many of my other 'oddities' were related to autism. It was not *me* who was wrong, it was my doctors, because they failed to listen to me and look beyond their tests to see a more holistic view of my experiences. I will remain forever grateful that I was fortunate enough to stumble onto a therapist who was willing to do more for me.

Through my experiences in therapy, I found that the naming of my conditions opened a gateway for me to learn about myself. As I began my journey of self-discovery, my research led me into the field of disability studies, which provided both the critical engagement that I sought and new ways of understanding myself and society. I learned that my physicians, and much of the world around me, largely viewed me and my conditions from a medical model of disability. The medical model sees me as a series of diagnoses in need of treatment, or maybe even a cure. I am 'not well.' My conditions are tested, listed, and described, yet as Melanie Yergeau observes, "in all of their describing, I find that little about me is described. Instead my body is reduced. Erased. Medicated."[5] The social model of disability recognizes that society and its norms play a significant role in defining disability, and that disability is not an individual problem but rather a social justice issue. The body and mind are not inherently disabled, but rather the societal conditions are themselves disabling to some minds and bodies. In my case, I was not born feeling like a different species, rather my classmates and my teachers made me feel like an outsider who would never fit in. My mind was 'other'—something inexplicable that was sometimes labeled 'gifted' and other times a 'problem' that was clearly an annoyance to everyone around me. Why did I ask SO MANY questions? Or, in

---

5   Melanie Yergeau, *Authoring Autism: On Rhetoric and Neurological Queerness* (Durham, NC: Duke University Press, 2018), 13.

college, why didn't I just cheer up? I cannot, and will not, fit within the structures society has constructed around me, and trust me, I've tried.

My experiences of failing to fit in align well with Rosemarie Garland-Thompson's conception of *fitting* and *misfitting*. Thompson explains that two things can "come together in either harmony or disjunction," and *fit* connotes the harmonious state. Misfitting, however, "describes an incongruent relationship between two things, a square peg in a round hole. The problem with a misfit, then, inheres not in either of the two things but rather in their juxtaposition, the awkward attempt to fit them together."[6] Thus I am not myself a misfit, but rather have experienced misfitting because the "round hole" of society and my chosen profession have refused to acknowledge that some of us are square pegs.

## Hiding in Plain Sight

Grade school taught me how to hide. Well, that's what my classmates taught me, anyhow. I was bullied throughout K-12, had suicidal thoughts for much of college, and then found myself in an abusive marriage for 15 years. Hiding seemed essential to my survival. So now I don't just mask, I embody identities outside of my own as I wear full costumes, makeup, and ways of being different than my own. I have developed stories to tell about my own history that don't expose my differences and don't reveal my trauma, stories to explain my quirkiness, my career choices, my need for quiet time. Only recently have I begun to share tiny pieces of the 'real' story–those pieces that have now been deemed socially acceptable in certain contexts. Anxiety, for example, I can now mention publicly, especially in academia where students and faculty alike are increasingly aware of the impact of anxiety on classroom learning. Yet even here, the full extent of my conditions remains hidden. Only the so-called tip of the iceberg shows—a small imperfection that can be made light of—but the full and sometimes crippling extent must never show, or I will be relegated back to my weirdo status and potentially subjected to further abuse.

I do not, for example, share that my career choice is the only one that I was allowed to pursue at the time, because my abusive former spouse

---

6    Rosemarie Garland-Thomson, "Misfits: A Feminist Materialist Disability Concept," *Hypatia* 26, no. 3 (August 2011): 592–93.

refused to allow me to do anything else. Instead. I have learned to tell a lovely story about my desire to help others pursue lifelong learning. My co-workers do not know that I am survivor of multiple sexual assaults, domestic abuse, and rape, nor do they know how often I am overcome by sensory inputs and overwhelming emotions that require me to hide in my office or in a restroom stall. My co-workers don't know about the time a book on a shelf triggered a panic attack so severe that I had to hide in the restroom for half an hour and continued to tremble for hours afterwards. I dismiss routines like fire alarm testing as 'annoying' rather than acknowledging that they are panic-inducing to the point of near- (or actual) meltdown. While I have begun to acknowledge my social anxiety at select conferences, this is yet another method for passing off my autism and anxiety as something more socially acceptable (thankfully the introverts in academia seem to find social anxiety quite relatable), but the conference itself is not really a welcoming space or experience.

At conferences, at job interviews, and in my everyday work life, I am constantly hiding my ways of being in the world, my cognitive overload, my fatigue, my need for a low-distraction environment, my facial blindness, my continual existential crises, my ADHD, my depression, my PTSD, and everything else I've already mentioned. I hear co-workers lament the emotional responses of colleagues in statements like, "I just wish some people were better at pretending to be interested," and the feeling that I need to hide all of these things continues. Additionally, I know that my mind does not always work in an orderly fashion, and I constantly worry about whether I make sense to anyone else. Who do I get to be in the workplace? Certainly not myself....

Unfortunately, experiences like mine are all too common in higher education and in libraries. However, and sadly not surprisingly, the literature has yet to reflect most of these experiences. The few studies that do exist concur that academics with mental disabilities tend to hide their conditions and "avoid the 'official' route of arranging accommodations through their employers, instead handling their accommodation needs informally or privately."[7] Potential risks of disclosing any disability, but especially those that are invisible, like mental disabilities, include fear of stigma, loss of privacy, lack of support from

---

7 Margaret Price et al., "Disclosure of Mental Disability by College and University Faculty: The Negotiation of Accommodations, Supports, and Barriers," *Disability Studies Quarterly* 37, no. 2 (2017), http://dsq-sds.org/article/view/5487.

supervisors and administrators, and navigating institutional procedures that may create additional barriers.[8] Librarians may write a lot of literature about how to serve those with mental illnesses and disabilities, but they are much less effective at looking inward and changing the profession itself to become more welcoming to all bodies and minds. For example, a recent survey of disabled academic librarians found that 68% of respondents did not request accommodations. When asked why they did not ask for accommodations, 71% "reported fearing an impact on their job, including colleague and supervisor reactions, being seen or treated differently, or negative impact on promotion or tenure opportunities."[9] These fears echo the lived experience of J. J. Pionke, whose attempts to obtain accommodations for his PTSD were met with disbelief, lack of cooperation, animosity from colleagues, and eventually required hiring a lawyer and investing significant time, money, and energy into a process that, professionally and ethically, should not have inflicted additional harm.[10] Instead of supporting library workers with mental disabilities, libraries continue to rely upon systems that create barriers to inclusion.

## Systemic Precarity across Higher Ed and Libraries

While companies like SAP, Microsoft, and J. P. Morgan Chase have initiated hiring programs to include autistic people in the workplace,[11] the same cannot be said of higher education, where mental differences of any type are largely viewed as conflicting with education's emphasis on mental productivity, predictability, and rigor. Disability scholar Tobin Siebers argues that academia imagines faculty and students as ideal personas that intentionally conceal "the distrust of thinking differently in academic life."[12] Different ways of thinking and being are typically unwelcome in academia. Additionally, individuals

---

8   Price et al., "Disclosure of Mental Disability by College and University Faculty."

9   Joanne Oud, "Academic Librarians with Disabilities: Job Perceptions and Factors Influencing Positive Workplace Experiences," *Partnership: The Canadian Journal of Library and Information Practice and Research* 13, no. 1 (2018): 9.

10   J. J. Pionke, "The Impact of Disbelief: On Being a Library Employee with a Disability," *Library Trends* 67, no. 3 (May 8, 2019): 429.

11   Dinah Eng, "Where Autistic Workers Thrive," Fortune, June 24, 2018, https://fortune.com/2018/06/24/where-autistic-workers-thrive/.

12   Tobin Siebers, "Foreword," in *Mad at School: Rhetorics of Mental Disability and Academic Life*, by Margaret Price (Ann Arbor: University of Michigan Press, 2011), xi.

with mental disabilities are presumed to be incompetent, mentally unsound, and incapable of contributing valuable work.[13] In the limited scholarship that does examine mental disabilities in higher education, those with mental disabilities are presumed to be students, are treated as something "other than" the norm, and are seen to only have value as research subjects for those without such disabilities.[14] In fact, the research on mental disabilities and autism in both higher education and libraries focuses mainly on students with these conditions, and the existence of academic faculty and staff with disabilities has remained largely unacknowledged. Despite the prevalence of the quirky 'absent-minded professor' stereotype, that way of being is only available to cis, heterosexual, hyper-able, white men of a certain age, and not to anyone whose identity does not align with these hegemonic norms. We remain impossibilities.

Library literature demonstrates that the profession has tended to label those with mental disabilities as "other" and those in need of "service." A content analysis of library literature conducted by Heather Hill in 2013 found that "significant literature themes begin and end with a focus on electronic accessibility," and that the main area of concern was the "services libraries are providing, what they need to improve upon, and their perception of those services."[15] Literature on learning disabilities and library employees with disabilities was virtually nonexistent, and the same has remained true for the most part. Publications such as those by Kumbier and Starkey,[16] Oud,[17] and Schomberg,[18] and the recent special issue of *Library Trends* dedicated to Disabled Adults in Libraries,[19] have remained exceptions, and may provide some hope that these conversations are beginning to emerge

---

13   Margaret Price, *Mad at School: Rhetorics of Mental Disability and Academic Life* (Ann Arbor: University of Michigan Press, 2011), 16.

14   Price, 52, *Mad at School*.

15   Heather Hill, "Disability and Accessibility in the Library and Information Science Literature: A Content Analysis," *Library & Information Science Research* 35, no. 2 (April 1, 2013): 140.

16   Alana Kumbier and Julia Starkey, "Access Is Not Problem Solving: Disability Justice and Libraries," *Library Trends* 64, no. 3 (Winter 2016): 468–91.

17   Oud, "Academic Librarians with Disabilities: Job Perceptions and Factors Influencing Positive Workplace Experiences."

18   Jessica Schomberg, "Disability at Work: Libraries, Built to Exclude," *Politics and Theory of Critical Librarianship*, February 1, 2018, 111–23.

19   Volume 67, Number 3, Winter 2019. (Missing rest of the citation)

in the profession. Yet librarianship is often viewed (even from within the profession) as a service-oriented profession, and guidelines created by professional organizations, such as the Reference and User Services Association's "Guidelines for Behavioral Performance of Reference and Information Service Providers," prioritize serving others and maintaining specified emotional responses.[20] This inability to account for the needs of disabled library workers, and a focus on policing professional behaviors, perpetuates the stigma of mental illness and disability and further contributes to the workplace precarity of library workers, who are increasingly experiencing insecure employment and inadequate compensation for their work.

The pressure to 'do more with less' is visible at most library conferences, in conversations across the profession, and often in decisions made by those in charge, but "as everyday lives are consumed extensively by the demands of the workplace, academics' bodyminds (as well as the bodyminds of those they love) are neglected and ignored."[21] As a substitute for actual care, many higher education institutions now offer wellness programs and resilience training, which yet again place responsibility on the individual, rather than on the systems that are neglecting and harming employees. Individuals must advocate for their own needs, without diminishing their workplace productivity, and any "failure to keep up with such demands becomes an individual's responsibility to fix in private in order to keep working as an academic."[22] These experiences are amplified for anyone with mental illness or disabilities, or any other form of invisible illness or disability. Mental illnesses and mental disabilities, in particular, are seen as somehow conflicting with higher education, a student-only affliction that must be corrected or weeded out. As a librarian, I see syllabi from many different faculty and I read their classroom policies and see the way they demand mental and physical compliance of their students (No knitting or fidgeting! No electronic devices! You must

---

20   For further discussion of these behavioral expectations, see Celia Emmelhainz, Erin Pappas, and Maura Seale, "Behavioral Expectations for the Mommy Librarian: The Successful Reference Transaction as Emotional Labor," in *The Feminist Reference Desk*, ed. Maria Accardi (Sacramento, CA: Library Juice Press, 2017), 27–45.

21   Akemi Nishida, "Neoliberal Academia and a Critique from Disability Studies," in *Occupying Disability: Critical Approaches to Community, Justice, and Decolonizing Disability*, ed. Pamela Block, Devva Kasnitz, and Nick Pollard (Dordrecht: Springer, 2016), 150, https://doi.org/10.1007/978-94-017-9984-3_10.

22   Nishida, 150, "Neoliberal Academia and a Critique from Disability Studies,"

pay close attention at all times, making eye contact with whomever is speaking!). The message is clear: this is what attention and engagement looks like, and anything else is unacceptable. In other words, the way I and many others function in the world is unacceptable.

Our society also sends clear messages about autism. Autism is that which must be avoided at all costs, even outbreaks of mumps and measles are better than autism. Autism is a state of being in desperate need of a cure. Autism is S~C~A~R~Y, and a terrible burden. *Even my therapist* told me I shouldn't tell people I was autistic–she didn't want that label for me or feel it would be helpful. She also told me she would not add that diagnosis to my chart, because it might be used to deny me further therapy. Apparently, insurance companies will allow me to see a therapist for anxiety and depression, but not for autism. Moreover, as a female, I am less likely to be diagnosed with autism, because my autism doesn't look like the male stereotype (Surprise! I am not Raymond from *Rain Man*, nor am I Sam from the television show "Atypical"). Autism research tells me I might have "extreme male brain" or lack a "theory of mind."[23] While I initially thought autism research might help me understand myself, approaches like those just mentioned furthered my outrage, and I'm not even going to talk about autism 'treatment' programs. Just...nope.

Melanie Yergeau observes, "Autistics haven't chosen their neurology, but who has?" and in a similar vein, I note that none of us struggling with mental illnesses or disabilities chose to have our brains, our minds, our body chemistries work this way, so why are we seen as wrong or at fault for our ways of being?[24] I can no longer wrap my head around this viewpoint. We are not to blame, and our ways of being must be accepted just like other ways already are.[25] Yet academic libraries are not currently accepting of difference, which was made quite clear to me at a previous workplace when I opted to disclose my autism after a successful first year of employment. When I asked who I should talk to about accommodations, I was given a warning about not asking for too much, and my continued employment there was

---

23   While my academic training tells me to cite these works, I simultaneously resist the idea of giving them merit.

24   Yergeau, *Authoring Autism*, 8.

25   Maybe my neurological difference is not a deficit, but rather the very genetic variation the human species needs to survive. Pass it on!

threatened. I needed that income, and I needed health insurance, so it was much easier to go back to hiding all of my conditions (and often hiding in the restroom since I worked in an open office space without any privacy) than it was to face the threats that clearly would lie ahead of me were I to seek the accommodations I legally deserved. As both Pionke and myself experienced, "employers do not rise enthusiastically to the challenge of access."[26] In a profession that claims to value equity, diversity, and inclusion,[27] this lack of acceptance for mind and body differences should be inexcusable, and yet the experiences of library workers continue to demonstrate that librarianship is currently failing to take action in support of these stated values.[28]

## Acknowledging and Valuing Difference

Although library workers have a legal right to seek accommodations for their mental disabilities, institutional compliance with the law is not enough. We all deserve more than the chance to merely survive our workplace. Compliance with the law is necessary but not sufficient for creating an inclusive environment that accepts and normalizes differences. Institutions may see the lack of complaints as a sign that they are immune to this issue, but the lack of complaints may in fact be evidence of the continued silencing of mentally ill or disabled faculty and staff.[29] Failure to revise and alter workplace norms will continue to exclude disabled library workers by requiring them to perform as something they are not.

In order to continue resisting the existing injustices, academic libraries need to heed the call for change. As Oud observes, "improving the workplace experience for librarians with disabilities requires a valuing of differences and a broader focus on cultural and social attitudes and

---

26   Price, *Mad at School*, 118.

27   American Library Association, "Core Values of Librarianship," Text, Advocacy, Legislation & Issues, July 26, 2006, http://www.ala.org/advocacy/intfreedom/corevalues.

28   Erin Burns and Kristin E. C. Green, "Academic Librarians' Experiences and Perceptions on Mental Illness Stigma and the Workplace," *College & Research Libraries* 80, no. 5 (July 2019): 638–57, https://doi.org/10.5860/crl.80.5.638; Joanne Oud, "Systemic Workplace Barriers for Academic Librarians with Disabilities," *College & Research Libraries* 80, no. 2 (2019), https://doi.org/10.5860/crl.80.2.169.

29   Price, *Mad at School*, 131.

on structural change, rather than on individuals."[30] Brown and Leigh also argue that "a societal shift in relation to our understanding of disabilities is needed. Rather than focusing on disabilities and illnesses, it is time to consider how ingrained the normalizations are in society that we all aspire to."[31] We need to normalize discussions around mental illness and disabilities and dismantle oppressive structures to create a supportive and inclusive environment for all library workers, not just those that appear to be 'normal.' As Schomberg states so effectively, "if we take an intersectional approach to the world, we quickly see that there are no true bodily experiences; instead, people come in a beautiful variety of shapes, sizes, colors, and movements."[32]

Library workers with mental illnesses and disabilities are not a liability or a disadvantage in the workplace, but have much to offer their institutions, organizations, and students. Academic libraries must recognize that "disabled academics bring value to the university, in their scholarship and their teaching, as well as their expertise. When they are required to waste time, energy, and emotion enacting 'optimal (non-disabled) academic' this is a waste of their unique skills, abilities and experiences, with significant costs to them, their students, the research community, and the broader public."[33] Library workers with mental illnesses and disabilities have much to contribute to this field, if only they are given the chance to do so without it exacting such an extreme cost for them personally and professionally. Rather than continuing to jeopardize the well-being of their employees, academic library leadership must take a proactive stance toward dismantling barriers to inclusion and normalizing human differences, especially mental differences, in the workplace. To fail to do so not only signals that library workers like myself are not welcome or desired, but also demonstrates that equity and inclusion are not, in fact, core values of librarianship, and nothing more than whitewashed words. How many

---

30  Oud, "Academic Librarians with Disabilities: Job Perceptions and Factors Influencing Positive Workplace Experiences," 40.

31  Nicole Brown and Jennifer Leigh, "Ableism in Academia: Where Are the Disabled and Ill Academics?," *Disability & Society* 33, no. 6 (2018): 988.

32  Schomberg, "Disability at Work," 121.

33  Bea Waterfield, Brenda B. Beagan, and Merlinda Weinberg, "Disabled Academics: A Case Study in Canadian Universities," *Disability & Society* 33, no. 3 (March 16, 2018): 327–48, https://doi.or g/10.1080/09687599.2017.1411251.

8tem.

(more) incredible human beings will this profession force out before enacting significant change?

Every morning I do my best to bring my full, enthusiastic self to my workplace, and every day I have to leave substantial pieces of my identity in the parking lot. I wanted librarianship to be my place and my people, but I am exhausted, and I am concerned that I will be unable to remain in a profession that does not welcome me or my way of being. Constraining my square-pegness to fit into the round hole that is librarianship is both frustrating and draining. Us square pegs need a space to exist as ourselves, so we might survive this profession and continue to do the work that motivates us. The only way we can do that is if the profession begins to carve out a more inclusive and welcoming space for those of us who don't currently fit.

Nishida, Akemi. "Neoliberal Academia and a Critique from Disability Studies." In *Occupying Disability: Critical Approaches to Community, Justice, and Decolonizing Disability*, edited by Pamela Block, Devva Kasnitz, and Nick Pollard, 145–57. Dordrecht: Springer, 2016.

Oud, Joanne. "Academic Librarians with Disabilities: Job Perceptions and Factors Influencing Positive Workplace Experiences." *Partnership: The Canadian Journal of Library and Information Practice and Research* 13, no. 1 (2018).

———. "Systemic Workplace Barriers for Academic Librarians with Disabilities." *College & Research Libraries* 80, no. 2 (2019): 169–94.

Pionke, J. J. "The Impact of Disbelief: On Being a Library Employee with a Disability." *Library Trends* 67, no. 3 (May 8, 2019): 423–35.

Price, Margaret. *Mad at School: Rhetorics of Mental Disability and Academic Life.* Ann Arbor: University of Michigan Press, 2011.

Price, Margaret, Mark S. Salzer, Amber O'Shea, and Stephanie L. Kerschbaum. "Disclosure of Mental Disability by College and University Faculty: The Negotiation of Accommodations, Supports, and Barriers." *Disability Studies Quarterly* 37, no. 2 (2017). http://dsq-sds.org/article/view/5487.

Schomberg, Jessica. "Disability at Work: Libraries, Built to Exclude." *Politics and Theory of Critical Librarianship*, February 1, 2018, 111–23.

Siebers, Tobin. "Foreword." In *Mad at School: Rhetorics of Mental Disability and Academic Life*, by Margaret Price, xi–xiv. Ann Arbor: University of Michigan Press, 2011.

Waterfield, Bea, Brenda B. Beagan, and Merlinda Weinberg. "Disabled Academics: A Case Study in Canadian Universities." *Disability & Society* 33, no. 3 (March 16, 2018): 327–48.

Yergeau, Melanie. *Authoring Autism: On Rhetoric and Neurological Queerness.* Durham, NC: Duke University Press, 2018.

# Bipolar Disorder and the Drive to Lead

**John Cohen**

*Content Warning*   Thoughts of Suicide

## Introduction

In 1987, I changed schools. I didn't know anyone, didn't connect with anyone, and my teachers noted to my parents that I was intelligent but had trouble connecting with the other students. I became sullen and unhappy; the teachers wrote on my report cards that I couldn't take any pride in my work—I had fallen into what I would later recognize as a major depression. I was ten years old and didn't understand why I felt like no one liked me; that the world would be better off without me. At ten, I didn't know that those feelings weren't true; I would remain undiagnosed for another 11 years.

Feelings of inadequacy and a little voice telling me I was worthless, that no one liked me, and I should kill myself, plagued me for the years following. When I was 18, I found a book called *Touched with Fire* by Kay Redfield Jamison. It was all about the connections between madness and genius, and as I read it I became uncomfortably certain that something was different with me; something reflected in the book. Reading this book was the beginning of my understanding that I had bipolar disorder.

## I.

I was 14 when Youth Employment Service hired me for a temporary job working at my local public library. When I was 16, that library hired me as a page. Paging was great for me; I could do it after school and on weekends. I worked in an air-conditioned building, and I was able to see everything in the library and learn what was there. My fellow pages were a mix of full time adults and shift-scheduled teens like me. Unfortunately, it wasn't a place where leadership was nurtured or valued. The supervisors were good people, but the problem was inherent in the position itself; it was a position where success hinged on completing everyday tasks and obeying what I was told to do. It was easy to do without thinking very hard about it. That was fine for people who want that kind of job, but it was difficult for those of us who saw problems with things we encountered and had no power to address.

Our library had a leaky roof, which was a major known flaw the building had but was never fixed. If it rained heavily, the circulation supervisor would tell the pages to cover specific stacks with tarps to avoid water damage. This system worked perfectly, until the night there wasn't a supervisor on duty. One of the clerks or the librarian on duty should have thought to tell the pages to break out the tarps, but no-one did. The pages acknowledged the leak and did nothing. Something wasn't right. We all knew the tarps needed to protect the stacks, we saw the leaks developing, but without permission none of us would do anything. I couldn't take it anymore and said "Hey, let's get the tarps rolled out." Everyone except me was waiting for permission to do something even slightly out of the routine—despite the fact we did this regularly—and while that's hardly a shining leadership moment, it's the first taste I had of leadership, and it felt good.

Feeling good was, unfortunately, quite rare for me—bipolar disorder led to me feeling awful far more often than I felt well. A job where thinking wasn't necessary was right for me at the time; turning off my brain was the only way to survive. I had manias far more often as a teen than as an adult, and I have scraps of paper with odd story ideas that make no sense in the light of day to prove it. Anger resulted from not understanding my own mind—rage, mania, and depression are all things I worked very hard to suppress, almost always successfully, because 'normal' people didn't feel this way. The only thing I could think of for people who had problems like me was that we end up in straitjackets.

That's not to say my way of thinking didn't offer up advantages; I often saw situations in unique ways and saw solutions that others did not that made me want to change things at my job. It would be years before I would gain the authority to so do, but I began to test the waters with my superiors and coworkers. While many times people didn't see it my way, there were times that I remember 'knowing best'—and sometimes I did have a good idea that could be implemented. Sometimes my approach was flawed in ways I hadn't foreseen.

For example, I did know that integrating our paperback collection so that mysteries, sci-fi, and westerns were all interfiled with non-genre specific titles was an error—people interested in those sub-collections wanted to browse that sub-collection and no others. I remember saying so, being ignored, and the department moving ahead with the idea. I also remember quietly undoing the interfiling about a year later, after the numerous complaints that started to pour into the suggestion box. On the other hand, another idea that makes me cringe amounted to lying to the patrons, and I'm glad someone stomped that idea out for me. Eventually, I was promoted to clerk, and in that job I worked on Thursday evenings; on those evenings we had no supervisor on duty. One thing I noticed during other shifts was that patrons would accept an answer from a supervisor, even if it was the same answer the clerk initially gave. Since we had no supervisor, I suggested each of us be ready to say we were the supervisor when a supervisor was requested—perhaps each clerk could turn to the person on their left whenever a supervisor was required. The other clerks didn't agree with this, and that's probably for the best; it was a little too outside the box and may have come back to haunt us.

The other advantage my mental illness offered up was an intense—INTENSE—sense of empathy. I could feel bad for others to such a degree that I often had to lop off those feelings to function, which made it look like quite the opposite—I could be an unfeeling jerk who didn't care. Sometimes, that's how it had to be, lest I not function at all. Other times, that empathy gave me the keen ability to do right by those with whom I had to interact. One of my clerk duties was to check-in magazines as they were received and to call EBSCO if they were not. The very first time I called EBSCO and navigated through the phone tree to reach the right person, I talked to Lauren (not her real name). She answered the phone with a heavy sigh and then said, "Hello. This is Lauren. How can I help you?" in a tone so defeated that I knew something was wrong; quickly, my empathy kicked in and I realized what it was. Lauren was a woman whose sole job it was to help people who were missing magazines they had paid for—her only job was to take information from people who were mad that the delivery had been missed.

That job sounded horrible to me, and I decided then and there to be Lauren's favorite client. I responded, peppy as can be (and I'm not a peppy person) "Hi Lauren! I'm the new magazine guy at my library! I'm hoping you can help me solve my problem!" I worked very hard to remain entirely positive throughout the interaction and to make it clear I was asking for her help, not filing a complaint. For the rest of my time at that library, Lauren always answered the phone with a heavy sigh, then "Hello. This is Lauren. How can I help you?" But the reply, "Hi Lauren! Its John!" always revealed a completely different woman, one who was happy and ready to help. I think she was sad when I had to leave. Luckily, I told my successor to treat Lauren well.

## II.

As I continued my journey at my first library, I eventually became a substitute library assistant in addition to being a clerk. Civil Service proved to be troublesome, as the training and experience ratings for a library assistant position didn't take into account any of my time as a page or a clerk, so I didn't score high enough to be permanently appointed to a higher position. And so informed that there was no room for advancement at my library, I applied at one of the local university libraries. I didn't realize it at the time, but I was applying for leadership roles.

I interviewed three times at one library. The first time, they had an internal candidate and I didn't get the position; the second, they had invited me back, but it wasn't a position for which I was appropriate. I wasn't going to apply for the third job made available there, except they once again invited me and this time, I was successful; they hired me as the evening and weekend supervisor of the library. They had seen something to keep asking me back; one might go as far as to say they had seen something in me I wasn't capable of seeing in myself.

My new schedule contained only evenings and weekends, and this is when I first realized how deeply impactful my schedule was on my mental health. Moving to a schedule where I went to sleep at 3 am and woke up at 11 am was strangely liberating for me–It was more in tune with my natural inclinations and I was better off for it. The schedule also allowed me to develop my leadership skills; I was responsible for supervising the student workers and participated in the hiring of those employees. Much of my time was spent as the responsible person for the facility, if only because there were no other non-student workers on the job in the evening (student workers couldn't be in charge of the facility). This responsibility was relatively unimportant in practice but crucial in my perception of the job; I was trusted, I was in charge. For a time, I was relatively happy—as happy as I was capable of being, which was, of course, not as happy as other people.

With staffing changes came a change in the workplace environment, and what was once good for me became very bad for me over a couple of years. Somehow, my brain convinced itself that I deserved this unhappiness, it wouldn't be better anywhere else, and I couldn't get anything better anyway. I stayed at the university far longer than could be considered healthy for me by any measure due to those issues, despite massive amounts of evidence that I was mentally unhealthy. I had the strongest suicide urge I had in years while walking across campus when an opportunity presented itself. I burst out in tears at a disciplinary discussion; I burst out laughing at my boss at a staff meeting because he was so insincere about something. In other words, my mental health was bad enough that I couldn't be counted on to remain professional. The opportunity for advancement came up at least twice, the first time the director said I wasn't ready for it; by the time the second opportunity came along, I no longer cared enough to even apply for it, though he said the job was mine if I wanted it. I had checked out of caring about work, and my work-life became nothing but a treadmill of toil.

I was sustained by my life outside of work, which was surprisingly positive: embracing good friends and finding love. That probably kept me from killing myself, because that's how things had become at work; death seemed like the solution to my work problems. I started on medication that I had been avoiding for years, for reasons ranging from "medications mean I'm sick" to "willpower is enough to power through it" to "medications will make me not feel like myself." Well, medication did make me feel unlike myself—they made me begin to feel better. As I came out of the fog of self-loathing and self-recrimination, as I began to value my time and myself again, I decided to apply for a job at the first library I worked at– that of volunteer coordinator.

Being volunteer coordinator helped me firm up a lot of what I had already started to see as ways to help myself. I was able to arrange for a schedule that more closely aligned with my natural patterns. This schedule not only helped me on a personal level but helped me meet with all our volunteers–over 125 in any given year–who could come in anywhere from opening to closing. Handling the interviewing, onboarding, supervising, and occasional dismissal of that group taught me a lot about how to do those things in a way that overseeing a handful of student workers at a university had not. Even though they weren't paid employees, they had the same basic needs for a supervisor and a leader that paid employees did. It also taught me about pushback—there was pushback from employees about volunteers "taking their jobs," so I needed to learn to thread the needle between what volunteers *could* do versus what they *should* do. The amazing thing was that with medication keeping my bipolar disorder under control, setbacks (such as workers complaining that volunteers might take their jobs) were just setbacks and not a devastating attack on my very existence.

For the first time, I was able to believe in myself. I moved to a small village outside the city I grew up and worked in and when that village's library needed a director, I applied and became the director. My first real solo leadership job, years before I earned my MLS, was an enormous game-changer. So were the challenges that came with the job.

My village library had staff that were long-term but had numerous changes of leadership along the way. They had also had a change in status—becoming a civil service library—that had threatened some jobs there. On the one hand, it's difficult to lead people who are used to getting their way; on the other, it's advantageous to have people who know their job. It was at the village library that I developed my "giving the people what you want them to want" style of leadership. I liked to be able to support my staff by giving them things they wanted. But it was also essential to get buy-in on things that were important to the library. Listening and helping achieve what they wanted helped lead to them respecting my opinions on what we could and couldn't do—a mutual build-up of trust that may have been harder in other circumstances.

Part of managing my bipolar disorder included medication changes at various points in my life. Such changes led to some unfortunate side-effects, such as an exceedingly messy and disorganized office to the point where my board addressed it with me—an event I found embarrassing and yet, thanks to medication, didn't drive me into the depression it could have. But it led to the further surety that empathy and kindness were positive leadership traits if you want to have employees that valued their job and their boss. For example, I had an employee whose father needed frequent intervention for his well-being.

Empathy and kindness led me to take on some of this employee's duties at the time, for example covering the desk when she needed to leave to care for her father for the day, even when it meant being in the building alone, was the kind of thing that employees saw as going above and beyond. This, too, was a leadership lesson. By staying in the trenches rather than walling myself up in my office; by being willing to make sacrifices such as working a 12-hour day, my staff recognized that I cared about their wellbeing and strove for fairness.

At the same time, I learned how to connect with my bosses. As a director, I no longer had a single boss, I answered to a board. At times, I've found board relationships to be odd; they are my boss and the representatives of the people, and yet I still need to guide them on all things library. But the same empathy and people skills that allowed me to succeed as a leader allowed me to succeed with the board. For example, there was a board meeting where my board president was acting strangely—acting forgetful, repeating herself, and generally seeming out of it. Despite my brain screaming at me to ignore it, I attempted to connect by asking her (privately) if everything was okay. The answer was no, and while it was, by and large, none of my business, giving her insight to see that it was affecting her performance was helpful to her; asking a question that was based on human connection rather than business dealings not only helped her feel heard and cared for, but also helped us build a beneficial relationship.

It was at this point that I developed enough confidence to tell both my staff and my bosses about my mental health condition. I felt the staff should know in case I was acting strangely, and my board should know about things that could impact my performance. I've received a lot of pushback over the years from people outside the role of staff or board about my willingness to share—that a) people don't have a right to know these things and b) it's dangerous for people to know these things about me. The people who have told me this are not wrong, but for myself, and for anyone who can summon up the courage to do it, it has been incredibly freeing to do so, and I have found nearly universal support from those with whom I've shared.

A little over a year later, a family situation forced me to move away from the village and forced me to resign from my position. It was difficult to leave the job so soon, especially given the high turnover in previous years. I should have predicted that such a radical change in circumstances would lead to a change in my mental health.

## III.

After the move, my wife and I determined we could live without my income; I remained in the MLS program I had entered, but the hope was that I wouldn't need to work again. This decision turned out to be unrealistic and unwise. Unrealistic simply because having more money has made life more comfortable, but unwise due to a deeper relationship between my mental illness, my self-worth, and how I occupied my time. There is absolutely nothing wrong with being a homemaker, but it felt like I wasn't spending my time on anything productive; worse, not living out my drive to be a librarian severely messed with my head. My wife later informed me that I was not in a good place in this period of our lives, something I didn't recognize at the time. It was around this time that I started seeing a therapist regularly.

What I did recognize was my intense frustration with the process of getting a degree. There were multiple kinds of frustration, but they all added up to an intense desire to quit. Sometimes subjects were hard for me to grasp, whether inherently difficult or obfuscated by the teaching methodology. Other times it was concepts that I had long since understood being taught to me as if I were new to the subject. But a strange transferal from one type of problem to another occurred—I was bipolar, yes, and that meant I spent more than my fair share of time thinking about committing suicide. It also meant I spent each day deciding *not* to commit suicide. That seemed directly transferrable to quitting school—I might get a stray thought about doing it every day, with more intense desires to do it now and again, but I could make an active decision to not act on those thoughts, to stick with it. And I did.

I was left with a degree, new debt, and no job. I was also left with a better understanding of my need to have something to fill my day, and I started looking for jobs. I don't remember how many I applied for, but the job I accepted was as a library assistant at a local community college. In this job, I worked closely with the director, acting as her assistant for much of my time and covering the reference desk for some of the rest. While I only worked this job for a short time—just over half a year—it was significant for two reasons. Firstly, this was the job where I decided to tell my boss about my bipolar disorder pretty much right off the bat, not in the interview, but on my first or second day. I felt that she should know and that if it was enough to make them not want me there, I could leave without much fuss. Instead, and as I always have, I received support from my superior. At the village library, I had waited some time, in this case, I let them know as early as reasonable. It's also a place where I had a significant mental health-related problem; my boss called me in to talk to me about something where I had made a mistake, and I suddenly burst into uncontrollable tears, a reaction that far outsized the problem. I was talking it over with my boss when I realized I hadn't cried in over two weeks; not coincidentally, that was the amount of time I had been on a new medication. The outsized reaction was due to pent-up volatility, not the immediate problem itself. Once we realized this, it was easier to move forward; it also made me much more aware of watching myself for unusual behaviors during medication changes.

After a short time with the community college, I was fortunate to get a job at a public library that, due to its nature, did not require time in grade for a civil service qualification. It was 15 minutes from my house, larger than my previous directorship but not so large as to drown me under the weight of doing the job. I wasted no time informing my bosses on the board and the staff about my condition. It wasn't the first thing I said to them, but within a month of my starting, both groups knew. While I think some were shocked that I would share this so easily and some were apprehensive (after all, mental illness is still worrisome to many) in the end all were supportive and saw that it not only didn't hinder my ability to do the job, in some ways it helped. I was not only able to implement my ideas for the library, but I was able to help others develop their ideas as well. My outside the box thinking could see problems and opportunities that others may have missed. Additionally, the staff had morale and confidence issues from problems with a previous director, and my improved empathy allowed me to detect the issues and work to solve them.

I had an employee who, after a process of escalating discipline, needed to be let go. One of the last things she said to me was, "You have a mental illness, you should be more compassionate to others who do!" While that situation did not lead to success, she was right that my mental illness informs my decision-making process even when evaluating others. I have learned that taking care of yourself is of high importance; that while you are suffering, you still have a job to do. I am willing to help where I can because I do know how difficult it can be.

It's not that my mental illness is gone forever. Quite the opposite, I live with it every day. I have friends who will tell you how much I agonized over the firing above; while I would certainly never say it's as traumatic to fire someone as it is to be fired, it was definitely a trying period for my mental health. If I hadn't been able to discuss the situation frankly with my therapist and other trusted individuals, if I hadn't been able to use them to reflect on my concerns regarding the situation, I'm not sure I'd have been as successful at getting through it. I spent much of every day for my first few years here convinced that I'd be fired, if not that day, then at the next board meeting. It's important to know that there was absolutely no real evidence that this was the case; quite the opposite, all the evidence was that I was doing well. Mental illness is, in a way, a processing disorder, and my mind processed my successes in such a way as to make me think I was in the middle of a cascading failure—that an entire house of cards was about to come down. It's only with hard work and support that I've been able to train my brain not to process this information incorrectly, and I'm proud to say that now I go into work each day, knowing that I am making a positive difference in both the lives of my employees and in the community I serve.

## Conclusion

At 42 years old, I find myself in the enviable position of being in a job that allows me to take care of myself. I answer to a board, of course, but they and my staff know of my condition and being in charge allows me some flexibility to take time for myself as needed. It also, at times, requires being there whether I want to or not, so it's a mixed bag. I'm comfortable enough with the diagnosis and the reactions from others about my mental illness that I no longer feel that it needs to be hidden. It wasn't easy to reach this point—I didn't get treatment for far too long and regret it now; it is incredible to look back and see the difficulties that were preventable if only I had taken care of myself earlier. Years of refusing to mention my pain to a doctor, years of refusing a diagnosis, years of refusing medication, all of which could have helped me clear a fog of negative thoughts that surrounded my life at that time. Years of work (and, admittedly, luck) have led me to the favorable situation I find myself in now, a job where I have the flexibility and the support to take care of myself while I do the job itself.

## Acknowledgements

My wife, for always supporting me, and my friends who are always there for me.

# Fog

**Avery Adams**

*Content Warning*   This chapter refers briefly to suicidal thoughts.

The fog doesn't come on little cat feet. It isn't cute or contemplative or observant. It isn't beautiful. It silently hisses itself to life, expanding inside my head, muffling and slowing everything inside. Sounds behave strangely in fog, seeming to come from perplexing directions with confusing volume. Thoughts drift, smothered by mist and sometimes by each other. The fog often dissolves only with adrenal fire, panic in its wake.

Or: Circuit breakers pop midsentence, the words gone without trace or never appearing at all. Speech falters, and faces around the meeting table grow perplexed, irritated, concerned, or all three at once. Sometimes someone will interrupt as if to save me. Sometimes they just interrupt, which angers me.

Or: Anger flashes at small things, or it doesn't appear at all when I'm being challenged and should respond with strength and clarity, defining and defending my boundaries. I cannot show anger; it costs too much later in shame, guilt, and impaired professional effectiveness. Anger is fickle with unpredictable power. That was my father's anger, and now it's mine. I am very afraid of it.

Or: One of my staff starts a passive-aggressive game, deftly riding the insubordination line, maybe for sport or maybe to deflect supervisory attention from some other issue. I think too slowly to call it out clearly, so I ignore it until I can understand it and shake the fear of confrontation, fear of uncontrollable anger. I hide, surf the news, not really fooling myself that I'm working through the problem by taking a break and letting it percolate. Sometimes a solution or the right language does come to me, but often it's far too late to address the issue. Among other things, supervisory feedback should be prompt, specific, and clear, and I grapple with all three.

I am a middle manager in an academic library, responsible for the collection, technical services, and the budgets for acquisitions and automation. I oversee a dozen staff, several million dollars, and overstuffed stacks in spaces coveted by non-library operations. Mental fog, insomnia, spotty concentration, erratic memory, and persistent anxiety all affect how I manage a high-performing department with some strong personalities; articulate vision and shape our collections, leading and guiding librarians I don't supervise; manage the acquisitions budget and collection spaces in a rapidly changing campus environment; teach and work in reference; negotiate some historically tense group relationships; conduct outreach to faculty, students, and administration about the library's integral place in campus intellectual life; and participate in the profession.

As I write this, the campus is currently in quiet turmoil over budget issues, with a personnel reduction in progress. Reassuring as I try to be, staff anxiety in my area is high and morale low. We're stretched thin and can't afford to lose anyone, not after the draconian cuts of 2008-2009. Sometimes that is clear to me, and sometimes nothing is clear, not the screen in front of me nor anything behind.

Behind me stretches a checkered résumé, a lengthy, indelible record of positions surrendered out of a depressive inability to manage the political as well as the logistical and philosophical challenges of a library—or any—profession. I'm fortunate not to have too many interpersonal conflicts among my staff, fortunate that my supervisor is hands-off but always available, very fortunate that the library's work culture is relaxed enough that no one so far has had to justify flextime or long-term leave, and extremely fortunate for the solid health insurance.

And yet...This somewhat isolated neighborhood is basically a small town with unpredictable attitudes toward mental health, and stigma is very present even on a supposedly progressive campus. Most people I know who seek therapy or psychopharmacology travel to other parts of the city for those services. I try to fight stigma by walking from the train into the counseling service with head held high, but I also walk fast, which sums up my conflicted feelings. If there's stigma-related trouble for me down the road, well, there would be no one to blame but myself. I doubt I've managed to escape all notice, not because of any overinflated sense of my own prominence but because I live and work among a lot of very observant and intelligent people. Sometimes I'm ready to move my treatment elsewhere, but that feels like a capitulation and betrayal of the cause, not to mention the fact that I'm currently blessed with some brilliant providers I don't want to give up.

Despite the social realities that I think I grasp, I habitually think of myself as invisible anyway and often prefer it. I also fight it, with a decades-long internal conflict between wanting to be recognized as a person and not wanting to be noticed, which seems like a perfectly logical result of relentless bullying from childhood into college, and other long-term emotional abuse. That abundant ill-treatment arose partly from my persistent lack of social awareness—its source being somewhere on the light end of the autism spectrum: I sometimes take things too literally or strictly, notice small details but overlook the obvious, miss social cues, don't understand or even perceive social rules that everyone knows, compulsively count things and sort M&Ms by color, etc., etc., etc. I think of Asperger's more as a lens than a diagnosis, not that it's a recognized diagnosis anymore anyway. It isn't a label I wear or talk about so much as just one way of understanding how I am and why I do the things I do (or don't do). Either way, feeling perpetually out of step with the world is one source of low self-esteem, but it's not the whole story.

I see my depression as a lifelong disease requiring constant management, dating to childhood, and hereditary in both genetics and family dynamics. This viewpoint is in itself a major advance for me; it's taken decades to begin thinking of depression as separate from me, a thing of its own, rather than as a vast set of deficiencies making me unable to cope with the world. Sometimes it's been severe, on two occasions enough so for hospitalization. The first time I wasn't sleeping, eating, or doing much of anything else; the second time I was going through a divorce and working in a thoroughly toxic place, and I had a suicide scare. That hospitalization probably wasn't necessary; it was an impulse, but it felt like a close call and I didn't feel safe. The hospitalization itself was nearly traumatic, pretty much counterproductive except for the temporary physical safety.

That's the background.

*Pseudodementia.* My father eventually died of Alzheimer's, as did his mother. His alcoholic father died not of dementia, but with dementia, well into his nineties. Somehow, he had beaten several cancers and showed no physical ill effects for all his drinking. After my grandmother's death, my father was so afraid of the disease that he grew increasingly obsessed with proving how solid his memory remained, to the point of ignoring what was happening around him. He naturally couldn't recall what he never noticed, and as he became so completely self-absorbed in proving himself, it was a very small step to dismissing anything he hadn't observed, which was an increasing amount of the world around him. That's its own form of dementia even if it's not in the *Diagnostic and Statistical Manual of Mental Disorders*, and the irony is desperately sad.

As my own symptoms of depression shifted and changed over the years, I became worried myself about what seemed to be signs of dementia: loss of memory, inability to locate words, occasional difficulty processing speech (i.e., making words out of what I'm thinking and then saying them), even physical disorientation at times. It was an immense relief after years and years to finally see a psychiatrist nod, completely unfazed and unsurprised, and say the word *pseudodementia*. The relief lasted a few days until I realized that the symptoms weren't going to just disappear now that I had a name for them. But being able to name the issue did help, along with the likelihood that I wasn't currently developing an early-onset problem that would burden my family for decades. That's not impossible, but for the moment I can worry a little less about it happening right now.

Still, I'm constantly frustrated by a lack of concentration and ease of distraction, which is a huge problem when I'm working on complex data analysis or on budget projections. It's not necessarily an interruption that throws me off track; all too often, it's internal, as if someone hit an "off" switch in my brain, and wherever I was in the mental process is lost. Nearly every day I have the experience of quickly switching windows or browser tabs to look something up, and in the split second it takes to hit *alt+tab*, whatever I meant to look up is gone. Instantly. I don't merely misplace my keys; I completely lose track of them within seconds of having had them in my hand. The worst of the mind-scatter coincides with poor sleep, and I think it's both cause and effect, a cycle of frustration and exhaustion that both feeds itself and spills over, spreading and drifting in every direction. But even when I'm sleeping half-decently (about as good as it gets), the inner circuits still spark and derail my thoughts at random moments.

Early in my career, when I worked full time in reference and instruction (when I was younger and not so greatly affected), I found the work exhilarating as a high-wire act, never knowing what was going to come across the desk, and facing the constant challenge of making sure I was expert enough with our resources to respond efficiently and accurately to whatever came. Fielding reference questions was a constant Zen dance, a focused exercise in staying present, asking deliberate questions, listening carefully, and responding with close attention to the patron's subsequent responses.

Instruction was a performance, also thrilling yet anxiety-inducing enough to overprepare and overprepare; that anxiety continues, although it's heightened these days by the fear of hissing fog. My work now involves a lot less time on the desk and in the classroom, which is just as well, although I do miss the public-centric work (see "positions surrendered...," above). Being overprepared for instruction isn't exactly a bad thing; I only wish it could be more reassuring that my mind won't suddenly dissolve midsentence in front of 20 people I'm trying to engage in an intellectual adventure. *Fear of fog, fog of fear. I cannot rely on my brain and I am afraid.*

I teach only a few times a year now, and while that particular fear still affects me, it doesn't come around constantly. Most of my work is different, more focused on long-range strategies and supervising continuous technical operations than on executing discrete tasks or working individually with students, faculty, and other patrons. It's on a different scale; the challenges are higher, the timelines longer, and the chasms deeper.

The big questions for me every day in my current role?

- How do I communicate with, encourage, and support the people who report to me, and especially bolster their morale, when so much of the time I just want to find some way to kill the pain, to crawl under a rock and die?

- How do I manage projects involving both overall direction and very detailed, complex work when I seem to have the concentration of a fruit fly?

- How do I communicate vision and discuss process and procedure clearly when I can't seem to maintain a line of thought from subject to verb, let alone to prepositional phrase?

- How do I maintain an image of leadership, mastery, and accuracy/trustworthiness when I take so long to remember things and can't keep stuff straight?

- How do I manage the frustration of all this, feeling unsafe disclosing it to anyone with whom I work?

Most of those questions would apply in any profession. How does mental illness affect my work in Library and Information Science (LIS) in particular? In two primary ways:

First, one fundamental element of our work is information, and my most constant challenge lies in processing information—taking it in, absorbing and understanding it, synthesizing it with other information, and responding to it. When I'm overwhelmed, written language is often incomprehensible. It's not that I suddenly can't read; rather, what I see is a collection of words on a page, without any meaning that I can put together.

Likewise, too much aural information turns everything to an unintelligible jumble. At that point, it's all just noise, and neither raised voices nor exaggeratedly slow speaking will get information through any better. Even if I hear the words, I can't make any meaning out of them. For instance, vendor reps frequently visit or ask to meet at conferences to talk about new products and new developments in products we already have. Depending on the rep's manner, I sometimes feel like I'm facing the proverbial firehose, and the information quickly becomes muddled. Sometimes I'll puzzle for a long time over a comment I don't understand, only to realize a week or two later that I'd been publicly challenged and either didn't respond or responded with a non-sequitur, or that I'd been lashed with sarcasm and sat there looking blank. *Too late to fix that now.*

Keeping up with and participating in LIS developments, news, and research is also a challenge; it's difficult keeping the thread of an article in mind, putting the pieces together as I go, and understanding the whole of what I read. I'm resorting more and more to executive summaries instead of the full text, unless I really need the details in order to grasp the argument. Even then it's difficult to remember what I've read for more than a few minutes, especially if I turn to reading something else next. I certainly won't be able to call it quickly to mind in discussions with colleagues, reps, and listservs later on; I'll vaguely remember reading something about the topic but will be too uncertain of what it was and afraid of getting it wrong to mention it at all.

The same problem appears in trying to keep track of news and developments within the library and on campus; this is slightly different in that it affects how I interact especially with the people who report to me. I don't want to appear careless, thoughtless, or uninformed, so when I feel lost and disconnected from what's going on, and unable to get a handle on it, I avoid conversations altogether. This, of course, only makes it look like I don't care, which is exactly what I don't want to do. It echoes far too closely what my father did to himself and his awareness of the world and the people around him. My preferred practice of "Management By Walking Around" falls off precipitously as I withdraw, further alienating my staff and cutting me off from a lot of day-to-day information about what's happening in my department.

In addition to trouble taking information in, I have trouble getting it out. Sometimes, I simply can't find the word I'm looking for, or the second part of a sentence will just disappear before I can say it. Other times, a completely wrong word comes out of nowhere. It might simply not be the right word for what I mean, but on occasion a word or phrase will come out of my mouth and I have no idea from where. It's as if someone else, in his own completely separate world, butted in with an utter irrelevance, absurdity, or wild exaggeration. *Where did that come from? That's not what I meant to say at all.*

Losing my place in expressing a thought, or losing words altogether, tremendously affects my work in reference, teaching, meetings, and supervisory conversations. Communication is absolutely key in LIS. In a very real sense, I make my living by talking to people in one way or another, but my current work also requires keeping a lot of complex, detailed information straight and mentally close at hand during those conversations. I deflect the embarrassment of struggling to remember by saying that once I've dealt with something, it's wiped from RAM, and then the tiny file clerk in my head has a lot of searching to do in order to retrieve it. Sometimes I explain that my indexing department is understaffed, which usually elicits enough of a chuckle to defuse others' irritation over my mental slowness. It's a risky self-deprecation—humor to which I'm prone in the first place and that not everyone understands or appreciates—and sometimes I can effectively undercut myself by trying to be funny or relieve an awkward moment. That helps only sometimes, and what I say seems to have a way of going astray amidst the noise.

Mack Hagood writes, "sleep, calm, concentration—these are presumably the states of a self in control...[and] noise is often conceived as the main threat to sleep, calm, and concentration."[1] The twenty-first century is a tremendously noisy world, and I'm easily overloaded with sensory information. The results of that overstimulation are 1) I can't absorb anything more; 2) I can't process the information I already have; and 3) I can't formulate a response. It's as if I've been turned to a mossy stump, unable to soak in anything more, unable to resist and unable to react. Vulnerability to sensory overload is one characteristic of autism, and to someone with depression as well, it's made-to-order for feeling alienated, out of control, and helpless. Worse, lack of sleep also makes me more vulnerable to noise and a sense of helplessness. In a corollary to Hagood's observation, inadequate rest lowers my resistance to noise, which in turn leaves me feeling less in control, not to mention less calm, which is not conducive to quality sleep.

I've spent my whole life working at coming to a place of peace with the world. I need rest, of which I can't get enough because of insomnia, and I need quiet—sensory, emotional, and spiritual.

Seeking quiet isn't why I went into librarianship, counter to the stereotype that we all know is nonsense. That decision was about being fascinated with the world of information, enjoying time spent with people who work in libraries, and loving any opportunity to help others find answers and learn how to find them. There's a kind of peace in doing worthwhile work well, and for me, helping people learn is the most worthwhile work possible.

Which brings me to the second core element of LIS service: Our work is about relationships, especially in academia. The scholarly world is fundamentally about conversations: among people, among people and ideas, and among ideas. In this environment, interactions between

---

1   Mack Hagood, *Hush: Media and Sonic Self-Control* (Durham, NC: Duke University Press, 2019), 108.

students and faculty, and students and ideas, are paramount. And when language and personal interactions can be so difficult, I feel for months on end that I'm unable to be effective, that I'm just groping blindly, despite knowing intellectually that I do have vision, I can successfully orchestrate logistics to realize vision, and I continue to solve complex problems on a large scale. I'm present, sharp, and helpful enough of the time to be considered competent, but I rarely see that myself, feeling separate and adrift as I do.

Being so sensitive and susceptible to feeling all my needles instantly peg when too much energy comes at me—say, in the form of an aggressive or devious colleague—I often find it impossible to defend my boundaries well, if at all. Managers routinely need to be assertive and clear; I sometimes have to defend my work, and I definitely have to back up my staff at times or give someone corrective feedback. When someone transgresses or offends, my first spurt of anger might burn off some mist, but hard on its heels are doubt and fear.

- What if I didn't really understand what was said? I've always been susceptible to misunderstanding things. One refrain of my childhood and adolescence:

- Mom: "If you weren't certain about it, why didn't you ask?"

- Me: "But I wasn't uncertain. I was just wrong."

- What if I'm overreacting? Is this not such a big deal?

- What if I shouldn't react at all? Or is this a challenge that I need to answer? I can't tell right off.

- I'm not sure I have the right to object. I have to think about that.

- Anger is wrong, wrong, wrong and I'm going to be annihilated for showing it. When I do give in to anger, for days afterward I burn with guilt and shame. There's no fog those days; all I can see then is flames everywhere around me. But mist or flame, it doesn't matter which, I can't think straight.

Cue the thermonuclear-scale impostor syndrome and the "I have no business being in this job" self-recriminations. It's clear how that line of thought can spiral downward in a hurry.

So, do I have any solutions? Coping mechanisms? Compensating strategies? Yes, a couple.

While in my MLS program, I came up with a different way of taking notes while reading, using a highlighter to mark only the subjects, verbs, and objects of sentences, which did help with comprehension. It worked for me because it forced a different kind of focus and attention, calling for not simply underlining whole sentences—which one can do without really absorbing them—but making myself physically parse out the meaningful components. It works, but it takes a lot of energy that I seldom feel I have.

In addition, one of the concepts I've been working on for some time is that of radical acceptance, which is pretty much what it sounds like: Taking the world, events, and people as they are. It doesn't mean approving, capitulating, enabling, or ignoring anything; it just means recognizing events and circumstances as what they are, nothing more and nothing less. It also means decoupling those realities from my own responses, and for me, that's the most important point.

For instance, working on and around college campuses in various roles for 30 years has made me a student of organizational behavior. That doesn't mean I claim any special expertise, but when the inevitable happens—say, a collaborative "pilot" project is unilaterally turned into a firm decision before any participant input or any discussion has taken place—I can remind myself that most institutions are more or less dysfunctional, and that's how they sometimes behave. I can still be irritated or unhappy about it, but I no longer expend much energy on impotent outrage, asking how "they" could possibly think that course of action would be okay. I already know the answer: That's how organizations behave. Having accepted that, I can then move on to choosing how to respond based on what I want to see happen, what's in my power to do, and what I think are the possible or likely outcomes of my choices. It's a powerful concept that has helped me begin to develop a stronger sense of agency and control, which is a potent repellant of despair. It's a way of separating what happens outside me from my own reactions and emotions, instead of jumping immediately from suffering injustice straight to feeling that I don't belong in this world. It hasn't been as simple to develop as I make it sound, but it's been helpful nonetheless, especially in academia where organizations are very complex, layered, and sometimes downright entangled with each other, quite literally in dysfunctional or even abusive relationships.

Therapy, of course, has been indispensable, along with medications, which have their own set of issues. Finding a balance between effectiveness and side effects is frequently difficult. A regimen will work for a while, even for years, and then suddenly cease its effectiveness. That's not news to anyone who's dealt with psychotropic medications, and it's not specific to LIS. But trying to comprehend clinical information consumes mental energy I need in order to do my job. I don't watch television and don't pay any attention to medication advertisements, so I'm not up to date in any way. Learning to rely on a psychopharmacologist has been a bit like learning to delegate work: It's about letting go. I still need to be engaged and want significant input, but I don't have to control everything about how it works or have absolutely all the information. But that's a challenge for a librarian used to mastering information. It feels like an inadequacy, like so much else, hazy and indistinct.

At sea, fog is a common and simple phenomenon, and some of the best tools for compensating are radar and GPS. Radar is susceptible to clutter and masking, though, from rain or ground structures that block radio waves from reflecting back to identify objects hidden in the mist. And radar can't always distinguish between another ship and a small island. Both are hazards, but one will never follow the legal rules of the sea and move out of your path.

Between humans, radar is even dicier. Some people with autism are very good at detecting patterns from partial information, and I count myself among them. This ability takes the form of being good at crossword puzzles, anagrams, and editing others' writing, sensing what they meant and how they intended their argument to unfold. Unfortunately, when trying to read human behavior, it's not hard to think erroneously that I have enough information and either over-extrapolate or completely misinterpret it.

GPS requires satellites that orbit the earth but remain in the same relative place geographically. The system of ground stations, satellites, and GPS receivers is a wholly external mechanism for locating ourselves in space. It's analogous to the social rules that help us navigate amongst other people, rules I have trouble interpreting or even noticing at times. It's as if I'm simply not wired to pick up the frequencies being transmitted and, supposedly, received. GPS's function is an electronic process, and most modern electronic circuits are well insulated, not vulnerable to short-circuits caused by moist air. Liquid water in the device will damage it, yes; fog, rarely.

Inside my head is an entire electrical system with circuits, switches, transistors, diodes, transmitters, receivers, capacitors, and connections among each of them everywhere. None of them is insulated, because the human brain naturally makes connections by association as well as by pure logic. It's supposed to skip and jump from one set of connections to another, as when applying an existing skill to a new problem or adding new information to what I already know. When even those normal skips and jumps begin to misfire and falter further, it's usually the fog.

We work with information and by making connections. Fog short-circuits things. It drifts, conceals, expands, redirects, impedes, deceives.

It silences.

---

### Bibliography

Hagood, Mack. *Hush: Media and Sonic Self-Control.* Durham, NC: Duke University Press, 2019.

Avery Adams is a pseudonym.

# Depression and Obsessive-Compulsive Personality Disorder (OCPD)

**Jodene R. Peck Pappas**

## Introduction

*Brief Background and Purpose*

I want to share my experience in the library and information science field of having depression and Obsessive-Compulsive Personality Disorder (OCPD) because I feel it is important to let others know they are not alone, to offer relief, and to end the stigma by discussing these disorders.

I have felt the symptoms of depressed moods lasting all day, nearly every day since I was a small child. For seemingly no reason feelings of sadness, emptiness, and hopelessness continued while growing up, during my teen years, and throughout my adult life in every job. My family never talked about depression other offering unhelpful suggestions to "Cheer up!" or "Smile!"

It was finally in my 30s—after completing all of my education, a short-lived marriage, and becoming married for a second time—when I was professionally counseled for depression. During this period— after multiple moves across the country with my husband following his career—I was unemployed, I became nonfunctioning and was barely able to let my husband take me to a doctor. Years later, at age 49, I was diagnosed with Severe Major Depressive Disorder and OCPD. The diagnoses felt like a relief. I could embrace it because it explained everything—all of my behaviors and thoughts from my whole life made sense. It also meant that there were other people who did things like me, because they were compelled to do it, and because they thought it was beneficial in some way.

While growing up, I always thought that I was different from most people because I couldn't tell anyone why I did things the way I did. I felt shame and embarrassment if anyone would discover that I put everything in order, especially when I knew that they would find it unnecessary. Who does unnecessary work? Why would anybody copy, in outline form, whole texts to study, because that takes forever!?

I later found out that one symptom of OCPD is that the individual views perfectionism as good or benevolent, whereas others may perceive these traits as problematic. For example, alphabetizing a list is helpful but not always necessary. I would do it because it pleases me. I like the order. In recent years, I have found out that there are many people with depression and OCPD, all with individual behaviors. Perhaps readers may identify with some of my traits as I share this with you all.

## Challenges As I Write This

Writing this book chapter, I have felt overwhelmed, extremely embarrassed, and anxious about the possibility of failing. I want to do my best. I want to get this right—to write it well—to be successful. For me that means I want to be complete and thorough. But it was too long. It was overwhelming to be thorough and then have to condense it.

As for perfectionism, I've been told in school or work, "It doesn't have to be perfect!" in order to get me to work faster. To me, that directive is annoying and unhelpful. I am not trying to be perfect. I am only trying to do my best. Perfection is an impossibility. I've also been told, "You can't do everything, Jodene!" But in my mind, I don't want to do everything.

For example, at home, I'm distracted by the things I like to do. These activities are my favorite, preferred tasks. An example of this is measuring the area in total square inches of pages in a notepad and filing it in order by size with the rest of the notepads of the same type. I use the notepads in order by the smallest area in total square inches. This is just one of my collections. This is a compulsive task. I am "in my happy place." I have done this ever since I had paper to organize, as a small child. Resisting these compulsive tasks is quite uncomfortable for me.

As for stigma, I am worried about other people thinking I'm strange, but I never thought of myself as having a mental illness. After all, I can function and have been successful and happy. But on the other hand, I've had tremendous support from family, teachers, and friends. However, there have also been times where I was not successful or functioning, or I refused support.

Despite all this, I am proud of the things I do because it is how I am.

## Definitions and My Symptoms

The DSM-5 Desk Reference says that for a diagnosis of Major Depressive Disorder, there needs to be five or more of the symptoms occurring in the same 2-week period and result in changes from previous life functions and that at least one of the symptoms must be either a depressed mood or a loss of interest or pleasure.[1] When I received the diagnosis, I was depressed all day, every day, for months. It felt like a painful, crushing sadness with no hope. I felt the pain in my head, chest, and other parts of my body at different times. I wanted it to stop and the only way I knew was to sleep as much as I could. All I did was lie on the couch, mindlessly watching TV or sleeping. I felt worthless. I couldn't verbalize what was wrong. I didn't want to take advice to help myself, like, get up and go outside for a walk. I was afraid to tell my parents and siblings. With these feelings, I didn't want to leave the house.

The symptoms of Obsessive-Compulsive Personality Disorder (OCPD) include "a pervasive pattern of preoccupation with orderliness, perfectionism, and mental and interpersonal control, at the expense of flexibility, openness, and efficiency, beginning by early adulthood and present in a variety of contexts."[2] For me, the symptoms manifested in my preoccupation with details, rules, lists, order, organization, or schedules to the extent that the major point of the activity can be lost.

People often confuse the two acronyms, so I want to point out the difference between OCPD and OCD (Obsessive Compulsive Disorder). I used to joke with others about having OCD. Behaviors like hoarding, orderliness, and a need for symmetry and organization are shared by both conditions. With OCD, it is unwanted and seen as unhealthy, while people with OCPD perceive these behaviors to be rational, desirable, and beneficial. It also helps to understand the difference between

---

1  American Psychiatric Association. *Desk Reference to the Diagnostic Criteria from DSM-5* (Arlington, VA: American Psychiatric Association, 2013), 94–97.

2  American Psychiatric Association. *Desk Reference to the Diagnostic Criteria from DSM-5*, 329–30.

obsession and compulsion. Obsession has to do with thoughts, feelings, ideas or sensations that are recurring and intrusive. Compulsion has to do with behavior that is conscious, standardized, or recurrent.[3]

## Background

### Child's Play

When I was young, I collected paper, pens, pencils, books, and any office supply that I could acquire for reading and writing. I saved up my money to collect my favorite BIC stick pens in different colors. I divided my pen collection by type: stick, click, felt tip, or magic marker. The click-type pens were mostly freebies with business' advertising, and I arranged them in alphabetical order. I had to decide whether to use the first word as it appeared on the pen or the name of the company as it was printed. I seemed to have early tendencies toward making up rules to alleviate decision-making and create order and consistency. I lined up my pen and pencil collections underneath my bed, away from my mom's intrusive vacuum. The pencils, if sharpened were in order by length, easily ascertained. If new, first chronologically by when I acquired them, second, alphabetically, by what was printed on them, or by color. I used them in order, shortest to longest, saving my new, unused pencils. I still have my collection of unused pencils from grade school that my sister gave me with my name printed on them plus many more that I've collected over my life. I always think that I will use them some day. Now I know my rules are too fixed. Right now I am using a pencil that is three inches long—because my rule says to "use up the shortest pencil first." I won't throw it away until it is too short to fit in the electric pencil sharpener. Efficiency, as I define it, is one of the highest values to me and I believed it should be of value to everyone. I felt my behavior was unusual, so I didn't tell anyone I did this. My collections continue to grow.

I also have always had a compelling need to put everything in order. Even chores like washing the dishes or hanging up the wash on the clothesline outside, I needed to do it in my order. My order felt aesthetically pleasing, but I couldn't have explained it at the time. I hung the clothes in order of my dad's, then my mom's, then mine (oldest to

---

3    Millamena, Sarah. "How to Deal with OCPD'S in the Workplace." *WIRED CHOICE*, April 3, 2009.
     http://wiredchoice.blogspot.com/2009/05/how-to-deal-with-ocpds-workplace.html?m=1

youngest). Then pants, shirts, shorts, socks (hanging longest to shortest). These rules made sense to me and I thought it was all a good thing. My mom was horrified at the length of time it took me to do this simple chore. Then the next wash load might not fit the pattern—so, I would have to rearrange the whole clothesline! This is an example where my mom was an authority figure, like a boss at work, and she insisted that I hang the clothes as fast as I could. This frustrated me to no end, and I tried my hardest to keep my order but do it faster, which was never fast enough. I could *not* stop this behavior and I feared getting caught and being reprimanded and I was. I thought I was doing a good thing. Wasting time was not an issue for me. I loved my processes.

## College, Music, and Pre-Professional Jobs

I started working in the college library during my sophomore year. As a student worker, it was okay to ask where things were. My junior year I worked at the reference desk. My main task was to hand write letters asking to have free materials sent to us for the vertical file. I had good handwriting. I took a list of topics the reference librarian marked and copied the same letter over and over, which I loved doing!

I had gone to college with a plan of becoming a music teacher. At this time, I was dealing with several life-changing issues, including marriage, pleasing my parents, and deep depression. During this I realized this teaching music didn't fit my natural behavior.

After college graduation, I desperately wanted to find a job in a library, thinking libraries had the kind of work I liked, and was hired at the University of Nebraska-Lincoln's Love Library and worked in the Serial Records department in Technical Services. This job is still my favorite job that I've ever had. Every procedure was outlined in a big binder. I was told that it would take six months to learn and become comfortable with the job. My supervisor was an excellent trainer who checked all of my work. She was kind and I wanted to please her. I typed each title of a serial on a thin strip of perforated cardstock, which was torn neatly after it had gone through the typewriter. Even though it was cumbersome and I hated to make a mistake, I enjoyed this work. All the individual strips' titles were alphabetized. I loved the daily routine in the department. When the mail arrived and was sorted each day, we would alphabetize the pile of journals further in our own section. All of these routines and tasks align with OCPD behavior. It was during this time that I believed I could do more than what I was doing. Someday I wanted to go to library school.

*Library School*

While going through a divorce, my mom suggested that it might be a good time to go to library school. I looked at Emporia State University in Emporia, Kansas, nearer to family. That is all I based it on. I could have gone anywhere if I had known how to assess Masters' programs. I needed the support of family, though, but with some sense of autonomy, which is what being at Emporia State offered me.

I enrolled in graduate school while working part-time at the Emporia Public Library (EPL). In library school, I learned that the profession was definitely a people profession and that I couldn't expect to hide my preferential behaviors behind my work at a public service desk. I questioned whether this was the right kind of work for me. I love books and organizing, but how can I be a leader and someone who helps people all the time? In my part-time job, I worked at both the Circulation and Reference desks. I didn't like either of those jobs, but I needed the experience interacting with people, and it proved beneficial. It forced me out of my comfort zone. I overcame my fear of answering the telephone. I gained confidence when I learned to find information on nearly any topic. I liked to help people when they showed appreciation. Ultimately, I learned to love my new profession. I felt proud of my experience.

## Professional Jobs

Ponca City Library in Oklahoma, was an ideal place for my first professional job. My co-workers were about the same age as me and I felt it was easy to work with and socialize with them. Besides reference work and collection development, my other duties were to plan and provide adult programming. This side of the job was not something I enjoyed because it involved asking people for help and that was not something I preferred to do. The things I asked people for help with were the very things that I didn't like to do. When I wished to channel my strong and preferred traits, I always expected to be told, "No." But I was able to plan a few programs by myself where I also presented.

Following my new husband, David, and his new job, I started a professional, part-time substitute reference librarian position at the Spokane Public Library (SPL) in Washington state and worked mostly downtown and at the Manito branch but eventually at the other branches too. Working reference was a steep learning curve for me after my small-town library. I had to learn fast, watch, and listen. They were good! They were fast! They made it look easy! I tried not to be in their way! This was hard for me and I tried my best. I improved but was disappointed when I didn't get hired for the next open full-time reference librarian position.

I started getting "headaches" more often. This really meant "depression" and I would stay home, call in sick, and feel guilty on top of feeling worthless. I didn't want to do this kind of job and didn't know what I was going to do. I spent a lot of time on the couch, not talking, not moving—just sleeping or watching TV. I wasn't really functioning. I went back to work, but it was difficult. I started declining requests to substitute at other branch libraries because it was so hard "shifting" to different locations.

David found a psychiatrist and made an appointment for me. The doctor prescribed Zoloft for my depression. I tried it and it made a tremendous difference. I went back to work. I still did not look forward to doing reference work, but I could stand it and I had hope for doing something better.

Next, I was hired full-time as a reference librarian at the Wichita Public Library (WPL) in Kansas. I found doing reference at WPL much easier than in Spokane, although I felt I had lost many hard-earned skills from SPL. I eventually burned out working on the reference desk, and one time I caught myself saying a bit too loudly while exiting the public area heading back to the workroom, that "people are so stupid!" I viewed my public service time as a type of teaching, helping individuals, one-on-one, on the spot, when-needed kind of teaching. I was good at it, and felt proud of my experience and referred to all of my public desk service as a time of "paying my dues." The reason I kept doing it because there were very few cataloging jobs available.

My favorite part of my job in Wichita was collection development. I loved reading reviews, selecting, analyzing, and weeding. Another selector and I moved to a smaller office that we shared. I loved that I was away from public service more and felt I could concentrate better in this two-person office. Some might have called me slow, but I had my own methodical system for selecting and I had difficulty keeping up with reading all the review journals. I was proud of knowing my collection. I loved the Literature collection. Developing it was almost as good as actually reading the books.

The head of the division knew I was interested in cataloging so when a position became available, I was allowed to transfer from reference to cataloging. I was finally in my "dream job." I wanted to learn as much as I possibly could. Several projects were highlights for me.

First, I completed the profile for our outsourcing of popular materials, beginning with adult fiction. This project was fun and it was challenging to figure out a more streamlined process from our highly customized processing. The project made me familiar with every aspect of processing; every category, collection, location, format, etc., for the library's branches and collections. I remember being extremely frustrated with many errors from the vendor and had to learn to let go and not obsess on every error with an email.

I loved original cataloging. It was like solving a puzzle and plugging in all the correct pieces in the right place. I loved AACR2r and MARC because they are rules and codes. One record that I'll be forever proud of, despite others saying I wasted my time, was the one I did for an unusual gift of the Guinness Book of World Records' largest book. At 8 feet x 5 feet, it was manufactured and uniquely created with digital photos and specially printed on carefully folded pages. This book was about the country, Bhutan. There were limited copies and I was determined to catalog it in OCLC first. I scoured AACR2r and MARC intending to put every detail I could where it was appropriate.

In 2006, David's job in Wichita ended and he started a new one in Sheridan, Wyoming. After nine months living in different states, a part-time information services assistant position came open at the Sheridan County Fulmer Public Library and David asked me if I would consider it if it meant we didn't have to live apart anymore. I did not want to do reference again. It wasn't even a professional position, and only paid $10.04 per hour. I think so often, I should have stayed in Wichita in my house with my good-paying job. Arriving in December for the icy, snowy winter in Wyoming, I was so depressed during this time that I couldn't appreciate much of anything. I still tried to appear friendly and happy to work at the reference desk on the worst hours—nights and weekends. I hated my life and didn't have my prescriptions anymore. Once, a co-worker exclaimed, "Jodene, it's okay!" This surprised me! I wondered if I had an expression on my face that looked worried or sad all the time! Over the years, I think my face did have a worried or sad expression because I tried to appear friendly and happy, even though I hated everything.

After only two years, David experienced another position change, a victim of the Wyoming economy. Soon, he secured a new position in

Harrisburg, Pennsylvania at the Harrisburg Area Community College (HACC). Harrisburg was a different kind of city for me because I couldn't find a job. I stayed home. I didn't get out much, so I never learned my way around or where things were. I used the local public library and it felt strange to be a real patron. I thought it would be fun, but instead, I was depressed because there just weren't any library jobs.

Our moves put stress on my relationship with David as I wasn't happy living with him and wasn't able to do things the way I wanted. I was lying on the couch in front of the TV, sleeping, and not talking. Basically, I wasn't functioning again. David took me to the doctor, and I was set up to go to a psychiatric institute for "partial hospitalization". It was like going to a job or to school, giving me a sense of purpose and I loved the social interaction and looked forward to it every day. I read my book, *Feeling Good*, by David Burns,[4] copying it in outline form in my planner. I copied the entire book while sitting in cafes and Starbucks over a few weeks. The doctors gave me new prescriptions for Cymbalta and Abilify. I had two bouts of severe depression and wound up at the institute a second time in the fall. It felt good to have people pay attention to me. Then, it happened again. After less than two years, HACC slashed some administrative positions, including David's.

David's next job landed us in Lufkin, Texas. In Nacogdoches, twenty miles to the north, was Stephen F. Austin State University. I got the cataloging librarian position that became available just at the right time. I was excited to start cataloging again. It was a nice campus, a nice library, and I had my very own office for the first time with nice, new, pretty furniture! I experienced imposter syndrome about being "faculty" and felt intimidated by younger faculty with Ph.D.s. The job wasn't hard but working out processes and workstyle differences with my supervisor was the biggest challenge.

I became stubborn and rigid in working with my supervisor because I believed she was wrong and that she didn't respect my level of experience. Others referred to us as a dysfunctional department. I hated this and I sat back and couldn't speak up because it was too much effort to defend myself with her strong, controlling personality and wagging tongue.

My OCPD-driven compulsion for ordering things has been with me in every job, even now. For instance, I have to put a truck of books in

---

4   David D. Burns, *Feeling Good: The New Mood Therapy* (New York, NY: HarperCollins Publishers, 1980, First WholeCare edition, 1999).

order by date and time received before I can start working on them. I have to process files of electronic records in order by date. I still try not to let anyone know that I do this.

I'm not sure I am well-suited to academic librarianship. I would rather catalog than constantly worry about writing for publication and presenting for tenure. I thought I would get to learn more about cutting-edge cataloging, but so much of my time is taken up with writing or administrative departmental duties. Despite my struggle, I was able to get tenure and now the clock has started over to meet requirements for post-tenure. I am jealous of anyone I perceive to have personal time to pursue their own interests outside of work.

I have feelings of worthlessness after disappointments, when not achieving whatever I was aiming for, especially if someone else got what I wanted. The worthlessness feeling feeds my loss of self-confidence. I have always felt guilty for many things and I always thought this was due to my upbringing, of respecting what is good and right. It is only in recent years that a co-worker has pointed out to me that I shouldn't feel so guilty.

## Treatments

Zoloft was the first antidepressant drug that I took, and it made an amazing difference when I started at the lowest dose. It meant I could face going back to work each day. I took it about twelve years and periodically the dosage was increased. Eventually my doctor added Wellbutrin as a supplement to Zoloft. The effectiveness of these drugs started to diminish toward the last few years I took them. I blamed the drugs for feeling fuzzy-headed and lethargic.

When I was hospitalized at the psychiatric institute in Pennsylvania, I started taking Cymbalta and Abilify together. They made a difference in relieving my painful sadness and I could function again. I have been taking them for about eight years now and am starting to wonder if the return of my fuzzy-headedness and forgetfulness is an effect from their long-term use.

I've had many therapists over the years from psychiatrists and psychologists to social workers and pastors. Some counselors were terrible; a few were wonderful, many were okay for a while. I was incapable of talking to the first one I went to. I was wrapped so tightly that I just sat there, miserable, embarrassed, and clammed up. She let me sit there pressuring me to talk, but I couldn't do it yet. With other counselors, I felt so comfortable, that I couldn't talk fast enough, for fear my hour would be up before I could tell them everything. I feel like I pay them to be my friend.

My supervisor didn't understand why I couldn't work faster. Attempting to impose her control, she continued directing me to move from one thing to another, to avoid boredom, instead of working on one thing until it was done. She would lose interest in one thing and change tasks constantly. I saw that as unproductive and it was counter to my OCPD traits. We simply had different work styles and I wanted her to respect mine.

I thought being honest and open was a good thing. When I told my supervisor that I had been diagnosed with OCPD and explained what it was, she said, she didn't know what to do with that. She had to tell her supervisor, the associate director. She asked if I should request "special accommodations" for a disability. I was shocked to think my disorder was a disability. I never thought of myself that way.

I had suspicions that she may have had the some of the same symptoms. With both of us needing control and lacking flexibility, we competed. She had a much stronger controlling personality than me and she was the boss. I let her overstep boundaries that I should have kept firm. In the end, I did not trust her. I feel very much like I failed and that she failed me as a supervisor.

## Conclusion

All of this self-reflection led me to wonder about other librarians and library workers I knew, and especially other catalogers, with similar behavioral tendencies. In various groups, we commonly joked about having OCD and having to fix books that are out of call number order on the shelf. I belong to a Facebook group for OCPD support where I've learned people with all types of vocations have similar symptoms. I believe that the library profession naturally attracts people who love order and organization. How do people with these tendencies find their way to work in a library?

I believe that my behavioral preferences do enhance my ability to care about details enough to focus on them while understanding the big picture and the purpose for those details. However, I also know that they can hinder my ability to complete work in a timely manner. So, how can I combat the constant nagging feeling that I am always be-hind and always busy? I feel I always work harder and care more than others. For hiring purposes, is there a way to find library workers with the "right" traits and filter out those with the "wrong" traits? Is it even possible to have the good traits without the bad ones?

The opportunity to write this chapter gives me hope. There have been times while writing this that I did not have hope—but they were times when I have felt discouraged, down, barely coping, and trying to hide my fears. I do have better days and many good days. Being understood is a very high value. The idea that someone else might identify with my narrative here is thrilling. I want them to know that living with depression and OCPD can get better if we eliminate the stigma of mental illness in all forms. This one chapter will help, I hope. We should be able to talk about it openly and find people like us, ourselves, throughout our paths in life. We can lean on and lift up each other as well as learn methods of coping from each other. Working in a library is not the only job for the personality traits we have, but it is a good one if we value learning, service to our communities, and all the opportunities that libraries offer. Whether in a public or an academic library, for me, it is the best work life I could imagine. If I am cataloging, I have my dream job!

---

## Bibliography

American Psychiatric Association. *Desk Reference to the Diagnostic Criteria from DSM-5*. Arlington, VA: American Psychiatric Association, 2013.

Burns, David D. *Feeling Good: The New Mood Therapy*. New York, NY: HarperCollins Publishers, 1980, First WholeCare edition, 1999.

Hochadel, MaryAnne. *Mosby's Drug Reference for Health Professions* 3rd ed. 2012, Mosby, Inc., Elsevier, Inc., MSDict Viewer, Version 9.0.274, MobiSystems, Inc. Mobile app from Google Play.

Millamena, Sarah. "How to Deal with OCPD'S in the Workplace." *WIRED CHOICE*. April 3, 2009. http://wiredchoice.blogspot.com/2009/05/how-to-deal-with-ocpds-workplace.html?m=1

# Librarian vs. The Machine That Goes Beep: Professional Adventures on the Autism Spectrum

**Jess Alexander**

## Environmental Challenger

Archenemies tend to be the bailiwick of superheroes and consulting detectives, not youth services librarians. However, when the library administration installed an industrial disc cleaner near my desk, I found myself locked in ultimate battle against my nemesis: The Machine That Goes Beep. Its beeps and whirs and screeches have the power to short-circuit my neurodivergent brain, turning a fairly useful mega-nerd into a twitching, rocking mass of otherness. Most of the time, I can hide my distress behind a veneer of normality, but one bad roll of the dice—a critical failure, if you will—and my dignity is forfeit.[1]

Do you see what I did there? I started this essay at the good part. Neurotypical people attend writing classes to learn how to do that. I, on the other hand, happen to be on the autism spectrum, and I start all of my stories at the good part. It is a conversational quirk that I share with quite a few people with Autism Spectrum Disorder (ASD). One might even say it's a talent, unless one converses with me on a regular basis. In that case, I am given to understand that the subsequent

---

1   For the layman, "critical failure" or "critical miss" is jargon used in roleplaying games. In Dungeons & Dragons, rolling a 1 on a twenty-sided die during your attack results in an automatic miss. Your friends yell "Fail!" and the monster is more likely to eat your faces.

wait to divine a story's intent, as well as the obligatory rehash of the good part—sandwiched between the logical beginning and the not-as-good-as-the-good-part conclusion—is frustrating beyond measure. However, that outlook ignores the question of why a person would stick around for a story without the assurance that it has a good part at all. Circling back, now that we are both assured that this essay has a good part, we can proceed.

In my everyday life, I work in youth services at a small suburban library, where I've nudged a fairly standard job into a configuration more in line with a belief that normal is optional. As such, the kids who grow up with me launch catapults at story time and expect trips to the library to include cardboard planetariums and riding T-rexes. My work makes me absurdly happy. What's more, on a day-to-day basis, it provides a socially acceptable platform in which to indulge some of my neurodivergent pleasures. Reference? People ask me non-personal questions, and I get to expound at great length on all manner of topics to an audience that actually wants to listen. They even commend my enthusiasm as an effort to interest the children. Interactions at the public service desk are stylized, and I hardly miss a social cue (unless there's subtext; I'm hopeless at subtext). When I'm in a particularly good or bad mood, I can disappear into the workroom and build things out of office supplies, and it is considered thrifty program prep. Librarianship is great.

However, my autism brain also complicates matters. Certain stimuli can trigger sensory processing issues and/or submerge my usual thought-processes in a seething morass of utter wrongness. At best, my ability to function is mildly restricted; at worst, I seem to lose connection with my mind for a span of time. I prefer to avoid this if at all possible.

In a professional setting, I'm most at-risk from bad auditory input. Cue The Machine That Goes Beep: my environmental challenger, my greatest foe.[2] When functioning properly, the disc cleaner shrieks and whirs

---

2  Let's take a moment to examine the pejorative I assigned to the disc cleaner: The Machine That Goes Beep. As of writing this chapter, I have spent upwards of 60 hours agonizing over its hyphenation (or lack thereof) in relation to a series about a certain Boy Wizard. Critical analysis of Harry Potter does not seem to extend to the implications of hyphenation. "He-Who-Must-Not-Be-Named" and "You-Know-Who" are written with hyphens, while "The Boy Who Lived" and "The Dark Lord" are written without. Is this related to grammar, word count, political affiliation of the title's user? Is it a type-setting consideration imposed by the publishing house? Do hyphens create a greater association to Voldemort (ideal), or do they indicate personal weakness or fear of the enemy (non-ideal)? I acknowledge that this mental bear trap is pointless, that I do not need a ruling on the matter or justification for that ruling. However, my brain will not let it go. I do not know if this fixation is related to being a nerd, being a youth services librarian, or being neurodivergent. Self-awareness has its limits.

and growls. The Machine ends its cycles by screaming its discontent with a perpetual BEEP, BEEP, BEEP: a Morse code message transmitted directly into my spine. It wears me down.

Anecdotally, I've heard that neurotypical people are able to tune out repetitive irritants after a while: for instance, they barely notice a faulty fire alarm that's been blaring for half a day. I don't have that luxury. For me, those noises never go away. If they trigger a sensory processing episode, then all of my auditory input gets remastered: background sound levels equal or surpass the foreground sounds. I can barely follow a conversation because the lights are also humming and the computer keys are pounding and The Machine That Goes Beep never stops beeping. My body physically reacts to the strain by tensing and my stress and anxiety rise, and it hurts. It hurts. In a normal year, I expect to experience one multi-day sensory processing episode and a handful of minor episodes in which my senses are thrown out of whack for an hour or two. With the Machine in play, my senses could phase at any time.

Not being of a milquetoast disposition, I alerted the higher ups at my library to my distress with regard to the Machine. Surely, a few emails or conversations or perhaps a weekly reminder would sort out the problem. Surely, this was just a case of library speed. After all, my brain pain was valid, right?

*"That new disc cleaner makes high-pitched beeping noises on a perpetual basis. [...] There is a small but real possibility that it will eventually drive me mad." (August, 2017)*

*"The beeping. Must. Make. It. Stop." (January, 2018)*

*"Sensory processing hell." (September, 2018)*

Maybe not.

## The Epiphany

Stepping back for a minute, I feel this is a good place to mention that I've only been aware of my neurodivergence for a few years. To be clear, I've always been on the autism spectrum. I just didn't recognize it. Think of it like walking around in public with your fly down. Some people might not notice—flannel shirts do cover a multitude of sins. Others might notice but find it prudent not to mention your trouser fail. Still others might attempt to clue you in with tact and subtlety. (In this analogy, my response to a well-meaning "XYZPDQ" would be a Jackson 5-style "A B C, one, two, three," rather than examining my zipper pretty darn quick.) However, when you finally do notice that your fly is down, you wonder how in the world you missed it in the first place.

It should come as no surprise that when I finally had my ASD epiphany, it was in the least subtle of all settings: a professional development session about library patrons on the autism spectrum. Our speaker had a PowerPoint presentation, and I was taking notes quite diligently... until I spotted an error. (Gasp!) What does it mean to be neurodivergent? Consult the chart! Column A lists ways in which a neurotypical person processes the world. Column B lists ways in which an autistic person experiences the same. Guys? Did you mislabel your columns? Column B is the normal one. We're all column B, right? Wait. None of you are column B? Shit.[3]

Unfortunately, this flash of self-awareness did not prove helpful for some time. First mistake: I consulted the internet for verification. As anyone who ever Googled their flu symptoms and discovered bubonic plague would tell you, this was a terrible idea. Take, for instance, "The Aspie Quiz," an online diagnostic that is particularly tempting to those who haven't yet kicked their ableist misconception that Asperger's syndrome is okay but autism is the end of the world.[4] Question 62 of the quiz asked: "Do you have odd hair (for example multiple whorls, standing up when short or other peculiarities)?"[5] I have two cowlicks, a subclinical whorl, and a predilection for silly hair. Aha! I must have Asperger's. Fortunately, I also have enough mathematics under my belt to give the quiz the side-eye and mutter that correlation does not imply causation.

My next plan had better potential, but it crashed and burned even worse: I consulted the experts. Autism sensitivity training was in vogue

---

3  This would mark the second time I experienced a rather personal epiphany while in a library. The first occurred in the summer of 1992, during a library screening of *A League of Their Own*. (Nope, not straight.) At least I'm consistent.

4  Asperger's syndrome first appeared in the *Diagnostic and Statistical Manual of Mental Disorders (DSM-IV)* in 1994. It described a less severe condition than autism. However, Asperger's ceased to exist as a diagnosis in 2013, when it was swallowed by autism spectrum disorder in the *DSM-5*; Barahona-Corrêa, J.B., and Carlos N. Filipe. "A Concise History of Asperger Syndrome: The Short Reign of a Troublesome Diagnosis," *Frontiers in Psychology* 6, no. 2024 (January 2016): 1–5, https://doi:10.3389/fpsyg.2015.02024.

5  Ekblad, Leif, "Aspie-Quiz: Final Version 4," 2019. https://rdos.net/eng/Aspie-quiz.php.

in library circles, so I'd amassed a respectable collection of business cards for various support organizations. It seemed an obvious choice to use them. "I'm pursuing an autism diagnosis," I wrote. "Can you point me in the right direction?" The answer was no, always no. "We do not diagnose functioning adults." "You don't want a diagnosis." "If you can ask on your own, you don't have autism." I didn't expect this outcome.

Suddenly, I was stricken by doubt. Perhaps I wasn't on the autism spectrum at all. Maybe the ability to look neurotypical in public about 90 percent of the time meant that I was, in fact, neurotypical. In that case, claiming an autistic identity and being wrong would make me an imposter. Imposters are jerks. Did I want to be a jerk? No! Therefore, I would not have ASD. If the Machine short-circuited my brain, would I merit reasonable workplace accommodations? Of course not! Regrettably, my logic was terrible. And, to reference an earlier analogy, my fly was still down.

## Acute Embarrassment

Let's return to the part where the Machine was winning. About a year had passed in Library Land. The Machine continued to beep. Weakened by this daily dose of kryptonite, my normie camouflage was failing with an alarming frequency. Stress stimming: unsubtle.[6] Ability to interpret conversational nuance: negligible. It turns out that social interactions tank pretty hard when you don't notice that you're irritating the other party. Heck, I still cringe at the memory of a book club I moderated while my bandwidth for social cues was critically low.

It's in this state that I found myself corralled into the worst of all department meetings: reorganizing the workroom. Technically, this was a reasonable course of action; the shelves were overflowing, and we'd begun to build stacks on the floor. However, as principal tinkerer of Youth Services, I'm the one who spent the most time turning spare parts into automatons and other pleasing curiosities. In my brain, this created an inconvenient sense of ownership toward communal

---

6   Stimming is a repetitive, self-stimulatory behavior that helps to regulate one or more senses or diffuse brain overload moments. In this piece, I'm referring mainly to motor stereotypies, that is, repetitive body movements: fingers, hands, head, whole body, etc. Stimming can be supremely useful for dealing with problematic input, is often soothing in stressful situations, and can be delightful in times of joy. For definition purposes, stimming can also manifest as repetitive vocal, oral, or tactile behaviors. Some neurotypical people stim, too. For instance, that guy who taps his foot all time and jiggles the conference table in meetings is totally stimming.

supplies. Thus, our mandatory hour of doom felt like it was devoted to discarding *my* things and moving *my* things and discussing why *my* things ought to live somewhere other than in their perfectly excellent schema. Naturally, this led to the pacing and the stimming and the blurting out of comments in a tone much louder than is socially acceptable. It was all too much.

Clinging to my last shred of composure, I fled the workroom. Three feet from the door, my brain switched off, and I dropped into a full-on meltdown on the floor of our office.

A colleague surrounded me with a barricade of book carts. I consider it an act of mercy: she spared me the role of carnival sideshow.

I can't tell you what happened while my brain was offline—for all intents and purposes, I wasn't there—so I'll fill the void with a story instead. Once upon a time, my library created a book cart drill team to march in the Fourth of July parade. It was one of those summers where the sun melted the asphalt and your skin would burn before you even broke a sweat; I can't believe we volunteered. After hours of practice, we maneuvered our carts in a series of twirls and formations past the entire community. It was legendary and utterly ridiculous, just like us.

In the recovery stage of a meltdown, my brain comes back online before I regain control over my body. I rocked back and forth on the carpet next to my desk, nonverbal and mortified––but a tiny piece of my brain noticed the book cart formation that hid me from display, and I thought appreciative thoughts about that drill team.

The hardest thing I ever had to do at my job was come into work the next day.

## Aftermaths and Allies

The Machine played the part of evil villain better than I ever imagined. In my moment of greatest weakness, it ripped away my mask and revealed to everybody the secret identity I concealed from even myself. I'm on the autism spectrum.

The days and weeks that followed were pretty bleak. My nemesis stood its ground, and I was a bundle of nerves, wondering if and when my brain would misfire again. I worried that my colleagues looked at me differently after witnessing my moment of shame—and I had no way of determining the answer because I'm dreadful at nonverbal cues and subtext (darn you, subtext!).

However, there was one bright spot. When I stopped fighting my neurodiversity, I gained the clarity to see that I wasn't alone. There are lots of people with ASD who share my origin story. As children, we learned to camouflage enough of our quirks to fly under the radar. We weren't given diagnoses because, for the most part, they weren't available: Asperger's syndrome only entered the *Diagnostic and Statistical Manual of Mental Disorders* in 1994.[7] Add to that a gender bias that rendered so many little girls invisible because they didn't present their autism in the same way as boys.[8] So instead of the autistic kid, we were the nerd or the band geek, the boy who talked over the teacher in class or the girl who broke down when the schedule changed. And I'm sure some of us had a special interest so fascinating that we were the most popular person wherever we went. Our neurodiversity was just part of the norm; heck, in a population as large as Homo sapiens, neurodiversity *is* normal.[9]

Later on, when the kids in our lives were given diagnoses or we stumbled upon autism awareness training or the stressors on our brains brought us low in ways we could not ignore, we finally began to make sense of ourselves. In the meantime, some of us became librarians and others became my library patrons—and, occasionally, allies in pursuit of justice.

A while back, I ran a Nintendo event in which most of the kiddos happened to be neurodivergent in one way or another. The adults skulked around the back of the room, per usual, though this time many of us were eyeing one mother who was reading a book about raising children with ASD. Suddenly, her video gaming son made a non-normative hand flap, and she called out, "Quiet hands!" I doubt she expected the response. Practically every other adult in the room started stimming, and a few of us reflexively yelled, "Noooo!" Classroom admonishments

---

7   Barahona-Corrêa and Filipe, "A Concise History of Asperger Syndrome," 3.

8   Ratto, Allison B., Lauren Kenworthy, Benjamin E. Yerys, Julia Bascom, Andrea Trubanova Wieckowski, Susan W. White, Gregory L. Wallace, et al. "What About the Girls? Sex-Based Differences in Autistic Traits and Adaptive Skills," *Journal of Autism and Developmental Disorders* 48, no. 5 (April 2017): 1702–1705. https://doi.org/10.1007/s10803-017-3413-9.

9   Walker, Nick, "Throw Away the Master's Tools: Liberating Ourselves from the Pathology Paradigm," in *Loud Hands: Autistic People, Speaking,* ed. Julia Bascom (Washington, DC: Autistic Press, 2012), 225–37.

silenced our hands when we were small and helpless, but now we were the mighty ones, and we would rise up. While the children raced their Mario-karts around Rainbow Road, my people neuro-converged on that unsuspecting mom for a brute force heart-to-heart[10].

We knew that little boy's language. It is expressive and nuanced, sometimes tortured and often beautiful. When we're happy flappy, it's because there is more joy than can possibly be contained in one body. When the monsters in the world threaten to overcome us, we stress stim to bring the focus inward, where we have control. There are a hundred different things our hands say and do, but if all you see is flapping, talk to us; we'll do our best to translate. Just don't take it away.

## Conclusion

I'm not much for endings when I tell stories. After all, if endings were any good, they would be tacked onto the beginnings with the good parts. This is to say that the final showdown of librarian vs. Machine did not quite live up to the dream. There was a distinct lack of baseball bat smashery with theme music grooving in the background. Nor did I exit in a swagger past a line of slow-clapping library folk and one jaded cataloger giving the head nod of respect. That would be a good ending. It just doesn't belong to this story.

Instead, I endured through the Machine's beeping for more than a year, nerves on edge and confidence tanking. My requests to move it remained unmet. You see, despite the strain, I loved my job and did not want to jeopardize it. Irrespective of my ASD, I'm a weird and quirky person. That my colleagues and my library community accepted me wholeheartedly was kind of amazing. I could teach algebra to kindergarteners while wearing a pirate hat and be considered innovative; if I fiddled with spare parts, people would gather around to watch me prototype; and when I thanked patrons for returning time and again to my oddball programs, they would look at me quizzically and respond, "But it's our family tradition."

Then, one day, it stopped being enough. I walked into work and laid down an ultimatum: relocate the disc cleaner or I leave. It was a move equal parts desperation and scraped together dignity. By that point, I

---

10   Thank you, editors, for letting me get away with that execrable portmanteau.

truly believed that my sanity mattered less to the library administration than the location of a midsize appliance. But you know what? In the end, my library chose me. I mattered, at least a little bit. Of course, it took another month and a second meltdown before the Machine got moved to its exile of shame... 50 feet away. Still, it was enough. Suck it, Machine: the librarian won.

I won't say that my faceoff with the disc cleaner was a valuable learning experience. It bothers me that moving the Machine and ending my misery barely took a couple of hours.[11] Still, the experience forced me to see myself more clearly. I *am* on the autism spectrum. I can own it without dithering about whether I'm "autistic enough" to deserve the identity. That's empowering. Should another environmental challenger threaten to bring me to my knees—or the carpet behind a blockade of book carts—I *will* assert my rights to reasonable accommodations in the workplace.[12] My experience of the world is valid even if it doesn't match yours.

It is a truism that Gotham City is never safe. Whenever Batman defeats his villainous foe, a new evildoer rises to take their place. While I might not be the Caped Crusader, it's in this spirit that I, Neurodivergent Librarian, must remain ever vigilant to the threat of my next adversary. I'm looking at you, Light That Goes Buzz.

### Bibliography

Barahona-Corrêa, J. B., and Carlos N. Filipe. "A Concise History of Asperger Syndrome: The Short Reign of a Troublesome Diagnosis," *Frontiers in Psychology* 6, no. 2024 (January 2016): 1–7, https://doi:10.3389/fpsyg.2015.02024.

Ekblad, Leif, "Aspie-Quiz: Final Version 4," 2019. https://rdos.net/eng/Aspie-quiz.php.

Ratto, Allison B., Lauren Kenworthy, Benjamin E. Yerys, Julia Bascom, Andrea Trubanova Wieckowski, Susan W. White, Gregory L. Wallace, et al. "What About the Girls? Sex-Based Differences in Autistic Traits and Adaptive

11  My ninja robots shall wear angry faces for the foreseeable future.

12  U.S. Equal Employment Opportunity Commission. "Depression, PTSD, & Other Mental Health Conditions in the Workplace: Your Legal Rights." Washington, DC. https://www.eeoc.gov/eeoc/publications/mental_health.cfm.

Skills." *Journal of Autism and Developmental Disorders* 48, no. 5 (April 2017): 1698–1711. https://doi.org/10.1007/s10803-017-3413-9.

U.S. Equal Employment Opportunity Commission. "Depression, PTSD, & Other Mental Health Conditions in the Workplace: Your Legal Rights." Washington, DC. https://www.eeoc.gov/eeoc/publications/mental_health.cfm.

Walker, Nick. "Throw Away the Master's Tools: Liberating Ourselves from the Pathology Paradigm." In *Loud Hands: Autistic People, Speaking*, edited by Julia Bascom, 225–37. Washington, DC: Autistic Press, 2012.

## Suggested Reading

Bargiela, Sarah, and Sophie Standing. *Camouflage: the Hidden Lives of Autistic Women*. London: Jessica Kingsley Publishers, 2019.

Bartmess, Elizabeth, ed. *Knowing Why: Adult-Diagnosed Autistic People on Life and Autism*. Washington, DC: Autistic Press, 2018.

Bascom, Julia, ed. *Loud Hands: Autistic People, Speaking*. Washington, DC: Autistic Press, 2012.

Kapp, Steven K., Robyn Steward, Laura Crane, Daisy Elliott, Chris Elphick, Elizabeth Pellicano, and Ginny Russell. "'People Should Be Allowed to Do What They Like': Autistic Adults' Views and Experiences of Stimming." *Autism*, 23, no. 7 (2019): 1782–92, https://doi.org/10.1177/1362361319829628.

# A Critical Conversation about LIS Interrupted

## With Miranda Dube and Carrie Wade

*Content Warning*  Discussion of mental illness, unsupportive work environments, substance misuse, domestic and sexual violence, and eating disorders.

CW   So how did you think up the idea for the book?

MD   I had my own experience with mental illness back when I was in undergrad and working in a university library and lacked options about disclosing what was happening with me as I underwent some serious personal, and often unavoidably public, crises that led to my diagnosis and treatment.

As a result, a lot of people knew about my mental illness and new diagnosis. Given the fear and uncertainty going on in my life at that time, I was pleasantly surprised by how supportive my colleagues and supervisors were at the library. My workplace became a special place to me because of their kindness, love, and support I received while I did what I needed to seek out help and treatment.

After I graduated with my Bachelor's degree I went into intimate partner violence and sexual assault victim and survivor advocacy work, and while I was in that field I started to miss the library workplace and labor I had been doing. I decided to go back to school for a Master's degree in Library and Information Studies (MLIS). During my degree program I found the same community that I felt like I had while working in the library as an undergraduate. I met lots of library workers—my professors as well as fellow students and other members of the field—who were doing important advocacy work, for not only mental illness but with the queer community and for Black, Indigenous, and People of Color (BIPOC). However, once I went back to working in libraries at the same University where I'd worked at as an undergrad that sense of community had disappeared, and so I was grappling with this idea that there are Library and Information Science (LIS) workers out there who want to have these conversations but I was not finding that in my everyday experience.

The idea for this book came from the thought, "How can I help create a space to have these conversations and hopefully create change in the field?" Maybe it will create more willingness to have honest conversations about mental illness in the workplace. One of my other motivations is also so people can feel heard because a lot of these conversations have been happening in the background—either on Twitter or over coffee breaks at conferences—and I want to do what I can to elevate these hidden voices in a way that would be meaningful and impactful, not only for the LIS field but also for the people who are sharing their stories.

MD    Why did you want to help create this book?

CW    I had some less than great experiences coming to terms with my own mental illness in and out of library workplaces, which has been my struggle for the last twelve years as a library worker. Part of this is a process of coming to own my mental illnesses and wanting to find ways to become more of an advocate for folks like me, which is something I want to do as part of my own journey to help others find their voices and share their stories.

I work as a Health Sciences librarian, so working on a project like this fits into that profile a little bit too, as far as scholarly output goes. There is some overlap with the knowledge I have about research and the more medical side of things—so as far as being someone interested in the more pathological side as well as the social and lived experience, I think that works in a certain way.

CW How much time did it take to evolve?

MD Like a lot of things that I do I get these grandiose ideas that feel very pie in the sky and I try to run with them but I have a harder time thinking about the smaller components. My ideas require another person to assist with that kind of thinking.

Because I felt unsettled about the incongruity between some of my experiences as a student worker, library sciences student, and then as a post-degreed professional the idea for the book came very quickly. However, I wanted to find some way to crystallize those ideas from my experiences and I realized I needed some assistance.

It was probably some random Tuesday where I thought about making an own-voices book and reached out to Emily Drabinski, who has edited and written great works that are similar in style to what I was envisioning. I reached out and asked, "what goes into this process of getting an idea to a finalized book?"

Then I sent out a tweet saying, "I have this idea and is anybody interested in partnering with me" and it was a stroke of fate that Carrie was the first and only person who messaged me. We'd met at the Gender and Sexuality in information Studies Colloquium (GSISC) in Boston and we engaged in similar conversations and as soon as I saw that she was interested I thought, "yes! this is exactly who I want to partner up with on this project!" and we just took it from there.

CW I was definitely surprised that I was the only person who responded but I suppose that's the wonderful way fate turns. I definitely wanted to get my feet wet with a book project, but I didn't want to have to do so much by myself. I thought you had a solid vision and idea that I always trusted.

I really appreciated how strong your vision has been and all along; it has been this great lighthouse for me in a lot of ways. I cannot say enough that I genuinely *love* editing, and that was something you communicated that you wanted from a partner in this project, and I felt like I could bring that, since I have a background in written communication. I'm a stickler for quality, and I wanted to find new ways to help other people tell their stories in clear and compelling ways, which was not always easy.

MD Balance between us was so important! I think that was one of the ways we really helped each other out, as I stated earlier, many of my thoughts about what we could accomplish were loftier and I tend to struggle with concrete things and you were always very capable of helping ground me and identifying next smaller steps. You helped me grow as an editor, teaching about constructive feedback, and how to produce that high quality work while also still being able to engage with my big dream of this book.

CW Was there anything else that you learned from Co-editing?

MD Oh gosh, I learned so many things. This entire process has been so educational in so many ways, but the one thing that sticks out in my mind when you ask me this question is the word, *patience*: Patience and compassion for myself and with myself.

There were times where I stumbled in this process of co-editing and there were times where it felt like I was never going to make it. It felt like having this big dream was too much and it would be my fault that it all crumbled. A lot of that tied directly into the myth that I had taught myself about being a person with a mental illness. I assumed I would never be capable of accomplishing much or that I would self-sabotage.

Some of these tendencies also get into massive feelings of impostor syndrome that a lot of folks with mental illness and in recovery from substance use disorders experience. I have questioned myself a lot, "Who am I to be successful in this book?" and having compassion towards myself helped in those stumbling moments and having patience in myself and with the process made a substantial difference. I had to learn that you cannot co-edit or author a book in three or even six months. I had to wrestle with wanting instant gratification but also balance putting out a magnificent work with the voices that we have in this manuscript.

CW On the opposite end of instant gratification, I move much more slowly, and I was nervous about not moving fast enough. I worried it would fail and I would be at fault too because I took my time editing and commenting. It was also emotionally difficult for me to read narrative after narrative in succession, and I felt like something was wrong with me for not being able to meet a certain pace.

Much the opposite of you, I prefer to delay gratification, but I am also deeply afraid of finishing things because I am so afraid of failure.

When this book comes out is it going to do justice to what we wanted it to do? Are people going to relate to it in the way we were hoping that they would relate to it? Those big hypothetical questions have lurked over me like massive black clouds and interfered with a lot of the work that had to be done, and I had to fight back against my anxiety to just, you know, get the shit done and hope that there is not much backlash.

MD    I do not have an easy time accepting compliments so I am equally as nervous for folks commenting on the book in a positive way.

CW    Much of that part of my anxiety comes from perfectionism but that perfectionism is a fear of failure. Similarly, I cannot handle compliments because I will only be able to fixate on what could have been better or done differently.

I think that's one huge thing I am learning throughout this process; that when you put something like this out into the world it is a very vulnerable act. Not just for us, but especially our authors, facing our feedback too. I am so impressed with how well they have taken the feedback and turned their work into these incredible chapters. It has been rigorous at times, but I am proud of every single person in this book including those who submitted chapters and were not accepted, that was brave and vulnerable on its own.

MD    Early on in this process, right after the Call for Proposals went live, we got some feedback on ALA Connect. Can you talk a bit about what we learned from that?

CW    On the ALA connect boards, some folks who work as social workers—that's a fair area for folks to provide feedback from—raised some valid issues about the language we used, which I think was something we learned from. We both refer to ourselves as people with mental illnesses and we both prefer to say mental illness and a lot of people took issue with that and they said, "well not everyone uses that term," which made us reconsider our language.

That was definitely an enlightening moment for me and I think that changed how we framed how we spoke with the authors because we did find out that even a lot of our authors had different preferences for how they referred to themselves so really trying to push that person-preferred language and trying to help authors identify themselves how they want to be identified was a good thing that came out of that.

MD    It really helped us create a space for people who were authoring chapters to be empowered to use whatever language they wanted and not feel like they had to use the language that somebody else uses.

CW    I am glad people raise those issues in some respects. I think when people challenge you like that it just gives you a chance to really crystallize your vision a little more.

So, have any of your ideas about the LIS field changed since working on the book?

MD    I've been on this rollercoaster of believing that LIS is such an inclusive field and people are responsive, caring, and educated about these topics whether that's about mental illness, substance use disorders, the queer community, and solidarity for BIPOC—but upon really entering the field it was a slap in the face to find out that many workplaces are not actually like that.

I am working to find ways to create space that is more in line with what I found prior to entering the field as a professional. But I am still quite jarred from the fact that my positive experience is a small portion of the field, and I am wondering how we can help elevate those voices or make that community larger?

I would say that the biggest thing for me was just coming to terms with: I cannot change everybody.

I *can* put my best foot forward, especially with this book and try and help create some type of change with and for others.

CW      My experience has been quite opposite, interestingly enough. I was not the most idealistic person when I entered the field 12 years ago as a library worker in a conservative public library district, so I never felt the field was inclusive. I am always surprised but delighted to meet more radically-oriented people.

        This surprise has been both professionally and personally incredibly fulfilling to be working on changing how we address mental disorders in LIS and it's quite shocking for me to think that, "oh! I can change things!" because I used to not think that was possible in my more cynical past of various library jobs. I have heard that normally people become more cynical as they grow older, but that all happened in reverse for me; I have become a bit more hopeful about our collective ability to enact change.

MD      I agree—there is so much power in the collective! We do not know until we talk with each other. I genuinely thought I was the only librarian who had my mental illness. For the longest time, I thought that I had snuck into the profession and that I was about to be exposed and the LIS field would blacklist me for having infiltrated its ranks. However, I met other library workers who had the same mental illness, which was so eye opening and created this even greater sense of community and helped me deal with my feelings. I no longer felt so isolated about my mental illness because of the community I found, which was wonderful!

CW      We have not really talked about what our specific conditions are, but I have a pretty common slate of mental conditions.

        My diagnosis is officially a major depressive disorder with mild social anxiety which I have done a lot of work with, because it used to not be mild. Depression is persistent and has some less-fun dips into major states while my social anxiety manifests in some particular ways that most people would not guess from interacting with me.

MD      I've had some interesting new developments around this actually, because even at this time (this book's publication) my diagnosis has evolved from when we started this project.

        I was originally diagnosed with borderline personality disorder (BPD) and it is one of the more stigmatized mental illnesses—some therapists will deny treatment because people with this condition will be seen as being manipulative or harmful to others, which contributes to the stigma and makes it harder to get help.

It is easier for me to be more open about my Post-Traumatic Stress Disorder (PTSD) because people tend to be more understanding and educated about it than BPD.

Just as an example, I remember telling someone about my BPD diagnosis once and they asked me, "are you going to be a different person every time I see you?" and completely lumped some of the more stigmatized mental illnesses together because people are uneducated about the differences between BPD and Dissociative Identity Disorder. When folks are uneducated about things, they experience an innate fear of the unknown. So, I try to be empathetic and I understand that people are unsure of how to interact with someone with a mental illness, but when you are the person with the mental illness, it can feel very terrifying to be open about it.

I recently started going back to therapy and after being re-assessed, I do not meet the diagnostic criteria for BPD anymore and that has been a process. For people who have known me, I have been open about my experience. This time around it was a more private process of dealing with my feelings. Heck, I still am trying to identify what those feelings are! I'm coping. It is like losing part of my identity. Now I ask myself, "how do I walk in a world where I don't fit the profile for this mental illness anymore? A mental illness that shaped a lot of who I am today. And what does it mean to be a person who is 'getting better?'"

I have reached a stage of grieving where I am dealing with it no longer being part of my identity and it has been a slow and natural progression. I remind myself that I started my treatment to get better, but I guess I did not think it would happen this quickly. And for me personally, quickly has been over the course of the last six years. In order to be diagnosed, a person needs to have five of the nine criteria. When I was first diagnosed and started treatment, I had eight of the nine and when I was reassessed, I had one of the nine. Day to day my life doesn't seem so much different but concrete measurements like the diagnostic criteria helped me see the changes. I do know though that if I am not diligent about my mental health then it is possible to become more symptomatic, so it is an ever evolving, ongoing process.

CW    I think the same goes for lots of conditions like ours. I have hairline triggers for depression, and social anxiety can be a problem in workplace situations.

MD    It is interesting how it is easier to talk about certain diagnoses over others because people will understand those more easily.

CW    I think that is one thing that we have encountered with reading some of these chapters and working with these amazing authors is learning how people talk about what they experience. Everyone talks about their own experiences quite differently and I think that is fascinating, even two people with similar conditions might have completely different experiences and talk about them completely differently.

MD    It is definitely a spectrum and I think if there is one thing that I hope readers take away it is that we cannot pigeonhole people to their diagnosis. Our ideas about how people with certain mental illnesses should behave needs to shift because it truly varies so much.

CW    Some of that touches on conversations about workplace accommodations and how so much of what allows accommodations to happen relies on consistency and the nature of mental illness is inconsistent at its core.

It almost requires us to change these pictures of what professionalism is and how that can be flexible. We are writing this intro during the COVID-19 pandemic right now and one thing that has shifted is the concept of presenteeism, which is a huge thing for someone with a mental illness because things like being at work on time can be difficult when someone has any variety of mental illness(es). I would say some mental illnesses make it an obstacle to be at work. If presenteeism is something that a particular workplace values, they need to reassess those policies. Unless the nature of the work is very situated within the physical environment, policies like these are ableist. I think what we are finding out from all these remote work situations is mandatory attendance is no longer necessary.

MD      For sure! I think when we start helping people to do things in a way that makes sense for themselves, we also help them become happier and healthier. I don't want to put an emphasis on "creating better workers" because I don't want to put a prominence on our ability to put out work, but if it comes down to it being more beneficial for someone to start their day at 9:00am because they have a rough time in the morning getting up and doing a medication routine, stretching or grounding exercises, it might be inherently better for everyone in the organization if that person starts at 9:00am instead of 8:00am. Supervisors, managers, and directors need to ask if the tradeoffs are worth it. The conversation really needs to be reframed around how to help folks bring their best selves, instead of caring about arcane rules or notions about what we think being a good worker is.

CW      The concept of changing expectations on what a good worker is grazes the surface of performing sanity in the workplace too. This topic, performing sanity, is something that we heard about a lot from our authors. Quite a few wrote about it in detail and this is something that is hugely challenging for a lot of us, especially when we face stressful situations in the workplace.

            What would happen if we removed this barrier of performing sanity? I think that is one thing that, to me, the encompassing ideas of time, the workday, and professionalism are comprehensively and individually huge barriers for me when I think about what it means to perform sanity.

            What if there existed a space where I could go freak out before a meeting? That would mean the world to me! Obviously, something like that is based on my own particular mental illness quirks because I hate meetings and they give me a lot of anxiety, but it is how we define professionalism and how ideas of sanity inform what professionalism means and what that means for workplace behavior. Workplaces need to make room both physically and emotionally for the needs of folks— like needing to sooth or cry or ground as they prepare and react to what happens in a day.

MD      To your point- crying at work–that is something that people have talked about a lot! Why is it so unacceptable to cry at work!? For many people, and particularly for me, crying is often just a body response to outside stimuli. It's largely out of my control but there is so much shame around doing it!

CW    I wish people would understand that so often it is a physical response. Personally, I am not a crier, but I understand it is a response. To be looked upon in a certain way if you cry at work is incredibly harmful, yes and it reinforces this idea that is also super gendered because women tend to cry more. It is looping back to professionalism being so male and white and ableist.

These concepts are major topics of exploration in this book, and how heavily these expectations weigh on us. If certain things about a workplace are not enabling a person to be their best self or even a part of their best self, how will they feel comfortable disclosing a disability if they feel judged or stigmatized?

CW    I think it is worth discussing some of the characteristics of an emotionally inclusive workplace.

MD    I think one of the biggest things that a workplace can do is recognize that not everybody's response to a given situation is going to be the same and that it is inherently harmful to expect people to do that. It is also harmful to judge or reprimand someone for having a response that is different than your own. So, if we start from a place of removing certain kinds of expectations for how people should respond to a situation, interaction, change, or stimuli we are just automatically going to be situated for more inclusivity.

CW    For instance, if you have a co-worker die suddenly, it is something that happens. How do you deal with grief in the workplace? That is one of those concrete examples of allowing people to experience what they need to experience. It might be difficult to be at work with that person's absence. But again, being able to dialog about how to grieve in a workplace is difficult and requires difficult conversations and opportunities for folks to feel what they need to feel.

MD    Workplaces want people to be working while also going through whatever emotional process they are going through in their personal lives. It is important to define what that might be. Does that mean extra breaks when someone has heightened feelings? It could mean working from home for a period of time or forming more informal solidarity or coping groups.

More broadly, the concept of making a workplace emotionally inclusive means coworkers, employers and employees working together to make workplaces accessible, allowing people to be their best self, and enabling them to accomplish what they need to do.

I loved doing my job when I was in libraries, and I love the job I do now. I know you love doing your job and so do lots of other library workers, but there are also things that occur outside of our jobs that impact our ability to be present and be focused. So how can a workplace help me when I am unable to focus? I still want to do my job and so how can I get assistance or support from my community and my job to balance that and do both. That is, sometimes doing my job and having a project to throw myself into because I can get release from whatever else going on. But maybe I need to cry too...

CW     or do whatever it is to process the situation or find emotional release safely.

MD     Yes, I completely agree because it is not like we do not want to be at work! We want to be at work! There is a myth from people who have not had experiences with mental illness either firsthand or secondhand that, because someone has a flashback or is emotionally heightened and needs some time or space, that they inherently must not want to be at work and that is not usually the case, at least for me.

CW     There were some periods where I was going through my worst depression but working a public service desk—fixing printers, checking in, and renewing books—was such a huge relief. Helping people kept me calm during a very tumultuous time for me.

Another thing I am thinking about in relation to emotional inclusivity in workplaces is how much burden is placed on folks with disabilities and mental illness to seek out accommodation and help. As someone who has been in a pretty dire depressive situation, coupled with the social anxiety, when you are drowning it is very difficult to save yourself, and you're often relying on people around you to be equipped and emotionally intelligent to know how to help you because you don't know how.

That is where a lot of shortcomings exist. Our mental health first aid skills are very lacking—either identification and/or referral too. So as someone who has gone through that experience it can feel like the suffering is your fault as well. I felt like I failed to articulate my pain enough to others around me or that my social anxiety prevented me from seeking assistance.

Also, I am very leery of the classic "employee assistance program" (EAP) line. I feel like a few of us have been fed that one before. For folks in more remote areas it can be difficult to access quality mental and behavioral health care and that EAP feels like a Band-Aid for a terminal illness. They are designed to be short-term solutions. For many of us, we might need something more intense and longer term and they are mostly designed to deal with workplace problems.

I will never forget my new employee orientation. They showed us this overly dramatized active shooter video without much warning—it was a mandatory intro about healthcare plans and stuff like that and boom! People running and crying while a dude with a gun runs around. Institutions need to consider how 1. trainings like that are ineffective and 2. trainings like that can be emotionally triggering and potentially cause flashbacks for folks with PTSD and similar conditions.

Within libraries, also considering police presence because many staff members may not have positive associations with police officers due to trauma as well.

But also dovetailing with that this book covers a lot of that in its chapters—crafting better workplaces for retaining and recruiting folks with mental illness.

MD  We had some wonderful people write incredible chapters about these things and really elaborated on the concepts, but I think kind of breaking it down to its simplest form, is having really transparent job descriptions and consistent job descriptions. I think a really big part of this too is having your salary listed. The amount of LIS jobs that don't have a salary listed- it's immediately a barrier for everybody because whether someone has a mental illness or not, they need to know how much they'll make to take care of basic needs.

CW    Also, the benefits package is something I always want to know about, especially given the state of healthcare in the United States, which is where we both live and work.

MD    Especially for me, as a person with mental illness, who really receives help from conventional therapy—knowing whether that is covered in your benefits package is the difference between whether I am spending a $20-$40 copay per visit or several hundred dollars per visit. It is much more helpful to candidates when workplaces are transparent about that information and it helps people make better decisions for themselves about whether a job is feasible for them and whether they could maintain care of themselves on that salary with that benefit package.

Speaking of benefits, which includes sick days—and we know that people reading this book are not necessarily in charge of these decisions—but advocating for them to be used is so important. One thing that drastically needs to end are sick day bonuses—so financial incentives for not taking sick leave or vacation. No one should ever be put in the position between taking care of their physical and mental health needs with sick days or getting an exceptionally generous sum of money at the end of the year that they might need to pay bills or they might use it to purchase Christmas presents, or fix their car. When workplaces make policies that force trade-offs like that—how do we help advocate that sick and vacation days are to be taken and used when you need them?

CW    Yeah, absolutely I take my sick days. Well, I have to because I can't do my work if I'm unwell, and policies like that actively discriminate against workers with chronic illness, various types of disability, etc. because what it does is financially punish folks who must take sick days for legitimate, medical reasons.

MD    Exactly! On top of that, another thing that we can do to help in terms of hiring and retaining is really looking at what those practices look like and whether they are inclusive.

I think an important thing to ask ourselves is why do we do the things the way we do them? So often the answer is, "because that's just the way it's always been done," and it's not necessarily the best way to do it or the most inclusive way to do it because those ways have been set by folks in culturally dominant (able-bodied, neurotypical, white, patriarchal) positions.

So unless you know you can answer, "why do we do it this way?" with a concrete, reasonable answer it is worth looking at ways that we can adjust and change our policies around interviewing, particularly in academic libraries.

I have turned down interviews because I cannot do the eight to ten hour day where I am repeatedly in meetings with a five minute bathroom break and forced to eat with the search committee. It is not physically and mentally possible for me to do that, so I have turned down jobs based on this hiring process.

CW Unfortunately, it is standard for professional academic librarian positions. As we talk about even the smallest things hiring committees can do to change hiring practices, something so simple is to make the meal optional for the candidate. By asking the candidate if they would like the meal or not demonstrates sensitivity to eating disorders (ED) and allows people a chance to show their best selves.

MD And sometimes it is nice to just have a break! People need breaks for lots of reasons beyond bathroom needs—like someone wants to call home and talk with their family. It could be the most mundane of things. Giving people this option like you were talking about earlier, you know, it really will help benefit those of us experiencing mental illness when those barriers aren't there but it also benefits people without mental illness.

CW The whole idea is that we need to get rid of this idea of academic hazing, which is the concept that certain oppressive conditions should be perpetuated because it's somehow good for new people. I don't want anyone to have to go through what I've been through because I've been through a lot of not great stuff. Honestly we should do better and try to do what we can to bring out the best in people both in an interview and in the workplace.

MD Truly, it does not showcase everyone's best self when you run them ragged for an entire day.

CW      Let's talk about your new work situation since you are out of the proper library world...

MD      Both my emotions and mental illness have changed in both positive and negative ways since leaving the proper LIS field.

        As a librarian, I was working in a place where almost everybody knew my history; they were either present while I was going through my diagnosis or had heard about it through the community and it followed me around, which was challenging. While I was ready to start fresh as a professional there were some people who were less inclined to let me be different or to see me in a different light than they had previously seen me—as a student.

        For the record, no one ever blatantly said anything when I went back to work as a professional at the library where I worked as an undergraduate, but it was there as a looming presence. Sometimes it would be a lighthearted comment like, "Oh yeah but not like back when you were a student!" Because when I was a student, I was a hot mess and actively addicted to substances and I struggled with undiagnosed mental illness in addition to a lot of family and personal issues.

        When it comes to people who have been in a work environment for a long time, to them that is the recent past—they did not see my student days as long ago. So, I was constantly under the cloud of people's ideas of who I was and what I was capable of and I was ready to break out of that. I was being limited by other people's ideas of what I could do, and you know what? That sucks.

CW      That's very intense and it makes sense, especially if someone is geographically limited because of a spouse or medical or family needs or even financial needs.

MD      Being in a new position in a new field has been a blessing because I do not feel the weight of my past mistakes or the things I worry about people judging me for—none of that follows me around like it used to. But I also work in a field where we punish people who I share some experiences with, so it does not necessarily feel safe to disclose even if I wanted to.

        In the law enforcement and legal field people are more judgmental about substance use and so I have had to be cautious about who and when I open up about my experience with that. Even putting this in the book is a little bit nerve wracking because I do not know if there will be repercussions for disclosing, but having the freedom to make that choice is empowering.

CW    Yes, that is wild, but that makes total sense. That's absolutely an environment where it would be more difficult to disclose a mental illness.

MD    In the general, non-mental illness population there is a scale of acceptability. With this in mind, I am more willing to be open about my substance use history because so many people will immediately characterize me as being a good example for people, although I do not particularly like being used that way. That part is frustrating, but it does make it safer to disclose that facet of myself, whereas disclosing my mental illness is more difficult. It is such a delicate balancing act.

Shifting back to the book, I am curious to hear what your vision is for where the conversation goes from here or where you hope it ends up.

CW    There has been so much good energy around generating more attention at least around certain areas of LIS with what the LIS Mental Health Week folks have done and the Zine that comes out, because they are absolutely wonderful and empowering happenings.

I am very encouraged that more people are paying attention too.

Also some of the articles coming out right now around burnout with Katraena Davis Kendricks' work and the Burns and Green article from ACRL—both of which are well cited here—have been monumental in furthering the conversations and actions that need to happen. We must fundamentally change systems that treat library workers and folks with mental illness who work in them like disposable labor.

While those works do a fantastic job highlighting Academic Library work, I think what this book does is it expands on the lived experiences and critically examines a bigger library world of different libraries and library workers.

We were intentional about what types of librarians we selected, wanting to get a range of types of librarians—people who work in a variety of environments both in and outside of the US. I hope people will start to realize that these are happening across the board whether or not they realize it.

There truly needs to be substantial movement around changing culture because systemic and cultural change is the biggest thing that needs to happen around how we talk about and work with folks with mental illness internally and externally in our workplace cultures and how we operate within structures of the contemporary capitalist library workplace.

I think a lot about how neoliberalism and capitalist culture impacts our lives as folks with mental disorders—the fact that we're viewed as "Human Resources" (HR)—that I'm a human resource has this underlying exploitive quality to it, and it's become a major annoyance to me, since a lot of the issues covered here are HR-related. We must consider how supervisors operate because so much of how we, as folks with mental illnesses, navigate our workplaces depends on supervisor relationships and relationships with how the institutions we work within view our labor and us as people.

There are some bigger library-systemic things too that are covered, like subject terms. However, when it takes a literal Act of Congress to change the Library of Congress classifications that makes some of our goals towards equity and systemic changes much more difficult.

The easier to attain goals must happen within our workplaces, or we will not survive as a profession. People are starting to wake up a little more—if people are not already starting to like, rub their eyes a little—I hope that this book will at least get them to crack their knuckles and start some work towards a better future.

But seriously, if people do not have to go through what I went through in my struggle to own and treat my mental illnesses as I have navigated my education and career, then this book has fulfilled its purpose.

MD      I agree on that. If one person does not have to go through what I went through this is an enormous success. I also hope that this book gives people a place for identifying. We are clear that this is not a diagnostic manual—do not use this for scientific purposes, please! This is about amplifying voices so hopefully folks can see themselves in these pages.

For a long time, I felt so lonely and isolated thinking I had infiltrated the profession and that there must be no one else like me, and that is a big reason that this book exists. I want to put an end to those feelings of impostorship and alienation. I want people to see that there are others like them and that we are also having workplace struggles that need to be addressed. And I hope people see that those struggles are not the result of us having mental illnesses nor are they our fault or responsibility- it's the culture that needs to change.

# Editor Bios

**Miranda Dube** is a librarian and criminal justice based advocate in New Hampshire. Her research interests include library services for domestic and sexual violence survivors, as well as the intersection of LIS workers with mental illness and addiction. Outside of work you can find Miranda tending to her houseplants while she dreams up new ways to help empower others.

**Carrie Wade** is a Health Sciences Librarian at the University of Wisconsin Milwaukee and a backpacking specialist at REI in Brookfield, Wisconsin. Within the library field, her work focuses on plotting out just, equitable, and liberated futures for the people who work within them. Outside of libraries she is an experimental musician, friend of cats, and avid outdoorsperson.

# Author Biographies

**Avery Adams** No biography.

**Jess Alexander** is a former mathematics editor. After determining that talking to humans is a rather nice thing, they transitioned to librarianship, earning an MS in Library and Information Science from the University of Illinois. Jess now works as a Youth Services Librarian in the Chicagoland area, where they specialize in STEM programming.

**Pamela Andrews** is a Public Services Librarian and Adjunct Instructor at Tarrant County College, Trinity River campus. She holds a MLIS from Florida State University and a MA in English from University of Central Florida. Prior to Public Services work, she enjoyed serving as the Repository Librarian at University of North Texas. Outside of librarianship and teaching, Pamela enjoys hiking, knitting, and catching Pokémon.

**Stacey Astill** is a senior library assistant at Keyll Darree Library on the Isle of Man. Prior to finding her home at KD she worked and volunteered at public libraries and archives from Douglas to Newcastle. Her professional interests include running as far as possible with unconventional ideas, riding high on the shocked "oooh" noise when demonstrating referencing software functionality, and the annual battling to keep the journal subscriptions within budget. Stacey has published about the benefits of monitoring in-library resource usage, spoken about 'being mad' at the 2018 Federation of European Psychodrama Training Organisations (FEPTO) conference, and presented at the Evidence Based Library and Information Practice (EBLIP) conference 2019 about the value of fucking up. In her spare time she researches the experience of Allied PoWs during the Second World War, her MLIS is next on the list!

**Christy Bailey-Tomecek** is the Project Archivist at the Fortunoff Video Archive for Holocaust Testimonies at Yale University. She received her MLS with an archives certificate at Queens College, City University of New York and her BA in English Literature at New York University. Her professional interests include description, metadata, and documenting cultural trauma.

**Andrew Barber** is a MLIS student at the University of Arizona and paraprofessional worker at Arizona State University where he supervises student workers and aids students and faculty with online reference. His past research focuses on the U.S. prison system, the history of economic thought, and labor theory with more recent interest in critical librarianship, prison libraries, and LGBTQIA+ information services.

**Alice Bennett** works for the library services for the University of York. She has an academic background in literature and medieval studies, before entering library work and qualifying as a librarian. Her research interests include information literacy, library history and improving accessibility, particularly around disabled access and services for patrons with English as a second language in academic libraries.

**Marie Campbell** has been working at a community college library for over 15 years. Her career thus far has been focused in Technical Services.

**Chaun "Moe" Campos** is a library specialist and library and information science student that advocates for diversity, equity, and inclusion through her participation in the Georgia Library Association and student research. She was born and raised in Atlanta, Georgia, where she worked as a visual artist until she joined the U. S. Army in 2012. After her time in service, she obtained her Bachelor of Arts degree in Anthropology from Augusta University in Augusta, Georgia and is currently pursuing her Masters in Library and Information Science at Valdosta State University.

**NIna Clements** currently works as a librarian in Madison, Wisconsin. She earned an MLIS from the University of Pittsburgh in 2007 and an MFA in creative writing from Sarah Lawrence College in 2004.

**John Cohen** has worked in libraries for 26 years, has been bipolar for 31 years, and has been officially diagnosed and treated for 21 of those years. He began his career as a page and has worked his way through multiple positions–clerk, library assistant, night manager, circulation supervisor, volunteer coordinator, and director–in both academic and public libraries. He has been the director of Ogden Farmers' Library, outside of Rochester, NY, for seven years.

**Melissa Freiley** is the Discovery and Access Librarian at University of Arkansas—Fort Smith. She graduated in 2018 with her Master of Science in Information Science from University of North Texas and is a graduate of Texas Woman's University and South Plains College. Before moving back to her home state of Arkansas, Melissa worked for 11 years as a cataloging technician at Denton (TX) Independent School District and at UNT. When not librarianing, she can be found beneath a pile o' cats.

**Michelle Ashley Gohr** is a First Year Experience Librarian with Arizona State University where she teaches critical information literacy to first year students and provides research assistance to students and faculty in women and gender studies, social justice/human rights, and other subject areas. Her research primarily focuses on radical librarianship and critical pedagogies.

**Karina Hagelin** is a disabled, (gender)queer, femme artist, librarian, and community organizer based in Ithaca, NY. Most recently, they served as an Outreach and Instruction Librarian at Cornell University and a First-Year Academic Librarian Blogger for the Association of College and Research Libraries. Karina has a BA in American Studies, a certificate in LGBT Studies, and a MLIS all from the University of Maryland, College Park. Their research interests include feminist pedagogy, critical librarianship, disability justice, creative instruction, trauma-informed librarianship, and zines. More about their work can be found at karinakilljoy.com.

**Carolyn Hansen** is an independent librarian and historian. She most recently held the position of Head of Cataloging & Metadata Services at Stony Brook University and has previously worked in metadata positions at multiple academic and special libraries, including: the University of Cincinnati, Eastern Washington University, the Brooklyn Historical Society, ProQuest, and the American Geographical Society Library. She holds a Master of Library and Information Science from the University of Wisconsin-Milwaukee, a Master of History from Marquette University, and a Graduate Certificate in Digital Humanities from the University of Victoria.

**Sara Harrington** is the branch librarian at the Eastern State Hospital psychiatric facility in Medical Lake, Washington. She has a Bachelor of Science in Psychology, and a Master's degree in Library and Information Science with a specialization in Cultural Heritage Resource Management. Her articles "Archivists, Donors, and the Grieving Process" and "Reading Horror Novels Helped Me Deal with OCD" have been featured in SAA's "Archivists on the Issues" blog series and Electric Literature Magazine, respectively.

**Ian Ross Hughes** has worked as a professional librarian for 6 years but has worked in academic libraries for over 10 years. He has helped organize two programs for the annual American Library Association (ALA) conference for the Intellectual Freedom Round Table (IFRT) as well as presented Information Literacy techniques at an Early Childhood Conference at Purdue University Northwest. Ian's interests in the field include instruction, information literacy, faculty and campus outreach, first year experience, librarian well-being, and open access publishing. He also writes comedy and is interested in how pop culture intertwines with librarianship. Ian currently works as an Instruction and Outreach Librarian at Purdue University Northwest.

**Clayton Hume** is a librarian working in the Midwest at a community college. She wanted to contribute to this work so others would not feel so alone in their own professional settings.

**Kaelyn Leonard** is a first-generation graduate student currently pursuing their MLIS, with an emphasis in archival studies. Prior to that, they earned a BA in English. Kaelyn's writing style blends analytical assessments with lyrical descriptions to create striking messages that make the reader hungry for more. Their poetry has appeared in iō Literary Journal & From Whispers to Roars. When they are not writing, Kaelyn can be found playing Dungeons & Dragons, on the hunt for an indestructible dog toy, and spending time with their family.

**Brady D. Lund** is a doctoral student at Emporia State University's School of Library and Information Management. He also received his Master of Library Science degree from Emporia State and his bachelor's degree in communication sciences and disorders from Wichita State University. He has extensive publication and presentation experience in the areas of accessibility in education and libraries and employment for individuals with special needs in libraries and information organizations.

**Evelyn E. Nalepinski** is an academic librarian who, in an alternate timeline, would have thrived personally and professionally. Instead, this librarian continues to struggle with fitting in and continually wonders if the library world will ever become a welcoming place for those with mental illnesses and disabilities. By the time you read this, they may no longer be part of the profession in the same way, but they will continue to advocate for inclusive workplaces.

**Zoë Nissen** is a Metadata Librarian at the University of Southern California and a graduate of the University of Wisconsin-Madison Information School. By day she organizes digital collections from community archives in the Los Angeles area, and by night she is a bellydancer and avid cat snuggler. She has been actively pursuing recovery for an eating disorder since 2016.

**Marisol Moreno Ortiz** finished her appointment as Diversity Scholar in the Diversity Scholars Program (DSP) at Oregon State University Libraries in June 2019. She holds a Master of Arts in English degree from Portland State University and received her Bachelor of Arts in English with a Writing Minor from Oregon State University. In May 2019, Marisol received her Master of Library and Information Science degree from Louisiana State University. She has been a panelist in the session, "The diverse workforce," at the Internet Librarian International (ILL) Conference 2018 in London, England. She is committed to equity, inclusion, and diversity in the library profession. Marisol is also a creative writer and poet.

**Jodene R. Peck Pappas** is the Head of Technical Services at University of Texas of the Permian Basin. As a librarian with thirty years of many varied experiences, she has worked in both public and academic libraries and in both public and technical services, in small towns and large cities. Her research interest focuses on linked data because of the promise of making library collections visible to the people who need them.

**Max Powers** is a librarian at a community college in Illinois where she focuses on digital library services. In addition to her library work, she has been teaching college courses online for the past ten years.

**Allison Rand** is an Instructional Design Librarian at Illinois State University. She has a BA in Writing, Literature, and Publishing from Emerson College and an MLIS from the iSchool at the University of Illinois at Urbana-Champaign. She has presented and published on first year information literacy, gaming programs in academic libraries, and intersectional pedagogy. She lives in Normal, Illinois with her dog Charles Wallace.

**Jasmine Rizer** is a serials cataloger at the University of Georgia. She has a B.A. in English from the University of Georgia and an M.L.I.S. from Drexel University. When not actively being a librarian, she writes fiction and essays and draws the occasional comic.

**Stephanie S. Rosen** is a librarian scholar who brings insights from disability studies (and its intersections with feminist, queer, and critical race studies) into library administration and digital education. She is Senior Associate Librarian and Accessibility Specialist at the University of Michigan Library and holds a PhD in English from University of Texas at Austin.

**Ann Sen** is currently a librarian at a private university in Illinois where she primarily serves online students. Before completing her MLIS she received a BFA in painting, and enjoys teaching arts and crafts to children in her spare time.

**Chelsea Tarwater** is a Master's candidate in the SIS program at the University of Tennessee Knoxville and a Youth Services Specialist at Blount County Public Library in Maryville, TN where she does storytimes for all ages and is constantly covered in paint regardless of whether or not she's actually used paint that day. In her free time, she yells about politics, practices archery and writes queer romance novels.

# Index